Family, Class, and Ideology in Early Industrial France

Life Course Studies
David L. Featherman
David I. Kertzer
Series Editors

Nancy W. Denney
Thomas J. Espenshade
Dennis P. Hogan
Jennie Keith
Maris A. Vinovskis
Associate Series Editors

Family and the Female Life Course: The Women of Verviers, Belgium, 1849–1880
George Alter

The Ageless Self: Sources of Meaning in Late Life
Sharon R. Kaufman

Family, Class, and Ideology in Early Industrial France: Social Policy and the Working-Class Family, 1825–1848
Katherine A. Lynch

Katherine A. Lynch

Family, Class, and Ideology in Early Industrial France

Social Policy and the Working-Class Family, 1825–1848

The University of Wisconsin Press

The University of Wisconsin Press
114 North Murray Street
Madison, Wisconsin 53715

The University of Wisconsin Press, Ltd.
1 Gower Street
London WC1E 6HA, England

5 4 3 2 1

Printed in the United States of America

Cover illustration: Cloth printing and spinning mill of MM. Schlumberger, Grosjean and Co., Mulhouse, by J. Mieg, 1822. From Société Industrielle de Mulhouse, *Histoire documentaire de l'industrie de Mulhouse et de ses environs au XIXe siècle*, vol. 1 (1902).

Library of Congress Cataloging-in-Publication Data
Lynch, Katherine A.
Family, class, and ideology in early industrial France.
(Life course studies)
Bibliography: pp. 251–268.
Includes index.
1. Family—France—History—19th century. 2. Family policy—France—History—19th century. 3. France—Social conditions—19th century. 4. Labor and laboring classes—France—History—19th century. I. Title. II. Series.
HQ623.L95 1988 306.8′5′0944 88-40198
ISBN 0-299-11790-1
ISBN 0-299-11794-4 (pbk.)

Contents

Figures

Tables

Preface

The present study represents my effort to understand how and why the subject of working-class family life emerged as a central concern of bourgeois social thinking and social action during the early phases of industrialization in nineteenth-century France. It seeks to bring together the sometimes separate stories of middle- and working-class life and family values by examining the way systematic thinking about the family was gradually concretized into social policy designed to effect changes in working-class family relations. In analyzing this process, I have sought to understand the impact of policy legacies of the Old Regime and Revolution, the importance of regional differences within France, and the political and institutional factors that shaped the debate and working-out of policies themselves.

The subject of the French family is one that has occupied my attention since graduate school; a first version of the present study, limited to a consideration of nineteenth-century trends, was contained in my doctoral dissertation. Additional research has permitted me to incorporate a longer-term historical dimension to the study by integrating my own and others' research into the social welfare institutions and traditions of the Old Regime and Revolution. My belief that policies directed towards the working-class family in late Restoration and July Monarchy France need to be understood with reference to currents of thought and social action handed down from the Old Regime and Revolution rather than as mere precursors of present-day family policies has stemmed in large part from this recent research. In formulating my ideas about the most fruitful lines of approach towards the study of family policy, I have also benefitted greatly from a deeper acquaintance with research on American social policy, which has helped me to see French developments in a wider comparative perspective.

It is a pleasure to acknowledge the advice and counsel of those who have contributed to the growth and improvement of my work. As a teacher and later a dissertation advisor, David S. Landes was a primary influence both in encouraging my interest in European social and economic history and in supervising my research. A graduate seminar with Theodore Zeldin allowed me to begin to explore the nature of bourgeois family life in nineteenth-century France. Louise Tilly and Peter Stearns both offered valuable criticisms of the first version of this study.

More recently, the manuscript has benefitted from readings by W. Andrew Achenbaum, who made helpful comments concerning American social welfare history, and Paul Spagnoli, who shared his knowledge of the Lille area and of the problems of illegitimacy and *concubinage*. Thanks are also due to Lee Shai Weissbach, who kindly allowed me to consult his manuscript on the history of child labor legislation in nineteenth-century France, and to Rachel Ginnis Fuchs, Guillaume de Bertier de Sauvigny, Paul Thomas, and Eugen Weber, who read all or parts of the text. Financial assistance from a President's Fund Grant in the Humanities at Carnegie Mellon permitted me to return to France to extend my archival research.

My research in France has been consistently facilitated by the staffs of all of the archives whose treasures I have explored. Special mention should be made of the ongoing help of M. Christian Wilsdorf, Head Archivist at the Archives départementales du Haut-Rhin, Colmar, who graciously continued to supply me with information relevant to my research into the demographic dimensions of working-class life in Alsace, and M. Raymond Oberlé, archivist at the Archives municipales de Mulhouse. In the past several years, my research trips to France have been enriched immeasurably by the collegiality, friendship, and hospitality of Jean-Pierre Bardet, Jean-Noël Biraben, Jacques Dupâquier, and Guillaume de Bertier de Sauvigny. Jean-Pierre Bardet and André Burguière kindly allowed me to present parts of the argument at their seminars at the Ecole des Hautes Etudes during the spring of 1987.

Closer to home, I would also like to thank the reference staff of the Hunt Library, Carnegie Mellon University, and in particular, Sheila Rosenthal for graciously accommodating my many requests for materials. Tracy Futhey's expertise was indispensable in producing successive drafts of the manuscript. Carol Goldburg lent valuable assistance in helping to prepare the final version. Unless otherwise noted, I am responsible for all translations in the text as well as any imperfections that remain.

Abbreviations

ABBL	Archives du Bureau de bienfaisance de Lille
ADHR	Archives départementales du Haut-Rhin, Colmar
ADN	Archives départementales du Nord, Lille
ADSM	Archives départementales de la Seine-Maritime, Rouen
AHL	Archives hospitalières de Lille
AMM	Archives municipales de Mulhouse
AN	Archives Nationales, Paris
ASVP	Archives de la Société de Saint Vincent-de-Paul, Paris
JF	Fonds Joly de Fleury, Bibliothèque Nationale, Paris
Moniteur	*Moniteur universel*

Family, Class, and Ideology in Early Industrial France

1
Class, Ideology, and Social Policy

During the years of the late Restoration and July Monarchy, French society was marked by the emergence of several distinctive ways of conceptualizing the fundamental problems of working-class family life in industrial society. The construction and dissemination of these views brought to the attention of the educated, middle-class public a close association between the processes of social and economic change and the growth of severe organizational and human problems within the working-class family. Over time, two of these conceptualizations or ideologies inspired the formulation and implementation of social policies that were intended to change the organization of human relations within the working-class family as it was understood by observers and policymakers themselves.

The two perspectives which gave rise to policy were those of a nascent Social Catholic movement and of a group defined here as "moral economists." Neither can be construed as a unified or tightly organized pressure group within French society of the Restoration or the July Monarchy, though Social Catholics did work through formal voluntaristic organizations. Broadly speaking, moral economists, both theoreticians and practitioners, tended towards a view of the world that advocated limited state intervention into public and private spheres in the interests of creating a moral and stable industrial society. Although some moral economists were sympathetic to a French style of laissez-faire in their writings on economic problems, their empirical examinations of French society frequently led them to defend a kind of social engineering that suggested intervention into family relations. Social Catholics, in contrast, were more ambivalent about state intervention, preferring the use of voluntary lay associations of believers in the movement to create a more solid and moral working-class family. These two perspectives on family problems were not, of course, the only ones to emerge in France during this period. Utopian socialist perspectives, for example, clearly offered an alternative to both.[1] During the period under consideration, however, the ideologies of moral economists and Social Catholics were those that had the greatest impact in shaping actual policy affecting working-class family life. The influence of these two groups stemmed both from their desire to effect changes in the family and their success in creating practical means for doing so.

When moral economists and Social Catholics referred to the family in the course of their publications and debates or when they referred to problems of working-class family life, what they usually had in mind was the family as a coresidential group—or, more exactly, the family as a nexus of relationships of which that group was composed.[2] Certainly there were points at which the rhetorical flourishes of debate exposed notions of the family as an abstraction, as a kind of reified, ill-defined institution that somehow served to buttress the social order. However, as this study will show, observers of industrial life and policymakers went beyond such posturing to examine some of the concrete circumstances of intrafamily relations that were characteristic of specific points in individuals' life courses. In particular, observers were preoccupied with two sets of relations—those between men and women who were in the process of forming a family, and those between parents and their children. Although observers of working-class family mores in the early years of industrialization were concerned about working-class family relations at all points in individuals' lives, their attention focused much more obviously on working-class family members as younger adults and as children.

The ways that observers thought about the effects of social change, largely brought on by changes in the economy, were inextricably linked to policies for family reform that they advocated and that their allies within private organizations or government agencies sought to implement. Although there was no coordinated effort to remodel working-class family life in a systematic way, we can detect a certain logic underlying the advocacy of policies designed to address three areas of family life that have been chosen for special consideration in this study: the problem of early marriages and common law unions among workers, the problem of child abandonment, and the problem of child labor in industrial work places. An examination of the manner in which policies on these issues were implemented in three of France's most heavily industrialized urban areas—Lille, Mulhouse, and Rouen—provides the empirical evidence permitting an assessment of the local effects of family policies.

The purpose of the study is thus to examine the nature of debates about

1. See, for example, Christopher H. Johnson, *Utopian Communism in France: Cabet and the Icarians, 1839–1851* (Ithaca, 1974), pp. 50, 91.

2. David I. Kertzer, "A Life-Course Approach to Coresidence," *Current Perspectives on Aging and the Life Cycle* 2 (1986): 1–22.

working-class family life and their policy consequences as they unfolded during the years of early industrialization. It compares the two major, identifiable schools of thought about the working-class family, examines the actual policies to which their perspectives gave rise, and assesses some of the consequences of policies for the working-class families and communities that were the objects of reform. The concerns of the study thus overlap the fields of the history of mentalities, the history of social policy, and the history of bourgeois and working-class life during the early period of French industrialization. In exploring the process by which policy was constructed and implemented, the study also seeks to illuminate relationships between the French bourgeoisie and working classes, particularly in those urban centers most affected by the process of industrialization.

A focus on social policy necessarily leads to a very particular way of understanding relations between social classes, and it is wise from the outset to clarify the limitations of such a perspective. Given the unequal access of bourgeoisie and working classes to political and social power during the first half of the nineteenth century, it was essentially within the bourgeoisie that policy towards the working-class family was formulated. Although this study seeks to demonstrate that individuals, couples, and larger groups of workers were not passive objects of policy, it is nonetheless true that middle-class observers of working-class life and middle-class policymakers provided the initiative and momentum for the specific *politiques familiales* under investigation.

However, archival records left by efforts to implement policy do provide some opportunity to equalize the conditions of the investigation by permitting an examination of workers' responses to policy decisions, responses that form the bases for a tentative reconstruction of workers' own familial values and attitudes under the conditions of early industrial society. To the extent that is possible, then, the study seeks to round out its understanding of the significance of family policies by examining popular responses to them.

The Ideological Bases of Family Policy

The use of the concept of ideology to characterize social thinking embedded in policy directed towards workers' families deserves particular attention, since it is closely associated with two very different modes of analysis and explanation, in particular those of Karl Mannheim and Karl Marx. Although there is an innate tension between the two analysts' use of the concept, their different perspectives can be used to achieve separate but complementary interpretive goals of this study.

The first of these is to reconstruct as well as possible the context in which social observers and the makers of policy thought about the social world, in order to understand the kinds of questions about working-class family life to which they were seeking answers. In his study of Karl Mannheim, A. P. Simonds has evoked R. G. Collingwood's ruminations on this very problem. Collingwood wrote: "you cannot find out what a man means by simply studying his spoken or written statements, even though he has spoken or written with perfect command of language and perfectly truthful intention. In order to find out his meaning you must also know what the question was (a question in his own mind, and presumed by him to be in yours) to which the thing he has said or written was meant as an answer." Mannheim's goal in constructing his "total conception" of ideology or the "sociology of knowledge" was to investigate the "social connectedness" of ideas, not in order to test their validity, but rather to "advance our understanding of [their] meaning."[3] The value of Mannheim's position lies in its emphasis on understanding both the social context and the context of meaning in which knowledge is produced.

Marx's analysis of ideology, on the other hand, was designed with less of a hermeneutic than a critical purpose in mind, concentrating on a critique of dominant "bourgeois" ideology on grounds of logic as well as validity.[4] As Bhikhu Parekh has recently argued, Marx's critique of ideology was torn between two emphases: one on ideology as idealism and the other on ideology as social apology.[5] The latter is by far the better known. Marx and Marxist critics have characterized ideological thinking as being at the same time distorted and self-serving, leading to a systematically false analysis of the world it seeks to understand.[6] Under this definition of ideology, the task of the critical historian is as much to expose the logical weakness and social function of dominant ideological thinking in maintaining the status quo as to understand the substantive meaning intended by its authors. At its most reductionist, the Marxist critique of ideology is vulnerable to easy attack, since no mode of thinking, including historical materialism, is exempt from the possibility of itself becoming ideological.

If Marx's own perspective on ideology were limited to the notion that the values or ideas defended by various social groups represented, *grosso modo,*

3. A. P. Simonds, *Karl Mannheim's Sociology of Knowledge* (Oxford, 1978), pp. 60, 31.

4. Bhiku Parekh, *Marx's Theory of Ideology* (Baltimore, 1982), pp. 44–45. Marx and Engels' principal analysis of the question is contained in "The German Ideology," in David McLellan, ed., *Karl Marx: Selected Writings* (Oxford, 1977), pp. 159–91. For an exhaustive account of the various usages of the term *ideology,* see Raymond Geuss, *The Idea of Critical Theory: Habermas and the Frankfurt School* (Cambridge, 1981), pp. 4–20.

5. Parekh, *Marx's Theory*, p. 10.

6. Nicos Poulantzas, *Political Power and Social Classes*, trans. Timothy O'Hagan (London, 1973), p. 207, defends this argument in the context of an Althusserian position that distinguishes ideology from science. A critical discussion of this aspect of Althusser's work appears in Ted Benton, *The Rise and Fall of Structural Marxism: Althusser and His Influence* (New York, 1984), pp. 46–49, 87.

their material interests, then the task of the social theorist or the historian of mentalities would consist simply in "unmasking" the ideological character of ideas by showing simple correspondences between interests and beliefs. In fact, as Parekh has shown, Marx's position was actually a great deal more interesting than this. For Marx, the ideological quality of much bourgeois thinking about the social world lay not solely or even primarily in its self-interestedness, but in its tendency to universalize social judgments on the basis of particularistic circumstances—to argue, for example, that conditions found in one place or time somehow exemplified *the* human condition, or the limits of historical possibility.[7] This aspect of Marx's critique of ideology is more promising as a source of insight into the evolution of bourgeois social consciousness and family policy in France. It seems to illuminate quite well several outstanding features of policy debates as well as policy itself.

One of the most powerful and novel features of writing and debate about working-class family life within the French bourgeoisie of the period under investigation was the prescriptive, normative tone that pervaded the writings of the two central groups of policy advocates examined in this study. Several historians have already studied the ways that normative critiques of working-class behavior contained in empirical studies of the period served to perpetuate the status quo of July Monarchy France.[8] Indeed, the simple correspondence between the desire for a more orderly working class and fundamental bourgeois interests is easy enough to depict. On the other hand, as William Coleman has noted in his analysis of the well-known moral economist physician Louis-René Villermé, "To view Villermé and his intellectual associates as apologists of class interests is perhaps exact but in itself is merely a claim, not an exposition of the precise terms in which that apology was expressed."[9] What has been less well understood than the "apologia" involved in many nineteenth-century discussions of reforms of the working-class family is the truly innovative character of a point of view that held that the problems of working-class families could be resolved in large part by workers' adoption of personal values and behavior identified with the bourgeoisie. This attitude, which was imbedded most clearly within the discourse and policies recommended by moral economists, is not at all an obvious or timeless one. It would have had no place, for example, in a society whose different classes or orders were believed to be hierarchically organized groups with essentially different needs, mores,

7. Parekh, *Marx's Theory*, p. 29. On the universalizing tendencies within French bourgeois ideology in this period, see also Yves Charbit, *Du malthusianisme au populationnisme: Les économistes français et la population 1840–1870* (Paris, 1981), p. 65.

8. Luc Boltanski, *Prime éducation et morale de classe*, 2d ed. (Paris, 1977); William Coleman, *Death Is a Social Disease: Public Health and Political Economy in Early Industrial France* (Madison, 1982).

9. Coleman, *Death*, p. xix.

and aspirations.[10] The prescriptive, normative nature of so much writing on the working-class family thus corresponded closely to what Marx saw as a peculiar universalizing feature of middle-class ideology.[11]

Although Marx's overall critique of ideology is helpful in illuminating some facets of the social values incorporated in French family policy, there is an important respect in which middle-class pronouncements on the family life of workers differed from what Marx and Marxist critics have identified as a central function of "bourgeois ideology." Both Marx and many of his followers have argued that a fundamental function of bourgeois ideology is to cloak or conceal radical divisions within capitalist society, such as those between dominant and dominated classes, in the interest of perpetuating the status quo.[12] Mannheim, in fact, shared this view of the function of ideology.[13] Yet, one of the most important initial themes in the pronouncements made by Social Catholics and moral economist observers about working-class families was that there was in fact an extraordinarily wide and dangerous social distance between industrial workers and their social superiors. Far from glossing over or concealing differences between bourgeois and worker, both moral economists and Social Catholics frequently had to work long and hard to convince their fellow bourgeois that there was such a gap, and that it represented a threat to the social and moral order. Thus, the Marxist view that bourgeois ideology necessarily functions to conceal sources of class conflict fails, at least at first view, to explain the importance of arguments that emphasized the salience of class distance.

Particular signs of the differences between workers and bourgeois in the first half of the nineteenth century resounded consistently in the texts of Social Catholics and moral economist commentators. As will be shown in the course of the study, the writings and pronouncements of both groups emphasized that the textile centers of early industrial France attracted migrant populations of rootless workers unconnected to the land, who dwelt in lodgings of unspeakable horror, frequently in ersatz family formations of dubious structure. Workers labored in the newly constructed mills of urban areas but did

10. Roland Mousnier, *Les hiérarchies sociales de 1450 à nos jours* (Paris, 1969). On Mousnier's concept of a society of "orders," see Armand Arriaza, "Mousnier and Barber: The Theoretical Underpinnings of the 'Society of Orders' in Early Modern Europe," *Past and Present*, no. 89 (1980): 39–57.

11. Parekh writes, for example, "The bourgeoisie . . . think that society would be much better off if *everyone* defined himself as a bourgeois and pursued appropriate objectives." Parekh, *Marx's Theory*, p. 28.

12. Poulantzas, *Political Power*, p. 207; Georg Luckács, "Class Consciousness," in *History and Class Consciousness: Studies in Marxist Dialectics*, trans. Rodney Livingstone (Cambridge, Mass., 1968), p. 48.

13. *Ideology and Utopia: An Introduction to the Sociology of Knowledge*, trans. Louis Wirth and Edward Shils (New York, 1946), p. 184.

not succeed in forming for themselves an independent existence that provided support for the family unit. Alcoholism, prostitution, and child abuse testified to the human costs of economic change. All of these features of working-class life added up to powerful images of the early industrial factory worker as the "other," as an outsider to French civilization as it was understood by bourgeois social observers during the Restoration and July Monarchy.[14]

This same theme was heard with some modifications later in the nineteenth century. In his study of rural France, Eugen Weber has argued that in the second half of the nineteenth century, another kind of Frenchman—the peasant—became the "outsider" in French society. Curiously enough, some of the characteristics that Weber identifies as central to late-nineteenth-century descriptions of peasants were, on the surface, the same ones attributed with such alarm to urban workers under the late Restoration and July Monarchy. Of the late nineteenth century, Weber writes: "The prevailing belief [was] that areas and groups of some importance were uncivilized, that is, unintegrated into, unassimilated to French civilization: poor, backward, ignorant, savage, barbarous, wild, living like beasts with their beasts. They had to be taught manners, morals, literacy, a knowledge of French, and of France, a sense of the legal and institutional structure beyond their immediate community."[15] Although late-nineteenth-century peasants and earlier-nineteenth-century urban workers were at different times characterized as savages or barbarians, it is important to understand the precise ways in which the gulf separating workers from bourgeois in the early part of the century differed from the distance between peasant and bourgeois articulated later on in the century. A key text for this comparison is provided by an example used by Weber himself, a two-part article by the eminent moral economist Adolphe Blanqui.[16] Blanqui's empirical studies of urban and rural workers in mid-nineteenth-century France illustrate the substantial differences that existed in middle-class evaluations of the relative "otherness" of these two groups at mid-century.

Whereas Blanqui demonstrated his belief in the savagery and backwardness of France's peasants, the reader is struck by the sympathetic vocabulary frequently used by the author to describe them, and the contrasting and characteristic denunciation of the conditions of urban working-class life. For Blanqui, peasants of the Pyrenees were "lively, alert, robust, intelligent, sober"; those of Alps "good, honest people." Even the "savage" Breton was also

14. Gérard Leclerc, *L'observation de l'homme: Une histoire des enquêtes sociales* (Paris, 1979), pp. 175–78.

15. Eugen Weber, *Peasants into Frenchmen: The Modernization of Rural France, 1870–1914* (Stanford, 1976), p. 5.

16. Blanqui, "Tableau des populations rurales de la France en 1850," *Journal des économistes* 28 (1851): 9–27; 30 (1851): 1–15. This text is also cited in Theodore Zeldin, *France, 1848–1945: Love, Ambition, and Politics* (Oxford, 1973), 1:131.

"loyal." In the author's view, the greatest menace to the rural populations of France was in fact the availability of industrial apprenticeships and the "false hope" of higher wages that they engendered. In fact, Blanqui had nothing good to say about city workers, emphasizing the viciousness of urban, working-class life and the preferability of rural labor to work in France's textile factories.[17] Far from being places of "civilization," the industrial cities of northern France that Blanqui knew best from personal experience were savage in a different, more troubling way than the countryside.[18] Whereas peasants in the most economically underdeveloped parts of France were by Blanqui's admission condemned to "almost savage conditions in which they have lived for so many centuries,"[19] the urban industrial worker of the time was condemned to a savagery that was all the more frightening because it was in many ways new.

Thus, whereas the later-nineteenth-century effort to integrate peasants more firmly into French society entailed bringing them out of the age-old ignorance and poverty of the past, earlier-nineteenth-century policies of reforming the family lives of industrial workers involved the more ambitious task of controlling the intensification of a cultural chasm between worker and bourgeois that appeared to threaten the future of French industrial society.[20] In essence, what bourgeois observers of peasant life in the later nineteenth century saw when they travelled to the most backward rural areas was a glimpse into France's past. What observers of urban industrial life saw earlier in the century was a troubling vision of France's possible future.

Social Inquiry and Sociological Knowledge

By the nineteenth century, the tradition of gathering information about society in the form of systematic empirical inquiry had a long history in France, emerging in its modern form in the seventeenth century. From these beginnings, the French state had been the main consumer of information gleaned from censuses and data on prices or fortifications exemplified in the work of such servants of the state as Vauban.[21] Tocqueville was perhaps the most

17. Blanqui, "Tableau," 28:14, 17, 22, 26; 30:13.

18. Weber, *Peasants*, p. 5.

19. Blanqui, "Tableau," 30:5.

20. Jean Lhomme, *La grande bourgeoisie au pouvoir, 1830–1880: Essai sur l'histoire sociale de la France* (Paris, 1960), pp. 32–33, identifies the haute bourgeoisie's fear of the lower classes with the 1830s.

21. Jacques Dupâquier and Eric Vilquin, "Le pouvoir royal et la statistique démographique," in Jacques Mairesse, ed., *Pour une histoire de la statistique* (Paris, 1977), pp. 83–104; Jacques Dupâquier and Michel Dupâquier, *Histoire de la démographie: La statistique de la population des origines à 1914* (Paris, 1985), pp. 83–91. On the early nineteenth century, see Marie-Noëlle Bourguet, "Race et folklore: L'image officielle de la France en 1800," *Annales, E.S.C.* 31 (1976): 802–3.

evocative observer of the Old Regime monarchy's gargantuan appetite for information that it demanded most aggressively of its *intendants* in the provinces.[22]

As Gérard Leclerc has demonstrated, however, there were several new features of the information-gathering process in the first half of the nineteenth century. The pursuit of information came increasingly to involve private citizens as well as prefects and their administrative staffs. Medical experts, technocrats, and other professionals sponsored by state ministries or by official learned societies such as the Académie des sciences morales et politiques gradually contributed to the information-gathering process. Another characteristic of nineteenth-century inquiry was its increasing preoccupation with the lives of the lower classes, whose daily existence, work habits, and family lives were scrutinized in ways inconceivable to earlier administrators or to a nineteenth-century bourgeois, with his concern for the privacy and sanctity of his own *foyer*.[23] This greater preoccupation with data on private mores, on information gleaned from the core of private life, was exemplified by data-gathering on workers' budgets and on what went on inside the dwelling place as well as public manifestations of political or economic contention.[24]

In long-term perspective, the focusing of sights on urban workers can be seen as part of a historical evolution by which the rulers of successive French regimes used the regional state apparatus as a conduit of information about those whom they believed most likely to threaten the status quo. Just as Richelieu, Colbert, or Louis XIV himself undertook to watch and to repress threats to the absolutist state originating among recalcitrant aristocrats, Huguenots, or disaffected peasants, so the nineteenth-century leaders of the *régime censitaire* attempted to exert scrutiny and control over those groups, in particular urban workers, whom they believed most likely to represent a challenge to their political and social power.

Publications containing details about working-class life could be read at several levels. As Louis Chevalier argued in his classic work centered on the Parisian experience, news items and published studies provided literate middle-class readers with chilling tales of an exotic, hidden world among them. The "working classes" gradually merged with the "dangerous classes" not only in these texts but also, Chevalier argues, in the minds of many bourgeois.[25] Political authorities and government administrators doubtless gained more than titillation from the growing number of observations of working-

22. Alexis de Tocqueville, *The Old Regime and the French Revolution*, trans. Stuart Gilbert (New York, 1955), pp. 61–72.

23. Leclerc, *L'observation*, p. 85.

24. William M. Reddy, *The Rise of Market Culture: The Textile Trade and French Society, 1750–1900* (Cambridge, 1984), pp. 147–57.

25. Louis Chevalier, *Labouring Classes and Dangerous Classes in Paris during the First Half of the Nineteenth Century*, trans. Frank Jellinek (London, 1973).

class life. Their interest, particularly in studies that observed workers' family behavior, stemmed from an apparent conviction that public disorder among the new working classes might be traced to patterns of private life. Stated simply, private life—read "family life"—of workers, was deserving of attention in large part because of its potential public consequences.

The specific interest in working-class life thus flowed from several sources: from the kind of "ethnographic" mentality discussed by Leclerc; from a long-standing spirit of *raison d'état* within the French monarchy that stimulated data-gathering on groups believed to represent the greatest threat to social and political stability; and from the specific values of the leaders of France from the late 1820s to 1840s, who placed a high premium on outward public order and gradually valorized the close linkages between private relations and public behavior.

Although the French monarchy had had a long tradition of activism in the charity or welfare field, supplementing and sometimes replacing activities of the Catholic church, there were few precedents for the precise social reform aspirations that came to characterize family-related policies under the late Restoration and July Monarchy. A brief example taken from the administration of foundling policy towards the end of the Old Regime and during the nineteenth century—a subject studied in detail in Chapter 4—illustrates this change. By the second half of the eighteenth century, administrative correspondence shows that the foundling problem was nearly as severe as it would be under the July Monarchy. Every year, thousands of unwanted infants were abandoned by their parents and transported to the capital. Although concerned by what they believed to be "abuses" of the king's generosity in aiding these children, and thus determined to make abandonment more difficult, Old Regime administrators never appear to have aspired to a thoroughgoing reform of parent-child relations as an appropriate solution to the problem. Nor does it appear that they seriously entertained the ambitious notion that the workers who were believed to be the source of foundlings should be gradually encouraged or forced by policy to adopt different family mores. In fact, in contrast to arguments expressed during the 1830s, especially by moral economists, the "foundling problem" of the waning years of the Old Regime was not considered to be essentially a family problem at all, but rather the result of a variety of economic conditions that affected individuals of the lower classes.

Questions of values or moral worth were very much present in welfare or charity administration policies under the Old Regime, and were perhaps most evident during the Reformation and Counter-Reformation, which witnessed the flourishing of urban social welfare activities inspired in part by militant lay piety. Local administrators of the most progressive urban charity movements in early modern Europe were especially concerned to aid those poor who were not only indigenous but "respectable" as well, frequently devising separate programs for illegitimate and legitimate children, for example.[26] The point is not that normative considerations of moral fitness were entirely new to policy discussions under the late Restoration and July Monarchy or that Old Regime welfare professionals were unconcerned about the morals of lower-class families. In contrast to what would come later, however, Old Regime administrators did not evince a belief that one universal model of family organization was either appropriate or attainable for all groups in the social order. Not until the first several decades of the nineteenth century do we find the gradual emergence of a model of family behavior that was believed to be not only appropriate for all social classes but vitally important for the stability and progress of the social order. While moral economists were the most active proponents of this model, moral economists and Social Catholics alike would be instrumental in reconceptualizing a growing number of social problems as family problems.

Thus, the incorporation of aspirations for family reform in local and national policy during the late Restoration and July Monarchy occurred simultaneously with an implicit but detectable consciousness of a model of values and behavior to which working-class families were to conform. In contrast to Old Regime policies in which the king and the church aided different categories of individuals *qua* individuals—foundlings, the poor, the insane—the most committed nineteenth-century interventionists, both secular and Catholic, came to believe that the family unit should be the target of policy. Their reasons for this preoccupation are explored in Chapter 2. Their goal to establish the nuclear, residential family as the policy target *par excellence* was heralded and accompanied by wide-ranging discussion among leaders of middle-class opinion about the social and moral functions this family should perform.

The Reception of Sociological Knowledge and the Formation of Middle-Class Consciousness

The investigation of working-class family life and the effort to understand its characteristics were part of the same process that saw the French bourgeoisie's growing cognizance of its own features—features that in many minds made it the legitimate guardian of French society's interests. In his study of Guizot, Pierre Rosanvallon has argued that the statesman-historian's pronouncements provide one of the clearest articulations of the bourgeoisie's claim to leadership of the French state and society. For Guizot, the middle classes were a

26. Natalie Davis, "Poor Relief, Humanism and Heresy," in idem, *Society and Culture in Early Modern France* (Stanford, 1975), p. 38; Olwen Hufton, *The Poor of Eighteenth-Century France* (Oxford, 1974), pp. 166, 171.

new kind of governing class, better fitted to the responsibilities of leadership because of their greater independence from the king as well as their unique qualities of gravity and stability that set them apart from the "frivolous" aristocracy of the Old Regime. These qualities made them the "regulatory pivot" of the new social order.[27] Guizot's larger views, if not his particular political practices while in office, incorporated other widely shared beliefs of the French bourgeoisie as it rose to social, political, and cultural power. One of these was his confidence in the efficacy of empirical social knowledge in informing the construction of a rational state mechanism. A second was his fear of social disorder.[28] The fear of social disorder, traceable to the experience of radical revolution in the previous generation and its echoes in the early 1830s, had manifested itself in a number of forms since the Revolution—for example, in the conservatism or reactionism of Bonald or deMaistre.

However, as one of the supreme defenders of the bourgeoisie's legitimate right to political dominance, Guizot rejected the desirability of recreating social stability on prerevolutionary bases. Rather, he tried to lead the bourgeoisie in creating a new social and moral order that took into account aspirations for civil equality born of the Revolution. Moreover, Guizot believed that only a state or administration that took cognizance of the sociological movements occurring within civil society and attempted to oversee and control them could hope to survive.[29] His belief in the accumulation of scientific knowledge needed to construct a rational and effective government was shared, at least in principle, by a large portion of France's bourgeoisie and lay at the root of the widespread interest in empirical, quantitative studies of working-class life.[30]

A taste for empirical knowledge about the social order had its limits, however. Rosanvallon has rightly evoked the consternation that Guizot, for one, began to feel by the 1840s in the face of an increasing number of studies that revealed the gloomier side of the social order. The government and even a number of esteemed observers of working-class life, including Villermé, began, Rosanvallon argues, to deviate from their own expressed desire to

27. Pierre Rosanvallon, *Le moment Guizot* (Paris, 1985), pp. 112–13, 146, 196.

28. Ibid., pp. 17–23, 75. Approaches to the problem of disorder in the work of early-nineteenth-century "Ideologues" are discussed in Thomas E. Kaiser, "Politics and Political Economy in the Thought of the Ideologues," *History of Political Economy* 12 (1980): 147.

29. Leclerc, *L'observation*, p. 196, views the flow of information about the lower classes as the countermovement of the flow of domination from the top of the social structure to the bottom. In his judgment, social domination increasingly required accurate information flowing upward to social and political leaders. He writes: "It is in the interest of the dominant class that [their] model [of society] be adequate, with as little bias as possible and that it has as an essential characteristic the goal of reflecting as precisely as possible this structure."

30. Rosanvallon, *Le moment Guizot*, p. 232, refers to Guizot's vision of the state as "l'état sociologique." On the Old Regime origins of such a view, see Keith Michael Baker, "French Political Thought at the Accession of Louis XVI," *Journal of Modern History* 50 (1978): 297–98.

base state administration on empirical knowledge of civil society and to slide imperceptibly into a more ideological or distorted style of thinking that was intent simply on maintaining the status quo.[31]

What is important to retain from Rosanvallon's analysis is the ambivalence that social inquiries about working-class life could and did arouse, not only in the minds of political leaders such as Guizot but also within informed middle-class opinion as a whole. Although Rosanvallon dates this ambivalence from the 1840s, divisions of opinion about the implications of observations of working-class life appear to have existed well before this time. During the whole period under examination, there were fundamental, if diminishing, differences of perspective within the French bourgeoisie about the nature and significance of class estrangement between workers and themselves, and the policies that might be used to address it.

The Heterogeneity of the French Bourgeoisie: Political Power and Social Policy

An understanding of the specific setting in which policy was advocated, debated, and implemented requires some attention to the distribution of social and political power during the period covered by this study. Both Tocqueville and Marx were convinced that it was the upper levels of the bourgeoisie that held real political power, particularly under the July Monarchy. In their judgment, the Revolution of 1830 marked a passage from the political dominance of land-owning elites loyal to the elder branch of the Bourbon dynasty to the rule of the wealthiest part of the bourgeoisie. Marx wrote: "It was not the French bourgeoisie that ruled under Louis Philippe, but *one section* of it: bankers, stock-exchange kings, railway kings, owners of coal and iron mines and forests, a part of the landed proprietors that rallied round them—the so-called *finance aristocracy*. It sat on the throne, it dictated laws in the Chambers, it distributed public offices, from cabinet portfolios to tobacco bureau posts."[32] Or again, speaking of the "Party of Order" after 1848, he wrote: "Under the Bourbons, *big landed property* had governed, with its priests and lackeys; under the Orléans, high finance, large-scale industry, large-scale trade, that is, *capital,* with its retinue of lawyers, professors and smooth-tongued orators. The Legitimate Monarchy was only the political expression of the hereditary rule of the lords of the soil, as the July Monarchy was only the political expression of the usurped rule of the bourgeois *parvenus*."[33] As

31. Rosanvallon, *Le moment Guizot*, pp. 261–62.

32. Karl Marx, "The Class Struggles in France," in Lewis S. Feuer, ed., *Karl Marx and Friedrich Engels: Basic Writings on Politics and Philosophy* (New York, 1959), p. 282.

33. Karl Marx, *The Eighteenth Brumaire of Louis Bonaparte* (New York, 1969), pp. 46–47.

so frequently happened, Tocqueville and Marx were nearly of the same mind in attributing the dreary and sordid tone of political life under the July Monarchy to bourgeois dominance, although Marx more than Tocqueville identified the upper reaches of that class as the bearers of power.[34]

More recent Marxists have attempted to refine Marx's analysis by emphasizing even further the divisions within the French bourgeoisie. For example, Nicos Poulantzas's formulation of the notion of "power bloc" emphasizes that while the "financial aristocracy" of July Monarchy France was the "hegemonic" portion of the bourgeoisie, seeking to defend its economic interests as those of the bourgeoisie as a whole, the ruling class—the men who actually governed, or those in charge of the state—were not necessarily drawn from it.[35]

Empirical studies of the composition of the legislative branch of government of July Monarchy France have attempted to explore the problem of bourgeois political power by examining the occupational backgrounds of members of the Chamber of Deputies and the Chamber of Peers. These studies have concurred in the judgment that members of the lower house were men with substantial wealth in land who had little personal involvement in either commerce or industry. Analyses have emphasized the numerical importance of *fonctionnaires,* particularly magistrates, *rentiers,* and *propriétaires* among the ranks of the lower house.[36] A composite portrait of the membership of the Chamber of Peers leaves a rather similar impression, although here military service loomed as a more important qualification for office. One historian has calculated that of the total of 550 men who sat in the upper chamber under Louis-Philippe, there were 121 generals and *maréchaux de France* and 54 military men of lower rank. Two-thirds of the members had served the state in some capacity, and of the 335 members nominated by the king, only 30 men acquired their status as merchants, industrialists, writers, or simply "propriétaires."[37] According to Paul Bastid's intriguing analysis of the men-

34. Alexis de Tocqueville, *Recollections*, ed. J. P. Mayer and A. P. Kerr, trans. George Lawrence (New York, 1971), pp. 5–6, 11–12. André Jardin's recent biography of Tocqueville illustrates the imperial nobility's participation in these same aspects of electoral politics under the July Monarchy. See his fascinating account of Tocqueville's election to the Chamber of Deputies and of his opponent, the Comte Polydor Le Marois, in *Alexis de Tocqueville* (Paris, 1984), pp. 275–83.

35. Poulantzas, *Political Power*, pp. 229–49.

36. Sherman Kent, *Electoral Procedure under Louis-Philippe* (New Haven, 1937); Patrick L. R. Higonnet and Trevor B. Higonnet, "Class, Corruption, and Politics in the French Chamber of Deputies, 1846–1848," *French Historical Studies* 5 (1967): 204–24; David H. Pinkney, *The Revolution of 1830* (Princeton, 1972), p. 279; and the citations in Rosanvallon, *Le moment Guizot*, p. 132. On the Chamber of Deputies under the Restoration, see Guillaume de Bertier de Sauvigny, *Au soir de la monarchie: La Restauration*, 3d ed. (Paris, 1974), pp. 290–91.

37. Lucien Labes, *Les pairs de France sous la monarchie de Juillet* (Lorient, 1938), p. 126.

tality of legislators under the *monarchie censitaire,* the legislative chambers under the Restoration and July Monarchy were composed of men who viewed themselves less as representatives of any opinion and more as government functionaries whose role was to help administer the state: "Chosen in the calm atmosphere of restricted suffrage, they acted less as representatives of the country than as functionaries assigned the task of bringing their help in the legislative sphere to the King's government."[38] Edward Fox has seconded this view, noting that "the real function of the new Chambers was to diffuse the enormous administrative power of the chief executive among the representatives of the country's elite, so that the regime could more accurately be called a corporate, than a constitutional monarchy."[39] These diverse arguments challenge the notion that the Chamber of Deputies in some simple or direct way represented bourgeois class interests as a whole.

Two features of the system of election to the lower chamber and the demands of life as a deputy helped to explain the weak direct participation of commercial and industrial elites. High rates of taxation on landed property that served as the basis for calculating eligibility for election and for membership in the electorate ensured that the possession of landed wealth was the precondition for membership in the *pays légal*.[40] Similarly, the fact that members of the Chamber were required to be in residence in the capital, and—in theory at least—in attendance at meetings of the Chamber made it unlikely that ambitious merchants or manufacturers who actually had to work for a living would devote their time to personal participation.[41]

Thus, even if the interests of the upper reaches of the financial bourgeoisie were represented in the Chamber, it was not necessarily by individuals drawn from their ranks. Thomas Beck has summarized this situation nicely: "The July Monarchy was supposed to be the businessman's regime, but his share of the deputies did not keep pace with his increased share of the eligibles. This may indicate that businessmen under the July Monarchy were more satisfied to have men of different occupations represent them than under the

38. Paul Bastid, *Les institutions politiques de la monarchie parlementaire française: 1814–1848* (Paris, 1954), p. 240. Saint-Marc Girardin assesses the strength of this attitude within the Chamber of Peers in "De la pairie en France depuis la révolution de juillet," *Revue des deux mondes* 12 (1845): 537–62.

39. Edward Whiting Fox, *History in Geographic Perspective: The Other France* (New York, 1971), p. 110. In this respect, Fox sees little difference between the chambers of the Restoration and July Monarchy. Cf. Bertier de Sauvigny, *Au soir de la monarchie*, p. 269.

40. Kent, *Electoral Procedure*, pp. 30–44.

41. François Julien-Laferrière, *Les députés-fonctionnaires sous la monarchie de Juillet* (Paris, 1970), pp. 79–81. On the importance of financial independence and leisure as prerequisites for a career in either Chamber, see William Fortescue, *Alphonse de Lamartine: A Political Biography* (London, 1983), p. 62. These strictures would not, of course, have inhibited the participation of men retired from commercial or industrial pursuits.

Restoration."[42] Such a phenomenon was echoed at the regional level, where even in the most industrialized *départements* considered in this study, men who had or were actively exercising commercial and industrial occupations constituted the minority of members elected to the *conseils généraux,* where family-related policies were sometimes discussed.[43] Thus, from recent empirical studies, it appears that there was a great deal of continuity in the elites who held national and regional government authority even after 1830. Ownership of land continued to figure largely as the criterion of membership in the lower legislative house, which was thus composed of men whose bourgeois status was not likely to rest primarily on the possession of or direct participation in industrial or commercial activities.

Although the authors of several of these empirical studies of deputies' backgrounds have seen their work as a refutation of Marx's or, for that matter, Tocqueville's belief that the July Monarchy was essentially a bourgeois regime,[44] the problem is rather in a misapprehension of the emphasis in Marx's understanding of the French bourgeoisie's relation to political power. Marx is difficult to pin down on this subject. It appears, however, that he as well as many others was quite aware that in France, the bourgeoisie was by no means led politically by men engaged in what he considered to be economically productive activities. Of the July Monarchy, he wrote: "Since the finance aristocracy made the laws, was at the head of the administration of the state, had command of all the organized public authorities, dominated public opinion through the actual state of affairs and through the press, the same prostitution, the same shameless cheating, the same mania to get rich were repeated in every sphere, from the court to the Café Borgne—to get rich not by production, but by pocketing the already available wealth of others."[45] Particularly in his polemical historical writings on French politics, Marx frequently expressed his scorn for the French bourgeoisie's deviation from the economically and politically revolutionary role history had assigned it.[46] Much to Marx and Engels' horror, the productive, economically active elements of the bourgeoisie allowed the less productive "finance aristocracy," along with the landowners and bureaucrats, to control state institutions. Their lack of

42. Thomas D. Beck, *French Legislators, 1830–1834: A Study in Quantitative History* (Berkeley and Los Angeles, 1974), p. 122.

43. The figures were 1/3 in Haut-Rhin, a bit over 1/5 in the Seine-Inférieure, and 1/10 in the Nord from 1840 to the 1848 revolution. André-Jean Tudesq, *Les conseillers-généraux en France au temps de Guizot, 1840–1848* (Paris, 1967), p. 146. On the Seine-Inférieure, see also Jean-Pierre Chaline, *Les bourgeois de Rouen: Une élite urbaine au XIXe siècle* (Paris, 1982), pp. 312, 375.

44. Pinkney, *The Revolution of 1830*, p. 275; Rosanvallon, *Le moment Guizot*, p. 132.

45. Marx, "The Class Struggles," pp. 284–85.

46. Karl Marx and Friedrich Engels, "Manifesto of the Communist Party," in Feuer, *Marx and Engels*, p. 12.

participation in the fight to liberate political institutions from the continued power of landed proprietors or finance aristocrats was in fact partly responsible for the lack of real political vigor of the regime. The problem was that the French bourgeoisie of this period, and especially their representatives in the Chamber or the government, were far from being the triumphant, ideal-typical bourgeois of the *Communist Manifesto*.

Marx was not, of course, the only one to criticize the industrial and commercial bourgeoisie's failure to claim a real place for themselves on the political stage of the July Monarchy. Rosanvallon has evoked Guizot's own disgust at the bourgeoisie's general lack of deep political consciousness.[47] In Guizot's view, it was only when national policy was likely to affect their very circumscribed short-term interests that members of the industrial and commercial bourgeoisie of July Monarchy France rose to the political occasion. For the most part, they seem to have been agreeable to having others rule in their name.

In his study of France's industrial bourgeoisie during this period, Peter Stearns has rightly emphasized the strong divisions in mentality that frequently distinguished industrialists from more traditional elements within the bourgeoisie. He goes so far as to identify industrialists as members of a new "middle class" that was separate and distinct from the bourgeoisie.[48] There is much truth in Stearns' argument, particularly for the late Restoration and early July Monarchy. However, as the discussion of child labor in Chapter 5 will show, the social consciousness of the most economically progressive French industrialists evolved considerably by the late 1830s, leading to their attempts to gain a stronger position in national policy debates and implementation. Their stronger participation in debates over child labor surely stemmed in part from the fact that their short-term material interests were at stake. But a more significant key to their growing ability to shape opinion on policy was their gradual success in demonstrating that their own *long-term* interests were entirely reconcilable with those of more traditional elements of the bourgeoisie. Here, moral economist ideology would establish a crucial bridge between industrialists who adhered to its precepts and more traditional elements of the bourgeoisie, showing as it did the ways policy could be used to reconcile the moral and economic needs of workers, different elements within the bourgeoisie, and the state.

The general lack of interest of France's bourgeoisie as a whole in policy questions of broad scope during this period was echoed by their frequent lethargy in the face of empirical evidence of social disorder stemming from the

47. Rosanvallon, *Le moment Guizot*, pp. 202–20, 311.

48. Peter N. Stearns, *Paths to Authority: The Middle Class and the Industrial Labor Force in France, 1820–1848* (Urbana, 1978), pp. 108–10.

lower classes.[49] Vitality and activity on policy issues came from other quarters, in particular from moral economist observers of working-class life who attempted to argue the case for intervention well before those who held power in the legislative chambers or the government. Marx believed that such observers emanated mainly from that part of the French bourgeoisie that had little institutional power under the July Monarchy: "The *petty bourgeoisie* of all gradations, and the *peasantry* also, were completely excluded from political power. Finally, in the official opposition or entirely outside the *pays légal,* there were the *ideological* representatives and spokesmen of the above classes, their savants, lawyers, doctors, etc.—in a word, their so-called *men of talent*."[50] Marx's characterization contains at least one idea worth retaining, and that is the conflict that could and did exist between "ideological" spokesmen and other bourgeois. In the story of policy debate and implementation, the role of social investigators, regional administrators, and a small number of concerned legislators was to act as harbingers of new ways of thinking about French society's future that did not always meet with the immediate assent of other legislative representatives or men within the state administration. Social investigators, more than anyone else, were the ones who transmitted information about the lower classes and recommendations for interventionist policy, but not always to attentive ears. The devotion of many of them to empirical social science did not keep their studies from bearing the marks of essentially middle-class concern. However, a number of their recommendations did reflect their belief that they, perhaps better than those in direct control of the central state, possessed the knowledge and capacity to direct policies towards the achievement of social peace and class reconciliation. Indeed, their documentation of the specific sources of estrangement between bourgeoisie and industrial working class frequently included suggestions on precise means of reconciliation.

Of the two groups of social reformers active in advocating intervention into family life under the Restoration and July Monarchy, only the moral economists truly believed that state power was the most appropriate tool for the implementation of policy. While Social Catholics gradually came to accept state funding for some of their efforts, and supported the legitimacy of state intervention into the problems of abandoned children and children's industrial labor, these activists strongly preferred individualized, personal intervention as a more legitimate means of bringing bourgeois and worker closer together, since for them many symptoms of working-class problems, familial and otherwise, were caused more by mutual estrangement *between* classes

49. Rosanvallon, *Le moment Guizot*, pp. 267–68, emphasizes Guizot's own relative lack of interest in economic matters. See also Stearns, *Paths*, pp. 111–13.

50. Marx, "The Class Struggles," p. 282.

than by workers' deviation from desirable behavioral norms epitomized by the bourgeoisie. Moral economists more effectively articulated a model of how state power might legitimately be used to intervene in working-class family life. At least until the late 1830s, however, the Social Catholic view provided an important alternative model of class reconciliation.

The State, Social Control, and the Intentions of Policy

In his book *The Policing of Families*, Jacques Donzelot has investigated the process by which the private lives of the French lower classes became the target of state policy in the nineteenth and twentieth centuries. Donzelot's work emphasizes the growth of state intervention into private human relations and has correctly identified several of the key policies that exemplified growing concern with problems of family disorder from the 1820s to the 1840s, particularly the problems of abandoned children and child labor. Moreover, he has succeeded in showing that there were strong differences of opinion within the bourgeoisie concerning the families of French workers.[51] Donzelot's study and the work of Michel Foucault, from which Donzelot's approach derives, have also focused attention on the modes of discourse that legitimized the intervention of the state and ultimately private "experts" into the family lives of the poor.

However, an important weakness of Donzelot's work for historians is that, particularly in its treatment of the nineteenth century, it tends to dwell at the level of discourse and plans for the execution of policy. Although it succeeds in exposing the self-serving quality of particular bourgeois writings in which authors dreamed of a social order populated only by people like themselves, Donzelot's study does not tell us very much about how policies directed towards this end came to be implemented or what effects they may have had on the lives of workers—whether, in fact, the policies fulfilled their stated intentions.[52] Similarly, Foucault's work was often marred by his inability to shed much light on the living, breathing human agents who participated in the state's intervention into lower-class life.[53]

51. Jacques Donzelot, *The Policing of Families*, trans. Robert Hurley (New York, 1979), pp. 54–62.

52. A critique of this same weakness within Foucault's work is articulated most fully in Jacques Léonard's "L'historien et le philosophe: A propos de *Surveiller et punir: Naissance de la prison*," in *L'impossible prison: Recherches sur le système pénitentiaire au XIXe siècle réunies par Michelle Perrot: Débat avec Michel Foucault* (Paris, 1980). See especially p. 12 and Foucault's response on p. 49 of the same volume.

53. See Foucault's ruminations on this problem in "The Confessions of the Flesh," contained in Colin Gordon, ed., *Power/Knowledge: Selected Interviews and Other Writings, 1972–1977, Michel Foucault* (New York, 1980), pp. 201–9.

The present study seeks to avoid these problems by tracing the interwoven stories of social-policy discourse and planning to their implementation within the social order. In doing so, it will show that the actual social power of those who recommended state intervention and attempted to carry it out was far weaker than concentration on the "discourse" of intervention has implied, at least during the late Restoration and July Monarchy. An understanding of the social consequences of family policies requires much closer attention to forces that could short-circuit the smooth translation of interventionist discourse into real social change.

The translation of new ideas about the social order into concrete administrative innovation was not an easy process in early industrial France. Nor does it appear that the process was much smoother in other nineteenth-century societies. In his study of social policy in the United States, Michael Katz has recently observed that public officials there always had a much greater sense of the complexities and difficulties that new policies would entail than social policy "theorists" did.[54] In the French situation, where there was disagreement among the different layers of power—ministries, *préfectures,* welfare bureaus, and legislature—not to mention the force of local public opinion, disagreements could and did contribute to making policy difficult to implement. In their own ways, divisions of opinion within the French bourgeoisie, the values and behavior of regional and local administrators, and the behavior of workers whom policy was supposed to change all played a role in disrupting the dream of a homogeneous family order constructed on the basis of bourgeois norms.

These divisions of opinion stemmed not only from divergent views of the bourgeoisie's and the state's short-term and long-term interests but also from conflicting views of the state as legitimate agent of social policy towards the family. When one goes beyond national debates to the day-to-day world of local and regional policy administrators whose task it was to translate emerging world views into social management, one frequently finds that the clear and systematic outlines of new visions of the social order became blurred. Agents of state policy, as well as members of local elites and workers themselves occasionally acted as if they were members of a conspiracy to undermine the best-laid plans for a new and orderly France.

In some cases, conspiracy did play a role. As will be shown in Chapter 5, some industrialists whose financial interests were threatened by plans for child labor reform did conspire to thwart policies with which they disagreed. Moreover, representatives of their view frequently expressed opposition to policy on the floor of the legislative chambers in terms indicating perspectives on the social and moral world that contrasted with those of both moral economists and Social Catholics. However, actual opposition to the imple-

54. Michael B. Katz, *Poverty and Policy in American History* (New York, 1983), p. 190.

mentation of policy more frequently took the form of mute inaction on the part of administrators or passive resistance on the part of workers.

Although the specific constraints within which policymakers, administrators, and workers maneuvered were peculiar to France, there are many points at which aspects of this French story resembled those taking place in other Western societies during the nineteenth century. In particular, there were obvious similarities between both moral economists' and Catholic activists' plans to control what they perceived as immoral and disorderly private conduct on the part of urban workers and the diverse reform projects that historians, particularly of the United States, have interpreted as examples of "social control." Although this study does not actively pursue comparisons between France and other Western societies in the nineteenth century, it does seek to advance beyond several problems that have led to an interpretive stalemate between proponents and opponents of social control approaches to social policy.

Recent discussions of the use of a social control model for understanding social policy seem to have polarized historians into extreme positions on three main issues: the causes for increased intervention into the lives of the lower classes, the motives underlying the expansion of intervention, and the functions that such intervention fulfilled. Proponents of a social control model tend to trace increased intervention by the state or voluntary organizations into working-class life to growing fears of social disorder. Under this formulation, fear, narrow self-interest, or class interests stimulated elites to design programs to respond to perceived disorder. Thus, the essential function of intervention was to quell disorder from below. On the other side, those who reject such a formulation trace the primary cause of intervention to a genuine compassion of the upper classes for the sufferings of the poor. In this analysis, underlying motives are understood as essentially humanitarian, and the essential function of intervention is viewed as the provision of assistance to those in need.[55]

More than perhaps any other scholars, Frances Fox Piven and Richard

55. For discussions of the social control approach, see Gerald N. Grob, "Welfare and Poverty in American History," *Reviews in American History*, no. 1 (1973): 43–52; William A. Muraskin, "The Social-Control Theory in American History: A Critique," *Journal of Social History* 9 (1975/76): 559–69; David J. Rothman, "The State as Parent: Social Policy in the Progressive Era," in Willard Gaylin, Ira Glasser, Steven Marcus, and David J. Rothman, *Doing Good: The Limits of Benevolence* (New York, 1978), pp. 67–96; the references in Walter I. Trattner, ed., *Social Welfare or Social Control? Some Historical Reflections on Regulating the Poor* (Knoxville, 1983), pp. 152–57; Gareth Stedman Jones, "Class Expression versus Social Control? A Critique of Recent Trends in the Social History of 'Leisure,' " in idem, *Languages of Class: Studies in English Working-Class History, 1832–1982* (Cambridge, 1983), pp. 76–89; Catharine Lis and Hugo Soly, "Policing the Early Modern Proletariat," in David Levine, ed., *Proletarianization and Family History* (Orlando, 1984), pp. 207–11; and Clarke A. Chambers, "Toward a Redefinition of Welfare History," *Journal of American History* 73 (1986): 407–33, esp. pp. 416–20.

Cloward, in their widely read *Regulating the Poor* emphasized the link between increases in social welfare funding and the threat of public disorder.[56] Their work also argued eloquently for the importance of bringing the actions and values of lower-class people back into the investigation of causes precipitating the flow of public monies to the poor. In revising an older kind of social welfare history that concentrated almost exclusively on elites, however, they sometimes appeared to think that an understanding of policy development could be based on a study of lower-class agitation alone.[57] In fact, although their general explanation of the way relief expands discounted the activities of members of social elites, their empirical work illustrated the important participation of middle-class groups in making lower-class protest more organized and effective.[58] More recently, Piven has stated her rejection of a "simplistic 'social control' perspective," and argued forcefully for the ability of social and gender groups to have an impact on policy formation and implementation.[59] Another recent analyst has urged historians to examine the interplay between the values and ambitions of the different constituencies affected by social policy and to become more aware of the fact that lower-class groups have historically used policy for the realization of their own ends.[60] Thus, if we are to understand the creation, implementation, and reception of social policies, it appears that the most fruitful approach is to explore the mentalities of all participants in the drama and the specific relations between different social groups.

On the issue of motivations underlying policy, one of the greatest problems is that the complexity of moral values underlying policy as well as the historic specificity of "humanitarianism" have tended to be lost. As the debate now stands, it appears that for a social policy to bear true moral authenticity, it must flow from motives that are demonstrably selfless and disinterested. An older generation of social welfare historians probably has only itself to blame for this rather astonishing notion, now defended by some proponents of the social control concept. Had earlier historians attempted to understand the moral values of policymakers in more detail, with a greater sense of those values' limitations, inconsistencies, and conflicts, current historians would

56. Frances Fox Piven and Richard Cloward, *Regulating the Poor: The Functions of Public Welfare* (New York, 1971). One critic has noted, however, that Piven and Cloward did not explicitly define or elaborate on their model of social control; see James Leiby, "Social Control and Historical Explanation: Historians View the Piven and Cloward Thesis," in Trattner, *Social Welfare*, p. 95.

57. Frances Fox Piven and Richard A. Cloward, "Humanitarianism in History: A Response to the Critics," in Trattner, *Social Welfare*, pp. 117–21.

58. Piven and Cloward, *Regulating the Poor*, pp. 290–92.

59. Frances Fox Piven, "Women and the State: Ideology, Power, and the Welfare State," in Alice S. Rossi, ed., *Gender and the Life Course* (New York, 1985), p. 279.

60. Chambers, "Toward a Redefinition," p. 420.

probably not be faced with such polarized opinion on the question of motivations. For it seems quite clear that the more social policy is imbued not only with specific moral goals in mind but with a conviction of how those values are to be expressed in specific behavior, the more repressive it will be towards behavior that conflicts or appears to conflict with the system of values on which it is based. Thus, the greater the apparent conflict between the moral values of reformers and the values of those to be reformed, the more policymakers will appear to be essentially self-interested.

Nevertheless, the possibility that the defense of moral principles and self-interest are quite compatible is illustrated in Piven and Cloward's analysis of lower-class Americans' agitation for changes in the system of public assistance. The authors show that poor people's application of their sense of the moral order could result in tangible material benefits for them. This should neither astonish us nor delegitimize the authenticity of their own moral critique of the social system under which they are disadvantaged. The notion that a group's idea of the moral social order needs to be entirely selfless in order to achieve authenticity seems not only unreasonable but deeply antihistorical. Similarly, while class factors are critical in shaping the basic outlines of moral-economic conflict, they do not dictate its specific features. As William A. Muraskin has argued, "The growth and development of ideas and their interaction with class interest is a complex phenomenon. It involves not only immediate self-interest, consciously or unconsciously perceived, but long-term developmental trends, of a material and nonmaterial form. Granted, 'pure' idealism or 'pure' humanitarianism do not exist, but while the material and social world places definite limitations on the power of ideas, socioeconomic factors determine boundaries or outer limits, not specific responses."[61] A critical problem is thus to show how different moral values about the social order are formed and the ways people of all classes bring them into the arena of social-policy debates or implementation. This is an eminently historical problem, one that suggests the importance of retaining a sense of the historicity of moral values.

For such reasons, it is unfortunate that the epithet "humanitarian" is used so loosely. The consequence of the very loose use of this label by both proponents and opponents of a social control model is that humanitarianism has been emptied of its specific historical associations. Self-proclaimed humanitarianism was a product of a very specific kind of secular, Enlightenment ideology propounded by members of the middle and upper classes who were struggling against monarchical and/or clerical institutions that were themselves imbued with historically specific notions of social subordination or Christian charity.[62]

61. "The Social-Control Theory," pp. 565–66.

62. On humanitarianism in its original historical setting, see Shelby T. McCloy, *The Humanitarian Movement in Eighteenth-Century France* (Louisville, 1957).

Intervention into the lives of the poor on the basis of humanitarianism was surely founded on the notion that the humanitarians themselves were the best judges of the interests of humanity and, given their social power, best able to implement policy in those interests. However, the idea that their own interests would be forwarded by humanitarian policies would have come as little surprise to eighteenth-century practitioners, since one of the fundamental features of their view of the world was that the interests of groups in the social order, properly understood, were reconcilable to the extent that each one understood its interests in the long rather than the short term.

The original humanitarians of the eighteenth century did not believe that they had a monopoly on compassion. They did, however, believe that they were the most intelligent proponents of social policy that would conform to new, progressive notions of the social order. The original humanitarians did not see themselves as entirely selfless or disinterested. Rather, they believed that their interests and the interests of the social order as a whole were entirely consonant. We may disagree with this perception. However, by using the term "humanitarian" so indiscriminately, we lose the moral vision and specific historical contours of the humanitarian perspective, and we are left with a term that conjurs up, in an ahistorical fashion, any effort whose proponents proclaim to be selfless and thus moral in nature. Thus, in response to their critics, Piven and Cloward attempt to characterize the struggles of the poor as the true source of humanitarianism. Besides concealing the fact that humanitarianism has historically been practiced by the upper and middle classes, their use of the term merely exacerbates the problem of imputing humanitarianism to any morally charged effort for redistributive social justice.[63]

While proponents and opponents of social control approaches have overused an ahistorical notion of humanitarianism in order to probe the motivations for a wide array of social policies, those employing the concept of social control are more vulnerable to committing what might be termed the "nothing but" fallacy. Because policies functioned to maintain the status quo does not mean that they were "nothing but" policies to do so. Those interested mainly in the history of the *longue durée,* in continuities in the functions of social policy, are of necessity preoccupied by this apparent function of social policy over the long term. Yet, historians concerned with shorter periods and with specific historical actors, while not neglecting longer-term perspectives, will doubtless wish to concentrate more on the particularities of historical situations and to probe the actual language and specific circumstances in which policy was debated. Importantly, too, historians must now devote greater attention to the effects that policies seem to have had once they began to be implemented.[64]

63. Piven and Cloward, "Humanitarianism," p. 117.

64. The need to examine the consequences of policy is developed in F.M.L. Thompson, "Social Control in Victorian Britain," *Economic History Review*, 2d ser., 34 (1981): 189–208.

However, of all the problems involved in understanding the significance of social policy, none is more difficult than probing the question of motivation. For several reasons, I have chosen in this study to concentrate on the stated intentions of policymakers rather than to search for their possibly hidden motivations. In an essay on the study of texts, Quentin Skinner has made a useful distinction between the interpretation of motivations and intentions that I have tried to follow in the analysis of the observers and policymakers under discussion.[65] He writes, "To speak of a writer's motives seems invariably to be to speak of a condition antecedent to, and contingently connected with, the appearance of his works." Skinner continues by distinguishing two approaches to the interpretation of writers' intentions, the latter of which engages the critic in an exploration of the work's larger setting.

> [To] speak of a writer's intentions may be either to refer to his plan or design to create a certain type of work . . . or to refer to and describe an actual work in a certain way. . . . In the former type of case we seem (as in talking about motives) to be alluding to a contingent antecedent condition of the appearance of the work. In the latter type of case, however, we seem to be alluding to a feature of the work itself, and to be characterizing it, in terms of its embodiment of a particular aim or intention, and thus in terms of its having a particular point.

The second approach to interpreting intentions, he argues, should be based on the understanding of "prevailing conventions governing the treatment of the issues or themes with which that text is concerned" and "focus on the writer's mental world, the world of his empirical beliefs."[66] This approach is, in fact, very similar to Mannheim's position on the need to understand the "connectedness" of ideas, though Mannheim placed greatest stress on ideas' "sociological" connectedness and the relation of ideas about the social world to their authors' place in the social structure.

The displacement of focus away from an emphasis on motivations also stems from my own skepticism about the possibilities of achieving a satisfactory historical understanding of the policy advocates and policymakers in this story by seeking to "unmask" them—by attempting to penetrate their minds in search of the "real" motivations behind their efforts. Hubert Dreyfus and Paul Rabinow, citing Paul Ricoeur, refer to such a plan of unmasking as "the hermeneutics of suspicion," which holds that "actors do not have direct access to the meaning of their discourse and practices [and] that our everyday understanding of things is superficial and distorted. It is, in fact, a motivated covering-up of the way things really are." This approach also holds that "there

65. See Quentin Skinner, "Motives, Intentions, and the Interpretation of Texts," *New Literary History* 3 (1972): 401–7, particularly the discussion of "illocutionary" intentions.

66. Ibid., pp. 401, 406–7.

is an essential continuity between everyday intelligibility and the deeper kind of intelligibility which the everyday view works to cover up. Since the deeper intelligibility is supposedly at work causing distortions on the everyday level, one can arrive at this motivating truth by sufficiently detailed attention to these distortions."[67] Mannheim, too believed that "unmasking" hidden motivations of individuals and groups lay within the purview of a "particular" conception of ideology, which by itself led only to radical skepticism about "human thought in general."[68]

Shifting the focus of attention from the motivation of reformers to their intentions does not, of course, obviate the problem of interpretation.[69] On the other hand, concentrating on intentions allows the human subjects of analysis to maintain a certain integrity. By concentrating on stated intentions, historians are more likely to succeed in meeting the subjects of their analysis on the subjects' terms, as the discussion of Mannheim at the beginning of this chapter has implied. The first task of the analysis is thus to try to understand what it was that social observers and policymakers said they intended to do. By concentrating on intentions, the study directs attention back towards the relationship of policymakers to their own society and to the working-class families they intended to change.

Having succeeded in understanding the stated intentions of policies, however, one must resort to a more obvious form of interpretation for an understanding of their larger significance, since critical readers frequently see other meanings in writings than those intended by their authors.[70] Historians have the added luxury of placing stories of social policy in longer-term perspective, thus imbuing them with meanings unimaginable to those who participated in their original plots. It is this advantage that leads historians to hazard

67. Hubert Dreyfus and Paul Rabinow, *Michel Foucault*, 2d ed. (Chicago, 1983), pp. 123–24. This book is the best available to historians on this elusive subject.

68. Mannheim, *Ideology and Utopia*, p. 37. See also Simonds, *Mannheim's Sociology*, pp. 101–3.

69. Joan Higgins has recently criticized social control theorists for ascribing intentions on the basis of effects of policy, for imputing conscious motives of social control when few are empirically documentable, and for "imply[ing] a coherence in social policy which it is difficult to identify in practice." She emphasizes the need to identify concretely those who make and implement policy and to trace their relation to the "ruling class." Higgins, "Social Control Theories of Social Policy," *Journal of Social Policy* 9 (1980): 21–22. E. P. Thompson, for his part, has voiced the opinion that even "intention is a bad measure of ideological interest and of historical consequences." Thompson, "The Moral Economy of the English Crowd in the Eighteenth Century," *Past and Present*, no. 50 (1971): 89. On the intentions underlying social policy, see also Piven and Cloward, "Humanitarianism," pp. 119–20.

70. See Dominick LaCapra, *Rethinking Intellectual History and Reading Texts* (Ithaca, 1983), p. 37, for a rejection of "the idea that authorial intentions constitute the ultimate criterion for arriving at a valid interpretation of a text."

speculations about the larger significance of particular policy stories, since we frequently wish to find links between past and present.

In this regard, it will become apparent that the present study is in some ways a "history of the present," considering as it does the gradual emergence of particular views of the family and a style of policy management that are still very much with us.[71] Not only the substantive views of the family but the whole integrated process of investigation, debate, and policy implementation in early-nineteenth-century France evokes features of the world in which we live. As two recent analysts of current family policy debates have written:

> To say that any object of experience is a "problem" implies at least two perceptions: First, there is the cognitive implication that this object "sticks out" from the rest of experience, that it invites attention, and that it does so because there is something not fully understood and perhaps not quite right about it. . . . At least in modern times, however, there is a second implication to a declaration that this or that has become a "problem" —namely, that we ought *to do* something about it. . . . This practical, activist implication is especially important when an institution is declared to be a problem, since one peculiarly modern assumption is that society . . . is a human construction and therefore may be *re*constructed if enough people think it should be.[72]

To argue, however, that French ideologies and family policies in the period from the mid-1820s to the late 1840s resemble more recent ones is not to say that the former were significant only or mainly as progenitors of policies that succeeded them. In order to understand why they evolved at all or why they evolved as they did requires an understanding of key policy legacies from the Old Regime and Revolution, specific features of relations between bourgeoisie and working class in cities of early industrial France, debates over policy implementation, and the ways policies were received by workers who were their targets.

A consideration of the ideological foundations of family policy begins in Chapter 2 in the analysis of the world views of Social Catholics and moral economists, where those views are discussed in the light of older traditions

71. This is an epithet used by Hubert L. Dreyfus and Paul Rabinow to characterize the historical work of Michel Foucault. Dreyfus and Rabinow, *Michel Foucault*, p. 119. La Capra argues: "Historians are involved in the effort to understand both what something meant in its own time and what it may mean for us today. The most engaging, if at time perplexing, dimensions of interpretation exist on the margin, where these two meanings are not simply disjoined from one another, for it is at this liminal point that the dialogue with the past becomes internal to the historian." *Rethinking Intellectual History*, p. 18.

72. Brigitte Berger and Peter L. Berger, *The War over the Family: Capturing the Middle Ground* (New York: 1983), p. 4.

of French policy and policy thinking as well as in the context of features that were historically new in both perspectives. Chapter 3 introduces the three urban settings under consideration and examines Social Catholics' and moral economists' understanding of and policies towards the problem of working-class marriage and common law unions. In Chapter 4, the focus shifts to the problem of foundlings and abandoned children in the three areas and the acrimonious debate at both the national and local levels over the relation of this age-old problem to the nineteenth-century working-class family. Chapter 5 considers the question of children's labor in the industrial work places of Lille, Rouen, and Mulhouse; the gradual construction and attempted resolution of the child labor problem; and the relation of children's industrial work to larger questions of working-class family life and its place in French society. In Chapter 6, the findings of the study are assessed in the larger context of class relations and group mentalities as they were expressed historically through social policy and its consequences.

2

Moral Economist and Catholic Perspectives on Working-Class Family Life

Since the publication of Edward Thompson's "The Moral Economy of the English Crowd in the Eighteenth Century," social historians have paid increasing attention to the ways popular values have informed patterns of social conflict between lower and upper classes and shaped the ways these conflicts were understood by their lower-class participants.[1] Thompson, in particular, has demonstrated the power that lower-class constructions of the eighteenth-century moral order had in encouraging popular resistance to a newer, capitalist organization of the marketplace. More recently, William Sewell has emphasized the persistence of French workers' corporate notions of social solidarity during the process of industrialization, showing how such traditions fired their systematic critique of the new economic order.[2] In his study of the organization of the French textile industry in the nineteenth century, William Reddy has gone further, arguing that the persistence of older world views among workers and bourgeois alike was symptomatic of France's failure to evolve into a truly capitalist society in the nineteenth century.[3]

The great contribution of these studies has been to recapture the specific values that inspired participants in conflicts over power, rights, and the basic nature of the modern social order. Although these historians associate the construction of world views and value systems with particular groups or social classes defined essentially in relation to the process of production, their studies have also helped to nuance a notion of class conflict by reintegrating moral values into an understanding of its causes. Their analyses have shown that

1. E. P. Thompson, "The Moral Economy of the English Crowd in the Eighteenth Century," *Past and Present*, no. 50 (1971): 76–136.

2. William H. Sewell, Jr., *Work and Revolution in France: The Language of Labor from the Old Regime to 1848* (Cambridge, 1980).

3. William M. Reddy, *The Rise of Market Culture: The Textile Trade and French Society, 1750–1900* (Cambridge, 1984).

though social solidarity was forged by groups who shared a similar place in the production process, it also resulted from specific shared experiences as consumers (Thompson), as skilled artisans with a corporate memory (Sewell), or as factory workers with a model of themselves as makers of goods rather than sellers of their labor (Reddy). In all three cases, workers' critique of the status quo stemmed in large part from their own construction of a collective consciousness in which elements of memory underlay claims for moral-economic justice in the face of economic change.

While these studies have illuminated the moral dimension of popular, working-class critiques of the capitalist social order, there has been less work on the moral dimension of middle-class or bourgeois views of the world. Although Reddy, in particular, has argued that the nineteenth-century French middle-class world view deviated sharply from a pure and unmitigated "capitalist" one, the specific elements of this view have remained relatively unexplored. The result has been a portrait of a rather undifferentiated bourgeois mentality to which workers' view of the moral elements of the capitalist economy may be contrasted.[4]

This chapter identifies the ways that values and beliefs about the family and its place in the industrial social order began to mobilize bourgeois thought and action from the late 1820s to the 1840s, tracing the evolution of Social Catholic and moral economist perspectives. Although these two world views about family and society appear to have been shaped most obviously by material changes in French society brought about by the early Industrial Revolution, conceptualizations of the problems of working-class family life showed vital and interesting links with traditions of thought and action deeply embedded in French history. Therefore, the discussion seeks to examine Social Catholic and moral economist views of the working-class family in the context of the historical traditions from which they derived.

Debates about the working-class family under the late Restoration and July Monarchy were emblematic of a larger examination of industrial capitalism's significance for French society. The critical examination of working-class family life, in fact, served as one of the more powerful vehicles for assessing the human consequences of industrial society, for articulating the proper relationship among family members, the role of the family in society, and the moral bases of social solidarity. Moreover, the empirical examination of working-class family life in France's centers of industry helped to crystallize and clarify fundamental values of the bourgeoisie. It stimulated observers to articulate what made them different from the industrial workers who so fascinated them and ultimately to ponder some of the latent similarities. In-

4. An exception to this generalization is provided in Peter N. Stearns, *Paths to Authority: The Middle Class and the Industrial Labor Force in France, 1820–1848* (Urbana, 1978).

quiries into working-class life also exposed important ideological differences within middle-class ranks, which later resonated with increasing force when specific policy decisions had to be made and executed.

Social Catholic and moral economist perspectives on policy towards workers' families developed within an intellectual and social context of profound disagreement less over the state of the working-class family in the 1830s and 1840s than over its fundamental causes or social implications. Analyses of workers' lives were used by both sides to capture the human face of industrialization and especially to extract the moral significance of social change. Although the moral bases of the Social Catholic critique of industrial capitalism were more obvious, framed as they were within an explicitly Christian world view with many links to Tridentine Catholicism, the moral economist position also resonated with its own fervor—its own notions of the moral bases of industrial society.

The New Foundations of a Catholic Perspective

One of the most lasting critiques of French industrialization and its human consequences was codified in the first recognizably Catholic, widely read study by Count Alban de Villeneuve-Bargemont, his *Economie politique chrétienne*. In a book whose form was to stand as a prototype of later studies, combining empirical data, personal observation, and a clear moral position, Villeneuve-Bargemont launched the first systematic critique of French industrial civilization, articulating some of the themes that were to be debated over the next twenty years. Responding to the early work of one of France's most eminent moral economists, Charles Dupin, whose book *Forces productives et commerciales de la France* described the infrastructure of France's new industrial civilization in detailed quantitative form, Villeneuve-Bargemont changed the focus of the discussion of French industrial capitalism to center on the problems of the human inhabitants of industrial areas, focusing as much on the issue of poverty as of wealth.[5]

The most salient elements of Villeneuve-Bargemont's magisterial work were its emphasis on the growing dimensions of poverty in France's richest

5. Alban de Villeneuve-Bargemont, *Economie politique chrétienne, ou recherches sur la nature et les causes du paupérisme en France et en Europe, et sur les moyens de le soulager et de le prévenir*, 3 vols. (Paris, 1834); Charles Dupin, *Forces productives et commerciales de la France*, 2 vols. (Paris, 1827). The most detailed discussion of Villeneuve-Bargemont is contained in Jean-Baptiste Duroselle, *Les débuts du catholicisme social en France, 1822–1870* (Paris, 1951), pp. 59–71. On the relation of Villeneuve's views to those of Villermé and Sismondi, see Ann LaBerge, "Public Health in France and the French Public Health Movement, 1815–1848" (Ph.D. diss., University of Tennessee, 1974), p. 101. On Dupin's work, see Reddy, *The Rise of Market Culture*, pp. 141–43.

industrial departments and his sense that the kind of poverty he observed there deviated sharply from its previous forms in the past. The characteristics of industrial civilization that aroused his greatest condemnation were to become classic features of a heterogeneous Catholic view. From the beginning of his work, Villeneuve took up the standard against Malthus: "It seemed to me that the deplorable poverty whose existence in England Malthus acknowledged could be more rationally attributed to the system of industry than to an excess of population, or at least to both causes acting simultaneously." The major critiques of industrial capitalism explicit in Villeneuve's work included its stimulation of rural emigration and the agglomeration of factory populations around cities such as Lille. Here, the dependency of thousands of workers on wages was tantamount to their ultimate dependency on an increasingly overburdened system of public relief. Aggregations of workers meant an excessive division of labor, dependency on markets outside France that could not be controlled, and the ultimate irony "*that the more entrepreneurs of wealthy industries an area contains, the more poor workers it has*." In this work, Villeneuve-Bargemont's remedy for the social problems of a nascent industrial society were systematic and economic, entailing the establishment of a national system of agricultural colonies designed to return workers to a way of life in which poverty was more manageable and moral relations between agricultural day laborers and their employers were based on values of human solidarity. As he wrote, "Among agricultural day laborers, there is not this passive and forced subjection experienced by industrial workers, which is born from excesses of competition and an excess of needs."[6]

Although Villeneuve-Bargemont criticized the systematic nature of a new pauperism, castigating the materialism of a Malthus or the greed of individual manufacturers, his indictment of industrial capitalist society was also firmly based on what he saw as its clear moral depredations, exemplified in the lives of urban industrial workers.

> The intelligence of the ignorant and immoral worker is rapidly extinguished. . . . For him, all ends by being reduced to the vegetation of physical life. Without foresight of the morrow, he consumes his modest earnings in cabarets or places of debauchery. If he marries, he blindly obeys a brutal and disorderly instinct. If he has a family, he neglects or abandons it as a burdensome charge. . . . His children do not render him the services he has failed to render to his own parents. They preceded him; others will follow him in the last degree of poverty. . . . This is the way that indigence is transmitted as the only inheritance in the fami-

6. Villeneuve-Bargemont, *Economie politique chrétienne*, 1:9, 379, 298. On the systematic and macrosociological qualities of Villeneuve's work, see Robert Goetz-Girey, *Croissance et progrès à l'origine des sociétés industrielles* (Paris, 1966), pp. 247, 251.

> lies of workers which the present system of industry leaves prey to the brutalization of intelligence and the depravation of mores.[7]

Many of Villeneuve-Bargemont's positions were not original. His antipathy for England's competitive, materialistic civilization, his critique of Dupin, his anti-urbanism and corresponding defense of agricultural colonies, even his sometimes instrumentalist view of the uses of religious instruction as a force for the pacification of the lower classes, echoed the work of Bigot de Morogues, which had been published several years earlier.[8] Villeneuve-Bargemont's study, however, carried more weight than some previously voiced opinions because of its length, its empirical documentation, and the count's position as a respected Restoration administrator in the department of the Nord in the years 1828–30.[9]

In addition, several features of Villeneuve-Bargemont's work made it a significant departure from previous volumes of inquiry into means of remedying the problem of human dependency. Unlike Gérando's *Le visiteur du pauvre* or Duchâtel's *La charité*,[10] Villeneuve-Bargemont's study was the first publication of note to analyze the problems of working-class families within the new social geography of industrial France. His book departed from earlier and some later investigations of working-class life by concentrating on those areas where a new France was being built. Moreover, he changed the terms of the discussion away from a relatively ahistorical focus on poverty and the poor to a greater focus on historically new features of poverty within working-class communities.[11] Villeneuve-Bargemont's ultimate vision of social policy relied less on rationalizing public and private charity systems, as Gérando or Duchâtel had recommended, and more on an ambitious, administratively driven restructuring of the French economy in order to alleviate the challenges

7. Villeneuve-Bargemont, *Economie politique chrétienne*, 1:479–80.

8. Pierre Bigot de Morogues, *De la misère des ouvriers et de la marche à suivre pour y remédier* (Paris, 1832).

9. Villeneuve-Bargemont's data on levels of indigence did incur some criticism. See, for example, Ambroise Clément, *Recherches sur les causes de l'indigence* (Paris, 1846), pp. 83–84. Three brothers of the count also served Louis XVIII as prefects. The king was reputed to have said of them, "If I had eighty Villeneuves, I'd make eighty prefects of them." Cited in Ernest Seillière, *Une académie à l'époque romantique* (Paris, 1926), p. 53.

10. J. M. de Gérando, *Le visiteur du pauvre* (Paris, 1820); Comte Tanneguy Duchâtel, *La charité dans ses rapports avec l'état moral et le bien-être des classes inférieures de la société* (Paris, 1829).

11. Other Catholic writers during the Restoration and July Monarchy continued to contribute to the older tradition that focused on the lower classes as the poor, and on the most efficient means to organize charity on their behalf. See, for example, J.B.F. Marbeau, *Du paupérisme en France et des moyens d'y remédier, ou principes d'économie charitable* (Paris, 1847). For a view of Villeneuve that downplays the innovative aspects of his work, see Jacques Donzelot, *The Policing of Families*, trans. Robert Hurley (New York, 1979), p. 62.

of systemic poverty and working-class dependency. His thorough critique of the societal sources of working-class poverty did not however, exclude administrative rigor in attempting to control the growth of dependency in the Nord. During his tenure there as prefect, Villeneuve-Bargemont was instrumental in ordering a thoroughgoing revision of relief rolls that resulted in important, if short-term, reductions of the number of poor receiving aid.[12] His larger and more visionary idea of reasserting moral bonds between workers and the owners of property on the basis of *colonies agricoles* won him the support of conservative Catholic observers of his own generation. However, his general critique of the social and moral consequences of industrial capitalism was more widely digested and admired than his specific proposals for reform.[13]

In the Catholic vision of working-class family life, a primary symptom of spiritual and moral decline was the loosening of parental-child bonds, a condition that was believed to mirror societal-level estrangement between classes. The underlying causes of intrafamilial estrangement, Catholics argued, could be traced directly to specific features of life in industrial cities. The first, as Villeneuve-Bargemont had shown, was the dependency of entire families on wages for their survival, a feature that in his view was tantamount to poverty.[14] His distaste for this form of veiled dependency was not a new one. For centuries, reliance upon wages had been intimately associated with poverty, signaling as it did the dependency of the wage earner on work supplied by another.[15]

Dependency upon wages and the concomitant lack of heritable property were closely linked by conservative Catholics to the breakdown of bonds between parents and their children that militated against the continuity of lineal consciousness: "To conceive of property without the family—the family without property—is impossible. Such is the strength of the bonds . . . that link these together. . . . [Without heritable property] there is no family, *and the*

12. Charles Engrand, "Les industries lilloises et la crise économique de 1826 à 1832," *Revue du Nord* 63 (1981): 249.

13. Bigot de Morogues was one of the best-known supporters of the *colonies agricoles,* in his *Du paupérisme, de la mendicité et des moyens d'en prévenir les funestes effets* (Paris, 1834), pt. 2. On Villeneuve's wider appeal, see Jean-Claude Lamberti, *Tocqueville et les deux démocraties* (Paris, 1983), pp. 229–30, for a discussion of Villeneuve-Bargemont's influence on Tocqueville's economic views. Tocqueville's brother Edouard, who was a contributor to the *Annales de la charité*, was a great admirer of Villeneuve and was probably the main link between the two students of society. See André Jardin, *Alexis de Tocqueville* (Paris, 1984), pp. 48–49.

14. On Englishmen's antipathy to wage labor, see Christopher Hill, "Pottage for Freeborn Englishmen: Attitudes to Wage Labour in the Sixteenth and Seventeenth Centuries," in C. H. Feinstein, ed., *Socialism, Capitalism, and Economic Growth: Essays Presented to Maurice Dobb* (Cambridge, 1967), pp. 338–50.

15. Jean-Pierre Gutton, *La société et les pauvres: L'exemple de la généralité de Lyon, 1534–1789* (Paris, 1970), p. 9.

poor man is proof. . . . His children disperse, succeeding generations soon forget their names. They have no names. Ask a poor man about his genealogy. He'll think you're kidding. The family is nothing, or nearly nonexistent for the poor."[16] Dependency on wages was most acute among newly developing communities of industrial workers whose families' proletarian status was believed to entail both moral and material deprivation:

> We should not confuse proletarians with workers. . . . a little capital, a strip of land, . . . sturdy arms, a head filled with some rudiments of useful knowledge, and fortified against immoral behavior by fundamental moral principles: these constitute what we can call the means and instrument of freedom, its signs and safeguard. Below the millions of people of the working class who do not possess this liberating instrument except in an incomplete manner [are] the many proletarians, condemned to the most complete destitution; who vegetate on others' land or in the area around factories, or in hideous urban hovels. Their master is called *wages,* whom circumstances render unmerciful.[17]

Moreover, Catholic observers strongly believed that industrial wage labor was increasingly carried out in distinctly unfamilial settings. Industrial labor in textile factories came to be associated in their minds with the individualistic, competitive, antifamilial values that underlay the new economic system as a whole. This link was illustrated in later, melodramatic portraits of the ravages supposedly effected in working-class families by industrial labor. In the following dialogues, two young spokeswomen for the values of a newer industrial working class were contrasted with girls representing an older way of thinking:

> HERMANCE: What have they done for me except to bring me into the world? . . . As a child, I was their servant, and they paid me by knocking me around and by cold and hunger. When I was older, they put me into the factory. They ate up my wages without giving me anything. . . . But since I'm flying with my own wings I've arranged things differently. . . . Don't you see, Marthe? It's a good way to be free and not to depend on a mother who's always grumbling and a father who could drink up the ocean and rivers.
>
> MARTHE: Don't talk like that of your parents, I beg you. It hurts me.
>
> HERMANCE: Ha! They've hurt me too! You should take me as your model, Marthe and not let people take advantage of you. We're young.

16. Roger Gougenot des Mousseaux, *Des prolétaires* (Paris, 1846), p. 353.
17. Ibid., pp. 49–50.

We should have a bit of freedom and fun. If we kill ourselves working, should our wages go to others or ourselves?

MARTHE: To others? A father and mother aren't others.[18]

Another similar drama echoed this theme. Julie, who was placed in the factory at the age of eight, is considering the prospect of becoming the mistress of the mill owner's son:

PAULINE: Poor girl, think of the consequences! Dishonor for you, your father and brother, who's a brave soldier.

JULIE: Ha! They should expect anything since they put me in the factory. It's a miracle that I haven't been the mistress of a half-dozen men, masters, and workmen.[19]

The conflicts here could be and were read at a number of levels. Marthe and Pauline represented the old, and Julie and Hermance the new model of working-class parent-child relations, the latter infused with a spirit of individual selfishness that resulted from a kind of family life in which affective bonds between parent and child were absent. It is important to note that in these two dramas, neither spokeswoman for the primacy of family bonds had entered the factory by parental choice. Both were *déclassées* who came from good artisan or lower-middle-class families fallen on hard times through no moral fault of their own. Although their factory work exposed them to corruption, they were able to resist its temptations because of the moral and religious values inculcated by their parents. Hermance and Julie, on the other hand, were themselves the daughters of factory workers who had sent their children to work because they had squandered their own earnings on high living. It was thus the first generations of factory workers whose values and behavior presaged a gloomy future for working-class family life in industrial capitalist society.

Villeneuve-Bargemont's antipathy to industrial capitalism and his concern for its putative effects on the families of industrial workers left their legacy in the commentaries of a variety of Catholic social observers. However, the strategies he advocated for dealing with these problems were not shared by the most important organized source of Catholic thinking and action on working-class family problems in the period under investigation. By the early

18. Mathilde Bourdon, *Marthe Blondel, ou l'ouvrière de fabrique* (Paris, 1863), p. 61. This source is discussed in Pierre Pierrard, *La vie ouvrière à Lille sous le Second Empire* (Paris, 1965), pp. 73, 276.

19. Emile Bosquet, *Le roman des ouvrières* (Paris, 1868), p. 96. The continuing appeal of this kind of didactic dialogue is illustrated in Luc Boltanski, *Prime éducation et morale de classe*, 2d ed. (Paris, 1977), pp. 19–21.

1830s, members of an emerging Social Catholic movement devised rather different means of dealing with the moral effects of social change hypothesized by Villeneuve-Bargemont and others. This new generation of Social Catholic activists brought a reinvigorated personal piety to their understanding of workers' family problems and a grass-roots rather than an administrative perspective to their solution.

Social Catholics' fundamental critique of industrial capitalism resonated in tones quite similar to Villeneuve-Bargemont's. In his address before Lille's chapter of the Société de Saint-Vincent-de-Paul, one of the organization's local leaders and an industrialist himself argued: "*Industry*, which wished to constitute itself outside the principle of Love, has come upon society as a disorderly, fatal force establishing war among all elements involved in work. In the name of competition—its essential condition of progress—[industry] has provoked hostility among those who should cooperate in the same task, and has contributed definitively to increasing immorality . . . and poverty among the lower classes to whom it had promised dignity and abundance."[20] In his classic work on French Social Catholicism, Jean-Baptiste Duroselle has identified lay organizations such as the Société de Saint-Vincent-de-Paul as precursors rather than pure examples of the Social Catholic movement. For Duroselle, Social Catholicism, "like socialism, assigned itself the task of eliminating social abuses engendered by the Industrial Revolution." It was not essentially charitable, concerned with helping those experiencing "inevitable" kinds of suffering, but rather, was concerned with "improving the life situation of those who, because of social injustice and economic conditions, could not live from their work."[21] Activists of the Société de Saint-Vincent-de-Paul did not conform entirely to this definition of Social Catholicism, since their work did include charitable activity. However, their efforts among working-class families were based at least originally on a view of society that identified the "social question" as a new and pressing issue. In this sense, Social Catholics of the late Restoration and July Monarchy were part of a larger tradition of "social Christianity" that was based on "organized and collective efforts to bring a contribution inspired by Christian principles to the solution of what is called the social question, that is, the situation of the working classes in modern capitalist society."[22]

20. Address by M. Kolb-Bernard to the Séance générale de la conférence de Saint-Vincent-de-Paul, Lille, 6 December 1840, ASVP, Paris, Dossier 1. Part of this speech is quoted in Pierrard, *La vie ouvrière*, p. 394.

21. Duroselle, *Les débuts*, p. 24.

22. Nadine-Josette Chaline, "Attitude et action sociale de l'Eglise dans le diocèse de Rouen au XIXe et au début du XXe siècle," *Revue des sociétés savantes de Haute Normandie*, no. 67 (1972): 71.

Social Catholicism in Action

The founder of the Société de Saint-Vincent-de-Paul, Frédéric Ozanam, was the source of the organization's perspective on the social question. In a letter of 1837, he articulated the outlines of this view:

> The question which divides men in our day is no longer a question of political forms, it is a social question—that of deciding whether the spirit of selfishness or the spirit of sacrifice is to carry the day; whether society is to be a huge traffic for the benefit of the strongest, or the consecration of each for the benefit of all, and above all for the protection of the weak. There are many who already have too much, and who wish to posseses still more; there are a greater number who do not have enough, and who want to seize it if it is not given to them. Between these two classes of men a struggle is imminent, and it threatens to be terrible—on one side the power of gold, on the other the power of despair. It is between these two opposing armies that we must precipitate ourselves, if not to prevent, at least to break, the shock. Our youth and the mediocrity of our [social] position facilitates this role of mediation which [our] title of Christians renders obligatory.[23]

One of the most powerful themes within Ozanam's view of the "social question" was the notion of class mediation. Significantly, neither he nor his original co-workers in the new confraternity represented by the Société de Saint-Vincent-de-Paul viewed themselves as protagonists in the class estrangement implied by the development of French industrial capitalism. As he argued, both the members' "youth" and their "position" combined to suggest their role of intermediary between the wealthy financial and industrial bourgeoisie and the working class. This theme was consistent throughout Ozanam's own career. In an 1841 letter, he emphasized the dramatic need for the group's mission within the new industrial social order: "Now, too, that an ever-increasing pauperism stands face to face, in rage and desperation, with a moneyed aristocracy whose bowels of mercy have hardened, it is well that there should be found mediators who may prevent a collision of which no man may foretell the horrible disasters."[24] As a young lawyer in Paris, Ozanam felt only revulsion at the demands of his profession, which required him to deal with businessmen. He confessed: "Relations with men of business are so painful, so humiliating, so unjust that I cannot become reconciled to them."[25]

The work of chapters, or *conférences,* of the Société de Saint-Vincent-

23. From a letter of 1837, cited in Kathleen O'Meara, *Frederic Ozanam: His Life and Works* (New York, 1891), p. 108.

24. Ibid., p. 131.

25. Ibid., p. 102.

de-Paul in the cities of industrial France after its initial founding in Paris of the early 1830s rested on the efforts of small local groups of laymen that were gradually linked together into a national network. The goals of the society and its related organizations were various: to visit the poor in their homes, bringing spiritual and modest material assistance; to organize young workers into informal groups that shared spiritual goals; and, in the case of the Société de Saint-François-Régis (to be discussed in Chapter 3), to aid workers to legitimize common law unions through civil and religious marriage. As far as can be determined, local chapters of the Société de Saint-Vincent-de-Paul included members whose backgrounds ranged from the upper working class to the bourgeoisie, though the leadership of the society and perhaps the majority of its membership were drawn from the families of local notables.[26] Young men frequently predominated as active members, as in the case of the first Parisian group surrounding Frédéric Ozanam, while older men served as honorary members.[27] The restriction of membership to men was attributed to the experience of a co-founder's wife as a home visitor in the infamous Rue Mouffetard district in Paris. Arriving at the home of a poor family to which she had been directed by the intervention of a local nun, Mme. Bailly was received "with vulgar insults" and is cited as observing that "this is not work for women. We need men, and young ones."[28]

Although the Société de Saint-Vincent-de-Paul was resolutely lay in character, some *conférences* included sympathetic members of the clergy. Lay-clergy relations seem to have varied widely by region. In the earliest days of the society, Ozanam encountered some problems with the church hierarchy or

26. On the members of Rouen's chapter, which was organized in 1841, see Jean-Pierre Chaline, ed., *Deux bourgeois en leur temps: Documents sur la société rouennaise du XIXe siècle* (Rouen, 1977), p. 165, n. 36; idem, *Les bourgeois de Rouen: Une élite urbaine au XIXe siècle* (Paris, 1982), p. 267; and Victor Duval, *La charité à Rouen: Les oeuvres catholiques* (Rouen, 1895), pp. 230–35. The original membership of Mulhouse's *conférence*, which was not organized until 1846, ranged from *négociant* to middle-class white-collar occupations, including an *instituteur,* a railroad inspector, a furniture dealer, and a designer for the cloth-printing industry. Minutes dated 15 August 1846, ASVP, Strasbourg, Dossier 1. Archival data on Rouen's membership in 1841 showed fifteen *propriétaires,* four clergymen, three clerks, four lawyers, three students, one doctor, two medical students, thirteen *commerçants,* and eleven diverse property owners. "Conférence de Rouen. Etat du personnel, 31 décembre 1842," ASVP, Rouen, Dossier 6. On Lille's chapter, organized in 1839, see Société de Saint-Vincent-de-Paul de Lille, *Notice historique de la Société de Saint-Vincent-de-Paul de Lille* (Lille, 1883).

27. O'Meara, *Frederic Ozanam*, pp. 121 and 130, noted that by 1841, when the Paris membership in the society had reached over 600, there were a large number of students, including *Normaliens* and *Polytechniciens*. The role of the older honorary members is discussed in Eugène de Margerie, *La société de Saint-Vincent-de-Paul: Lettres, entretiens, récits et souvenirs* (Paris, 1876), 1:46.

28. Abbé J. Schall, *Un disciple de Saint Vincent de Paul au XIXe siècle: Adolphe Baudon, 1819–1888* (Paris, 1897), p. xx.

parish clergy, who occasionally regarded this lay organization with suspicion or downright hostility.[29] The founder of the society could be bitter about what he felt was the church's neglect of working-class communities. In an 1848 letter to his brother, he wrote: "If a greater number of Christians, and above all of priests, had but occupied themselves with the working class these last ten years, we should be more secure of the future, and all our hopes rest on the little that has been done in this direction up to the present." [30] Tension between the church hierarchy and lay members of the society was not apparent in the Rouen and Lille areas, however. In Rouen, the society enjoyed the support of parish clergy from the beginning of its efforts there.[31] The *conférence* of Lille attracted the elite of the Catholic bourgeoisie, including at least one member of the clergy who was a relative of the founders of the local chapter.[32] Provincial chapters of the society were clearly marked by the spirit of their local membership. In Lille, the rich variety of Social Catholic organizations bore the imprint of their leaders' Legitimist political and social values. Nevertheless, it would be erroneous to view the Société de Saint-Vincent-de-Paul, particularly in its early days, as a bastion of either Legitimism or social conservatism. Both the spiritual attitudes and the attitudes towards church and state of Ozanam and some of his early collaborators distinguished them strongly from the church hierarchy's continuing defense of both Gallicanism and Legitimism. Ozanam himself was a republican, and though he stopped far short of support for Lamennais's rebellion from the Catholic church, he was, like the renegade, consistently critical of the church hierarchy's support of political reaction.[33] It does appear that over time, the society gradually became less militant on the social question, more preoccupied with its charitable mission, and more secure in its relationship to the church hierarchy, gaining the approval of the pope for its works in 1845.[34] By the second half of the nineteenth century, leaders of the society in some areas were decrying a certain loss of vigorous commitment, especially among the young. One historian of the society, for example, lamented the flagging interest of young men in the

29. Ozanam's problems with the clergy of Lyon are discussed in O'Meara, *Frederic Ozanam*, p. 113.

30. Cited in O'Meara, *Frederic Ozanam*, p. 236.

31. Duval, *La charité à Rouen*, p. 232.

32. Pierrard, *La vie ouvrière*, pp. 392–94.

33. On Lamennais and his relations with the nascent Social Catholic movement, see Adrien Dansette, *Religious History of Modern France*, trans. John Dingle (Freiburg, 1961), 1:216, 224, and Ruth L. White, *"L'Avenir" de Lamennais: Son rôle dans la presse de son temps* (Paris, 1974), p. 161.

34. As one historian has noted, "The defiance of the prelates towards the lay character of the society disappeared when Gregory XVI gave it his approval in 1845." Georges Weill, *Histoire du catholicisme libéral en France, 1828–1908* (Paris, 1909), p. 66. See also Schall, *Un disciple*, pp. 66–68.

works of the Société de Saint-Vincent-de-Paul and at several points seemed to be counseling participation as a remedy for boredom among well-heeled Parisian young men.[35]

Social Catholicism in Historical Perspective

The affinities of nineteenth-century lay Catholic organizations with those of seventeenth-century France were obvious, the name of the main organization —the Société de Saint-Vincent-de-Paul—reminding adherents of the greatest of French Counter-Reformation saints. Grass-roots activities of such Social Catholic organizations also bore clear resemblances to lay charitable confraternities of the later Middle Ages, but more particularly to those of the Counter-Reformation that had gradually extended their "works" beyond the limits of their membership, giving rise to a wide variety of charitable activities among the urban poor.[36] Many of these Tridentine confraternities in fact exemplified the efficiently organized, systematic charity which Saint Vincent himself had practiced.[37]

Although there was a strong tradition of lay Catholic activism to which nineteenth-century members of the Société de Saint-Vincent-de-Paul could look for inspiration, their goals, the focus of their work, and the society in which it took place contrasted in important ways from those of previous centuries. Nineteenth-century Social Catholics, who by their activities in working-class communities sought to address the "social question," viewed the world rather differently from earlier groups. In 1848, Ozanam spoke to one of these differences: "God did not make the poor; He sends no human creatures into the charges of this world without providing them with those

35. Margerie, *La société*, 1:50, 58. A real sense of decadence pervades this book, contrasting sharply with the militance of Ozanam's generation of the 1830s and 1840s. Lille's Charles Kolb-Bernard voiced his own concern about the flagging commitment of members there as early as 1855. One of his co-workers characterized the declining vigor of the society as a descent into "philanthropy." Pierrard, *La vie ouvrière*, p. 397.

36. On the variety of late-medieval and early modern confraternities, see Jacques Heers, *L'Occident aux XIVe et XVe siècles: Aspects économiques et sociaux* (Paris, 1963); Charles Ouin-Lacroix, *Histoire des anciennes corporations d'arts et métiers et des confréries religieuses de la capitale de la Normandie* (Rouen, 1850); Etienne Martin Saint-Léon, *Histoire des corporations de métiers* (Paris, 1941); Gabriel LeBras, *Etudes de sociologie religieuse* (Paris, 1956), 2:418–62. The spread of good works to the urban community is summarized by John Bossy: "After 1500 or so the abstract view of charity had passed from civic humanist to civic patriciates and was spreading from Italy to the north. One of its symptoms was the reconstruction of the smarter fraternities in such a way that their charity came to consist less in how their members behaved to each other, and more in what they or their officers did on behalf of defined categories of needy outsiders." *Christianity in the West: 1400–1700* (Oxford, 1985), p. 145.

37. Jean Delumeau, *Catholicism between Luther and Voltaire: A New View of the Counter-Reformation*, trans. Jeremy Moiser (London, 1977), p. 58.

two sources of riches which are the fountain of all others—intelligence and will. . . . Why should we hide from the people what they know, and flatter them like bad kings? It is human liberty that makes the poor; it is this that dries up those two primitive fountains of wealth by allowing intelligence to be quenched in ignorance and the will to be weakened by misconduct."[38] Ozanam's argument that large-scale poverty was largely man-made helped to distinguish his view of the world from that of Counter-Reformation charity activists. Furthermore, the father of the Société de Saint-Vincent-de-Paul held that the behavior of both bourgeois and workers lay at the root of the social question. His belief that poverty among workers was exacerbated by their tendency to debauchery, gambling, and other vices was not a new one. Even within the highly spiritualized view of the poor among noble Catholic activists of Counter-Reformation France, there had been room for this belief and for ambivalence about the poor themselves.[39] However, Ozanam's point was to emphasize the societal and systemic rather than the accidental or individual causes of poverty and, furthermore, to implicate the behavior and mores of both worker and bourgeois in the class estrangement of industrial capitalist society.

Other significant features distinguished nineteenth-century lay activism from earlier traditions. One was the overwhelming importance that Social Catholic activists attributed to bonds within the nuclear family, a view that seems to have been strengthened by a growing convergence of their secular and religious values. Although it may appear axiomatic that Catholic values have always served to defend the family, there is some evidence to show that this was not always the case. According to at least one historian, Counter-Reformation legislation on marriage reflected the church hierarchy's mistrust of the family as a competitor in the struggle for Christians' hearts and minds. To be sure, the family in these texts could be understood as a complex web of kin relationships and not just as a nuclear grouping. But during seventeenth century, the church hierarchy seems not to have viewed the interests of the family in either of its senses as entirely consonant with those of the church. As John Bossy has argued,

> What made the medieval Church on the popular plane a real, if ignorant and misguided community, was its admission of the kin-group, natural and artificial, as a constituent element in its life; where the Tridentine Church . . . most damagingly failed was in its reluctance to admit the nuclear family or household on the same terms. This may be felt a surprising suggestion to make, considering how prominent a position has

38. Cited in O'Meara, *Frederic Ozanam*, p. 248.

39. Kathryn Norberg, *Rich and Poor in Grenoble, 1600–1814* (Berkeley and Los Angeles, 1985), p. 63. Ambivalence towards the poor is also discussed in Gutton, *La société*, p. 215.

> been occupied in modern catholic apologetics by propaganda about the social rights and spiritual importance of the family. But there was little precedent for this in the activity of the Counter-Reformation hierarchy, in whom the notion of the nuclear family as an autonomous entity inspired indifference or distaste. There seems to be no reference to the *familia,* in either of its senses, in the decrees of the Council of Trent; the council enacted only two reforms which affected it, about marriage and catechism, and both, if anything, diminished the rights of parents and the independence of the family.[40]

Bossy's position has been somewhat moderated by historians of France, where Counter-Reformation legislation on marriage was implemented only in piecemeal fashion and frequently in competition with the monarchy's own rulings. Jean-Louis Flandrin, for example, has argued that "the Church of the Counter-Reformation made the family one of the privileged places of Christian life." Even Flandrin, however, has noted the ambiguity of the Catholic church's endorsement of the family when compared with Reformation Protestantism, and has traced the former's interest in family life per se as increasing steadily over the period from the fifteenth to the eighteenth century.[41]

Whatever ambiguity there may have been in the church hierarchy's view of the family in the early modern period seems to have disappeared by the advent of Social Catholicism in the nineteenth century. In fact, one of the notable features of lay Catholic activism during the 1830s and 1840s was its emphasis on the nuclear family as the institution through which the spiritualization of French workers was to proceed. The family, now considered in its residential, nuclear form was not seen as a threat to the church's authority, but rather as one of its main supports. Social Catholics' intervention into the worker's family conveyed their belief in its moral, spiritual, and social centrality.

This valorization of the nuclear family helps to explain the importance ascribed by organizations such as the Société de Saint-Vincent-de-Paul to visits into the homes of workers. There were, of course, precedents for this, too,

40. John Bossy, "The Counter-Reformation and the People of Catholic Europe," *Past and Present*, no. 47 (1970): 68.

41. Jean-Louis Flandrin, *Families in Former Times: Kinship, Household, and Sexuality* (Cambridge, 1979), p. 121. The debate over the Catholic church's mistrust of the autonomous authority of family groups is clarified in R. M. Smith, "Marriage Processes in the English Past: Some Continuities," in Lloyd Bonfield, Richard M. Smith, and Keith Wrightson, eds., *The World We Have Gained: Histories of Population and Social Structure* (Oxford, 1986), pp. 78–80, 92–93, 96. On the competition between the French church and state over marriage legislation, see also René Pillorget, *La tige et le rameau: Familles anglaise et française, XVIe–XVIIIe siècles* (Paris, 1979), pp. 17, 33–41. For the church's struggle with the marriage traditions embedded in popular culture, see André Burguière, "Le rituel du mariage en France: Pratiques ecclésiastiques et pratiques populaires (XVIe–XVIIIe siècle)," *Annales, E.S.C.* 33 (1978): 637–49.

in militant Tridentine Catholicism. Home visits had long been a part of the multifaceted good works that expressed a Catholic activist's vigorous spirituality. However, late-sixteenth and seventeenth-century urban charity workers and confraternity members appear to have directed more of their attention to ministering to the needs of the poor within quintessentially antifamilial institutions such as the *hôpitaux généraux*—monuments that attested to the inability of families to protect and care for their own members.[42] In contrast, Social Catholic activists of early industrial France believed that the nuclear family could and should form the nexus of human relationships on which moral community was to be based.

There is little doubt that the weekly visits into workers' homes by members of the Société de Saint-Vincent-de-Paul provided visitors an opportunity for scrutinizing those receiving aid. Indeed, this goal was freely admitted by some. It would be erroneous, however, to see this function of the home visit as the primary one.[43] Visits into the homes of workers by members of the society had a different intention. The home visit constituted the ritual that served symbolically to dissolve the estrangement between bourgeoisie and workers that Social Catholics attributed to industrial capitalism as a system. The following description of a home visit is typical: "Arriving at his home, we place our modest offering in his hand. Then we sit down, if there is room in his little home. We talk casually with him about his work, his family, his poverty, and we ask him to bear all of it with patience for the love of God. We also ask him to send his children to mass, catechism, and school."[44] Although such descriptions emphasized the primacy of the visitor's role in offering moral counsel to the worker, the face-to-face contact between visitor and worker was also designed as a vehicle for mutual edification, which was one of the rea-

42. On the incompatibility between total institutions and family life, see Erving Goffman, *Asylums: Essays on the Social Situation of Mental Patients and Other Inmates* (New York, 1961), pp. 11–12. Cf. Donzelot, *The Policing of Families*, who argues that "the construction of general hospitals corresponded in part to the express desire to furnish poor families with a means of coercion against their undisciplined members" (p. 51). See also pp. 25–26 of the same volume.

43. One historian of the society stated that members of the society in Paris altered the days of the week they visited families in order to counter "cheating." Margerie, *La société*, 1:206–7. However, Joseph Isaac seriously underestimates the difference between the function of home visits by members of the Société de Saint-Vincent-de-Paul and those made by "hygienists" or proponents of scientific charity, such as de Gérando, cited in note 10. It was the latter who stressed the need for systematic scrutiny of the poor aided by the government charity bureaus for whom the visitors worked. Joseph Isaac, "Tactiques et figures disciplinaires," in Joseph Isaac, Philippe Fritsch, and Alain Battegay, *Disciplines à domicile: L'édification de la famille* (Fontenay-sous-Bois, 1977), pp. 88–94. The primacy of the home visit in the works of the society is emphasized in Albert Foucault, *La société de Saint-Vincent-de-Paul: Histoire de cent ans* (Paris, 1933), p. 110.

44. Rapport du conseil central de Lille, 29 May 1855, ASVP, Paris, Dossier 1.

sons that material assistance remained very modest. The argument was that since spiritual exchange was reciprocal, it was less humiliating than material aid alone. Moreover, personal contact between members of the society and the families they visited led Social Catholics to criticize the depersonalized, quantitative approach to working-class family problems characteristic of their moral economist contemporaries.[45]

Social Catholics' visits into the homes of workers were thus part of their effort to spiritualize working-class families and themselves by dissolving estrangement both symbolically and practically. They lamented what they saw as excessive individualism or egotism in all of its manifestations and believed that the shoring up of family bonds within working-class communities of industrial France, like the reaffirmation of bonds between bourgeoisie and worker, required changes in both material conditions and moral sensibilities. Their vision of working-class family life included efforts to create more solid bonds between parents and children under the auspices of spiritual values to which both bourgeois and workers needed to conform. Realizing this vision of a more spiritualized working-class family required changes in the morality of France's bourgeoisie, who were to be inspired by face-to-face contact with workers to renew the social and spiritual bonds that economic change had weakened.

Although such organizations of lay activists as the Société de Saint-Vincent-de-Paul led the way in applying a new kind of Catholic vision of the working-class family under the impact of industrialization, their efforts were not the only ones that reflected the appeal of this view. As will be shown in the chapters that follow, efforts to devise administrative or legislative solutions to working-class family problems involved such parliamentarians as Lamartine and Montalembert, whose religious sensibilities clearly incorporated some of the same values as the Social Catholic efforts discussed here.[46] For the present, it is sufficient to note that the infusion of a liberal Catholic or Social Catholic point of view into policies born of administrative or legislative change was generally more difficult than organizing and carrying out voluntaristic intervention into working-class family life through face-to-face relations between individuals. In discussion and debate about working-class family problems and their solutions, parliamentarians and administrators sympathetic to Social

45. Kathryn Norberg has observed that charity givers' antipathy towards the poor in seventeenth-century Grenoble was often softened after upper-class visitors established face-to-face bonds with them through charity activities. *Rich and Poor in Grenoble*, p. 63.

46. White, *L'Avenir*, pp. 56, 66–67, 75, discusses Lamartine's and Montalembert's relations with the Social Catholic movements. On Montalembert's early career in the Chamber of Peers, see R. P. Lecanuet, *Montalembert: D'après son journal et sa correspondance* (Paris, 1899–1902), 2:11–13. On Lamartine's Catholicism, see Christian Maréchal, *Lamennais et Lamartine* (Paris, 1907), pp. 302–20. Maréchal (p. 365) characterizes Lamartine's views as those of an "independent Social Christian."

Catholic views would have to confront representatives of another, quite different way of conceptualizing the moral and material problems of working-class families.

The Formulation of a Secular Moral Economy

In his 1847 work *Du paupérisme,* J.B.F. Marbeau offered this distinction between "political economy" and "moral economy": "Political economy says to men: 'Work and you shall be happy.' Moral economy [says]: 'Behave well and you shall be happy.' "[47] His distinction was actually a little too neat, since in the minds of moral economists, assiduity in work as well as moral conduct was a key to happiness. However, his distinction hints at a real difference in emphasis. Proponents of a moral economist approach included observers of society, professional men, and administrators who were generally favorable to the advent of industrial capitalism, yet were deeply ambivalent about its human and social consequences. Like Social Catholics, they seized upon the disruptive features of industrial capitalism and more than any other group in French society up to 1848 worked to gather the kind of data that could be used by the government and administration to control them. They were not economists in either the late-twentieth or even the early-nineteenth-century sense. By the latc Restoration and July Monarchy, *économiste* was generally used to refer to proponents of free trade, men such as Jean-Baptiste Say, who shared the economic views of England's own classical political economists. There were frequent examples of close relations between political economists and moral economists during the period under discussion as well as a tendency for clear lines of demarcation between the two to become blurred over the course of time.[48] At least one of France's eminent moral economists of the period, Jérôme-Adolphe Blanqui, was also a proponent of free trade.[49] However, the approach of several of his key empirical texts on working-class life, such as that discussed in Chapter 1, placed him squarely in the tradition of moral economy.

47. J.B.F. Marbeau, *Du paupérisme en France et des moyens d'y remédier, ou principes d'économie charitable* (Paris, 1847), p. 9.

48. See, for example, William Coleman's discussion of Villermé's collaboration at the *Journal des économistes*, the bastion of 1840s political economist thinking, in *Death Is a Social Disease: Public Health and Political Economy in Early Industrial France* (Madison, 1982), p. 9. But cf. the same author's remarks on the differences between Villermé and the orthodox free trader Charles Dunoyer (ibid., pp. 262–64). I place much more emphasis on the differences between political and moral economists than do Coleman or Jacques Donzelot. The latter aggregates important members of the two groups together under the label "social economists." Donzelot, *The Policing of Families*, p. 63.

49. Blanqui was the author of *Des classes ouvrières en France pendant l'année 1848* (Paris, 1849).

The style moral economists used to make sense of the social world also distinguished them from classical political economists of the period. Whereas political economists of the July Monarchy tended to express their views in fairly abstract theoretical texts, moral economist writers were masters of a style of inquiry and social thought that, like Villeneuve-Bargemont's, was based on empirical data. While political economists of the Restoration and July Monarchy published works on economics that were generally historical and didactic in a rather dry, academic way, moral economists concentrated on the concrete, the recent, the palpable symptoms of industrial capitalism in the making. The distance between political and moral economy was evoked in the irate preface to F.C.-P. d'Esterno's *De la misère, de ses causes, de ses remèdes*. The author had submitted his work to a competition sponsored by the Académie des sciences morales et politiques in 1840, but was told by the judges that they did not want a work of "political economy." The aggrieved author vented his spleen against the academy for its prejudice against political economy, insinuating that had competitors known who was going to be head of the prize selection committee—whom d'Esterno referred to as a "distinguished statistician"—they would have made adjustments in the works they submitted. D'Esterno also cited Eugène Buret's complaint about the vagueness of the subject of the competition, on "poverty, its signs and its causes in different countries." [50] The academy's rejection of d'Esterno's and others' texts of "political economy" was based not merely on disagreement with their approach. The small number of proponents of free trade, of "true" political economy in France during the years under discussion, were in fact institutionally isolated and rather unpopular in official circles at least until the mid-1840s. Political economists' pronouncements on economic problems could make confirmed Orleanists as well as many others quite nervous because of their free-trade political agenda, which was extremely unpopular among most commercial and industrial interests. Moreover, some still associated political economy with its free-thinking Ideologue proponents of the earlier nineteenth century.[51]

Furthermore, whereas political economists, as free traders and rather uncritical proponents of capitalist economic development, tended to emulate the style and substance of classical Anglo-Saxon economic thinking, moral

50. F.C.-P. d'Esterno, *De la misère, de ses causes, de ses remèdes* (Paris, 1842), pp. 5–13. His crack about the statistician seems to have been directed at Villermé.

51. Lucette LeVan-Lemesle, "La promotion de l'économie politique en France au XIXe siècle jusqu'à son introduction dans les facultés (1815–1881)," *Revue d'histoire moderne et contemporaine* 27 (1980): 270–94. Also see Yves Charbit, *Du malthusianisme au populationnisme: Les économistes français et la population, 1840–1870* (Paris, 1981), pp. 4–20, and Thomas E. Kaiser, "Politics and Political Economy in the Thought of the Ideologues," *History of Political Economy* 12 (1980): 141–60.

economists conformed to an older French tradition of examining economic questions more in terms of their social and administrative implications. The moral economists were not full-fledged Anglophiles like the political economists, and in fact seem to have derived their fear of the human consequences of industrial capitalism from the specter of the administratively uncontrolled example of English industrial growth during the first half of the nineteenth century. Moral economists could thus view the relatively sluggish pace of French economic growth during this period as a potentially desirable feature of their society, to the extent that it inhibited the untrammeled growth of urban working-class communities that epitomized the social dislocations of industrial capitalism.

The Historical Foundations of Moral Economy

Moral economists' ambivalence about industrial capitalism stemmed from their concern for its social and human consequences and echoed some of the ambivalence of eighteenth-century Physiocrats about capitalism *tout court*. Their larger affinities with the Physiocratic school lay not in a philosophy of wealth based on agriculture but rather in moral economists' approach to economic problems. Like the Physiocrats, moral economists conceived of economic problems in a way that bound them intimately to the larger question of social governance. Furthermore, their approach was essentially administrative and not political in nature.[52] Like Mirabeau, moral economists were ambivalent about the progress of capitalist economic development in French society. On the one hand they welcomed the possibilities that it provided for generating new wealth, but on the other they were sobered by the disruptive social consequences that it could entail, including the aggregation of workers in industrial towns, the growth of exaggerated forms of economic individualism, and the loosening of social bonds. The advent of *industrial* capitalism, of new industrial working-class communities and the factories in which work was now carried out, seems to have made nineteenth-century moral economists even more ambivalent than the Physiocrats about the disruptive potential of economic change, magnifying as it did those particular features of capitalist society that late-eighteenth-century Physiocrats had feared.

Moral economists' texts also resonated with Physiocratic notions of a state whose administration was founded on the active role of rational, scientific inquirers with special access to the means of reform.[53] The view of

52. Elizabeth Fox-Genovese, *The Origins of Physiocracy: Economic Revolution and Social Order in Eighteenth-Century France* (Ithaca, 1976), p. 244. Fox-Genovese continues her discussion of the Physiocrats' antipathy to politics in the introduction to *The Autobiography of DuPont de Nemours* (Wilmington, 1984), pp. 12–14.

53. Fox-Genovese, *The Origins of Physiocracy*, pp. 49, 304, 310. See also Harvey Mitchell,

moral economists that the social problems of industrial society could best be addressed through the vehicle of administrative rather than political reform made a great deal of sense under the Restoration and July Monarchy, given the lack of interest in social questions among legislators in both the Chamber of Deputies and the Chamber of Peers.[54] Like the latter-day Physiocrats, moral economists were also marked by the legacy of the most radical phases of the Revolution, a legacy that helped shape their fear of popular politics or politics in general.

However, moral economists were less sanguine than prerevolutionary Physiocrats about the inherent desirability of state-administrative intervention in civil society. By the time of the Restoration, the monarchy, upon whose strength the Physiocrats' efforts had so depended, had been transformed both concretely and ideologically into an institution with limited power. Although moral economists would recommend the reform of working-class families through administrative and legislative instruments, their advocacy was tempered by a sense of the limitations placed on these means of reform. In their writings about the social problems of industrial society, moral economists, like Social Catholics, argued that the working-class family was a key institution to which policy should be directed. They also believed, however, that the nuclear family could be manipulated by social policy only with great difficulty. The Physiocrats' defense of administrative intervention into the life of French civil society in order to control some of the deleterious consequences of socioeconomic development was thus difficult for the moral economists to share wholeheartedly once they had identified the working-class family as a primary source of problems. Moral economists' advocacy of administrative intervention had of necessity to be rather timid, since they themselves construed the family as an essentially private domain into which the administrative state of the July Monarchy had only a tenuous right of intervention.[55]

This particular position distinguished the moral economists' world view from an older tradition that had legitimized royal intervention into families to maintain their good order. Writing of the system of the *lettres de cachet* at the

---

"Politics in the Service of Knowledge: The Debate over the Administration of Medicine and Welfare in Late-Eighteenth-Century France," *Social History* 6 (1981): 185–207, especially pp. 196–207.

54. In his *Recollections* Tocqueville, of course, argued that members of the two bodies were not interested in political questions either. Speaking of the Chamber of Deputies of the July Monarchy, he wrote, "What was lacking, especially at the end, was political life itself." Alexis de Tocqueville, *Recollections*, ed. J. P. Mayer and A. P. Kerr, trans. George Lawrence (New York, 1971), p. 11.

55. In his classic work of moral economy, *Des classes dangereuses de la société dans les grandes villes et des moyens de les rendre meilleures* (Paris, 1840), Honoré Frégier wrote, "It would be unjust and unreasonable to make the government responsible for private mores, when philosophy itself has posited that domestic life should be immured" (1:5–6).

end of the Old Regime, Arlette Farge and Michel Foucault have argued: "The familial *lettre de cachet* [was] a royal order no different from others. Like other social groupings, the family owed the king [a certain] transparency. Private and public life were confounded here by the necessity for order. The family [was] the privileged place where private tranquility created a certain form of public order; thus, the king had the right to scrutinize its functioning and its lapses."[56] The demise of divine right monarchy and the central tenets of the moral economists' own value system combined to delegitimize this older view.

The moral economist perspective on family and society was also marked by an increasing consciousness of the nuclear family's unique role in a post-revolutionary society in which bonds between social classes had been weakened and habits of subordination made more difficult to enforce. Signs presaging this new social role for the family had appeared in nascent form among the Physiocrats themselves. As Fox-Genovese has argued, "Mirabeau's use of the family as the prototype for social subordination . . . reflect[ed] his position halfway between a divine and a material sanction for natural law. It also suggest[ed] that the authority of the father, rather than that of the master or seigneur, constitute[d] the irreducible minimum of paternalist sensibility. This doctrine render[ed] paternalism assimilable to bourgeois values, as its subsequent endorsement in the Napoleonic Code show[ed]."[57] However, moral economists' concern with working-class family life entailed much more than a simple desire to reinforce paternal authority in new ways. Their insistence on examining in detail the valuative or "moral" implications of working-class life in part through an examination of the family gradually led them into a new and vaguely charted territory where mores and morals met. Yet, even these English translations do not quite capture the sense of what the moral economists were up to, since the French term for "mores," *les moeurs,* even today retains a more inherently valuative sense than its English equivalent.[58] Similarly, *sci-*

56. Arlette Farge and Michel Foucault, *Le désordre des familles: Lettres de cachet de la Bastille au XVIIIe siècle* (Paris, 1982), p. 15. See also Pillorget, *La tige*, p. 285.

57. Fox-Genovese, *The Origins of Physiocracy*, p. 212.

58. The most recent *Robert* still gives as the first definition of *moeurs,* "Habits (of a society or an individual) relative to the practice of good and bad." The more neutral sense, "Habits of life, customs of a people, of a society," comes fourth. Thus, in his *Tableau de l'état moral et physique des ouvriers employés dans les manufactures de coton, de laine et de soie* (Paris, 1840), 1:109–10, Villermé wrote, "The weavers who live in villages and work at home have *mores/morals and habits* that are generally very good; whereas workers in large workshops vie with each other in spending and debauchery that alter their health and ruin their future" (italics added). In his study of America, Tocqueville explained his own use of the term: "I here mean the term 'mores' (*moeurs*) to have its original Latin meaning; I mean it to apply not only to *'moeurs'* in the strict sense, which might be called the habits of the heart, but also to the different notions possessed by men, the various opinions current among them, and the sum of ideas that shape mental habits." Alexis de Tocqueville, *Democracy in America*, ed. J. P. Mayer, trans. George Lawrence (New York, 1966), 1:287. Even Crane Brinton admitted, "*Moeurs* is an

ences morales, in the sense of its title in the name of the Académie des sciences morales et politiques, referred less to questions of abstract moral principles or of systematic moral philsophy than to the art and science of observing *les moeurs*.[59] In his *Classes dangereuses,* Honoré Frégier articulated the nature of and justification for this new kind of inquiry by introducing his book with the announcement that the work was at the same time "a book of administration and of morals,"[60] complaining that up until his day, "moralists" had tended to speak in high-falutin' language that was overly didactic and speculative, whereas what was needed was practical and empirical investigation. Since the decline of morals (*moeurs*) lay at the cause of crime, "a statesman who [was] both prudent and skilled ha[d] a right to be concerned about the moral improvement of the country which he [wa]s called to govern."[61]

Several authors of central texts of moral economy during the 1830s and 1840s attempted, however timidly, to cast a critical eye on the mores of the bourgeoisie as well as the working classes. Thus, Frégier began from the premise that his study should have dealt more substantively with the depravity of the literate classes, "because of the role that intelligence plays in the depravity of [certain] individuals." However, the Académie des sciences morales et politiques in its wisdom had constrained this and other, future observers to concentrate on those classes of people who were both dangerous *and* ignorant. Frégier, among others, had answered the charge given by the academy to "seek by empirical observation what are the elements, in Paris or in other large cities, of the part of the population that forms a dangerous class by its vices, its ignorance, and its poverty; to indicate the means that could be taken by the administration, the wealthy, or comfortably-off, or by intelligent and assiduous workers to improve this dangerous and depraved class."[62] In practical terms, a writer like Frégier understood very well why the Académie des sciences morales et politiques sponsored studies with these focuses. Whereas in principle prudent statesmen and administrators were concerned about deviant behavior among all ranks of society, they were more preoccupied with the lower classes than the upper classes because the latter were better able to conceal their habits and maintain some sense of prudence about their financial affairs, thus resisting the inevitable passage workers were likely to follow from private disorder to public menace.[63] The priorities set by the academy,

exceedingly hard word to translate." *French Revolutionary Legislation on Illegitimacy, 1789–1804* (Cambridge, Mass., 1936), p. 66.

59. Thus, the first definition of the adjective *moral* is "that which concerns *les moeurs,* habits, and especially the rules of conduct admitted and practiced by a society."

60. Un ouvrage d'administration et de morale." Frégier, *Classes dangereuses*, 1:vij.

61. Ibid., p. 5.

62. Ibid., pp. vj, i.

63. Ibid., pp. 6–7.

as Frégier well knew, resulted from the government's and the academy's own preoccupation with social disorder emanating from the urban lower classes.[64]

A focus on working-class mores also stemmed from moral economists' belief that nearly every class in French society had made admirable moral progress in recent years. After vaunting the new purity of French men and women of letters compared to their eighteenth-century counterparts, Baron Charles Dupin provided other significant evidence of Frenchmen's improving mores. His location of the lower social boundaries of this improvement is instructive:

> If I consider the mores of [our] society, I observe the same progress as in the writings of novelists and poets. From the steps of the throne to the humblest bourgeois home, I see everywhere the happy effects of this great improvement. I would look in vain within our kings' palace for those vile prostitutes, drawn from the lower classes so as to soil the scepter with all the more effect. Cowardly calumnies notwithstanding, the mores of the ladies of the court are today purer not only than the sadly infamous time of the Medicis, of the Regent, and of Louis XV, but even of Louis XIV and Louis XVI. Suffering has reinvigorated the virtues of our illustrious families. Domestic life has regained its charm for them. Conjugal love is no longer ridiculous in their eyes.[65]

Dupin's gallantry apparently fueled his keen optimism about the moral as well as economic improvement of France since 1814. Certainly not all moral economists were as sanguine about the purity of upper- and middle-class mores as Dupin. Frégier's skepticism on this score has already been mentioned. It is clear, too, that Social Catholics would not have entirely concurred with Dupin's judgments. However, Dupin's expressed belief that the monarchy, upper classes, and French bourgeoisie were now conforming to a more sober style of family life was an important one that marked moral economists' critical examination of the family lives of workers.

Investigations of family mores among France's urban industrial working classes permitted moral economist observers to initiate an important cognitive process in which they began to crystallize at the ideological level key features of a bourgeois family model by illustrating how workers deviated from it. But then, in a stunning twist of logic, moral economists gradually turned

64. Hilde Rigaudias-Weiss, *Les enquêtes ouvrières en France entre 1830 et 1848* (Paris, 1936), pp. 25, 237. The larger role of the academy in lending support to the government through its research had been outlined by Guizot. Elise Feller and Jean-Claude Goeury, "Les archives de l'Académie des sciences morales et politiques, 1832–1848," *Annales historiques de la révolution française*, nos. 219–22 (1975): 567–68.

65. Dupin, *Forces*, 1:xxxvij–xxxviij. As proof of this improvement, Dupin contrasted the works of Laclos and deSade on the one hand with those of Thierry and Guizot on the other!

back upon this judgment to reveal certain latent affinities between bourgeoisie and working class that could be strengthened by the skillful use of social policy. These two stages of their argument are worth exploring in more detail.

Bourgeois and Working-Class Families

Key features of working-class family life that struck moral economist investigators and that will be studied in the chapters that follow centered on problems of early marriage and lack of sexual self-control, the weakness of both financial and affective bonds between parents and their children, and the apparent inability of workers to create nuclear households that were financially self-sufficient. Bourgeois families of the late Restoration and July Monarchy were not, of course, completely free of the particular moral blemishes that moral economists identified systematically with industrial workers' families. If they had been, the tone of moral economist discourse would presumably have been much more indulgent. However, industrial workers, at least at first glance, appeared to violate precisely those norms of family life that members of the bourgeoisie sometimes found difficult to enforce within their own families.

The central ideal of bourgeois family life that moral economists appear to have brought to bear on their examinations of workers' family lives was its balance between financial prudence and rationality on the one hand and bonds of affection on the other. Such a balance lay at the source of group security, permitting the development and success of both individuals and the nuclear family core. This high value placed on financial security and stability has long been recognized as a central feature of nineteenth-century French bourgeois family ideals, one that shaped the conduct of business affairs.[66] The intimate relationship between prudent business management and the maintenance of bonds of affection between parents and children, however, has been less clearly understood.

Diverse portraits of bourgeois families, particularly those in provincial centers of industry in the first part of the nineteenth century, support the idea

66. That the values of prudence and caution in French businesses devolved from their familial character was set forth in David S. Landes, "French Entrepreneurship and Industrial Growth in the Nineteenth Century," *Journal of Economic History* 9 (1949): 45–61. See idem, "French Business and the Businessmen: A Social and Cultural Analysis," in Edward M. Earle, ed., *Modern France: Problems of the Third and Fourth Republics* (New York, 1964), pp. 334–53, and more recently, "Religion and Enterprise: The Case of the French Textile Industry," in Edward Carter II, Robert Forster, and Joseph N. Moody, eds., *Enterprise and Entrepreneurs in Nineteenth- and Twentieth-Century France* (Baltimore, 1976), pp. 41–86. Although there has been a recent tendency to revise the gloomy picture painted by Landes and others of France's economic growth in the nineteenth century, no one has seriously questioned the importance of these values to the French bourgeoisie as a group.

that bourgeois families did try to practice at least the financial values that they preached. Thrift, sobriety, and real austerity appear to have characterized the bourgeoisie of those cities where French industrial civilization was born.[67] The Calvinist bourgeoisie of Mulhouse, in particular, continued to conform to a style of life reminiscent of the Reformation, when piety and frugality were paramount.[68] In 1821, a rather jaded subprefect of the arrondissement of Altkirch, where Mulhouse was located, observed these values in action even as he decried some of their less attractive consequences. Writing of Mulhouse's bourgeoisie, he observed: "For many years formed into a republic, a poor ally of the Swiss, they have conserved the spirit of order, frugality, and economy of their ancestors with a local selfishness that recognizes only themselves and those who surround them. Good fathers, good husbands, charitable and even generous among themselves, their philanthropy rarely goes beyond the limits of their area."[69] Although Mulhouse's bourgeoisie lay perhaps at the extreme end of a rigorist spectrum, their values appear to have been largely shared by families of the industrial bourgeoisie in other towns of the period. Lille's industrial *patronat* of the first half of the nineteenth century was strongly Catholic rather than Protestant. Yet its family values seem to have been quite similar to those of Mulhouse's bourgeoisie.[70]

Rouen's bourgeoisie does not emerge from contemporary or historical depictions with quite the same degree of austerity seen in the lives of Mulhouse's or Lille's *patronat*.[71] However, the memoirs of one of its members do permit a close-up view of one bourgeois family's effort to reconcile the values of fi-

67. Stearns, *Paths*, p. 124.

68. Paul-René Zuber, "La famille bourgeoise mulhousienne vers la fin du 18e siècle," *Revue d'Alsace* 83 (1936): 254–63.

69. Cited in P. Leuilliot, "La 'situation morale et politique' de l'arrondissement d'Altkirch en 1821," *Revue d'Alsace* 79 (1932): 28. Mulhouse's leaders had voted for incorporation into France in 1798. For an account of this decision, see Albert Metzger, *La république de Mulhouse* (Basel, 1888), pp. 64–68.

70. Bonnie Smith, *Ladies of the Leisure Class: The Bourgeoises of Northern France in the Nineteenth Century* (Princeton, 1981). Despite its title, one of the themes of this book is the contrast between the workful and austere family life of the Lille industrialists during the first part of the century and their development into a "leisure class" as their wealth grew. See, in particular, pp. 21, 37, 41–43. The same point is made by Paul Leuilliot, "Bourgeois et bourgeoisies," *Annales, E.S.C.* 11 (1956): 87–101, reviewing the increasing size of dowries among the Nord's *patronat*. On the growing wealth of Lille's richest inhabitants over the course of the nineteenth century, see Adeline Daumard et al., *Les fortunes françaises au XIXe siècle: Enquête sur la répartition et la composition des capitaux privés à Paris, Lyon, Lille, Bordeaux et Toulouse d'après l'enregistrement des déclarations de succession* (Paris, 1973), p. 274. On the austere character of the bourgeoisie of Rouen, see Chaline, *Les bourgeois de Rouen*, pp. 257–58.

71. Louis Bergeron, "La tradition du textile," in Yves Lequin, ed., *Histoire des Français, XIXe–XXe siècles: La société* (Paris, 1983), pp. 184–86.

nancial prudence and affection that it had constructed for itself.[72] Jean-Baptiste Curmer, a solid bourgeois of Rouen during the July Monarchy, was the son of a rather irresponsible father whose lack of financial acumen was associated in the author's mind with his proposal for a marriage of interest for his son when Curmer was only nineteen years old. Curmer recalled his father's proposition: "Do you want to get married? I have a good arrangement to propose to you—a very young Parisian girl, an only child, an association with very important industrial affairs." Curmer replied: "I'm only just nineteen; we'll see later." His own friends, he argued, "thought it abusive to sacrifice me, as young as I was, to an alliance based on money."[73] It was not so much the principle of a "marriage of reason" to which Curmer objected, but rather his youth at the time that his father proposed it. It was perhaps not a coincidence that the possibility of a marriage based purely on considerations of fortune involved a Parisienne. Although the capital's bourgeois were surely not the only ones to place high consideration on financial security through advantageous marriages, they were the main culprits in increasing the financial stakes of the bourgeois marriage market, particularly later in the century.[74] Curmer's own fate, he happily reported, was to achieve what he considered a much better balance between financial prudence and affection in his own marriage. When he was eight years old, Curmer had become friends with the "family from which [he] later took his wife," his father and his future father-in-law having begun to envisage the possibility of an alliance from the time Curmer and his future wife were born. Curmer and his future wife gradually built an affectionate relationship, but he hesitated to ask for her hand because he believed that her father "wanted to place his daughter in a good financial situation." However, this relationship ultimately triumphed, and Curmer entered what he viewed as a "marriage of inclination."[75]

Curmer's memoirs illustrate how affection and prudence could be balanced despite frequent tension between these separate considerations. Yet they also show how bourgeois families had to cope with distressing deviations from

72. Jean-Baptiste Curmer, "Souvenirs d'un bourgeois de Rouen," in Chaline, *Deux bourgeois*, pp. 29–133.

73. Ibid., p. 68.

74. The growing luxury of bourgeois family life, already noted in Bonnie Smith's discussion of the Nord, became the subject of heated social criticism late in the nineteenth century, centering on Parisian life. The rising levels of dowries here, and the decline of marriage itself gradually, became part of the "depopulation" controversy. Expressions of these lines of argument appear in Hugues Leroux, *Les filles, qu'en ferons-nous?* (Paris, 1898); Jules Simon, *La liberté civile* (Paris, 1872); Clarisse Bader, *La femme française dans les temps modernes* (Paris, 1883); Louis Delzons, *La famille française et son évolution* (Paris, 1913); and Frédéric LePlay, *La Réforme sociale en France* (Paris, 1864).

75. Curmer, "Souvenirs d'un bourgeois de Rouen," pp. 45, 82, 84, 87.

their cherished values. Not only did Curmer himself have to serve as a kind of father to his own father,[76] but he also admitted the painful fact that he had a brother-in-law living in a common law union. Despite the scandal, Curmer himself took care of the "wife" and the child born of the union after his brother-in-law's death. Happily for Curmer, his own daughter's marriage exemplified his ideal. He noted that "[it was] perfectly matched in all respects of fortune, tastes, and social position."[77] Curmer's memoirs show that the ideals of bourgeois family life were not easy to maintain. Their actualization required a delicate balance between strictly individual interests and those of group solidarity. Yet, far from being viewed as antithetical to one another, bonds of affection and bonds of property were in principle thought to be the complementary foundations of family solidarity.[78] An excess of individual desires or individual failings could threaten the continued existence of the group and its status, while an excessive attention to group interests could lead to an oppression of the individuals who composed it.

The bourgeois family model that informed moral economist investigations of workers was never completely articulated, nor does it appear that moral economists were consciously constructing a vision of their own family system to use in the examination of the mores of workers. Indeed, their failure to articulate explicity the values and mores of bourgeois family life was itself evidence of the power of their shared assumptions. It was simply unnecessary, given the shared context of meaning in which moral economists wrote, to belabor discussions of values that all of them shared and that played such a central role in shaping the bourgeoisie's own image of itself. However, moral economists did attempt to purvey their own ideals as universalizable ones and on occasion faced head on the idea that their conformity to these values could have important social consequences. In an 1851 publication, for example, Alphonse Grün, editor of the *Moniteur universel*, evoked the nature of this burden in fine polemical style:

> The family! We must demonstrate it to the worker as the point of departure of all civic virtues, as the center of all legitimate happiness. But we must ourselves provide him with the model. What will this worker think, what will he do, if, looking above himself he sees marriages contracted

76. Of whom he wrote, "my poor father, whose habits were not above reproach." Ibid., p. 67.

77. Ibid., p. 112.

78. Hans Medick and David Warren Sabean, "Interest and Emotion in Family and Kinship Studies: A Critique of Social History and Anthropology," in idem, eds., *Interest and Emotion: Essays on the Study of Family and Kinship* (Cambridge, 1984), pp. 9–27, have recently made this point most eloquently, arguing against some historians' tendency to see the family's foundations as built either on emotion or on material interests. Their point is to show how families have historically tried to mediate these two facets of their existence.

> without affection, where self-interest replaces sentiments; households whose entire morality consists in avoiding scandal and where infidelity has broken with all scruples; a kind of education that constantly separates parents from their children, that corrupts the character by vanity [and] dries up the heart with selfishness![79]

These reminders constituted more than ritualized breast-beating. Although the author was unusual in dwelling at length upon the need for bourgeois families to set an example (one senses here the tone of a rueful post-1848 sensibility), he revealed in explicit form a style of social thinking and analysis that was shared, albeit tacitly, by moral economists of the late Restoration and July Monarchy. Grün's text shows its author characteristically thinking in class terms, mentally shuttling back and forth between workers and bourgeois in musing about family life. Through such a juxtaposition, he and earlier moral economists were able to isolate the specific qualities of bourgeois family life that gradually came to serve as the foundation of its claim to legitimate moral, political, and economic ascendancy. It was ironic but certainly not unusual that moral economists attested most eloquently to the powerful hold of their social ideals in their writings about working-class family life by their relative silence about them. For moral economists, the virtues of the bourgeois family did not have to be spelled out to readers. They were already part of the core of social values whose existence needed only be hinted at, and only when the clearest deviations from it were under discussion.

Moral economists and Social Catholics were in essential agreement about the external signs of working-class family problems. However, in the moral economist analysis, estrangement between members of working-class families and between working class and bourgeoisie did not result primarily from the estrangement of all parties from the religious ideals of moral and spiritual community. Indeed, moral economists had surprisingly little of substance to say about religion. Rather, they traced the source of family and social estrangement to workers' deviation from specific behaviors that bourgeois families attempted to enforce among their own members.

Moral economists' evaluation of working-class family problems did not, however, remain centered exclusively on industrial workers' deviations from bourgeois mores, though these deviations were initially uppermost in their own minds. Rather, within their texts there were signs of latent affinities between industrial workers and bourgeois that at the level of both ideology and policy would be used to try to overcome workers' family problems and ultimately the social distance that separated worker from bourgeois. Their analyses demonstrated that industrial workers' families shared, albeit in distorted and embry-

79. Alphonse Grün, *De la moralisation des ouvriers* (Paris, 1851), p. 14.

onic form, some structural features of the bourgeois families—features that well-conceived policy might use to encourage the establishment of a new kind of working-class family.

One of the most obvious similarities was both groups' need to work. Like the bourgeoisie, especially the industrial bourgeoisie, industrial workers could be assiduous in their labors. Moral economist texts based on empirical data from France's industrial centers attested to the relatively regular working habits of factory workers that distinguished them from many better-paid artisans, who, as was well-known, had a tendency to slip into their preindustrial work rhythms when wages were too high.[80] Nor were workers in France's new textile areas the same as the idlers and loafers who composed such an important proportion of the lower class in large, traditional cities such as Paris, and who were generally responsible for the ideational merging of the "working and dangerous classes" anatomized by Frégier.[81] The existence of these groups was, in a real sense, timeless. They had populated the urban landscape for centuries, whereas the factory working class had the potential of being more modern and disciplined, just like the industrial bourgeoisie who employed them. The workfulness of the newer working classes brought them, in theory at least, closer to the bourgeoisie.[82] Such a notion was reinforced by economic arguments which had gained currency since the eighteenth century and which stood in sharp contrast to those espoused by Social Catholic writers. Montesquieu himself had argued, "Man is not poor because he has nothing, but because he does not work."[83] A 1787 memoir on poor relief reiterated this theme: "It is not a want of property that constitutes poverty. It is a lack of work. An artisan who exercises a craft is as rich as he who cultivates six acres of land of which he is the owner."[84] The result of these pronouncements, which would be taken up wholeheartedly by moral economists of July Monarchy France, was to break the conceptual link between wage earning

80. See, for example, Achille Penot, *Recherches statistiques sur Mulhouse* (Mulhouse, 1843), p. 34.

81. Frégier, *Classes dangereuses*, 1:44. In Frégier's inimitable typology, which deserves to be cited in its original, he described the class that was "both vicious and dangerous" as comprising "joueurs, filles publiques, leur amans et souteneurs, maîtresses des maisons de prostitution, vagabonds, fraudeurs, les escrocs, les filous et voleurs, les voleuses et les receleurs," whose vices were "la paresse, le jeu, l'intempérance, la débauche, et en général toutes les passions basses et immorales."

82. This is only one of the reasons that Peter Stearns has cited for the less censorious tone of industrialists' estimation of their workers' immorality, in contrast to opinion emanating from Parisian observers. See *Paths*, pp. 111–13. Whereas Stearns sees this view as emanating from the *patronat*'s "traditionalism," the present study emphasizes the importance of an innovative, moral economist ideology in shaping this view of workers and their families.

83. Cited in Gutton, *La société*, p. 432.

84. Cited in Alan Forrest, *The French Revolution and the Poor* (New York, 1981), p. 100.

and poverty so critical to Social Catholics' indictment of industrial capitalist society.

In recognizing some of the more promising characteristics of France's new industrial working classes, moral economists also began to demonstrate a new approach to the understanding of wage labor, one that articulated another latent affinity between workers and bourgeois. Here, the moral economist position contrasted sharply with the Catholic perspective. Whereas Social Catholic writers and activists emphasized and decried the structural link between wage labor and poverty, moral economists subtly shifted the discussion of wages to the behavioral link between wage work and prosperity. Projecting into the future of industrial capitalist society, moral economists realized that wage labor was destined to include an increasing proportion of France's population. Moreover, whereas wage labor had in previous centuries been associated with an underclass of laborers, large proportions of them unmarried, or with young men and women before marriage, it was now destined to engage the activities of individual family members throughout much of their lives. The dependency of a whole family upon wages instead of on the product of landed or invested wealth or the possession of a skill made it imperative that industrial workers learn to handle their wages, to create a true family economy just as bourgeois families living off their income did. To do this, workers had only to save, thereby transforming their family's wages into family capital.

This was one of the most important implications of moral economist thinking about working-class family problems and about the clear relationship between material and moral problems. Moral economists tried in essence to show that in an industrial capitalist society, the "moral economy" should exist first at the level of the family. Not until this task was accomplished could workers' families be truly integrated into a moral community at the societal level. In their discussions of workers' need to accumulate and to save wages, moral economists had to show that wages transformed into small savings could, if properly managed, serve to support a family. Like capital, workers' savings gained a moral personality to the extent that they were used to support and enhance bonds of blood and affection. All of these facts help to explain the growing fixation of moral economists on working-class budgets, budgets that William Reddy has very rightly referred to as "imaginary."[85] There is no doubt that their accounts contained unrealistic calculations. From another point of view, however, these budgets and the larger attempt to demonstrate the possible ways that workers *could* build savings from wages reinforced a sense of the affinities between worker and bourgeois. Thus, moral economists' discussions of the work habits and budget-making potential of industrial workers

85. Reddy, *The Rise of Market Culture*, p. 147. On the relation between savings and family autonomy, see Donzelot, *The Policing of Families*, p. 57.

represented a first hesitant, ideological step towards overcoming the view of industrial workers as cultural others and, if only fantastically, demonstrating their potential affinities with the bourgeoisie itself.

Moral economist critiques of industrial workers' failure to garner their resources to plan for the future thus flowed from some of their deepest values and from their fears of their own families' inability to avoid dependency on outside resources. It was therefore not surprising that moral economists emphasized the need for greater interdependency within workers' families and less dependency of the group on resources outside of itself. Here, there were particular administrative problems to be resolved, since it could be shown that the families of some industrial working-class communities believed themselves entitled by right to public resources during difficult periods of the year or at key stages of their lives. The administrative commission of Lille's Bureau de bienfaisance, for example, lamented:

> For too long a certain class of individuals has viewed the subsidies we have given them as a right, one that is heritable and of which we cannot deprive them. This opinion is due perhaps to [the fact that] aid has been given too periodically and based *more on custom and a sort of tradition* than on the real need of individuals. Thus, on the one hand [we have] the growth of the indigent population which threatens . . . to perpetuate the abuses . . . of a poor tax and on the other [the problem of] dividing the feeble resources of [our] charitable establishment into too many parts, thereby making it impossible to give solace in an efficient manner to the truly unfortunate.[86]

Moral economists' desire to see the working-class family moralized began with wages that when properly managed could be turned into a modest family capital to support a household. A concomitant problem, however, was to break down some workers' notion that they were entitled by right to community resources. Moral economists gradually came to view workers' claims to these entitlements as expressions of a rational, grasping selfishness, an egotism that threatened to destroy the financial and moral autonomy of working-class families while undermining the social order in the same manner as calculative and excessive individualism of any kind. However, moral economists' sense of the importance of this propensity to rational calculation among workers provided another example of a latent similarity between workers and themselves. The problem created by workers' claims to public funds was not only that they cost money, though the specter of the English Poor Law loomed large in moral

86. Bureau de bienfaisance de Lille, Commission administrative, "Registre aux délibérations," meeting of 6 March 1833, "Révision de la liste des indigents," p. 275, ABBL, E. 71, vol. 14.

economists' writings until the early 1840s.[87] In addition, workers' idea that they were entitled to public resources to see their families through difficult times weakened the lesson that moral economists thought they needed to learn: that the family, and not society at large, was the seat of financial and moral solidarity.[88]

Like the perspective of their Social Catholic contemporaries, moral economists' views had evolved from the combined influence of older ways of thinking about the relation of economy, society, and family as they were confronted by the new conditions of industrial society. Both Social Catholics and moral economists, like many of their contemporaries, had a great fear of social disorder, stemming not only from the Revolution but from the exacerbation of interclass tension during the early days of the July Monarchy. Social Catholics and moral economists were somewhat unusual in concentrating on the importance of domestic life and private mores of the industrial working classes rather than on public, political behavior as a primary long-term threat to the social order. However, this feature of their world views was not particularly surprising, given that workers in France's industrializing areas before 1848 were less likely than artisans in more traditional crafts to participate in movements of political contestation, work stoppages, or strikes.[89] By their interest in the newly conceptualized moral problems of industrial society, moral

87. Duchâtel, *La charité*, p. 170; d'Esterno, *De la misère*, p. 179. Villeneuve-Bargemont believed that elements of an English-style poor law already existed in many communities of the Nord during the late Restoration. See "Le département du Nord sous la Restauration: Rapport du Préfet de Villeneuve-Bargemont en 1828," *Revue du Nord* 26 (1943): 41.

88. Richard Smith's work on England has shown that local communities had through the centuries exercised a welfare role in family life, particularly at stages when impoverishment was expected—for example, when family heads reached old age. See "Transfer Incomes, Risk, and Security," in R. Schofield and D. Coleman, eds., *The State of Population Theory: Forward from Malthus* (Oxford, 1985), pp. 200–201. He argues, though, that reluctance to fulfill these entitlements occurred during periods when demographic changes increased the dependency burden of key groups (children, the aged). Although the organization of relief institutions was not the same in France, the fact that charity under the Old Regime had so frequently to target children, the aged, and widows with children does suggest the family's—or at least the urban family's—inability to provide alone for its members' welfare.

89. On factory workers' political contention and strike activity, see, for the Nord, Jean-Paul Courthéoux, "Naissance d'une conscience de classe dans le prolétariat textile du Nord?" *Revue économique*, no. 1 (1957): 114–39. Other sources include Peter N. Stearns, "Patterns of Industrial Strike Activity in France during the July Monarchy," *American Historical Review* 70 (1965): 371–94, and more recently, Ronald Aminzade, "Capitalist Industrialization and Patterns of Industrial Protest: A Comparative Urban Study of Nineteenth-Century France," *American Sociological Review* 49 (1984): 437–53. Aminzade argues that while class antagonisms between factory workers in Rouen and owners were "intense," these workers had "weak capacities for sustained action" and launched few strikes against whole trades, as artisans in other towns were able to do. See especially pp. 445–48. For a contrasting view of workers' contestation, see William Reddy, *The Rise of Market Culture*, pp. 185–204.

economists shared the concerns of Social Catholic activists, but given their more secularized vision of the world, they necessarily reached conclusions different from those of lay Catholics concerning remedies to the kind of family problems they attributed to French industrial workers.

The specific policy studies that follow illustrate the difficulties that moral economists and Social Catholics had to face in attempting to implement measures of reform that targeted working-class family life within France's industrializing areas. Moral economist projects, based essentially upon administrative initiatives, were bound to meet with greater resistance than those proposed by Social Catholic organizations, which remained voluntary. Unlike Social Catholics, moral economist publicists and administrators rarely had the occasion or the desire to sustain face-to-face relations with families of the industrial working classes who were to be the targets of reform. The most gifted of them, men such as Villermé or Adolphe Blanqui, did interview workers in the course of their explorations of working-class life, but these encounters could easily dissolve into rather one-sided affairs.[90]

One of the greatest challenges moral economists faced was to find the exact way to use administrative measures effectively.[91] The problem was that administrative measures, in contrast to the highly motivated efforts of Social Catholic volunteers, sometimes had to be translated into action through sluggish bureaucracies and competing layers of local and/or regional government. Furthermore, proposals for reform occasionally became highly charged subjects of public debate suffused with an inordinate level of ideological *Sturm und Drang*. Thus, the discovery of the mores of France's industrial working classes and the gradual, if tentative elaboration of a bourgeois family model were only the beginning of the story. The design and implementation of policies intended to change working-class family life constitute its real heart.

90. See, for example, the confrontation between Blanqui and a worker in Rouen in 1848, which ended with Blanqui's teaching a lesson in moral economy to his interlocutor. Cited in Francis Demier, "Les ouvriers de Rouen parlent à un économiste en juillet 1848," *Le mouvement social*, no. 119 (1982): 24–25.

91. Frégier argued that government ministers had gradually been convinced that power should be used not only for the repression of behavior but also for a greater control over the individual intentions that led to behavior. Frégier, *Classes dangereuses*, 1:270.

3

Industrialization, Urbanization, and the Problem of Working-Class Marriage

In their observations of working-class life under the late Restoration and July Monarchy, moral economists and Social Catholics identified a number of practices that they believed distinguished workers' family values and behavior from those of other classes. Workers were thought to begin their distinctive family lives with early entry into marriage, or alternatively with their participation in common law unions that placed them outside the social and religious status quo. Although the two groups of social observers and policy advocates would emphasize different aspects of workers' behavior in this regard, both gradually came to associate these behaviors most strongly with lower-class life in France's newly industrializing cities.

Consequently, in this chapter, discussion will focus first on the processes of urbanization and industrialization within the areas under study, concentrating on the commonalities and then the local differences which marked these processes of social change in the cities of Lille, Mulhouse, and Rouen. I examine the constituent elements of each area's working class as well as relations between local bourgeoisie and working class in order to begin to explain the differential appeal of moral economist and Social Catholic policies towards the problem of workers' marital unions. These considerations prepare the way for an examination of the policies themselves, and of workers' reactions to them.

Socioeconomic Development in Urban Industrial France

In very obvious ways, the cities of Lille, Rouen, and Mulhouse epitomized the kinds of environments that were believed to give rise to distinctive patterns of working-class family formation. All three were cities that grew, albeit at radically different rates, primarily as the result of migration. All three contained large numbers of working-class poor, many of whom worked in the first generation of cotton mills of early industrial France.

The evolution of industrial society in France, beginning under the late Restoration and continuing to the time of the 1848 Revolution, was relatively slow compared both with England's contemporaneous development and with France's later evolution under the Second Empire.[1] As in England, economic growth resulted in part from gains in productivity brought on by mechanization in the textile sector, particularly cotton. However, even more so than England, France's development in the first half of the nineteenth century was more regionally specific and highly concentrated. Both economically and demographically, France's expanding textile regions of the period deviated from the economic and demographic experience of the nation as a whole. Within a national setting of slow demographic and economic growth, regional textile centers such as those under study provided a sometimes startling contrast that in the minds of many observers resembled the intrusion of a new form of social evolution more evocative of English than indigenous French trends.[2] Although the urban areas in which the cotton industry developed were socially and historically diverse, they shared key economic and demographic features.

The demographic and economic histories of the cities of Lille, Rouen, and Mulhouse in the first half of the nineteenth century were clearly shaped by the rise and fall of the protoindustrialization process.[3] In all three regions, textile industries had gained increasing importance in the eighteenth century, expanding the number of households and individuals dependent upon cottage industry in cotton, in particular, for a measure of financial stability. Spinning and handloom weaving recruited workers from land-poor, rural proletariats in

1. On the present state of the debate on the comparative structure and pace of French economic growth in the nineteenth century, see Rondo Cameron and Charles E. Freedeman, "French Economic Growth: A Radical Revision," *Social Science History* 7 (1983): 3–30, and N.F.R. Crafts, "Economic Growth in France and Britain, 1830–1910: A Review of the Evidence," *Journal of Economic History* 44 (1984): 49–67. A useful survey of the literature is contained in Roger Price, "Recent Work on the Economic History of Nineteenth-Century France," *Economic History Review*, 2d ser., 37 (1984): 417–34.

2. Paul G. Spagnoli, "Industrialization, Proletarianization, and Marriage: A Reconsideration," *Journal of Family History* 8 (1983): 234, cites Philippe Ariès' argument that these textile centers demonstrated more of an "English" demographic pattern. See also Marie-Pascale Buriez-Duez, "Le mouvement de la population dans le département du Nord au XIXe siècle," in Marcel Gillet, ed., *L'homme, la vie et la mort dans le Nord au 19e siècle* (Lille, 1972), p. 24.

3. Franklin Mendels, "Protoindustrialization: The First Phase of the Industrialization Process," *Journal of Economic History* 32 (1972): 241–61. François Crouzet, "Quelques problèmes de l'histoire de l'industrialisation au XIXe siècle," *Revue d'histoire économique et sociale* 53 (1975): 529, has argued that "in western and central Europe, nineteenth-century industrialization was accomplished on the basis of protoindustrialization that nearly all industrial regions of the nineteenth century experienced during the eighteenth century and sometimes even since the end of the Middle Ages."

areas adjacent to the three cities, providing a partial brake to migration in the presence of late-eighteenth-century population increases.[4] Although the cotton industry provided the most spectacular growth in the eighteenth century in the regions of Rouen and Mulhouse, extending its tentacles respectively into the households of eastern Normandy and the Vosges mountains, linen also played a part in the Lille area's protoindustrial economic development, reaching its economic apogee during the last years of the Old Regime.[5]

But it was the decline of rural protoindustry that most obviously shaped the economic and demographic fortunes of the three cities from the 1820s to the 1840s. The decline of protoindustry was a slow and painful one, beginning in the regions of Rouen and Lille with the Commercial Treaty of 1786 with England, but extending well into the 1830s and 1840s.[6] As in England, home spinning was the first economic casualty, being gradually replaced by factory production during the first decades of the nineteenth century. The demise of handloom weaving was much slower. As late as the mid-1840s, there were still thousands of handloom weavers in the three regions.[7]

Like recent economic historians, observers of working-class life under the July Monarchy were aware that the process of industrialization in the Mulhouse region was more dramatic, faster-paced, and more reminiscent of English regional development than either Rouen's or Lille's. By the mid-1840s, there were fewer cotton mills in Mulhouse than in Rouen or Lille, but

4. For economic histories of the three regions' protoindustrial textile development, see, for the Nord: Georges Lefebvre, *Les paysans du Nord pendant la révolution française* (Lille, 1924), pp. 279–305; Serge Chassagne, "La diffusion rurale de l'industrie cotonnière en France (1750–1850)," *Revue du Nord* 61 (1979): 97–114; and Pierre Deyon, "La diffusion rurale des industries textiles en Flandre française à la fin de l'Ancien Régime et au début du XIXe siècle," *Revue du Nord* 61 (1979): 83–96. For Normandy: Jules Sion, *Les paysans de la Normandie orientale: Pays de Caux, Bray, Vexin normand, vallée de la Seine: Etude géographique* (Paris, 1909), pp. 182–88; J. Levainville, *Rouen: Etude d'une agglomération urbaine* (Paris, 1913), pp. 204–13; E. LeParquier, *Une enquête sur le paupérisme et la crise industrielle dans la région rouennaise en 1788* (Rouen, 1936), pp. 3–4; Marie-Odile Deschamps, "Le dépôt de mendicité de Rouen (1768–1820)," *Bulletin d'histoire économique et sociale de la révolution française*, 1977, pp. 81–93, 88, 91; William M. Reddy, *The Rise of Market Culture: The Textile Trade and French Society, 1750–1900* (Cambridge, 1984), pp. 24–31; and Gay L. Gullickson, *Spinners and Weavers of Auffay: Rural Industry and the Sexual Division of Labor in a French Village, 1750–1850* (Cambridge, 1986), pp. 56–65. On the process of protoindustrialization in the eighteenth century in Alsace, the classic source remains Henry Laufenberger, *Cours d'économie alsacienne* (Paris, 1930), 1:116–20.

5. Deyon, "La diffusion," p. 89.

6. On the effects of the 1786 treaty in the Rouen area, see Reddy, *Rise of Market Culture*, pp. 54–57, and Gullickson, *Spinners and Weavers*, pp. 86–88.

7. On Mulhouse and the Haut-Rhin, see Francis Hordern, "L'évolution de la condition individuelle et collective des travailleurs en Alsace, XIXe siècle (1800–1870)" (Thèse de doctorat, Université de Paris, Faculté de droit et des sciences économiques, 1970), p. 69.

Table 3.1. Size and Composition of Labor Force, Cotton-Spinning Mills, Mulhouse, Mid-1840s

A. Size and Composition of Total Labor Force

Number employed	Percentage of mill force
942 men	30.2
926 women	29.7
1,249 children[a]	40.1
3,117	100.0

B. Size of Mills, Total of Workers in Each Size Category, and the Percentage of Mill Force in Each Category

Number of mills	Number of workers	Workers in category	Percentage of mill force
3	151–200	576	18.5
1	201–250	219	7.0
1	301–350	337	10.8
1	651–700	670	21.5
1	1,301–1,350	1,315	42.2
		3,117	100.0

C. Number and Percentages of Men, Women, and Children in Each Size of Mill

	Number of workers			
Size of mill	Men	Women	Children	Total
151–200	181 (19.2%)	154 (16.6%)	241 (19.3%)	576
201–250	70 (7.4)	65 (7.0)	84 (6.7)	219
301–350	159 (16.9)	63 (6.8)	115 (9.2)	337
651–700	200 (21.2)	180 (19.4)	290 (23.2)	670
1,301–1,350	332 (35.2)	464 (50.1)	519 (41.6)	1,315
	942 (99.9%)	926 (99.9%)	1,249 (100.0%)	3,117

Source: France, Statistique générale, *Statistique de la France publiée par le Ministère de l'Agriculture et du Commerce*, ser. 1, vol. 10 (Industrie, vol. 1) (Paris, 1847), pp. 136–49.

[a]Under age 16.

they were on average larger and more mechanized, generally producing higher grades of cotton thread.[8] Mulhouse's mills also employed higher proportions of children. (See Tables 3.1. to 3.3.) Data from the *Statistique de la France*

8. In his memoirs, Charles Noiret noted: "Rouen's mill owners seldom produce [high grade] threads. If cloth producers wish [them], they must have them sent from Flanders or Alsace." *Mémoires d'un ouvrier rouennais* (Rouen, 1836), p. 36.

Table 3.2. Size and Composition of Labor Force, Cotton-Spinning Mills, Rouen, Mid-1840s

A. Size and Composition of Total Labor Force

Number employed	Percentage of mill force
633 men	30.0
887 women	42.1
587 children[a]	27.9
2,107	100.0

B. Size of Mills, Total of Workers in Each Size Category, and the Percentage of Mill Force in Each Category

Number of mills	Number of workers	Workers in category	Percentage of mill force
5	1–50	210	10.0
9	51–100	596	28.3
6	101–150	716	34.0
1	151–200	185	8.8
1	351–400	400	19.0
		2,107	100.1

C. Number and Percentages of Men, Women, and Children in Each Size of Mill

	Number of workers			
Size of mill	Men	Women	Children	Total
1–50	76 (12.0%)	85 (9.6%)	49 (8.3%)	210
51–100	234 (37.0)	183 (20.6)	179 (30.5)	596
101–150	223 (35.2)	344 (38.8)	149 (25.4)	716
151–200	50 (7.9)	75 (8.5)	60 (10.2)	185
351–400	50 (7.9)	200 (22.5)	150 (25.6)	400
	633 (100.0%)	887 (100.0%)	587 (100.0%)	2,107

Source: France, Statistique générale, *Statistique de la France publiée par le Ministère de l'Agriculture et du Commerce*, ser. 1, vol. 12 (Industrie, vol. 3) (Paris, 1850), pp. 26–47.
[a]Under age 16.

gathered at this time show that 81.5 percent of Mulhouse's cotton-mill workers were employed in factories of 201 or more workers, while the comparable figures for Rouen and Lille were 19 and 34.6 percent, respectively. Data from the same and other archival sources to be discussed in this chapter showed the longer persistence in Rouen and Lille of smaller units of production in the linen-spinning trade, handloom weaving, and cotton spinning.

Although mechanization in the textile sector occurred most rapidly in Mulhouse, one of the city's most important trades, the cloth-printing industry,

Table 3.3. Size and Composition of Labor Force, Cotton-Spinning Mills, Lille, Mid-1840s

A. Size and Composition of Total Labor Force

Number employed	Percentage of mill force
2,022 men	50.8
1,086 women	27.3
876 children[a]	22.0
3,984	100.1

B. Size of Mills, Total of Workers in Each Size Category, and the Percentage of Mill Force in Each Category

Number of mills	Number of workers	Workers in category	Percentage of mill force
7	1–50	265	6.7
15	51–100	1,101	27.6
7	101–150	881	22.1
2	151–200	360	9.0
1	201–250	250	6.3
4	251–300	1,127	28.3
		3,984	100.0

C. Number and Percentages of Men, Women, and Children in Each Size of Mill

	Number of workers			
Size of mill	Men	Women	Children	Total
1–50	162 (8.0%)	55 (5.1%)	48 (5.5%)	265
51–100	595 (29.4)	286 (26.3)	220 (25.1)	1,101
101–150	395 (19.5)	245 (22.6)	241 (27.5)	881
151–200	160 (7.9)	120 (11.0)	80 (9.1)	360
201–250	150 (7.4)	60 (5.5)	40 (4.6)	250
251–300	560 (27.7)	320 (29.5)	247 (28.2)	1,127
	2,022 (99.9%)	1,086 (100.0%)	876 (100.0%)	3,984

Source: France, Statistique générale, *Statistique de la France publiée par le Ministère de l'Agriculture et du Commerce*, ser. 1, vol. 10 (Industrie, vol. 1) (Paris, 1847), pp. 16–43.

Note: Data includes the suburban communes of Wazemmes and Esquermes.

[a]Under age 16.

remained an important employer of skilled labor. The historical foundation of the city's cotton trade lay in the cloth-printing industry, one that required a well-trained labor force to design and print the cloths that had long been sought out for their unusually beautiful designs and workmanship.[9] Cloth printing

9. On the history of cloth printing in modern Switzerland and France, see Pierre Caspard, "La fabrique au village," *Le mouvement social*, no. 97 (1976): 15–37; idem, "L'accumulation

Table 3.4. Population of Lille, Mulhouse, and Rouen, 1831–1846

	Lille[a]	Mulhouse[b]	Rouen
1831	69,073	13,300	88,086
1836	72,005	13,932	92,083
1841	72,537	18,076	96,002
1846	75,430	29,085	99,295

Sources: AN, F20/498, 499, 501; *Bulletin des lois*, nos. 163 (1832), 958 (1842), 1,367 (1847); Adolf Burger, *Beiträge zur Statistik der Stadt Mülhausen* (Mulhouse, 1914), p. 7; Charles Pouthas, *La population française pendant la première moitié du XIXe siècle* (Paris, 1956), p. 98; Emile Levasseur, *La population française* (Paris, 1891), 2:345.

[a]Population *intra muros*.

[b]Settled population.

was gradually transformed in the course of the 1830s from hand to machine production, but printers' work still demanded skill and concentration, and paid wages superior to those of other textile-factory workers.[10]

The demise of rural industry and the growth of manufacturing in and around Lille, Rouen, and Mulhouse provided the impetus for urban migration from the middle of the 1820s. Population data for the three cities point to radically different levels of growth but a similar importance of migration as the source of what growth there was. Between the censuses of 1831 and 1846, Mulhouse's population rose by over 118 percent, from 13,300 to 29,085. Of this increase of 15,785, however, only 18.4 percent was the result of natural increase. For Lille in the same period, where the population increased by 9.2 percent—from 69,073 to 75,430—births exceeded deaths by only 23, making natural increase responsible for less that 1 percent of the total growth. Figures for Rouen in the years 1830–45 are even more dramatic. The city's population would have declined had it not been for inmigration. Although deaths here exceeded births by 2,993, the city's population showed an increase of over 12 percent, rising from 88,086 to 99,295 (see Table 3.4).[11]

---

du capital dans l'indiennage au XVIIIème siècle," *Revue du Nord* 61 (1979): 115–23; and Serge Chassagne, *Oberkampf: Un entrepreneur capitaliste au siècle des lumières* (Paris, 1980).

10. Wage records of the Stackler cloth-printing works near Rouen in the 1840s also revealed a higher pay scale for skilled workers in the cloth-printing trade. Workers who engraved the designs on wooden planks for hand printing earned 5 francs a day; those engraving on metal, mechanized plates earned 4 francs a day; cloth dyers, 2.5 francs; and unskilled laborers, 0.75 to 1.75 francs. See "Etat de la somme nécessaire pour faire marcher une fabrique," ADSM, 4 J/1. On the wages and organization of work in one successful French cloth-printing works near Paris in the late eighteenth and early nineteenth century, see Chassagne, *Oberkampf*, pp. 226–58.

11. For vital events in the years 1825–35, see *Statistique de la France*, ser. 1, 2 (Paris, 1837): 446, 464; for the years 1826–46, AN, F20/ 440 4, 499, 504. For Mulhouse, see Adolf Burger, *Beiträge zur Statistik der Stadt Mülhausen* (Mulhouse, 1914), p. 7. On the importance of migration to Mulhouse between 1798 and the mid-nineteenth century, see Arthur Borghese, "In-

The importance of migration in the nineteenth century was not, of course, limited to textile-factory towns but was, rather, a characteristic of urban growth in general.[12] However, inmigration was especially critical to industrial cities of northern France because of high rates of mortality stemming not only from the occurrence of epidemics such as cholera in the early 1830s, but also from the more chronic problems of high infant and child mortality. As the moral economist Eugène Buret argued, "Large industrial cities would lose their working populations in a short time unless they continuously received healthy recruits . . . from the surrounding countryside."[13] Data from both Lille and Mulhouse indicate that the proportion of children born in the cities surviving to age five ranged from 55 percent in Mulhouse in the 1820s to 68 percent in Lille in the 1840s.[14] Results of studies of infant and child mortality reveal the importance of class and spatial variations. For example, in the period 1840–49, when the mortality rate for children under age three in Lille was 317 per thousand, the figure for the poor, working-class quarters of the city was 420 to 630 per thousand.[15] A more recent study of infant mor-

---

dustrialist Paternalism and Lower-Class Agitation: The Case of Mulhouse, 1848–1851," *Histoire Sociale / Social History* 13, no. 25 (1980): 57–58.

12. William H. Sewell, Jr., for example, has shown that 94% of Marseille's growth over the period 1821–72 was attributable to net immigration. See *Structure and Mobility: The Men and Women of Marseille, 1820–1870* (Cambridge, 1985), p. 152.

13. *De la misère des classes laborieuses en Angleterre et en France: De la nature de la misère, de son existence, de ses effets, de ses causes et de l'insuffisance des remèdes qu'on lui a opposés jusqu'ici; avec l'indication des moyens propres à en affranchir les sociétés* (Paris, 1840), 1:362. As Allan Sharlin pointed out, it is impossible to gauge the relative effects of migration, fertility, and mortality levels on population growth without data on age-specific fertility rates among migrants and more stable residents of cities. However, the weight of the aggregate evidence on the three cities under consideration here lends support to the hypothesis that migration and not natural increase was the more important factor in population growth. See Allan Sharlin, "Natural Decrease in Early Modern Cities: A Reconsideration," *Past and Present*, no. 79 (1978): 126–38, and the exchange between Sharlin and Roger Finlay in "Debate: Natural Decrease in Early Modern Cities," *Past and Present*, no. 92 (1981): 169–80.

14. For Mulhouse, see the commentary on vital event data in the *Industriel Alsacien* of 9 January 1836. According to this report, of 1,000 children born in the city, 450 were dead before age five and 500 before age ten. Thus, the commentator noted: "Half of the children come into the world only to consume, without producing anything." Cited in Burger, *Beiträge*, p. 11. Life tables calculated for Lille from data contained in AN, F20/440 4, indicate a life expectancy at birth of 33.4 and 35.5 years for both sexes combined for the 1820s and 1840s, respectively. The latter figures are consistent with those for the urbanized departments of the Rhône, Seine, and Bouches-du-Rhône calculated in Samuel H. Preston and Etienne van de Walle, "Urban French Mortality in the Nineteenth Century," *Population Studies* 32 (1978): 278. See also Etienne van de Walle and Samuel H. Preston, "Mortalité de l'enfance au XIXe siècle à Paris et dans le département de la Seine," *Population* 29 (1974): 89–107, who estimate a constant rate of infant mortality for the area at 190–200 per thousand during the nineteenth century.

15. Aline Lesaege-Dugied, "La mortalité infantile dans le département du Nord de 1815 à 1914," in Gillet, *L'homme, la vie et la mort*, p. 101. On Mulhouse, see Louis-René Villermé,

tality by fathers' occupations for a slightly later period has found an infant mortality rate of 189 per thousand for children born between 1800 and 1860 in the urbanized Rouen area to fathers working in the cloth-printing industry, an increase over the rate for previous generations.[16]

The formation of the populations of Lille, Mulhouse, and Rouen during the Restoration and July Monarchy was marked by the infusion of largely proletarianized migrants who were both "pushed" from adjacent rural areas by the demise of economic opportunities there and "pulled" to the cities by work opportunities in the areas' factories. Many members of the indigenous part of Lille's and Rouen's working class doubtless experienced the transition to factory textile production as a decline in the status that their crafts had previously enjoyed. For migrant men and women, however, work in urban factories offered higher wages than they could hope to earn in rural labor, the main alternative in regional economies marked by the demise of protoindustry.

In a recent work, Charles Tilly has hypothesized a direct and positive relationship between the capacity of urban proletariats to reproduce themselves and the growth of an "autonomous, persistent proletarian culture." He believes that during the nineteenth century an increasing proportion of Europe's workers began to experience proletarianization once they had migrated to the city, in contrast to an earlier situation in which proletarianization occurred mainly in the countryside. He emphasizes that urban workers' capacity to reproduce would tend to raise their consciousness of class, while the greater ongoing infusion of rural proletarians would tend to dilute it.[17] Data from Lille, Mulhouse, and Rouen have suggested that in all three, migration and not natural increase played the greater role in the formation of the urban working classes. However, the relative demographic importance of indigenous and migrant workers in forming the populations and working-class families of the three urban areas is extremely difficult to determine even with demographic records. Marriage records and, after mid-century, census records can help identify individuals who were not born in cities under observation. Yet neither

---

Tableau de l'état physique et moral des ouvriers employés dans les manufactures de coton, de laine et de soie (Paris, 1840), 2:376. A critique of Villermé's methodology is contained in Edmonde de Védrenne-Villeneuve, "L'inégalité devant la mort dans la première moitié du XIXe siècle," *Population* 16 (1961): 665–98. For a discussion of Villermé's work on mortality, see William Coleman, *Death Is a Social Disease: Public Health and Political Economy in Early Industrial France* (Madison, 1982), ch. 6.

16. Chassagne characterizes this as a "biological drama of industrialization in an urban milieu," arguing that contemporary rates among workers in rural cloth printing were generally lower. Serge Chassagne, "Les ouvriers en indiennes," in Société de démographie historique, *La France d'Ancien Régime: Etudes réunies en l'honneur de Pierre Goubert* (Toulouse, 1984), 1:123.

17. Charles Tilly, "Demographic Origins of the European Proletariat," in David Levine, ed., *Proletarianization and Family History* (Orlando, 1984), p. 11.

source pinpoints the timing of migration in individuals' lives, thus increasing the difficulty of analyzing whether and how the marriage behavior of people who chose to migrate of their own volition rather than as children may have differed from the behavior of indigenous workers.[18] Understanding the impact of migration or of proletarianization, whether in countryside or city, on the formation of marriages or consensual unions is thus rendered extremely difficult.

Another problem in understanding the locus and experience of proletarianization for working-class families is that the plight of traditional urban working classes—those who were likely to experience the transition to factory production as a decline in status—was more obvious and more likely to capture the attention of urban observers, both working-class and bourgeois alike. This was particularly the case in Lille and Rouen, whose indigenous crafts suffered severe decline as the result of industrialization. Workers such as Lille's lacemakers or thread spinners (*filtiers*) or Rouen's indigenous fancy weavers, who had epitomized a distinctively urban, skilled *artisanat,* experienced an obvious social decline. The demise of their trades in the course of the 1830s and 1840s did not necessarily lead to their own adjustment to factory work, but more likely to its adoption by their children.[19] This loss of status among the traditional crafts workers of both Lille and Rouen was portrayed in fictional accounts as one of the causes of an increasing and painful distance between the experience of working-class parents and their children. In one such account, a young mill worker complained that the work habits of her handloom-weaver father were dying too slowly: "I can understand that at his age, when one has always worked at home, one doesn't just pick up and go into the factory. But instead of making fancier cloths on a Jacquart, he has continued to weave simple blue cloths as they did twenty years ago."[20] Similarly, one of Lille's *filtiers,*

18. For a discussion of these problems, see Katherine A. Lynch, "Marriage Age among French Factory Workers: An Alsatian Example," *Journal of Interdisciplinary History* 16 (1986): 421.

19. On Rouen's handloom weavers, see Hiromasa Suzuki, "L'évolution de l'industrie cotonnière dans la région rouennaise au XIXe siècle: 1789–1880" (Thèse du 3e cycle, Université de Rouen, 1969), p. 141; Georges Guérif, "Charles Noiret et l'enquête de 1848 sur la profession de tisserand," *Revue d'histoire économique et sociale* 49 (1971): 94–112. On Lille, see Dr. Thouvenin, "De l'influence que l'industrie exerce sur la santé des populations dans les grands centres manufacturiers," *Annales d'hygiène publique et de médecine légale* 36 (1846): 32–33; Jérôme-Adolphe Blanqui, *Des classes ouvrières en France pendant l'année 1848* (Paris, 1849), pp. 84–85; Charles Engrand, "Les ouvriers lillois de 1829 à 1832" (Diplôme d'études supérieures, Université de Lille, 1957), pp. 39–40, 70. On the recruitment of the early factory labor force in England, see Michael Anderson, "Sociological History and the Working-Class Family: Smelser Revisited," *Social History* 3 (1976): 326–27.

20. Emile Bosquet, *Le roman des ouvrières* (Paris, 1868), pp. 96–97, a novel about Rouen's working class in the 1830s.

accustomed to supporting his family in decent style, lamented his daughter's entry into the factory as the sign of his inability to provide sufficient income.[21] Both quantitative and qualitative sources suggest a more gradual emergence of urban industrial society in Rouen and Lille. Nevertheless, the transition appears to have been more traumatic for workers in the two towns' traditional trades. Immigration of rural proletarians was crucial in all three instances of urban growth, with the pace of growth significantly more rapid in Mulhouse.

The rise of an urban industrial civilization in France resulted not only from the labors of a new working class but also from the entrepreneurial activities of provincial industrial bourgeois whose mentalities were strongly marked by traditions within the cities where they dwelt, specific regional features of the industrialization process, and their own attitudes towards workers and industrial pursuits. The different pace of industrialization in the three areas and the formation of rather different senses of class solidarity within local industrial bourgeoisies were both caused and perpetuated by fundamental attitudes towards their engagement in industry. Available evidence suggests both similarities and differences of social mentality among the bourgeois of the three cities that resulted in rather different attitudes towards the urgency and means of intervention in the working-class family problems of industrial society.

Mulhouse's *patronat,* organized very early into the powerful Société industrielle de Mulhouse, appears to have shared a high level of class solidarity and devotion to the long-term fortunes of industry. Their shared religious commitment to Reformed Protestantism and the persistence of family dynasties in the cotton trade there underpinned this sense of cohesiveness. Differences in religious affiliation also helped demarcate broader lines of social class. Whereas city administrators and industrialists in Mulhouse were by and large members of the Protestant Reformed Church, the working class, particularly those who were least skilled, were overwhelmingly and in an increasing proportion Catholics.[22] "Dynastic" elements were not lacking in either Lille or Rouen. Here, too, there were a number of industrialists who could trace both their business training and the source of their capital to their families' earlier successes.[23] However, members of Rouen's bourgeoisie, in contrast to the industrialists of Lille or especially those of Mulhouse, seem to have viewed their

21. Mathile Bourdon, *Marthe Blondel ou l'ouvrière de fabrique* (Paris, 1862), p. 56, cited in Pierre Pierrard, *La vie ouvrière à Lille sous le second Empire* (Paris, 1965), p. 73.

22. Borghese, "Industrialist Paternalism," pp. 62–63.

23. Jean-Pierre Chaline, *Les bourgeois de Rouen: Une élite urbaine au XIXe siècle* (Paris, 1982), pp. 71–72, has traced some of these links. In contrast, Suzuki, "L'évolution de l'industrie cotonnière," p. 108, has argued that very few of Rouen's spinning-mill owners under the Restoration and July Monarchy were the product of long-lived dynasties, compared with the *patronat* of Alsace. Noiret, *Mémoires*, pp. 2, 6, also emphasizes the recent working-class origins of some of Rouen's manufacturers.

engagement in the textile industry less as a long-standing commitment and more as a commercial investment. Each generation tended to divide up profits among family members.[24] Mulhouse's *patronat* was distinguished not only by its commitment to industry, but also by its apparently greater control over the local administration than industrialists achieved in the other two cities. It was not that industrialists in either Rouen or Lille were unable to convince their cities' administrations to defend their economic interests.[25] Rather, in Mulhouse there was simply a greater overlap between economic and administrative elites, contributing to the bourgeoisie's consciousness of itself as a group capable of wielding power both inside and outside the industrial work place.

Moral Economist Perspectives on Workers' Marriages

In attempting to understand the impact of social change on the marriage behavior of industrial workers, moral economists and Social Catholics would emphasize different but complementary features of the urban working-class marriage problem. Moral economists were much more concerned than Social Catholics about what they identified as industrial workers' proclivity to enter marriage too young. As far as the moral economists were concerned, the best attitude that workers could take towards marriage was to postpone it until they were in a secure financial position, since they would soon be burdened with the costs of child-rearing:

> We wish to have workers be on guard against their lack of foresight, against the ease with which they contract early marriages. We cannot exaggerate the burdens and cares of poverty which a large family can bring in the city. . . . The sturdy young worker can support himself, his wife and first child. But [what if] his earnings do not increase in proportion to the number of children, if there is unemployment, sickness or death! Without presupposing any accidents . . . nature brings with age the diminution of strength, and it is when the worker has most need of it that he has it the least. Young people should think before they marry.[26]

Young workers were urged to take moral as well as financial responsibility for their families' future. As Sismondi had pointed out in the first edition of

24. Suzuki, "L'évolution de l'industrie cotonnière," p. 126. See also Chaline, *Les bourgeois de Rouen*, pp. 373–74, on the failure of the Rouen bourgeoisie to develop a distinctively "industrial" mentality.

25. The promulgation of stricter rules on workers' *livrets* and factory discipline during and following the Revolution of 1830 in the Rouen area was undertaken with the aid of the city administration. See Départment de la Seine Inférieure, "Police des fabriques et des manufactures," 6 July 1832, ADSM, 10 MP/1302.

26. Alphonse Grün, *De la moralisation des classes laborieuses* (Paris, 1851), pp. 22–23.

his *Nouveaux principes d'économie politique*, guilds and workers' corporations had historically controlled skilled urban workers' access to marriage and reproduction by limiting it to masters.[27] But since this traditional collective restraint on marriage no longer existed, he advised young working couples to modify their individual behavior in order to adjust to the necessarily undependable supply of work in an industrial capitalist economy.[28]

As Sismondi himself realized, however, workers frequently seemed unable or unwilling to organize their lives this way. He lamented the fact that the modern factory operative "often suffers hunger and does not refuse marriage. . . . He has become accustomed to the fact that he never knows a future beyond the next Saturday when he is paid for his week's work. His moral and sympathetic qualities have been dulled. He has too often been led to think about present comforts so as not to be too afraid of the future suffering that his wife and children may bear."[29] It was Villermé who argued most persuasively that young industrial workers were tempted to marry during their early twenties because it was at that age that their wages often reached their maximum.[30] The fact that in some areas such as Mulhouse, workers' ages at first marriage were higher than this was not in itself very consoling to moral economists in particular because the figures did not take into consideration workers' tendency to enter sexual unions, either stable or unstable, before marrying.[31] As one of Lille's own moral economists observed, there was really no reason for working-class women to refrain from common law unions, since their communities did not reproach them for such conduct: "Since they often marry the father of their children or another worker, they see no harm in giving rein to their passions."[32] Given a de facto choice between early marriage and

27. Jean-Charles Simonde de Sismondi, *Nouveaux principes d'économie politique* (Paris, 1819), 1:403–8. On the moral aspects of guild solidarity, see William M. Reddy, *Rise of Market Culture*, pp. 35–36.

28. While sharing certain of Malthus's concerns about the growth of population, Sismondi argued that in "civilized" societies the demand for labor, and not the supply of food, was the main regulator of population growth. J.C.L. Simonde de Sismondi, *Political Economy* (New York, 1966), p. 119.

29. Simonde de Sismondi, *Nouveaux principes*, 2:265.

30. *Tableau*, 1:113. See also Société libre pour concourir aux progrès du commerce et de l'industrie de Rouen, "De l'état des enfants employés dans les manufactures," AN, F12/4705, which noted: "Men [in the cotton mills] who have reached age eighteen generally receive about fourteen francs a week, rarely more. This wage is the highest a spinner can earn."

31. Earlier in his work, Villermé had noted that the average age at first marriage for Mulhouse's workers was 26 years, 10 months for women, and 28 years, 5 months for men. See *Tableau*, 1:51, and Katherine A. Lynch, "Marriage Age," pp. 402–29, for a discussion of the ages at marriage of industrial workers during the first half of the nineteenth century.

32. Thouvenin, "De l'influence," *Annales d'hygiène publique et de médecine légale* 37 (1847): 86.

consensual unions, moral economists emphatically preferred the former: "If you scare [young workers] too much about marriage, you will have illicit relations without consecration or responsibility—young men without moderation, young women without modesty, children without families—in a word, all the inconveniences of hastily conceived marriages minus the moral bond and sanctity of legitimate unions."[33] Although several German states and Swiss cantons had begun to reimplement restrictive laws on marriage for their poor inhabitants during the 1820s and 1830s, this idea appears never to have gained more than very marginal support in France, in part for the reasons adduced by Grün himself.[34] A petition submitted to the French Chamber of Deputies in the session of 23 September 1830 in which legal restrictions on marriage for the poor were suggested seems to have fallen on deaf ears. The petition did evoke some scandalized responses after the fact, which cited several problems to which the legislation could give rise.[35]

As early as the late 1820s, Baron Charles Dupin had advocated a French moral economist version of policy towards workers' common law unions.

> It is not by coercive measures or by the help of the law or the arm of authority that we will force members of the working class to refrain from living in the dissolution of *concubinage*. But it seems that it would be easy to bring about an immense amelioration . . . by the simplest, easiest and most natural means. I would advocate that the *livrets* held by each male and female worker regularly receive an inscription attesting to their legitimate marriage and children . . . from the municipal authority. When they present themselves for work . . . and there is not enough . . . it would be natural that all other things being equal, married men with legitimate children be preferred. It would be easy to interest honest factory owners and their honorable wives in this preference. In hard

33. Grün, *De la moralisation*, p. 24.

34. On the history of restrictions on marriage in Switzerland, Germany, and Austria, see D. V. Glass, ed., *Introduction to Malthus* (London, 1953), pp. 42–45, and John Knodel, "Law, Marriage, and Illegitimacy in Nineteenth-Century Germany," *Population Studies* 20 (1967): 280–81.

35. Pierre-Marie-Sébastien Bigot de Morogues, *Du paupérisme, de la mendicité et des moyens d'en prévenir les funestes effets* (Paris, 1834), p. 114. One observer noted that restrictive marriage legislation in Switzerland was frequently very local in nature and that cantonal authorities sometimes overruled particularly harsh laws. These laws could require couples to repay any welfare funds received before marriage, establish their ineligibility for funds for a period before the marriage could occur, and require their contributions to poor-relief coffers. See F.M.L. Naville, *De la charité légale, de ses effets, de ses causes, et spécialement des maisons de travail et de la proscription de la mendicité* (Paris, 1836), 1:107–12, 158. The author described the implementation of this legislative repertoire in Freiburg-im-Breisgau, Frankfurt-am-Main, and the Swiss cantons of St. Gall, Fribourg, and Appenzell.

> times, workers would soon learn that one of the most efficacious ways of escaping misery and famine would be to sanctify their reprehensible relations by marriage. Gradually, the men who now live a scandalous life would be called back into the gentle empire of moral habits.[36]

Dupin's suggestion did not entail the same means of legal coercion as those implemented in parts of Germany and Switzerland. His kind of policy was intended to operate, rather, through factory owners or municipal authorities newly conscious of the moral leadership their position demanded. Workers' desire to eat would inspire their cooperation. Echoes of Dupin's recommendation would appear in particular regions, as will be shown. However, his dream of eliciting the cooperation of factory owners or municipal authorities nationwide would remain just that.

When moral economist commentators on working-class life began to attack the problem of illegitimate unions, what they had in mind was not primarily short-term sexual relationships, nor the kind of bohemian liaisons widespread in Paris that might represent a stage in a bourgeois student's life. These unions certainly earned their disapproval, but moral economists began to concentrate more of their attention on the longer-lived coresidential unions of working-class men and women that in some ways—frequently their duration and child-rearing functions—actually emulated features of legitimate marriage. This kind of union became the focus of concern for several reasons. First, during the period under observation, common law unions seemed to become more numerous and more obvious, both because of their duration and because workers made little effort to conceal them, at least from their neighbors.[37] Second, workers seemed to feel little shame about them, this in a society whose moral standards on such matters Dupin had shown to be undergoing a process of purification. Third, moral economist commentators and policymakers as well as Social Catholics may well have believed that policy to encourage legitimate marriage would enjoy greater success among *concubinaires* than among couples engaged in only casual sexual encounters.

Although workers themselves may not have viewed common law unions as proof of their rejection of legitimate marriage, both moral economists and Social Catholics clearly did. Moral economists saw such arrangements as the origins of a deviant kind of family life and, very importantly, as the source of illegitimate children who might well redound to the public charge. At least initially, the response of moral economists at the national and local level was to suggest policies designed simply to repress the practice by instruments of coercion that stopped just short of Swiss and German legislation.

36. *Des forces productives et commerciales de la France* (Paris, 1827), 1:101–2.

37. It seems extremely likely, however, that large numbers of residential common law unions would have been reported to census takers as legitimate marriages.

Table 3.5. Geographic Origins of Foreigners Living in Mulhouse, 1823

Place of origin	Number of individuals
Baden	543
Bavaria	150
Hesse	75
Prussia	145
Saxony	86
Württemberg	268
Total Germany	1,267
Switzerland	1,449
Austria	265
Netherlands	21
Italy	14
Russia	5
England	1
Total excluding Germany	1,755
Grand total	3,022[a]

Source: "Etat des étrangers demeurant à Mulhouse à l'époque du 29 Octobre 1823," AMM, F I/Da2.

Note: The compiler of these figures expressed his view that the true total was higher, given that a number of the foreigners failed to keep their *cartes de sureté* up to date.

[a]There were an additional 26 cases whose origin was illegible.

Controlling the Concubinage Problem: Mulhouse in the 1820s and 1830s

A consideration of the way Mulhouse's city administration attempted to deal with the problem of working-class consensual unions reveals that the city administrators were moral economists *avant la lettre,* a feature stemming from several local circumstances. As early as the 1820s, Mulhouse had large numbers of foreigners, drawn from densely populated areas of Baden, Württemberg, and northern Switzerland as well as from adjacent departments of eastern France (see Table 3.5 and Fig. 3.1). The numerical importance of non-native workers to Mulhouse's industrial working class was a constant source of amazement to some departmental-level administrators, though surely not to the city's own administration. As late as 1845, after receiving a letter indicating that approximately 25 percent of the city population was composed of foreigners, the subprefect of the arrondissement of Altkirch asked whether this figure could possibly be accurate, to which the mayor, André Koechlin, responded, "I can assure you . . . that the information is very exact."[38] He

38. Letter of 20 February 1845, AMM, F I/Da 23.

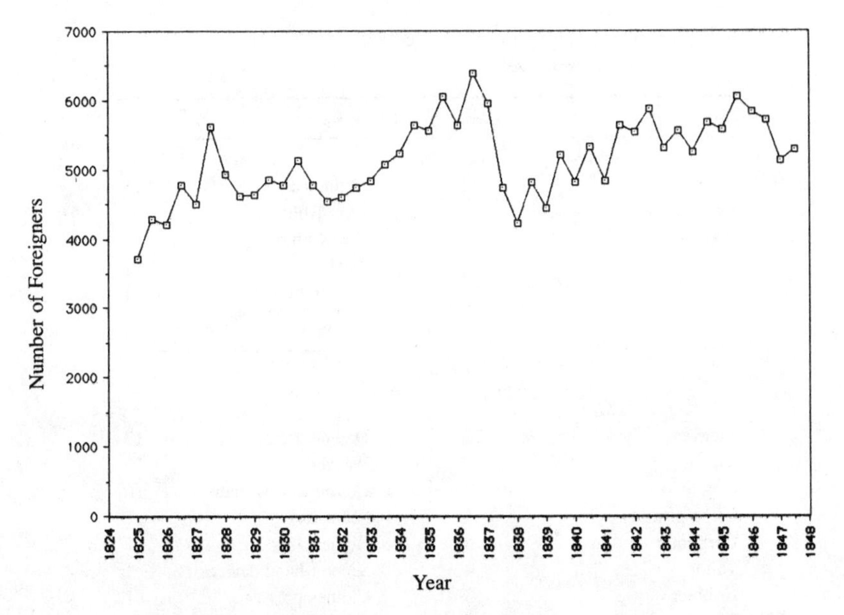

Figure 3.1 Number of Foreigners in Mulhouse, 1825–1847. Source: AMM, F VI/Da2-25.

was reporting a feature of the city that had existed for decades. As shown in Figure 3.1, which indicates the number of foreigners on 1 January and 1 July of each year, some of this migration continued to be seasonal, particularly for men in the building trades. Many migrants arrived in spring and left in the autumn. However, Mulhouse also became the destination of longer-term migrants, whose presence lay at the source of a new social problem.

A record of 75 concubinaire couples in the city in 1824 showed the importance of the major sending areas already cited. It also showed foreigners living in common law unions both with French citizens and with other foreigners (see Table 3.6). Foreign males (54) outnumbered foreign females (36) somewhat in the group of concubinaires included in this survey, whose occupations indicate that nearly all were members of the city's working class.[39] Besides the information presented in Table 3.6, the survey revealed that the 75 couples had 62 living children of a total of 85 born to them and that two of the women were 8½ months pregnant. Of the 54 foreign men listed, 23, or 42.6 percent, had been living in Mulhouse for five years or less; 13, or 24.1 percent, had been there from five to nine years; and the rest had been residents of the city for ten years or more.[40]

39. Cf. Michel Frey, "Du mariage et du concubinage dans les classes populaires à Paris (1846–1847)," *Annales, E.S.C.* 33 (1978): 803–29, who argues that concubinage in the capital was not specific to the working class.

40. This record was also updated with annotations of five marriages that took place during

Table 3.6. Geographic Origins and Occupations of Concubinaires in Mulhouse, 1824

Geographic Origin			
Foreign[a]		*French*[b]	
Germany	34	Mulhouse	18
Switzerland	46	Haut-Rhin[c]	37
Austria	10	Bas-Rhin	3
Total	90	Doubs	1
		Uncertain	1
		Total	60

Occupation			
Men		*Women*	
Weaver	23	Day laborer	17
Mason	9	Weaver	16
Day laborer	8	Cotton-mill worker	16
Cloth printer	6	Seamstress	7
Carpenter	5	Homemaker	7
Tailor	4	Second-hand dealer	1
Cobbler	3	Clothes presser	1
Farm servant	2		75
Cloth worker	2		
Cloth shearer	1		
Woodworker	1		
Brewer	1		
Engraver	1		
Locksmith	1		
Gardener	1		
Teacher	1		
Glass worker	1		
Winegrower	1		
Second-hand dealer	1		
Unknown or uncertain	1		
	75		

Source: AMM, J II/La1.

[a]Foreigners included 54 men (half of whom were living with Frenchwomen) and 36 women (of whom 9 were living with Frenchmen).

[b]French included 21 men (9 of whom were living with foreigners) and 39 women (of whom 27 were living with foreigners).

[c]Excluding Mulhouse.

A policy of keeping a close watch on the number of non-native people living in the city had had a long history in Mulhouse, antedating by many years the city's annexation to France in 1798. As an independent republic

1825, the death of one of the women, and a laconic note of "mauvaise vie" next to one couple's name.

during most of the early modern period, Mulhouse extended citizenship to outsiders reluctantly and with an eye to candidates' financial and moral capital. During the sixteenth and seventeenth centuries, the bourgeoisie of the town had comprised two levels, the lower of which, the *bourgeois manants,* first admitted newcomers. Members of this group enjoyed fewer privileges than the indigenous bourgeoisie and could be more readily expelled from the town for misconduct. By the late seventeenth century, another class of non-natives —those admitted to simple resident status on a conditional basis—began to assume a greater numerical importance as the distinction between the two bourgeois statuses declined. The beginnings of the cloth-printing industry in 1736 increased the number of workers admitted only as temporary residents.[41] This traditional, restrictive policy gained renewed impetus during the period of industrialization as a result of the sheer size of the migrant population, its dependency on the cotton industry for its income, and the documented proclivity of migrants to form consensual unions.

Administrative surveillance of migrants was also fundamental to the city's welfare policy: "Knowing all the strangers who are in Mulhouse [as a result] of their obligation to leave identification papers at city hall when they arrive, we can get them to leave the city as soon as they have no resources left by telling them that available aid must above all be given to citizens of the city. By allowing strangers to receive aid, we would in a way be encouraging them to stay here and multiply." [42] For non-natives, both French and foreign, residency in Mulhouse was in principle conditional on employment and good conduct. Although, as we have seen, foreign workers were not the only ones living in common law unions in the city, they were the ones most associated with the practice. City officials ascribed their conduct to a variety of causes: "Lack of foresight, heedlessness, their precarious position, even a sort of real economy keeps them from contracting legal engagements. . . . Most often the difficulty they have in procuring documents from their governments, those . . . required by French law, retards or hinders the accomplishment of civil and religious marriage. They call this sort of union 'marriage *à la parisienne*' and have made a German verb, *parisieren—pariser* means to do as in Paris." [43]

The city administration was apprehensive lest the habit of consensual unions among the migrant working class spread to indigenous workers. For this and other reasons, concubinaires were the first workers to be expelled from the city during periods of economic crisis in the cotton industry and the least likely

41. See Philippe Mieg, "Bourgeois et manants à Mulhouse du XVIe au XVIIe siècle" in Société savante d'Alsace et des régions de l'Est, *La bourgeoisie alsacienne: Etudes d'histoire sociale* (Strasbourg, 1954), pp. 103–15.

42. Mairie de Mulhouse, "Extinction de la mendicité: Sociétés du travail," 12 April 1839, AMM, Q I/Aa5.

43. Société industrielle de Mulhouse, *Documents relatifs au travail des jeunes ouvriers dans les établissements manufacturiers*, n.d. (but early 1840s), AN, F12/4704.

to be granted residency status in France.[44] Those migrants, the vast majority of them males, who successfully applied for residency status were likely to be married to a French woman, own real property, or have a dependable income. Good conduct was also a prerequisite, as indicated by the *conseil municipal*'s note that "it is moral and politic to admit those foreign workers who by their good conduct show us that they are worthy of this favor."[45] German and Swiss workers often wished to legalize their common law unions by marriage. But they were in many cases prohibited from doing so by the fact that their own governments would not recognize their marriages as legal or agree to admit them back into their homeland until the couple met the requirements of their more restrictive marriage legislation. The mayor of Mulhouse, André Koechlin, thus cautioned other French officials that they should not agree to marry any foreigner with a French national or another foreigner until it was proven that the couple had complied with the marriage regulations of their respective countries.

To illustrate the problems that could arise, Koechlin cited the case of Jean-Georges Bauer from Württemberg, who had married Marguerite Flury of Glarus, Switzerland, while both were living in France. They had been married by a well-meaning French official without paying the fees—in this case the *droits de bourgeoisie*—required by both of their governments to insure that neither the new couple nor their children would become dependent on public relief. Bauer returned to Württemberg without his wife, who then applied for financial assistance from Mulhouse's welfare coffers. Bauer's own government refused to recognize the marriage as legal or to admit Bauer's wife into Württemberg. This is when the Malthusian marriage legislation of the kingdom of Württemberg became a problem for the mayor. In order to get Bauer's penniless wife out of Mulhouse, the mayor required her to return to *her* birthplace, without success: "When she entered Switzerland at Basel, she was led back onto French territory under armed guard. . . . [S]ince she had married a Württemberger, she had lost her Swiss citizenship and had lost her right to aid and domicile [there]. She is not French, since she was born in Switzerland, and is married to a Württemberger. However, she will remain on French [charity] rolls since, given her indigent state, neither Switzerland

44. On the economic cycles of the cotton industry in the Mulhouse area, see Francis Hordern, *Les crises industrielles en Alsace au XIXe siècle (1800–1870) et leur répercussion sur l'emploi des travailleurs* (Aix-en Provence, 1970), p. 6. Hordern notes that the cotton crisis of 1810–11 brought the first modern expulsions of unemployed workers from Mulhouse.

45. Conseil municipal de Mulhouse, "Procès-verbaux" (1834–38), p. 163, AMM, D I/A1. For other examples of deliberations on granting residency status, see "Procès-verbaux" (1826–30), pp. 25, 38, 312, 346, 398, 408. Those rejected included workers living in consensual unions, those "not sufficiently known," and those who did not own real property. For cases of rejection, see ibid., p. 289, and "Procès-verbaux" (1830–34), pp. 165, 523.

nor Württemberg will receive her."[46] The mayor also explained that if other French officials continued to marry foreign workers without their governments' permission, the Mulhouse administration would no longer be able to have the workers expelled from France when, by "their scandalous and immoral conduct and their lack of means of subsistence, they disturb public order . . . and absorb part of the resources designated for the relief of French citizens."[47]

Koechlin recommended changes in French marriage legislation to the minister of justice, and urged that other mayors follow his example. He believed that his conflicts with French legal authorities and with the prefect and subprefect over his refusal to marry foreign workers without the permission of their governments were worth his trouble, even though many workers succeeded in circumventing Mulhouse's restrictions by getting married in neighboring communes.[48]

Another case provides a closer look into the lives of workers caught in this dilemma. It concerned a Marc Schellenberg, originally of Zurich, who was living in Mulhouse with his common law wife. He was denied *admission à domicile* twice by the city council and suffered expulsion twice. In a meeting of 3 January 1827, the council noted that "despite delays accorded to him since October 1824 to procure the documents necessary to legitimize the illicit union in which he lives, he has justified no action on this matter. Only when he was expelled by superior order from France did he finally produce a certificate delivered by his government, which expressly states 'that the certificate is valid only for one year and cannot be interpreted as consent to his marriage.'"[49] Schellenberg appeared again in the records on 13 March 1829, when he once more applied for residency status. This time the record indicated that he "has lived for the past eleven years in Mulhouse with a French woman and several children whom he has [legally] recognized as his own. But failing to legitimize his union, he was expelled from the kingdom. He was allowed back by ministerial order and now requests *admission à domicile* so that he may obtain the documents necessary for his marriage."[50] Nevertheless, the minutes went on, since residency status in France was the "last thing required for his legitimate marriage," admission was denied. Schellenberg and other foreigners like him apparently had to earn the money required to purchase the right to marry somewhere other than Mulhouse.

Efforts to stamp out the practice of common law unions in Mulhouse

46. André Koechlin, mayor, to the minister of justice, 8 November 1840, cited in Achille Penot, *Recherches statistiques sur Mulhouse* (Mulhouse, 1843), pp. 49–50.

47. Ibid., p. 50.

48. Ibid., pp. 48, 54. Koechlin noted that mayors violated French law by marrying couples when neither spouse was legally domiciled in their communes.

49. Conseil municipal de Mulhouse, "Procès-verbaux" (1826–30), p. 290, AMM, D I/A1.

50. Ibid., p. 426.

had begun as early as 1821. In that year, Mayor Emile Dolfuss summoned city workers living in consensual unions to separate from their partners. His attempts, however, met both with resistance from the workers affected and shock on the part of higher regional officials. Male workers ordered to separate from their common law wives under threat of expulsion from the city brought their case before the *procureur* of Altkirch. It ultimately reached the minister of justice, who wrote to the minister of the interior: "The mayor was no doubt guided by praiseworthy intentions, but his zeal for proper morality pushed him too far. The measures are more likely to increase than diminish scandal."[51] The prefect of the Haut-Rhin, more familiar with the spirit of the Mulhouse city administration and also more sympathetic, wrote to the subprefect of Altkirch: "I do not regard the mayor's conduct as reprehensible. In limiting himself to suggesting that factory workers legitimize their unions, he has not gone beyond his powers."[52] However, the mayor had clearly gone beyond mere suggestion, as the next sentence of the prefect's letter indicated: "Only the courts can decide if he has placed himself [outside the bounds] of article 184 of the Penal Code," which restrained public officials from illegal entry into the domiciles of citizens.[53]

Although the records do not indicate whether the mayor or the workers triumphed in this particular instance, it is clear that the policy of expulsions continued. In 1825, Mayor Dolfuss responded to a request from the subprefect of Altkirch for a list of the foreigners living in Mulhouse. The list he sent was entitled "List of foreign individuals whom the mayor of Mulhouse proposes to expel from the kingdom as a result of the scandal caused by their [living in] common law."[54] Expulsions of concubinaires reoccurred regularly along with expulsions of unemployed and indigent outsiders. Local police described one expulsion in 1837: "The measures taken by the authorities for the renewal of identity cards [for non-native workers] and the expulsion of workers without resources is being executed. . . . As of 2 May, 273 households and about 30 single workers had to leave the city." In their report, the police also noted that at the same time there was a "coalition against wage reductions at the spinning mill of Messieurs Koechlin/Dolfuss."[55]

Industrial crises, attempts by workers to form coalitions, and the expul-

51. Paul Leuilliot, *L'Alsace au début du XIXe siècle* (Paris, 1959), 2:493.

52. Letter of 21 February 1821, AMM, F I/Da2.

53. Article 184 reads: "Any judge, *procureur général* or *procureur du roi*, or substitute, any administrator or officer or justice of the police who has entered the domicile of a citizen outside cases provided for by law, and without the formalities prescribed, shall be punished with a fine of at least 16 francs and no more than 200 francs." The penalties for breaking this law were strengthened by an amendment of 1832. See Joseph-André Rogron, *Codes français expliqués par leurs motifs, par des exemples et par la jurisprudence*, 2d ed. (Paris, 1843), vol. 2.

54. "Renvoi des étrangers . . . ," AMM, J II/La1.

55. Commissariat de Police, "Rapport sur la deuxième quinzaine d'avril," ADHR, 1M 124/1.

sion of concubinaires were closely related in the period from the 1820s to the 1840s. Mulhouse was not the only place in Alsace to employ this kind of policy, though it seems to have been the most active in expelling concubinaires specifically.[56] In order to ensure workers' passage out of the area, Mulhouse's Bureau de bienfaisance had a special fund for the distribution of small sums to those expelled by the city administration. In 1833, for example, a total of 7,161 francs in general aid was given to the city's indigenous poor along with 1,300 francs in cash to "the temporarily impoverished and also to nearly 200 workers to facilitate their travelling with their families to another place when they were without work."[57]

Of the three industrial cities under consideration, it is clear that Mulhouse's leaders were most concerned about concubinage. They viewed it against the background of working-class immigration and poverty and bore in mind the possible labor problems to which this combination of circumstances could give rise. That Mulhouse's working class was being so obviously fed by the rapid influx of outsiders and that its demographic increase was so much more vigorous than growth in the other two towns were central to the city administration's intense concern for the problem of common law marriages. The policy of Mulhouse's city leaders exemplified a moral economist approach to the problem of concubinage. Their fear of the dangers of social disruption resulting from the industrialization process, combined with the local practice of expelling "undesirables" from the town helped shape their approach to the problem during the 1820s and 1830s. Leaders' fear of the multifaceted dangers of inmigration and consensual unions gained urgency too because of the religious difference between the city's bourgeoisie and large elements of its settled working class on the one hand, and the migrants on the other.

56. See the letter from the prefect of the Haut-Rhin to the subprefect of Belfort advising him to send away the unemployed with "prudent firmness" and the letter from the minister of the interior to the prefect, dated 7 May 1837, congratulating the latter on his decision to advise these expulsions, ADHR, 1M 124/1. On expulsions of the unemployed, see letters in AMM, J II/La 1 on Colmar in 1825, J II/La 4–5 on Mulhouse between 1836 and 1839, and J II/Hf 4 for expulsions from Mulhouse in the 1840s. On the expulsion of unemployed foreigners from Roubaix in the 1840s, see Judy A. Reardon, "Belgian and French Workers in Nineteenth-Century Roubaix," in Louise A. Tilly and Charles Tilly, eds., *Class Conflict and Collective Action* (Beverly Hills, 1981), p. 168.

57. Commune de Mulhouse, "Tableau de la situation financière du Bureau de bienfaisance et autres établissements analogues au 1er janvier 1835," AMM, Q I/Aa 6. These 7,161 francs were not the whole sum distributed to the indigenous poor during that year. The city's special fund for the "extinction of pauperism" also distributed a total of 13,865 francs. On payments to workers being expelled, see also the letter from an unidentified source to the subprefect of Altkirch, 27 February 1826, AMM, Q I/Aa1; "Observations du Bureau de bienfaisance de Mulhouse sur le budget de 1830," AMM, Q I/Aa5; and Yvette Tschill, "Le Bureau de bienfaisance de Mulhouse, 1798–1848," in Georges Livet and Georges Shaff, eds., *Médecine et assistance en Alsace* (Strasbourg, 1976), p. 247.

The Work of the Société de Saint-François-Régis

Religious factors also seem to have affected the treatment of the concubinage question in Lille and Rouen, where, however, the question of Protestant-Catholic differences between city leaders and working class was not an issue. In both of these towns, it was Social Catholic activists and not city administrators who took the initiative in suggesting and implementing policy towards concubinaires. In the Catholic view, couples cohabiting outside the married state and their illegitimate children were in principle living outside the boundaries of the religious community. Social Catholic activists thus determined to work through an organization of laymen to bring concubinaires and their children back into a moral and spiritual community that was bounded by the accomplishment of marriage under the laws of both state and the church. Although the church hierarchy and individual members of the clergy were doubtless concerned by the problem of common law unions, efforts to deal with this problem were initiated and led by pious laymen gradually organized into a nationwide, voluntary organization, the Société de Saint-François-Régis.[58]

The Société de Saint-François-Régis was originally created under the Empire to help soldiers contract marriages while they were away from home. By the time of the Restoration, however, it had evolved into an organization concerned specifically with rehabilitating common law unions among the urban working class.[59] Lay members of the society carried out their work among poor couples in part by helping them obtain and pay for the many legal documents necessary for marriage. Chapters of the society frequently grew out of the work of local *conférences* of the Société de Saint-Vincent-de-Paul. This was the case in Lille, where a chapter of the Société de Saint-François-Régis was officially constituted in 1839. In Rouen, however, the existence of the Société de Saint-François-Régis preceded that of the Société de Saint-Vincent-de-Paul by four years, beginning its own efforts there in 1836. The Mulhouse chapter of the Société de Saint-Vincent-de-Paul, created only in 1846, apparently devoted part of its efforts to the rehabilitation of workers' consensual unions until the creation of a chapter of the Société de Saint-François-Régis there in 1851.[60] By the early 1850s, one source shows that from the time of its

58. Information on the church hierarchy's activities in addressing the problem of common law unions is sparse. Rouen's Archbishop Cröy, who served from 1823 to 1844, followed a policy of keeping a register of concubinaires within his diocese and advocated posting lists of noncommunicants on church doors. See Adrien Dansette, *Religious History of Modern France*, trans. John Dingle (Freiburg, 1961), 1:193.

59. Eugène Gossin, *La vie de M. Jules Gossin* (Paris, 1907), p. 50; Jacques Donzelot, *The Policing of Families*, trans. Robert Hurley (New York, 1979), pp. 31–33.

60. For an overview of the society, see Jules Gossin, *Manuel de la Société charitable de Saint-Régis de Paris* (Paris, 1851), p. 15. For Lille, Société de Saint-Vincent-de-Paul de Lille,

record-keeping in 1826, the Société de Saint-François-Régis was responsible for facilitating nearly 42,000 marriages nationwide (see Table 3.7).[61]

In the diagnosis of both moral economists and Social Catholics working through the Société de Saint-François-Régis, common law unions were believed to have diverse contributory causes. While moral economists tended to emphasize individual moral choice as the ultimate precipitating cause, Social Catholics were instrumental in shedding further light on the importance of migration in preparing workers to make that choice. The origins of the work of the Société de Saint-François-Régis among soldiers serving away from home attested to the importance of migration in complicating the process of contracting legitimate marriage. However, the return of peace and the growth of migration caused by industrialization led the society to focus more specifically on problems of contracting legitimate marriage as experienced by civilian populations, particularly workers.

More than any other force in French society during the Restoration and July Monarchy, the Société de Saint-François-Régis began to understand and to cope with the formation of working-class consensual unions. While decrying this problem and working towards its extirpation, the society recognized the multidimensional aspects of a phenomenon that had important roots in law, social change, human psychology, and popular culture. It is worth quot-

---

Notice historique sur la Société de Saint-Vincent-de-Paul à Lille, 1838–1883 (Lille, 1883), pp. 236, 325; the letter from M. Fiévet-Chombart, one of the founders of the Société de Saint-François-Régis in Lille, to the prefect of the Nord, 2 September 1839, ADN, M222/373; and Pierrard, *La vie ouvrière*, pp. 119–20, 383–84. For Rouen, see an unclassified document, "Note sur la Société de Saint-Vincent-de-Paul et quelques autres associations religieuses de Rouen," 7 January 1861, ADSM; and Société de Saint-Vincent-de-Paul de Rouen, "Etat du personnel," 31 December 1843, which dates the first meeting of the Rouen chapter of the Société de Saint-Vincent-de-Paul on 25 February 1840 (ASVP, Rouen, Dossier 6, under "Extrait du procès-verbal de la conférence de Rouen"). Jean-Pierre Chaline, "Le dix-neuvième siècle," in Nadine-Josette Chaline, *Le diocèse de Rouen-LeHavre* (Paris, 1976), p. 258, and Jean-Pierre Chaline., ed., *Deux bourgeois en leur temps: Documents sur la société rouennaise du XIXe siècle* (Rouen, 1977), p. 165, dates the founding of the *conférence* of the Société de Saint-Vincent-de-Paul in Rouen to 1841. He notes that the founder of the Rouen chapter of the Société de Saint-Vincent-de-Paul included a friend of Ozanam's, Auguste LeTaillandier, who was "related to various local bourgeois families." For Mulhouse, see "Compte rendu du trésorier de la conférence de Saint-Vincent-de-Paul, Mulhouse," January 1872, and the "Bulletin d'aggrégation" for the *conférence* of 15 August 1846, both in ASVP, Strasbourg, Dossier 1. The first mention of a Société de Saint-François-Régis is in 1850. A "Tableau statistique" from 1851 noted that the work of the Société de Saint-François-Régis had been instituted regularly that year. Cf. Ernest Meinenger, *Essai de description, de statistique et d'histoire de Mulhouse* (Mulhouse, 1885), p. 134, who dates the work of the Société de Saint-François-Régis here from 1861.

61. Jules Gossin, *Manuel*, p. 112. This figure is certainly too low. It does not, for example, include some 743 marriages facilitated by the society in Rouen between 1836 and 1843, documented in Société de Saint-Vincent-de-Paul de Rouen, "Etat du personnel," 31 December 1843, ASVP, Rouen, Dossier 6.

Table 3.7. Marriages Celebrated and Children Legitimized through the Efforts of the Société de Saint-François-Régis

City	Dates	Marriages celebrated	Children legitimized
Alger	1845–June 1850	328	74
Bordeaux	Jan. 1839–1850	1,400	350
Dieppe	1842–1850	238	173
Dunkerque	1843–1850	243	87
Grenoble	1840–Jan. 1850	147	76
LeHavre	1839–Dec. 1849	490	257
Lille	1840–Dec. 1850	2,209	925
Lyon	1837–Dec. 1850	4,700	1,950
Marseille	1838–May 1850	2,661	1,077
Metz	1839–June 1850	741	373
Nancy	1838–Dec. 1850	1,889	1,550
Nantes	May 1841–Dec. 1850	2,195	938
Orléans	1840–1850	180	74
Paris	1826–Dec. 1850	21,692	15,207
Roubaix	1842–Nov. 1850	965	332
Rouen	1844–Dec. 1850	711	140
Toulouse	1840–1850	1,052	364
Versailles	1845–1846	31	16
		41,872	23,963
Ratio of children to marriages		.57	

Source: Jules Gossin, *Manuel de la société charitable de Saint-Régis de Paris* (Paris, 1851), p. 112. The author noted: "The figure for Paris is only approximate, because at the beginning [of the society] no exact figures . . . were kept. This figure of 21,692 [marriages] is probably below the actual one."

ing at length from their president's analysis of one of the primary causes of consensual unions among workers:

> To marry, the couple must produce several *actes de l'état civil*. Often they are numerous: birth certificates to be gotten from other places when the future spouses are not native to the commune where they are marrying; death certificates of father and mother, in certain cases of other relatives; notarized acts of consent if the parents are living but not present or cannot come to the town hall; "family assemblies" for minors; consent of regiment heads for soldiers, of hospital administrators for former foundlings; publication of banns in different communes; legalization of foreign documents. All this is without mentioning unusual cases where they have to have notarized acts to replace lost birth certificates, to rectify names improperly spelled, or to seek dispensations for marriage among [certain] relatives. There are almost always costs occasioned by procuring these

documents, and it is rare that a sum of from 10 to 12 francs is not necessary, even if the parties are informed or educated enough to obtain them by themselves. Very often the cost rises to 25–40 or 50 francs. Sometimes, even 100–200 francs do not suffice. Thus, it is evident that civil marriage, *which must always* precede religious marriage, is in fact impossible *for most indigent people,* properly speaking, if we do not come to their aid.[62]

In the effort to moralize the family life of workers, the emphasis of the Société de Saint-François-Régis was, of course, on religious marriage, to which civil marriage was only the prelude. The goal of rehabilitating common law unions was to eliminate the sinful status of workers' unions and ultimately to integrate couples and their illegitimate children into the Catholic community, whose influence was felt to be particularly weak among workers in most French industrial cities. The society held weekly office hours to receive interested couples who were referred to them by members of the clergy, certain civil officials including administrators of local *bureaux de bienfaisance,* or hospital officials. However, members of the society also noted with satisfaction that neighbors and couples who had already received their help also served to publicize the work of the organization. The society's authorities in Lille cited the example of a widow from one of the city's working-class parishes who knew of an old couple living in common law because of the difficulty they had had in obtaining documents required for marriage. Informed by her priest of the existence of the Société de Saint-François-Régis, she herself accompanied them to the Lille office.[63]

Once arrived at the society's office, the man and woman were questioned about their circumstances and encouraged to be patient while members of the society carried out all the correspondence necessary to gather needed documents. If the couple had not already been living together but were simply seeking help in order to marry, they were enjoined to abstain from sexual relations until the marriage had been accomplished. Members of the society were often shocked, however, by the apparent shamelessness of some of the couples they encountered. The president of the Société de Saint-François-Régis warned his fellow members to be prepared:

62. Société de Saint-Vincent-de-Paul de Lille, *Notice historique*, p. 329. On dispensations for marriages among relatives and other special cases, and a list of all the documents and costs involved in civil marriage, see Jules Gossin, *Manuel*, pp. 72–88.

63. Société de Saint-Vincent-de-Paul, "Séance trimestrielle du 15 mai 1840," ASVP, Paris, Dossier 1. The "Procès-verbal de la séance générale de la conférence de Saint-Vincent-de Paul à Lille," 6 December 1840, noted: "Many couples come to our presentations each Sunday. . . . [A] happy indication of the progress of moralization is that often it is by the advice and encouragement of a legitimately married couple that a common law couple comes to ask for our help." ASVP, Paris, Dossier 1.

> Gentleness is useful on all occasions that the society has relations with the poor. [But] this is particularly true of the [couple's] first visit. . . . Often the future [husband] comes only half-heartedly. The woman often has to drag him there. Thus, if the reception is not overwhelmingly cordial and charitable, all is lost. The man, hoping for a pretext for dissatisfaction, will violently take the hand of his common law wife and children and leave with a satisfied look. . . . [S]ometimes . . . we have to listen to the protestations of a kind of vice that refuses to admit that their situation is counter to all morality and religion . . . but there is a way [for us] to remain calm, by remembering that these people are immersed in profound ignorance—that their words are the echo of the antireligious passions in which they live.[64]

Like the Société de Saint-Vincent-de-Paul, the work of the Société de Saint-François-Régis entailed face-to-face relations with the working-class families whose mission it was to help and to moralize, with the lay volunteers of the society serving as mediators between working-class concubinaires and the written culture of legal documents which they were required to enter in order to contract marriage. Despite his counsel of using "gentleness" in facing working-class males in particular, Gossin illustrated that the society's goal of moral reform consisted of more than external changes in behavior. Confronted by one man's refusal to admit his error at having cohabited in common law, the president of the society related the following dialogue:

> GOSSIN: I'm quite upset that we cannot agree. What! You persist in maintaining that when, eighteen years ago, you corrupted this woman who is now by your side, you did nothing wrong?
>
> MAN: Not at all. I'm an honest man. I've never stolen or killed. When I was young I had a bit of fun, but that's not wrong. Besides, I didn't *force* her. Why did she allow herself to be caught?
>
> GOSSIN: Let's talk about something else. . . . Are those all your children?
>
> MAN: No sir. We also have a little girl at home.
>
> GOSSIN: In two or three years, the girl will be a young woman . . . what would you say if a worker did the same thing that you did to her mother, debauched and dishonored her?
>
> MAN (*getting up furiously, out of control*): What would I say? I'd say nothing, and I'd kill the sinner who had stolen my daughter.

64. Jules Gossin, *Manuel*, pp. 141–42.

GOSSIN: You'd be wrong because this boy, from what you just said, would be a perfectly honest man, having neither killed nor stolen, nor forced your daughter into it.

MAN (*still furious*): I said that I'd kill the scoundrel, the monster. . . .

GOSSIN: My friend, remember what you yourself did and judge yourself.

MAN: Sir, you must forgive me. I was lying to myself when I said what I did. I was joking . . . but I'm worth more than that.[65]

Members of the society sometimes had to use these and similar strategems to evoke a consciousness of sin and shame among concubinaires that was believed to be the first step towards their spiritual and moral regeneration.[66]

Beyond the sanctification of the union itself, another one of the society's goals was to urge couples to legitimize their children. As the society stressed, this could occur only at the time of marriage. For children to be legitimized, both parents had first to make a formal declaration recognizing the child to an *officier de l'état civil*. Only after formal recognition and civil marriage could the children of a consensual union enjoy the full legal rights of any legitimate child.[67] For this reason, the head of the Société de Saint-François-Régis urged couples: "If as a result of false shame you have concealed the birth of children who have or have not been deposited in foundling homes . . . it is urgent that you declare this at the town hall before the celebration of [civil] marriage. Without this essential precaution the children will not and

65. Ibid., pp. 144–45. Part of this passage is quoted in Donzelot, *The Policing of Families*, pp. 34–35.

66. Another chapter of the Société de Saint-François-Régis, near Rouen, observed: "We show them the hideous evil which degrades them and try to enhance their dignity by making them understand the blessings of rehabilitation." Oeuvre de Saint-Vincent-de-Paul, conférence d'Elbeuf, "Rapport de l'année 1846," ASVP, Rouen, Dossier 6.

67. On the laws regarding the recognition and legitimation of children, see Code Civil, arts. 331–35 and Alfred Nizard, "Droit et statistiques de filiation en France: Le droit de la filiation depuis 1804," *Population* 32 (1977): 91–122. Nizard notes that "during the nineteenth century, legitimation was possible only if recognition took place before marriage, or at the latest at the moment of its celebration" (p. 115). There is some disagreement among scholars in interpreting these rules in nineteenth-century France. Etienne van de Walle states that in the case of illegitimate unions, "registering the birth was the normal way of establishing legitimacy." See "Illegitimacy in France during the Nineteenth Century," in Peter Laslett, Karla Oosterveen, and Richard M. Smith, eds., *Bastardy and Its Comparative History* (Cambridge, Mass., 1980), p. 265. However, this does not seem to have been the case in the first half of the nineteenth century. Lenard R. Berlanstein, "Illegitimacy, Concubinage, and Proletarianization in a French Town, 1760–1914," *Journal of Family History* 5 (1980): 365, implies that the law allowed couples to legitimize children after marriage.

can never be legitimized."[68] Couples with children were of particular interest to the society, since they already constituted a new family in the making.[69] Information contained in Tables 3.7 and 3.8 lends support to the hypothesis that the society enjoyed its greatest success among couples who had been together for only several years. Besides figures on the duration of cohabitation contained in Table 3.8, the data in Table 3.7 also show that there were only 0.57 children legitimized for each marriage facilitated by the Société de Saint-François-Régis, suggesting among other hypotheses that couples may have been in the early stage of their lives together at the time they sought the society's help. It is obvious that mortality would have reduced both the number of children surviving to be eligible for legitimation at the time of marriage and the number of couples in the higher-duration groups. However, the figure on the average number of children legitimized per marriage is quite low compared to a figure for the late nineteenth century, which showed that for France as a whole, the average number of children per marriage for those marriages that legitimized children was 1.42.[70]

Besides providing for the legitimation of children, the Société de Saint-François-Régis tried to reinforce bonds between young concubinaires and their own parents by supporting parental control over the marriage of their children. The Civil Code stated that parental permission was required for the marriage of women under age twenty-two and men under twenty-six. In cases of disagreement between parents the father's permission was sufficient. If parents refused to give consent to daughters between ages twenty-two and twenty-five or sons between twenty-six and thirty, the couple was obliged to make three formal written requests for permission, or *sommations respectueuses,* to their parents at one-month intervals. If after the third request consent was still withheld, the marriage could take place one month after the issuance of the last *sommation*. For men over age thirty and women over twenty-five, only

68. Jules Gossin, *Manuel*, p. 107. On the role of the Société de Saint-François-Régis in encouraging parents to take back children whom they had abandoned as foundlings, see Abbé A. H. Gaillard, *Recherches administratives, statistiques et morales sur les enfants trouvés, les enfants naturels et les orphelins* (Paris, 1837), p. 383.

69. "Instruction given to future spouses before the marriage and a moralizing influence exercised after marriage are two important tasks in which we have not been entirely successful. By taking care of the couples most worthy of our pity and help, those with the most children, we will contribute mightily to the solution we seek." Société de Saint-Vincent-de-Paul à Lille, "Séance trimestrielle du 15 mai 1840," ASVP, Paris, Dossier 1.

70. This figure, for 1893, is cited in van de Walle, "Illegitimacy," p. 269. Figures from the Société de Saint-François-Régis would also tend to be lower than van de Walle's because they undoubtedly include some childless marriages. According to figures from Lille in the late 1850s and early 1860s, city marriages that legitimized children had an average of 1.23–1.25 children at the time of marriage. These data, from the mayor's annual reports on population movements, contained in ADN, M475, were kindly supplied by Paul Spagnoli.

Table 3.8. Duration of Cohabitation among Couples Aided by the Société de Saint-François-Régis of Paris, 1826–1841

	Number of couples	Percentage of total known[a]	Cumulative percentage of total known[a]
≤ 6 mos.	681	9.9	9.9
6 mos.–1 yr.	869	12.7	22.6
1–3 yrs.	1,710	24.9	47.5
3–6 yrs.	1,448	21.1	68.6
6–9 yrs.	821	12.0	80.5
9–12 yrs.	545	7.9	88.5
12–15 yrs.	330	4.8	93.3
15–18 yrs.	180	2.6	95.9
18–21 yrs.	101	1.5	97.3
21–24 yrs.	61	.9	98.2
24–27 yrs.	40	.6	98.8
27–30 yrs.	37	.5	99.4
> 30 yrs.	44	.6	100.0
Total for known length of cohabitation	6,867		
Unknown length of cohabitation	298		
Total	7,165		

Source: Gossin, *Manuel de la société charitable de Saint-Régis de Paris*, pp. 162, 168.

Note: Durations are those at the time the couples presented themselves to the society.

[a]Percentage of total whose length of cohabitation was known.

one *sommation respectueuse* was required. Although the society was aware of the difficulties young couples often encountered in obtaining permission, they warned:

> It sometimes happens that parents learn of their children's plan to marry only through the actions of the society—as if fathers and mothers did not have the sacred right to be the first to receive such confidences from a son or daughter who had retained his natural affections. Never make yourself guilty of such a grave oversight. . . . *In order to avoid the legitimate complaints of parents on this point, the Société de Saint-François-Régis has decided not to admit future spouses who do not bear recent letters of expressed parental approval for the planned marriage*.[71]

71. Jules Gossin, *Manuel*, pp. 101–2.

Having said this, however, the society believed that parental power was not absolute and that in some cases it needed to bow to larger considerations of religious morality.

One case from the Nord illustrated this theme, while also showing the importance of the Société de Saint-Vincent-de-Paul in advancing the goals of the Société de Saint-François-Régis. M. Plével, head of the Société de Saint-Vincent-de-Paul in Cambrai, a town fifty kilometers south of Lille, wrote to the president of that society in Paris

> concerning François LeCroix, aged twenty-three years, toymaker in Cambrai, born in the arrondissement of Arras but now residing in Cambrai, where he has been living maritally with a Mlle. Wyart, age twenty-eight, daughter of François-Joseph Wyart living in Vaugirard, and Louise-Marceline Bocquet of Cambrai. These two young people have greatly wished to marry for a long time, but the father's refusal to consent to the marriage [of his daughter] has created a barrier. The father's refusal is inexplicable. The young people are perfectly suited. The husband is hard-working, intelligent, his little business is developing and seems sure to succeed. . . . There is another interest of which M. Wyart is aware —that of a child already born and one about to be born. Thus, not only is it important to have the father's consent, but we need it as soon as possible. Not only is the woman pregnant, but her health is so frail that we fear she may lose her own life in giving it to her child. Thus I beg you, my friend, to ask the president of the society of Vaugirard, if there is one in that town, or any other person, to make a final effort to convince the father to give consent to the marriage of his daughter. If the father is not troubled by the position of his unhappy daughter, we must have recourse to *sommations respectueuses* or at least once, since the woman is twenty-eight years old. One month after it is issued, she will have the right to bypass paternal consent.[72]

In cases of conflict between couples' desire to marry and the reluctance of parents to approve, the interests of religion and the younger couple appear to have taken precedence, particularly when children had already been born of the union. Although the society did not wish to challenge paternal authority, the national network of the lay Catholic organization could function as an advocate of the interests of the concubinaires, going so far as to help put moral pressure on irate parents.

Members of the Société de Saint-François-Régis struggled against a va-

72. "Résumé analytique des réponses faites par les conférences du diocèse de Cambrai dans la circonscription du conseil de Lille aux questions du tableau statistique pour 1853," ASVP, Paris, Dossier 1.

riety of structural socioeconomic conditions and human problems to rehabilitate consensual unions. As in Mulhouse, migration both foreign and indigenous was identified as a primary cause of concubinage. This was particularly the case in the Lille region, which attracted a large number of Belgian migrants. Although Lille had proportionately many fewer Belgians living within its limits than smaller factory towns like Roubaix or Tourcoing, its vast size made the absolute numbers of these migrants important. At the end of the 1840s, when the arrondissement of Lille had a Belgian population of approximately 14.4 percent, Roubaix showed a figure of 40 percent, Wattrelos and Halluin 37 percent, and Tourcoing 22 percent. While Lille *intra muros* had a population that was only 3 percent Belgian, its suburb of Wazemmes, called "little Belgium," had a population that was 38 percent Belgian. Public authorities attributed the large number of Belgian migrants both to the demise of rural putting-out industries in Belgian Flanders and to overpopulation there. Lille's status as a garrison town was also an important source of migrants. In the years 1831 and 1832, there were, respectively, 6,900 and 7,300 soldiers stationed there.[73]

The importance of migrants in the work of Lille's Société de Saint-François-Régis can be illustrated in figures for the year 1844 (see Table 3.9). Belgians in particular remained an important part of the society's clientele well into the 1850s. During 1857, for example, 64 percent of the individuals seeking aid from the society were Belgians. During that year the president of the Lille chapter had to assemble a total of twenty-three documents to permit one marriage between a Belgian man and a French woman.[74] Officials of the society argued that it was migrants who had the greatest difficulty in marrying because they had frequently "broken off relations with their birthplace. Besides, they do not know the laws or the way to carry out regular correspondence. They do not know the information they must have, or from whom

73. On Belgian migration see F. Lentacker, "Les ouvriers belges dans le département du Nord au milieu du XIXe siècle," *Revue du Nord* 38 (1956): 5–7. Speaking of foreigners in the Nord, authorities noted that "the great majority [are from] Belgian Flanders, whose traditional economy is experiencing an irreversible decline caused by the decrease of home spinning and weaving." See also Buriez-Duez, "Le mouvement dans le Nord," p. 30. On the basis of similarities between several demographic parameters of border areas of Belgium and those of French communities receiving substantial numbers of migrants, Paul Spagnoli has hypothesized that a portion of the migrants to the arrondissement of Lille in the middle of the nineteenth century must have come from the province of Hainaut as well as from Belgian Flanders. See "High Fertility in Mid-Nineteenth-Century France: A Multivariate Analysis of Fertility Patterns in the Arrondissement of Lille," *Research in Economic History* 2 (1977): 298. On soldiers in Lille, see Engrand, "Les ouvriers lillois," p. 149.

74. Claude Hélène Dewaepenaere, "L'enfance illégitime dans le département du Nord au XIXe siècle," in Gillet, *L'homme, la vie et la mort*, p. 160; Pierrard, *La vie ouvrière*, pp. 119–20.

Table 3.9. Geographic Origins of Individuals Aided by the Société de Saint-François-Régis of Lille, 1844

Foreign		*French*	
Belgium	113	Lille	126
Netherlands	4	Arrondissement of Lille[a]	95
Prussia	1	Nord[b]	49
Poland	1	Pas-de-Calais	28
Saxony	1	Other departments	37
Italy	2	Total	335
Germany	2		
Total	124		

Source: Société de Saint-Vincent-de-Paul de Lille, *Notice Historique sur la Société de Saint-Vincent-de-Paul à Lille* (Lille, 1883), p. 330.
[a]Excluding Lille.
[b]Excluding the arrondissement of Lille.

to request it. Most often they do not know what to write and have only confused ideas about their place and date of birth or the [place and date] of their parents' deaths."[75]

There is some evidence that public officials in Lille, if not in Rouen, tried to encourage the legitimation of common law unions among workers, but their efforts were weak and amateurish by comparison with those in Mulhouse. As has already been mentioned, common law couples might be referred to the Société de Saint-François-Régis through officials of the city welfare bureau. On the occasion of an 1841 census of the city's poor, the Lille administration urged welfare commissioners to "seek out the individuals living in consensual unions and use persuasion to convince them to regularize their unions in the eyes of the law and religion."[76] The explicit wish of the Lille authorities to encourage religious as well as civil marriage marked a difference with the treatment of concubinaires in Mulhouse, testifying to the long-standing vigor of Catholic traditions in Lille and the contentious nature of the religious issue in Mulhouse.

In thinking about the reasons for the occasional failure of their efforts, the Lille authorities of the Société de Saint-François-Régis summarized the causes that made their task more difficult. These included parents' refusal, "difficulties in military law, the inconstancy and bad faith of the couples, lack of work, changes in residence, [and] death."[77] The "bad faith" of couples could be expressed in a number of ways. After all the documents had been

75. Société de Saint-Vincent-de-Paul de Lille, *Notice historique*, p. 330.

76. Bureau de Bienfaisance de Lille, Commission administrative, "Registre aux délibérations," meeting of 24 August 1841, p. 146, ABBL, E. 72, vol. 17.

77. Société de Saint-Vincent-de-Paul de Lille, *Notice historique*, p. 328.

laboriously assembled and the wedding date set, officials of the society sometimes encountered a final but important cause of reluctance on the part of the couple itself—the lack of decent clothing in which to be married. Gossin's manual cited this "pretext" three times and urged couples to borrow decent clothing if necessary instead of postponing the ceremony.[78] The importance of this problem was confirmed by the fact that Rouen's *conférence* of the Société de Saint-Vincent-de-Paul felt it fitting to allocate a credit of 400 francs to the city's Société de Saint-François-Régis to pay for wedding clothes for couples ready to complete the ceremony.[79] Another example of this situation was provided by Henry Mayhew's investigations among London's East End slop-workers in the late 1840s:

> During my stay in this quarter an incident occurred, which may be cited as illustrative of the poverty of slop-workers. The friend who had conducted me to the spot, and who knew the workmen well, had long been striving to induce one of the men—a Dutchman—to marry one of the females working with him in the room, and with whom he had been living for many months. That the man might raise no objection on the score of poverty, my friend requested me to bear with him half the expense of publishing the banns. To this I readily consented, but the man still urged that he was unable to wed the girl just yet. On inquiring the reason we were taken outside the door by the Dutchman, and there told that he had been forced to pawn his coat for 6s., and as yet he had saved only half the amount towards the redemption of it. It would take him upwards of a month to lay by the remainder. This was literally the fact, and the poor fellow said, with a shrug of his shoulders, he could not go to be married in his shirt sleeves. He was told to make himself easy about the wedding garment, and our kind-hearted friend left delighted with the day's work.[80]

Officials of the Société de Saint-François-Régis also complained about couples' lack of perseverance in the struggle to marry when faced with the complexities of French officialdom. Certain readers may empathize with the broad outlines of the situation described:

> Ignorance is the primary suffering of the poor. If at city hall someone gives them any trouble, however slight, about the documents they've presented, they wrongly persuade themselves that their papers have been re-

78. Jules Gossin, *Manuel*, pp. 106, 109, 140.

79. Conférence de Rouen, "Etat du personnel, 31 décembre 1843," ASVP, Rouen, Dossier 5. The Paris chapter of the Société de Saint-François-Régis also budgeted funds for this expense. See the speech by Villeneuve-Bargemont in the Chamber of Deputies on 19 June 1846, which is reproduced in *Annales de la charité*, 1846, pp. 383–91, and is discussed below in greater detail.

80. Eileen Yeo and E. P. Thompson, *The Unknown Mayhew* (New York, 1971), p. 120.

> fused and that their shameful position is without remedy. They no longer think of marrying. Unable to explain themselves or to understand exactly what is being said to them, unable to repeat what [we've] told them to say, or repeating it wrong, they consume entire days going from office to office. And when from a lack of understanding everything fails, they get the mistaken idea that their horrible position is irreversible and remain in vice without shame and nearly without regret.[81]

Members of the Société de Saint-François-Régis, in frequent collaboration with local chapters of the Société de Saint-Vincent-de-Paul, characteristically favored a policy of voluntary persuasion among common law couples to rehabilitate their unions. While decrying the practice of consensual unions, members of the two societies were instrumental in recognizing the similarities that could exist between common law unions and legitimate marriages. In principle, of course, the longer that common law unions lasted without the benefit of religious sanction, the more sinful they were. On the other hand, the long duration of illegitimate unions made them seem even more like marriages and thus less blameworthy than short-lived sexual encounters. This was in fact the main reason that organized Catholic laymen devoted their efforts towards concubinaires, using a kind of moral suasion that at times could become quite vigorous indeed.

The Evolution of Moral Economist Policy in Mulhouse

The story of policies towards concubinage under the Restoration and July Monarchy did not entail a simple dichotomy between the use of moral suasion by Social Catholic activists on the one hand and expulsion from the city by Mulhouse's leaders, who were convinced practitioners of a moral economist approach to the problem. The moral economist perspective as implemented in Mulhouse evolved over the period from the 1820s to the 1840s, indicating a growing consciousness of the latent similarities between concubinaires and legitimately married couples. In contrast to the work of the Société de Saint-François-Régis, the policy of Mulhouse's leaders remained completely secular, but the analysis of the problem of concubinage within the moral economist perspective began to emphasize more actively the ways that policy might be used to integrate concubinaires into the urban social order rather than simply expelling them. It also seems likely that the increasing scale of the problem and city leaders' desire for a more stable and settled industrial labor force helped to lead to a revision of older, more coercive policy. As in the past, Mulhouse's city administration took responsibility for implementing

81. Société de Saint-Vincent-de-Paul de Lille, *Notice historique*, p. 331.

Table 3.10. Recognized and Unrecognized Illegitimate Live Births in Mulhouse, 1835–1847

Year	Recognized	Unrecognized	Total	Percentage recognized
1835	81	78	159	50.9
1836	110	90	200	55.0
1837	132	77	209	63.2
1838	127	90	217	58.5
1839	142	90	232	61.2
1840	117	102	219	53.4
1841	86	82	168	51.2
1842	81	80	161	50.3
1843	84	85	169	49.7
1844	86	88	174	49.4
1845	96	100	196	49.0
1846	79	136	215	36.7
1847	63	107	170	37.1
Total	1,284	1,205	2,489	51.6

Source: Yearly figures published in the *Industriel Alsacien* distinguish between these two groups of illegitimate children. See issues of 2 January 1836; 7 January 1837; 13 January 1838; 19 January 1839; 26 January 1840; 3 January 1841; 1 January 1842; 29 January 1843; 7 January 1844; 5 January 1845; 4 January 1846; 17 January 1847; 12 January 1848. The totals of illegitimate and legitimate live births given in this yearly record coincide almost exactly with totals in Adolf Burger, *Beiträge zur Statistik der Stadt Mülhausen* (Mulhouse, 1914), p. 7.

a new strategy. Charles Dupin's early recommendation that factory owners become involved in such a project seems also to have been realized here. Conveniently, in Mulhouse the city council and the factory owners were the same people.

A change in Mulhouse's policy of dealing with the problem of concubinage was shaped by the research and writing of Mulhouse's leading and nationally recognized moral economist, Dr. Achille Penot. As early as the 1820s, Penot had cited the difficulties that Mulhouse's workers experienced in gaining permission to marry and his belief that concubinage there was less shocking than in other French towns.[82] Penot expanded this line of argument in his later work, *Recherches statistiques sur Mulhouse*, adding more data and emphasizing what he saw as the *sui generis* nature of Mulhouse's concubinaires by demonstrating the high proportion of illegitimate children born in the city who were legally recognized by their fathers compared to most other French cities (see Tables 3.10 and 3.11). Penot argued that recognized children

82. Achille Penot, *Discours sur quelques recherches de statistique comparée faites sur la ville de Mulhouse* (Mulhouse, 1828), p. 21.

Table 3.11. Percentage of Illegitimate Live Births Legally Recognized, Selected French Cities, Early 1840s

City	Year(s)	Percentage of illegitimate births recognized
Clermont	1841	85
Nîmes	1841	67
Avignon	1841	45
Metz	1841	29
Strasbourg	1841–42	25
Angers	1841	20
Montauban	1840–41	19
Besançon	1840–41	16
Colmar	1841–42	10
Troyes	1840–41	9
Reims	1840	6
Montpellier	1841	6
Grenoble	1841	5
Laval	1840	4
St.-Quentin	1840–41	4
St.-Etienne	1841	4
Orléans	1841	4
Dijon	1840–41	2

Source: Figures calculated from Dr. Achille Penot, *Recherches statistiques sur Mulhouse* (Mulhouse, 1843), p. 26.

were those born to female factory workers living with foreign workers, usually of the same occupation, while the unrecognized were born to "servants, laundresses, etc., and the fathers often men of a higher social position."[83] He could also have cited the fact that rates of infant mortality were quite similar among legally recognized illegitimate children and legitimate children (see Table 3.12). Penot's belief that in some important ways concubinaires in Mulhouse resembled legitimately married couples appears to have been critical in helping to change the local moral economist perspective from its emphasis on concubinaires as outsiders threatening the urban social order to concubinaires as individuals whose lives it might be possible to rehabilitate.

Not all moral economists were willing to accept Penot's judgments. In his generally favorable review of Penot's 1843 publication, Villermé did not entirely share the author's sanguine view of working-class illegitimacy and concubinage in Mulhouse, in part because of the very short-term statistics Penot offered. Moreover, Villermé pointed out that Mulhouse did not contain large numbers of soldiers or a hospital for the reception of foundlings, two conditions that were widely believed to raise the number of illegitimate births

83. Penot, *Recherches statistiques*, p. 36.

Table 3.12. Infant Mortality among Legitimate, Recognized Illegitimate, and Unrecognized Illegitimate Children Born in Mulhouse, 1835–1847

	Legitimate		Recognized illegitimate		Unrecognized illegitimate	
Year	Live births	Deaths	Live births	Deaths	Live births	Deaths
1835	608	136	81	20	78	43
1836	736	198	110	46	90	36
1837	651	235	132	21	77	20
1838	698	166	127	40	90	45
1839	756	175	142	33	90	39
1840	756	131	117	26	102	39
1841	886	189	86	21	82	48
1842	921	194	81	22	80	36
1843	895	154	84	20	85	44
1844	—	—	—	—	—	—
1845	964	178	96	16	100	54
1846	979	168	79	14	136	53
1847	837	208	63	24	107	71
	9,687	2,132	1,198	303	1,117	528
Infant mortality (per 1,000), 1835–47		220		253		473

Source: See Table 3.10.

and depress levels of legal recognition in other cities. However, after citing the "curious considerations" of Mulhouse's mayor on these questions, including his policy of publishing names of mothers of illegitimate as well as legitimate children in the city's newspapers and of expelling foreign workers, Villermé averred that "all these measures are not perhaps very legal, but certainly they are [part of] an intelligent and skillful administration."[84]

Mulhouse's "skillful" administration began to move towards a new policy on common law unions in the early 1840s. The new plan towards foreign concubinaires in particular, which began to be implemented in April 1840,

84. Villermé did concur with Penot's judgment that working-class life in Mulhouse had improved significantly since the former's visit to the city in 1835. See "Rapport de M. Villermé sur l'ouvrage intitulé *Recherches statistiques sur Mulhouse*," *Séances et travaux de l'Académie des sciences morales et politiques*, 1843, p. 119. Another review of Penot's work in the same volume, which offered longer time series of data on the proportion of illegitimate children in French cities who were legally recognized by their fathers, supported Penot's conclusion that the level of recognition was unusually high in Mulhouse. See M. Berriat Saint-Prix, "Observations relatives aux *Recherches statistiques sur Mulhouse*," ibid., pp. 126–30. On the evolution of Penot's work, which was supported by the Société industrielle de Mulhouse, see Peter N. Stearns, *Paths to Authority: The Middle Class and the Industrial Labor Force in France, 1820–1848* (Urbana, 1978), p. 15.

was described in a city council meeting in spring of 1842. After reiterating the importance of workers' lack of financial means to purchase the right to marry from their home governments, the council mandated a policy by which these workers would be required to make weekly deposits to the *caisse d'épargne* in order to save enough money to make the required payments. Deposits were made proportional to wages, and in the event that workers refused, expulsion was still retained as an option.[85] Participation was limited to couples in which the woman was pregnant and the man had already recognized the child as his own, or to those who already had children. Other concubinaires were still liable to expulsion.

Penot cited the results of this policy during the two years of its operation, from April 1840 to April 1842. At the earlier date there were 317 male concubinaires identified, who with their "wives" and children totalled 958 persons. Five couples were expelled from the city, presumably as a result of their unwillingness to comply with the policy. By the latter date, 63 couples had married, legitimizing 78 children; 51 couples had left the city voluntarily, taking with them money that had been saved. As of April 1842, a total of over 19,833 francs in savings and interest had been accumulated by the 203 couples who had not yet married but who were allowed to remain in the city.[86]

The implementation of the policy, Penot thought, was responsible for a declining number of illegitimate births in the years 1841–42. It was in all probability also a contributing cause of the rising number of children legitimized by the marriage of their parents (see Table 3.13).[87] Penot was clearly pleased with the initial results of the new policy, believing that the encouragement of marriage moralized workers both by strengthening bonds with their children and by encouraging the habit of thrift so essential to stable family life.[88]

Moral Economist and Social Catholic Policy in Comparative Perspective

This analysis of attitudes and policies towards consensual unions in the late Restoration and July Monarchy has revealed important variations by region. The appeal to Mulhouse's leaders of active, interventionist, and repressive policy had clear roots in long-standing traditions of defending the urban social order against outsiders. This tradition, and the leadership's concern about the rapid growth of a migrant industrial working class, doubtless help account

85. Conseil municipal de Mulhouse, "Procès-verbaux" (1841–44), meeting of 24 May 1842, pp. 81–82, AMM, D I/A1.

86. Penot, *Recherches statistiques*, pp. 58–59.

87. Illegitimate live births, both recognized and unrecognized, fell from 23.5% and 22.5% of total live births in 1839 and 1840, respectively, to 16.7% and 14.9% in 1841 and 1842.

88. Penot, *Recherches statistiques*, p. 61.

Table 3.13. Children Legitimitized by the Marriage of Their Parents, Mulhouse, 1835–1847

Year	Number of children legitimized
1835	14
1836	20
1837	26
1838	22
1839	29
1840	62
1841	76
1842	49
1843	62
1844	93
1845	66
1846	50
1847	50

Source: See Table 3.10.

for the intensity of their efforts. Important, too, was the fact that Social Catholic organizations that might have acted more vigorously here, as in Lille and Rouen, were initially viewed with great suspicion by the city's Protestant administration, though the leadership's suspicion began to wane towards the end of the 1840s. As one of the founders of the Société de Saint-Vincent-de-Paul in Mulhouse wrote, "We have been able to do little good for the poor in the last several months and have tried to counter the restrictions placed on our efforts by the Protestants and the Protestant administration. [However], we are led to think that the restrictions are now gone. The Bureau de bienfaisance has even given us a little help." [89]

Furthermore, it is clear that illegitimacy, concubinage, and massive urban poverty had been much more familiar to city administrators in Lille and Rouen than in Mulhouse since well before the end of the Old Regime. At the end of the eighteenth century it was not at all unusual for large proportions of Lille and Rouen's population—from one-third to one-half—to depend on local welfare funds for part or all of their subsistence needs.[90] Illegitimacy, too, was

89. M. Ravenèz to the Société de Saint-Vincent-de-Paul, Paris, 12 February 1847, ASVP, Strasbourg, Dossier 1. See also his letter of 15 February 1848, in which he notes, "Our report of 1847 had at the same time to satisfy local Catholics and dissipate the restrictions, I would even say the anxiety, of the Protestants."

90. On Lille, see Evelyne B. Henaux, "Paupérisme et assistance à Lille au XVIIIe siècle" (Maîtrise d'histoire, Université de Lille, 1968), pp. 25–46. Henaux shows that the proportion of the population assisted was normally one-third, rising to one-half during crisis years. For the end of the Old Regime, Jean-Pierre Bardet shows that 40% of newborns in Rouen received local

a familiar problem in Rouen and Lille, as it was in nearly all large cities of the kingdom, particularly since the middle of the eighteenth century.[91] However, high levels of dependency on local charity and high proportions of illegitimate births were not a part of the social history of Mulhouse, which since before its integration into France had developed a welfare system effectively restricting residency rights and eligibility for public assistance.[92] Thus, Mulhouse also differed from the other two towns by the novelty of its experience with concubinage, which came to be associated more clearly with the impact of industrialization itself. Beyond differences in their historical experiences with poverty and illegitimacy, Mulhouse's city administration seems to have enjoyed more autonomy from regional and central state officials in dealing with this and other social problems than was typical of the other two cities. Such relative autonomy may be explained in part by the *régime censitaire*'s adherence to the French monarchy's historic policy of allowing more leeway for regionally specific practices in areas most recently integrated into the kingdom.

Although moral economists such as Dupin could argue as long as they wished for wide-ranging action by employers and city authorities in the interests of controlling the problem of consensual unions among workers, the idea of the French central state implementing an orthodox, if evolving, moral economist approach to the problem from the center would have been difficult to imagine. This was not because government or administrative leaders failed to share a certain horror at the growth of common law unions. But French legislators and administrators were working under different constraints than local authorities in Germany and Switzerland, who had enacted legislation restricting marriage among the poor. Although the French central administration was willing for a time to look the other way while Alsatian authorities expelled concubinaires or, after 1840, devised more innovative policy, it is quite unlikely that any national-level legislation of the kind extant in Germany and Switzerland would have been possible given the continued power of the Catholic church and French bourgeois fears about possible violations of the privacy of domestic life.

These kinds of concerns combined to make the work of the Société de

---

assistance and that after 1760, "the great majority of proletarian households received grants at one time or another." *Rouen aux XVIIe et XVIIIe siècles: Les mutations d'un espace social* (Paris, 1983), 1:292, 294. By 1849, 42% of the population of Lille's working-class quarter of Saint-Sauveur was still receiving some form of assistance from the city's Bureau de bienfaisance. See Pierrard, *La vie ouvrière*, p. 49.

91. Alain Lottin, "Naissances illégitimes et filles-mères à Lille au XVIIIe siècle," *Revue d'histoire moderne et contemporaine* 8 (1970): 278–99; Bardet, *Rouen*, 1:320–31.

92. Raymond Oberlé, "Société et assistance à Mulhouse à la fin du XVIIIe siècle," in Livet and Shaff, *Médecine et assistance*, pp. 121–23. The author notes, however, that city authorities did sometimes distribute aid to poor inhabitants outside the city limits.

Saint-François-Régis seemed to work. When asked, for example, to discuss the causes which increased the legal recognition of illegitimate children in bourgeois opinion. The society intervened into the families of workers, but only on a voluntary basis, thus avoiding the kind of possible judicial problems encountered early on by the city administration in Mulhouse. The society attempted to convince working-class couples to join the religious as well as the civil community—an attractive prospect even for the most religiously indifferent members of the bourgeoisie. The society's efforts also had the advantage of being inexpensive, given the contributions of volunteer members. Finally, as local and national statistics attested, the efforts of the Société de Saint-François-Régis seemed to work. When asked, for example, to discuss the causes which increased the legal recognition of illegitimate children in the Nord, the prefect cited marriages concluded as a result of the society's efforts as the primary cause, especially in the manufacturing districts.[93] For all of these reasons, government aid to the Paris chapter of the Société de Saint-François-Régis had begun to flow as early as 1836, if only in a sporadic manner.[94]

By the late 1840s, support for government contributions to the society and for legislative changes that would facilitate marriage among the poor began to gain ground. An 1846 report by the Institut royal de France recommended using central government funds to support the work of the society, since "one of the surest means of preventing misdemeanors and crime, of extending civilization's blessings and inspiring the poor with respect for law and property consists of substituting the sacred bond of marriage [and] peaceful habits contracted in the home, for the disorder of the street; and joys of the family for uncontrolled license."[95] A speech by Villeneuve-Bargemont in the Chamber of Deputies on 19 June 1846 which quoted from this report of the Institut's commission was one of the first signs of a legislative effort to translate the society's private mission into state-supported policy.[96] Villeneuve-Bargemont

93. Prefect of the Nord to the minister of agriculture and commerce, 22 February 1848, AN, F20/282 39.

94. The Ministry of the Interior had granted funds to the society in 1836 but had informed members that "it would promise nothing for the future." Gaillard, *Recherches*, p. 385. The Société de Saint-François-Régis in Lille requested departmental funds in 1844, though it is unclear whether it received any. See the letter from the society to the conseil général du Nord, 24 August 1844, ADN, M222/373. In the *Manuel de la société charitable de Saint-Régis de Paris*, Gossin noted that the Paris chapter received funds from both the hospitals of Paris and the Ministry of the Interior, but that these resources were "uncertain" (p. 28). The most dependable source of funds seems to have been monies raised from members, private subscribers, and local churches.

95. Institut Royal de France, *Statistique: Mariage civil et religieux des pauvres* (Paris, 1846), p. 1.

96. This speech, reproduced in the *Annales de la charité*, 1846, pp. 383–91, is cited in

recognized that on the issue of common law marriage, "Christian charity has preceded the action of government, just as it has always preceded science in the art of recognizing the most intimate afflictions of society and of bringing remedies to them. While political economy and the administration sought (and are still seeking) means to repress disorders that have become more and more intolerable, there was formed in Paris and then in several principal cities of the kingdom a charitable society known under the name of Saint-Régis."[97] Support for the secular benefits of the society's work continued after the 1848 revolution, when concubinage began to appear even more sinister because of its growing reputation as a kind of consciously self-styled institution among workers. An 1849 report to the Assemblée Nationale advocated that "public assistance be formed into a civil Société de Saint-François-Régis . . . and that it try, with all its means to check this habit of common law unions, which are valid neither in law, morality, nor religion. We must extirpate this sytem of regularized concubinage, which forms only households and not marriages, and which is even more threatening to society because fundamentally it constitutes an organization of the proletariat."[98] However, it was not until 1850 that new legislation addressed the financial problems that workers encountered in assembling the documents necessary for marriage. By this law, charges for copies of all documents necessary for marriage were reduced to 30 centimes for those qualifying as indigents.[99]

A certain convergence of views on the value of strategies pursued by the Société de Saint-François-Régis by the late 1840s should not, however, distract us from the important differences that characterized moral economist and Social Catholic treatment of the problem.[100] Although legislators, administrators, and the bourgeoisie in general concurred on the undesirability of common law unions as early as the 1820s and 1830s, policies of intervention remained mainly within the purview of local groups both inside and outside

---

Jean-Baptiste Duroselle, *Les débuts du catholicisme social en France, 1822–1870* (Paris, 1951), p. 235, and is discussed in Philippe Fritsch, "De la famille-cible à l'objet-famille," in Joseph Isaac, Philippe Fritsch, and Alain Battegay, *Disciplines à domicile: L'édification de la famille* (Fontenay-sous-Bois, 1977), pp. 249–54.

97. *Annales de la charité*, 1846, p. 385. Villeneuve also recognized here the participation in the works of the society of the "worthy mother" of his "illustrious colleague, M. de Lamartine."

98. "Rapport fait par le citoyen Athanase Coquerel au nom de la commission chargée d'examiner le project de loi sur l'organisation de l'Assistance publique," *Moniteur*, 6 March 1849, p. 735. Part of this passage is cited in Eugène Gossin, *La vie de M. Jules Gossin*, p. 329.

99. Edouard Lévy, *Les difficultés du mariage* (Paris, 1923), p. 183. On the law, see also *Bulletin de la Société de Saint-Vincent-de-Paul*, no. 6 (March 1849): 161.

100. On the rapprochement of secular and Catholic attitudes to workers' common law unions, see Jeffrey Kaplow, "Concubinage and the Working Class in Early-Nineteenth-Century Paris," in Ernst Hinrichs, Eberhard Schmitt, and Rudolf Vierhaus, eds., *De l'ancien régime à la révolution française* (Göttingen, 1978), p. 372.

city and regional administrations. Policies formulated essentially at the local level were strongly marked by historical traditions and in some ways by the local peculiarities of the industrialization process. In Lille and Rouen, a specifically industrial working class seems to have been formed more gradually than in Mulhouse, with elements of an older and skilled *artisanat* attempting, albeit unsuccessfully, to hold onto their trades. The obvious and visible proletarianization of these workers was viewed with concern and even sympathy on the part of some indigenous leaders. In Mulhouse on the other hand, the more rapid influx of industrial workers as well as the religious differences between them and the city's leaders seem to have contributed to the latter's greater fear of the problem of concubinage. The city's long habit of tightly controlling the urban order also made its leaders receptive to moral economist perspectives on the world during the process of industrialization.

Having examined policies towards the problem of common law unions that were the products of moral economists' and Social Catholics' different perspectives on the problem, we must now determine whether the available sources permit any insight into the significance of this social practice for the workers concerned. Records of the successes of the Société de Saint-François-Régis and of the policies of Mulhouse's city council beginning in the early 1840s suggest that moral, psychological, and financial pressure exerted particularly on male workers could encourage them to legitimize the bonds of consensual unions. The earlier Mulhouse policy of using *force majeure* may also have had some effect, though this is impossible to judge with any confidence.

Concubinage and Working-Class Culture

In the 1970s, historical scholarship on the causes and significance of illegitimacy and consensual unions among workers was divided between the views of Edward Shorter on the one hand and those of Louise Tilly, Joan Scott, and Miriam Cohen on the other. In this well-known debate, Shorter held that women's willingness to engage either in short- or long-term sexual unions before marriage stemmed from working women's sense of personal liberation from the constraints of rural preindustrial life, while Tilly, Scott, and Cohen argued that such behavior stemmed more from the persistence of women's desire to marry even within conditions of urban life that sometimes militated against this wish.[101] The present analysis provides greater support for the latter

101. Edward N. Shorter, "Female Emancipation, Birth Control, and Fertility in European History," *American Historical Review* 78 (1973): 624; Louise A. Tilly, Joan W. Scott, and Miriam Cohen, "Women's Work and European Fertility Patterns," *Journal of Interdisciplinary History* 6 (1976): 447–76.

argument, while emphasizing more than Tilly, Scott, and Cohen the disruption of family life that urban migration could entail.

Quite obviously, as officials of the Société de Saint-François-Régis realized, highly motivated workers could and did succeed by themselves in assembling all the documents needed for their marriage, even if they were impoverished and illiterate. If they were French nationals, they could with persistent effort ultimately triumph against the forces of French bureaucratic life and obtain required papers. The same was perhaps least true of foreign workers in the Mulhouse area, constrained as they were by greater financial and legal restrictions from their places of origin. However, as the triumphant mayor of Mulhouse in the 1840s was able to show, workers constrained by moral economist policy could, by prudence and thrift, ultimately accumulate the financial resources that legitimate marriage required.

Nevertheless, a great many working-class couples seem to have been daunted by the complexities and cost of a "decent" marriage, rendered even more difficult by the effects of migration. The appearance of large numbers of migrants in the records of the Société de Saint-François-Régis in places such as Lille does not, of course, prove that migration was the main cause of consensual unions. Since migrants formed such an important part of the working-class populations of industrial towns, we would expect them to appear in the records in large numbers. However, information from the Société de Saint-François-Régis—admittedly not an unbiased source—has implied that migration to the city in the period under study may have led to a greater suspension in relations between migrants and their families of origin than the analysis of Tilly, Scott, and Cohen led us to believe. Breaks in these relations, sometimes caused by parental death at the migrants' place of origin, only exacerbated the difficulties facing younger couples who needed a variety of documents in order to marry.

The evidence does lend support to Tilly, Scott, and Cohen's belief that legitimate and "decent" marriage continued to represent an ideal to which many working-class couples, and women in particular, still aspired. Evidence, albeit slim, suggests that it was women who were more highly motivated in seeking out help in the desire to marry, at least from the Société de Saint-François-Régis. This fact may have stemmed from their higher level of religious observance, or from more frequent contact with a *curé* or female neighbor who might have recommended them to the society. Urban female networks may thus have played an important part in familiarizing women with the organization.

The kind of pressure that volunteers of the society exerted on couples to marry legitimately was reminiscent of the type of family, community, and clerical pressure that had existed in preindustrial Europe since the Counter-Reformation. Here, as is well known, the force of community opinion was fundamental and often very vigorous in overseeing the marriage of men and women who had become engaged and who had begun sexual relations. In an urban milieu increasingly cut off from some of these traditional pressures, the work of the Société de Saint-François-Régis seems to have filled the same kind of function. The fact that volunteers of the society actually helped working-class couples with the practical details and costs of contracting marriage doubtless modulated somewhat the moral pressures they brought to bear.

Although the dialogue between Jules Gossin and the reluctant husband presented earlier in this chapter was more likely an edifying example for members of the Société de Saint-François-Régis than an accurate description of one particular interview, it nonetheless suggests several ways of understanding working-class men's attitudes towards the question of concubinage and legitimate marriage. First of all, it appears that these men were well aware of the social disapprobation that living in common law entailed, although it is doubtful that verbal expressions of disapproval ever came from anyone other than a member of the clergy, if indeed they ever encountered one, or members of the bourgeoisie such as Gossin and his fellow volunteers in the society. At the level of daily life, common law husbands were probably not plagued by constant feelings of guilt, in part because of arguments like those expressed to Gossin. The common law wife had accepted voluntarily to enter the union. Common law husbands and wives had entered a relationship that exemplified even more than the civil or religious marriage ceremony the value of freely given individual choice of partner emphasized by post-Reformation values, both Protestant and Catholic. In the formation of the common law union, even parental and community pressures were absent. As Tilly, Scott, and Cohen have pointed out, of course, single working-class women could have significant material reasons to enter a coresidential common law union. They did not dwell in a world devoid of pressures affecting their conduct. However, there was a sense of social and perhaps psychological equality underlying these unions.

The importance of "decent" clothing, far from being a pretext or a trivial matter in the minds of working-class men recruited to marriage by the Société de Saint-François-Régis, suggests the persistence of other traditions related to marriage. For them as for any bourgeois, entering a legitimate marriage conjured up a variety of symbols as well as enduring material obligations. Although appearance in decent clothing on one's wedding day may well have been as important for the most rustic peasants as it was for urban workers, there is evidence that urban workers, much to the distress of many a nineteenth-century commentator, placed particularly high value on clothing as an external sign of decency.[102] Accounts of the traditional male textile workers of Lille and Rouen in particular evoked the importance to workers not merely

102. See, for example, the comments of Villermé in *Tableau*, 1:363, cited in Coleman, *Death*, p. 235.

of "decent" but at times dandyish clothing. A Lille source from the early 1830s recalled an earlier time in which male workers were readily distinguishable: "The linen thread spinner [*filtier*] is noted for his agility, [and] by his costume, composed of a turquoise shirt, nankin pants, a jacket of the same cloth and a small-brimmed cap tipped over the left eye. A cotton spinner is distinguished by a more refined appearance: black boots, polished and shining, a finer hat, and a frock coat of good cloth. He is as robust as the *filtier*, the natural effect of a more difficult but better paid kind of work."[103] Failure to appear at one's marriage dressed decently would have defeated the whole point of a ceremony that marked men's passage to a new and more respectable status within the eyes of their own individual community and that of the larger society. Given the propertylessness of the vast majority of France's industrial working class during these years and the long-standing belief that the possession of property was a precondition for marriage, men's unwillingness to marry without the most basic, outward symbols of decency becomes more understandable. Important, too, were the obligations of the working-class husband to mark his marriage by correspondingly "respectable" generosity in celebrating the marriage with friends and family.

Thus, while new economic and social conditions stimulated by industrialization, particularly migration, gave rise to structural conditions favoring common law unions, it was the persistence of old values about marriage that ironically helped to perpetuate them. Although both moral economists and Social Catholics at first considered these unions to counter the very foundations of traditional marriage values, their closer examination of the subject and their policy experience led to a greater sense of the possible affinities between concubinage and the ideals of legitimate marriage. For moral economists in particular the first stage of their analysis had emphasized the valuative and behavioral chasm between concubinage and legitimate marriage. However, experience in actually implementing policy, combined with a certain evolution in the moral economist approach, seemed to indicate that the social chasm could be breached. The modulation of moral economist policy in the Mulhouse area was doubtless encouraged by city administrators' and factory owners' desire to establish a more settled working class. Moreover, as the number of migrant workers to Mulhouse grew, the earlier policy of close surveillance of concubinaires and their large-scale expulsion probably became less feasible.

Common law marriages in industrial areas of France up to the 1848 revolution do not seem to have represented a conscious rejection of the whole

103. Jean-Baptiste Dupont, *Topographie historique, statistique et médicale de l'arrondissement de Lille* (Paris, 1833), p. 80. Charles Noiret, a handloom weaver in Rouen, also believed that a lack of the financial resources for a "decent" marriage explained the prevalence of common law unions among city workers there. Noiret, *Mémoires*, p. 41. For Noiret's critique of the legal formalities of marriage, see pp. 83–84.

repertoire of family values associated with legitimate marriage. They do not, for example, appear to have stemmed from the kind of rejection of bourgeois values associated with the later practice of "free unions" by social or political militants, particularly in the nation's capital. It is possible that already-proletarianized workers arriving in the cities of Lille, Mulhouse, and Rouen were more prepared to accept the possibility of living in common law than were skilled, indigenous workers; however, the proletarianization of these crafts workers, particularly in Lille and Rouen, may have gradually worked a similar effect upon them.

Recent work on the marriage experience of migrants to French cities in the later nineteenth century seems at first glance to contradict the notion that migrant members of the working class were particularly likely to engage in common law unions. Basing their conclusions on the study of marriage records and census listings, several historians have shown that there were almost no differences between migrant and indigenous workers' propensity to marry and that migration frequently did not cut people off from rich networks of kin.[104] The thrust of these studies is to emphasize that migration was not the uprooting experience portrayed in earlier literature because it recruited a large proportion of well-off people, took place in family groups, or drew on populations that were educationally if not always occupationally qualified for life in the city. Yet, as William Sewell has himself shown, marriage records and census listings are not perhaps the best source for understanding the more disruptive consequences of urban migration.[105] More importantly, the presence of large numbers of migrants in marriage registers or in legitimate unions recorded by census takers is entirely compatible with the present analysis. The vast majority of working-class migrants, even to the cities of early industrial France, probably married at rates similar to those of indigenous workers. However, it does appear that concubinage played a larger role in the experience of migrant workers, at least for part of their "married" lives. Taking seriously the impact of migration in encouraging consensual unions does not imply a reversion to earlier images of working-class couples and families as nomadic savages, consciously opposed to traditional values of marriage and family life. As has been shown, some of the evidence gathered by moral economists and Social Catholic organizations in the early industrial period showed that working-class concubinaires dwelt, with at least part of their hearts and minds, in a valuative world quite compatible with that of the larger society.

104. Leslie Page Moch, *Paths to the City: Regional Migration in Nineteenth-Century France* (Beverly Hills, 1983); Sewell, *Structure and Mobility*.

105. Sewell, *Structure and Mobility*, pp. 159–233.

4

National and Local Policy on Foundlings and Abandoned Children

Social Catholics and moral economists viewed the struggle to abolish consensual unions as a first step towards workers' firmer integration into the moral and social order of early industrial France. However, the shoring-up of family bonds, in their judgment, only began here. Beyond the effort to reinforce the foundations of legitimate families under civil and religious law lay a more formidable task of strengthening parent-child bonds, thereby serving to make nuclear families more viable affective and economic units. Towards this end, moral economists and Social Catholics gradually engaged in a second front on policy that was directed towards working-class families, entailing a confrontation with the problem of foundlings and abandoned children.

By the late 1820s, policy on foundlings and abandoned children had a very long history, and it was the legacy of key policies inherited from the Old Regime, Revolution, and Empire that became central focuses of debates involving the central administration, prefects, conseils généraux, and local hospital administrators as they attempted to agree on the best position to take towards the problem of children becoming dependents of the state. Discussion involved a large number of observers whose publications were routinely cited by different parties as expert opinion on the moral, financial, and administrative implications of policy development. At one critical point, "public opinion" also came to bear on the formulation of policy. Removed from center stage of debates, in the wings, were the parents of foundlings and the nurses who cared for the children. Although parents and nurses did not participate in forming policy, their attitudes and behavior, as analyzed by participants in the debate, played a key role in shaping it.

Discussions of policy towards foundlings and abandoned children in the period from the 1830s and 1840s differed from those of earlier times in two principal ways. First, they entailed an increasingly close examination of the hypothesized effects of older policies on the families of France's working classes. Second, they were marked by the growing appeal of a moral economist analysis for regional and national administrators as well as for most "experts." In contrast to Social Catholics, who defended older ways of envisaging the obligations of French state and society towards foundlings and abandoned children, moral economist theorists and administrators began to construct a new way of understanding the problem of children's dependency on state relief.

To understand the debates and policy concerning foundlings and abandoned children, one must be aware of policies handed down to nineteenth-century society from the Old Regime, Revolution and Empire. The following discussion considers this legacy and then turns to an examination of the moral economist and Catholic perspectives on the problem, evoking the terms in which the two groups understood the causes and implications of child abandonment. An analysis of the administration of foundling policy in the regions of Rouen, Lille, and Mulhouse is designed to show the growing resonance of the moral economist perspective at the local and regional levels, to assess the relative accuracy of Catholic and moral economist judgments about the problem, and to bring parents and children into clearer focus. The culmination of debates on foundlings and abandoned children, which saw the issue of family life become a central focus, is seen in the evolution of significant policy changes in the late 1830s.

The administration of foundling policy in the areas of Lille, Mulhouse and Rouen generally mirrored struggles of opinion at the national level. At the beginning of the period, Lille and Rouen's hospital institutions were more typical of prevailing French administrative approaches. However, the attitudes and administrative procedures used by Alsatian authorities, which deviated from national policy at the beginning of the period, gradually lost their marginal character. From the middle of the 1820s to the late 1840s, the repressive strategies they had long followed gradually gained in appeal, so that by the end of the period under examination the spirit underlying services to foundlings and abandoned children in Lille and Rouen came to resemble Alsatian strategies much more closely.

Policy Legacies: The Old Regime, Revolution, and Empire

The early modern history of policy towards foundlings in France reflected the main outlines of a changing relationship between monarchical, clerical, and seigneurial authority. Already by the sixteenth century, seigneurial authorities, in their capacity as *hauts-justiciers,* were attempting to divest themselves of responsibility for caring for foundlings in their areas, a factor that helped to inspire the monarchy and the Tridentine church to become more actively involved.[1] The best-known advocate and spiritual mentor of aid to foundlings and abandoned children was Saint Vincent-de-Paul, whose work in seventeenth-century Paris called Louis XIII's attention to their plight. Vincent was inspired to his efforts by a growing traffic in homeless children, who were purchased or taken off the streets of the capital to serve as cheap labor or as assistants to professional beggars. Aided by a group of his own creation, the Dames de la charité, Vincent worked to establish the Maison de la couche in Paris in 1638, leading directly to Louis XIV's 1670 edict that established the Hôpital des enfants trouvés.[2] Royal policy in the seventeenth and eighteenth centuries proclaimed the king's interest in these children on the basis of obligations of Catholic piety and paternal authority as well as considerations of *raison d'état*. Louis XIV's edict of 1670 establishing the Hôpital des enfants trouvés decreed: "There is no obligation more natural nor one conforming more to Christian piety than to care for poor abandoned children whose weakness and misfortune render them . . . deserving of compassion."[3] However, the king's plan was that children received by the hospital could legitimately be required to serve the state either as soldiers or as colonists. In this regard as in so many others, royal policy expressed the several sides of its nature: its paternalism, its piety, and its *raison d'état*. Writing of royal policy on the problem of subsistence, a recent historian of the Old Regime has captured this sense of the monarchy's variegated natures:

> Whereas social control spoke the chilling language of *raison d'état* and stressed the checks placed upon the people and the supremacy of the interests of the State, this brand of paternalism exuded the compassion characteristic of familial ties, emphasized not the constraints upon the subjects but their claims upon the State, not the prerogatives of the government but its obligations, and found its rationale in the very nature of the royal mission, consecrated by tradition and religion.[4]

Expectations of the usefulness of foundlings in serving the interests of the state never seem to have been fully realized, at least according to statements

1. On relations between the monarchy and seigneurial authorities, both lay and religious, and the conflict between royal legislation against child abandonment and the provision of services for foundlings, see Ernest Semichon, *Histoire des enfants abandonnés depuis l'antiquité jusqu'à nos jours: Le tour* (Paris, 1880), pp. 98–133, and Jehanne Charpentier, *Le droit de l'enfance abandonnée: Son évolution sous l'influence de la psychologie, 1552–1791* (Paris, 1967), pp. 21–24.

2. Charpentier, *Le droit*, pp. 11–12; Hélène Bergues et al., *La prévention des naissances dans la famille: Ses origines dans les temps modernes* (Paris, 1960), pp. 167–68; L. F. Benoiston de Châteauneuf, *Considérations sur les enfants trouvés* (Paris, 1824), pp. ix–xiii.

3. JF, 1236/1–2.

4. Steven L. Kaplan, *Bread, Politics, and Political Economy in the Reign of Louis XV* (The Hague, 1976), 1:5–6.

made by hospital authorities writing in 1761.[5] However, some of the traditional antipathy towards illegitimate children, as foundlings were assumed to be, was overcome in policies initiated by Louis XIV in consideration of other interests central to the monarchy. Royal involvement in aid to foundlings through the creation of the new hospital, as in so many other areas, was both result and cause of a progressive erosion of seigneurial obligations. By the middle of the eighteenth century, administrators of the Parisian hospital spoke the truth when they declared that foundlings "belonged to the state."[6]

From the time of its establishment, the annual number of children brought to the Parisian foundling hospital grew rapidly. In 1670, there were 312 children admitted; in 1680, 890; in 1700, 1,738; in 1740, 3,150. By the end of the Old Regime, over 6,000 children were being admitted each year.[7] One of the reasons for the increases was the inability of the hospital to restrict its services effectively to the children for whom it had been established. The foundling population gradually came to include legitimate as well as illegitimate children, the proportion of the former being estimated as high as one-half to two-thirds of the total by 1761.[8] Such an abuse of the system evoked some ambivalence on the part of the royal administration. On the one hand administrators decried the growth of the problem and looked back longingly to a time when laws had been used vigorously to repress the abandonment of children. On the other hand, hospital authorities and royal administrators such as Joly de Fleury joined with others in speaking a new language of "humanity" which gave a different but no less powerful legitimacy to the monarchy's original way of framing its obligations to foundlings. Joly de Fleury cited the "inhumanity" of a policy that would pursue parents who abandoned their legitimate children and advised provincial administrators to "close their eyes" to this abuse of the system unless abandonment was accompanied by a criminal act.[9] This spirit did not preclude vigorous prosecution of third parties who were discovered to be illegally transporting children or abandoning them on the high road. However, the same rigor was not apparently shown towards parents, even though there were cases of women brought to justice as a result of abandoning their

5. "Extrait du registre des délibérations du bureau de l'Hôpital-Général," 7 January 1761, JF, 1223/277. Cf. Jacques Donzelot, *The Policing of Families*, trans. Robert Hurley (New York, 1979), p. 10.

6. Administrators of the hôpital-général to the contrôleur-général des finances, undated, but probably 1758, JF,: 1236/157–58.

7. Bergues et al., *La prévention des naissances*, p. 173; Jean-François Terme and Jean-Baptiste Monfalcon, *Histoire des enfants trouvés*, rev. ed. (Paris, 1840), p. 101.

8. See "Extrait du registre des délibérations du bureau de l'Hôpital-Général," 7 January 1761, JF, 1223/277.

9. Joly de Fleury to the administrators of the Hôpital du Mans, 17 March 1754, JF, 1271/100.

child.[10] Royal judicial authorities in the late eighteenth century, when asked whether poor parents whose identities were known should be allowed to leave their children as foundlings in the care of hospitals, advised local *procureurs du roi* to proceed with their admission.[11]

Paris was not the only city to create an institution for foundlings, nor the only one in which their growing numbers rapidly created financial problems for hospital administrators. However, it was the rapid growth of the capital's foundling population that led to Louis XVI's declaration of 1779 that prohibited the transportation of provincial foundlings into Paris and provided for the establishment of hospitals for them throughout the kingdom.[12] It was well known that the Parisian hospital received large numbers of provincial children, which several sources estimated at nearly one-third of the total.[13] Indeed, transport of foundlings from countryside to city was not restricted to the Paris region, but occurred whenever a provincial town established its own services. Parents often paid midwives, wet nurses, and men known as *meneurs* to undertake the journey.[14]

Generalizations about the method of admission to foundling homes under the Old Regime are difficult to make. In some regions, the person bringing the infant did not hesitate to reveal information about the parents, including names and the child's place of birth or its parents' residence, even though legal sanctions could be brought against them. In other areas, parents attempting to leave a child were required to give authorities this information. Investigations could ensue, with hospital authorities attempting to convince parents to take back the children they had left.[15] Such local variations would persist well into the nineteenth century.

10. For one prosecution, see the case of Jacques Moriceau (a.k.a. Morizot) and his accomplices in Angers, contained in JF, 1270/62–77; and Semichon, *Histoire*, p. 155.

11. Procureur général to the Procureur du roi in Châlons-sur-Marne, 30 May 1781, JF, 1270/123, which noted, "Hospitals and *Hôtels-Dieu* were founded to come to the aid of those in need and indigency." See also Procureur général to Procureur du roi in Château-du-Loir, 29 September 1781, JF, 1270/128.

12. This decree also stated the belief that a large portion of foundlings were legitimate children. See "Arrêt du conseil d'état du roi concernant les enfants trouvés," 10 January 1779, JF, 1270/137. For excerpts of the 1779 decree, see Bergues et al., *La prévention*, pp. 177–78, and Antoinette Chamoux, "L'enfance abandonée à Reims à la fin du XVIII siècle," *Annales de démographie historique*, 1973, 263. On Necker's role in this decree, see Camille Bloch, *L'assistance et l'état en France à la veille de la révolution* (Paris, 1908), p. 233.

13. This estimate was cited in Benoiston de Châteauneuf, *Considérations*, p. xv, who stated, "Of 56,800 children received in the [Paris] hospital during nine years from 1764 to 1772, 16,200 came from the provinces." Chamoux, "L'enfance," p. 265, gives a figure of 28% for the years 1773–77.

14. Etienne Hélin, "Une sollicitude ambiguë: L'évacuation des enfants abandonnés," *Annales de démographie historique*, 1973, pp. 225–29.

15. Chamoux, "L'enfance," pp. 266–69; Charpentier, *Le droit*, pp. 10–11. On the history of Rouen's foundling services under the Old Regime, see G. Panel, *Documents concernant*

By the end of the eighteenth century, there was growing administrative concern about the problem. Necker, who in 1789 estimated the total number of foundlings in France at 40,000, offered a prophetic commentary on the debate to come:

> Of all the institutions created by a humanitarian spirit, those whose utility is most inmixed with inconveniences are . . . asylums for abandoned children. These praiseworthy institutions have doubtless kept these children, worthy of compassion, from being the victims of parental depravity. But imperceptibly, we have become accustomed to regarding hospitals for foundlings as public homes in which the king finds it just to feed and support the children of his poor subjects. The abuses are growing daily and will one day become a great nuisance, because the remedy is difficult using only palliatives . . . [E]xtreme measures will not be approved until [this] disorder becomes an excess obvious to everyone.[16]

The Revolution's legacy to the policy on foundlings was an ambiguous one. On the one hand, liberal and republican legislators viewed the state's responsibility to foundlings and illegitimate children as very wide, and attempted to legislate away the stigma attached to bastardy by a law of 26 Brumaire, Year II.[17] However, revolutionary upheavals and the seizure of the funds of individual hospitals devastated resources used to care for foundlings, or *enfants de la patrie*, as they were now called.[18] By the last years of the century, regional administrators flooded the Ministries of the Interior and Finances with correspondence attesting to the impoverishment of their foundling services.[19] The decline in hospital resources for foundlings made it nearly impossible for their administrators to engage suppliers or to pay wet nurses in the countryside for their care. During the darkest hours, unpaid wet nurses returned children to the hospitals where they had originally been left.[20]

Under the Directory and Consulate, lawmakers searched for means of

les pauvres de Rouen: Extraits des archives de l'hôtel de ville, 3 vols. (Rouen, 1917), and Dr. François Hué, *Histoire de l'hospice général de Rouen, 1602–1840* (Rouen, 1903), pp. 81–86.

16. Cited in Henri Derbigny, *Analyse raisonnée des ouvrages de MM. l'Abbé Gaillard, Terme et Monfalcon, Remacle et de Gérando sur la question des enfants trouvés* (Bordeaux, 1840), pp. 21–22. Necker's speech was widely cited by moral economists in the nineteenth century, figuring prominently in a speech by the minister of the interior, Montalivet, in the Chamber of Deputies on 30 May 1838. See *Moniteur*, 31 May 1838, p. 1468.

17. Crane Brinton, *French Revolutionary Legislation on Illegitimacy, 1789–1804* (Cambridge, Mass., 1936), pp. 29, 36.

18. On aid to foundlings from the Republic to the Consulate, see Alan Forrest, *The French Revolution and the Poor* (New York, 1981), ch. 7.

19. On the departments of the Nord and Seine-Inférieure, see AN, F15/440 (Years IV–VIII); Nord (Year VII) F15/349 and (Year IX) F15/387; Seine-Inférieure (Year IV) F15/274, (Year V) F15/302, and (Year VII) F15/367.

20. Léon Lallemand, *La révolution et les pauvres* (Paris, 1898), pp. 231–39.

undoing earlier legislation, attempting, for example, to restore the fundamental distinction between legitimate and illegitimate children as it pertained to inheritance. As Crane Brinton has shown, this period witnessed a new understanding of the relationship between laws of "nature" or "humanity" and concrete civil law. Legislators' desire to reestablish order meant that they now gave precedence to revising previous revolutionaries' understanding of the laws of "humanity" in the interests of making civil law a proper anchor for the social order. Laws regulating such an important family matter as inheritance, for example, now needed to be applied "as nearly as possible in accordance with the sentiments of nature, combined with the principles of political economy, . . . of morals, and of the preservation of societies."[21] Brinton also showed that legislative debate under the Directory helped prepare the way for key aspects of the Code Civil's view of the family and in particular its prohibition of the *recherche de la paternité,* the right of either authorities or women pregnant with illegitimate children to identify the father legally.[22]

Nineteenth-century commentators on the foundling problem, however, held the emperor himself responsible for the substance and tone of his legislation on foundlings, which was contained in a decree of 1811. By this law, Napoleon attempted to standardize the administration of aid to foundlings, abandoned children, and poor orphans throughout the country, much as kings before him had tried. By the 1811 decree, foundlings were defined as "those who, born of unknown fathers and mothers, have been found abandoned in whatever place, or carried to hospitals designated to receive them." Abandoned children were "those who, born of known fathers and mothers, and first raised by them, or by other persons at their release, are abandoned by them, without anyone knowing what has happened to the parents, or without the possibility of recourse to them."[23] Under Napoleon's decree the state, through individual hospitals, had responsibility for foundlings and abandoned children until they could be apprenticed at age twelve or were reclaimed by their parents or adopted by third parties. One of the key points of the decree was that foundlings were supposed to be children absolutely without family to support them. They were in principle supposed to be illegitimate children whose mothers had abandoned them—the kind of children whom Saint Vincent-de-Paul had rescued from the streets of the capital in the seventeenth century.

21. Brinton, *French Revolutionary Legislation*, p. 53, citing Siméon, "Rapport sur la successibilité des enfans naturels," 18 Messidor An V, *Conseil des Cinq-Cents* (Paris, 1797), p. 13.

22. Brinton, *French Revolutionary Legislation*, p. 52.

23. Orphans were defined as "those who, having neither father nor mother, have no means of existence." "Décret impérial concernant les enfants trouvés ou abandonnés et les orphelins pauvres," 19 January 1811, *Bulletin des lois*, 1811, pp. 82–86. The text of the decree of 1811 is reproduced in French in Rachel Ginnis Fuchs, *Abandoned Children: Foundlings and Child Welfare in Nineteenth-Century France* (Albany, 1984), pp. 282–85.

The 1811 decree, which was to regulate administration into the 1830s, and with some modifications until 1904, provided for the establishment of one receiving hospital for foundlings with a *tour* in each arrondissement. *Tours* were revolving wooden cylinders placed in the wall of each receiving hospital, with one side facing the street. The person who wished to leave an infant placed it into the *tour* and rang a bell, alerting a staff member, who turned it 180 degrees, bringing the infant into the hospital.[24] Before 1811, the establishment of hospital *tours* had been by local choice. Now, in theory, it was made mandatory for each hospital designated to receive foundlings. However, since there were some departments, including the Haut-Rhin, that did not have such hospitals, there were also a number that had no *tours*.[25] Departments that never established *tours* were usually more restrictive in their admission of foundlings to public assistance, demanding, for example, that persons who left infants supply parents' names and addresses to hospital authorities.

One explanation for the establishment of *tours* in certain countries was advanced by L. F. Benoiston de Châteauneuf, who argued that they were more compatible with Catholic than with Protestant values. Citing their absence in England and in the Protestant parts of Switzerland, he also noted that in England, the *recherche de la paternité* was legal. Women who bore illegitimate children there were pressured to declare the name of their child's father, and the law would in theory try to enforce his obligation of support.[26] In France and other Catholic countries, on the other hand, the mother was not permitted this right and was thus in a more vulnerable position. *Tours,* he believed, thus filled women's need to rid themselves of a burden they bore alone and to protect their own and their family's honor. Importantly, too, *tours* were also designed to prevent infanticide.

Catholic and Moral Economist Views on the Foundling Problem

From the end of the Empire until the mid-1830s, the number of foundlings admitted annually to the hospitals of France held steady at approximately 33,000 a year, rising above this number during times of economic and social crisis, as in the early 1830s. However, the total number of foundlings dependent on state aid tended to increase over time (see Tables 4.1 and 4.2). Some observers, looking back over the period of the 1820s and 1830s, retrospectively ascribed

24. For illustrations of the *tour,* see Edward Shorter, *The Making of the Modern Family* (New York, 1975), between p. 128 and p. 129, and Fuchs, *Abandoned Children*, pp. 22, 112.

25. Abbé A. H. Gaillard, *Recherches administratives, statistiques et morales sur les enfants trouvés, les enfants naturels et les orphelins* (Paris, 1837), p. 110. As of 1827 this group of departments also included the Bas-Rhin, Meuse, Vosges, Côte d'Or, Jura, Haute-Saône, Nièvre, and Orne.

26. L. F. Benoiston de Châteauneuf, "Sur les enfants trouvés," *Annales d'hygiène publique et de médecine légale* 21 (1839): 94.

Table 4.1. Number of Foundlings Admitted Yearly to the *Tours* and Hospices of France, 1815–1845

Year	Number of foundlings	Year	Number of foundlings
1815	28,429	1834	31,771
1821	33,792	1835	31,415
1825	32,278	1838	26,950
1826	32,870	1839	26,266
1827	32,501	1840	26,547
1828	33,749	1841	25,677
1829	33,141	1842	25,846
1830	33,431	1843	25,146
1831	35,814	1844	24,770
1832	35,884	1845	25,239
1833	33,191		

Sources: Abbé A. H. Gaillard, *Résumé de la discussion sur les enfants trouvés* (Paris, 1853), pp. 12–23; Alfred Legoyt, *La France statistique* (Paris, 1843), table B; Ad. de Watteville, *Statistique des établissements de bienfaisance: Rapport à M. le Ministre de l'Intérieur sur la situation administrative, morale et financière du service des enfants trouvés et abandonnés* (Paris, 1849), p. 6.

the growing population of foundlings and abandoned children in part to declines in the level of their mortality, while other authors emphasized that the extent of the increase in foundlings was merely the result of overall population increase. The fact remained, however, that the total cost of supporting the foundling population rose from four million francs in 1819 to eleven million by 1838.[27]

One of the main factors shaping the debate to come was that the cost of supporting foundlings and abandoned children fell very heavily on departmental administrations. Receiving hospitals were responsible for feeding and clothing the children for the first day or two after they had been received. However, the bulk of the costs, which went as payment of wages to nurses for the home care of the children until they reached age twelve, was part of departmental budgets.[28] Although nurses' wages were extremely low, averaging four

27. Authors who emphasized the decline in mortality argument included Alphonse Esquiros, *Paris, ou les sciences, les institutions et les moeurs au XIXe siècle* (Paris, 1847), 2:288, 355, and Ulysse Laget, "Extrait de l'histoire des enfants trouvés," *Société de la morale chrétienne* 2, no. 3 (1853): 50. Gaillard, *Recherches*, pp. 103, 149, cited declines in mortality, but also argued that many observers were exaggerating the level of increase. Budget figures are cited in Benoiston de Châteauneuf, "Sur les enfants trouvés," p. 89.

28. The story of one prefect's conflict with his local hospital administration over who was going to pay the costs of foundling services is found in François M. de T., Vicomte de Bondy, *Mémoire sur la nécessité de réviser la législation actuelle concernant les enfans trouvés et abandonnés et orphelins pauvres* (Auxerre, 1835), pp. 27–28, 44, 66. Bondy was prefect of the Yonne in the mid-1830s.

Table 4.2. Total Number of Foundlings on Rolls in France, 1784–1845

Year	Number of foundlings	Year	Number of foundlings
1784	40,000	1828	114,307
1790	30,000	1829	115,472
1798	51,000	1830	118,073
1809	69,000	1831	123,869
1815	84,500	1832	127,982
1816	87,700	1833	127,507
1817	92,200	1834	129,629
1818	98,100	1836	130,000
1819	99,346	1838	95,624
1821	105,700	1839	96,088
1822	109,410	1840	97,770
1823	116,452	1841	97,948
1824	116,767	1842	97,500
1825	117,305	1843	96,938
1826	116,377	1844	96,514
1827	114,384	1845	96,788

Sources: Jean-François Terme and Jean-Baptiste Monfalcon, *Histoire des enfants trouvés*, rev. ed (Paris, 1840), pp. 128, 180; Abbé A. H. Gaillard, *Recherches administratives, statistiques et morales sur les enfants trouvés, les enfants naturels et les orphelins* (Paris, 1837), pp. 100, 108; Louis Desloges, *Des enfants trouvés, des femmes publiques et des moyens à employer pour en diminuer le nombre* (Paris, 1836), p. 18; Ulysse Laget, "Extrait de l'histoire des enfants trouvés," *Société de la morale chrétienne*, 2 (1853): 20; Ad. de Watteville, *Statistique des établissements de bienfaisance: Rapport à M. le Ministre de l'Intérieur sur la situation administrative, morale et financière du service des enfants trouvés et abandonnés* (Paris, 1849), p. 6; Yves Turin, "Enfants trouvés, colonisation et utopie: Etude d'un comportement social au XIXe siècle," *Revue historique*, no. 496 (1970): 33; *Rapport au Roi sur les hôpitaux, les hospices et les services de bienfaisance par M. Gasparin* (Paris, 1837), p. 4. Figures for 1824–33 are from Gaillard, *Recherches*, p. 108, and probably represent mid-year estimates. Pre-1815 figures probably indicate the number of foundlings at year end, as do the 1838 and 1845 figures, respectively from Laget and Turin. Watteville noted that the figure of 69,000 attributed by most sources to 1809, but by Watteville to 1811, included children in the whole Empire, a population of 40 million, which he contrasted with the 1789 base population of 26 million. In his judgment, it was only in 1819 that figures once again became comparable to Old Regime data.

to eight francs per month, the total costs for support of the children frequently constituted the largest single item in departmental budgets.[29] A shortage of

29. In the Haut-Rhin, nurses received seven francs for children of all ages. In the Seine-Inférieure, wages declined as the child grew. They began at eight francs to age one, declined to six francs between ages one and two, five francs between ages two and seven, and four francs between ages seven and twelve. There was a twenty-franc bonus when infants received

funds at the departmental level meant that the conseils généraux of many departments had to add a percentage tax onto the *contributions directes* of some or all communes, making the foundling problem an issue of local as well as national interest.[30]

In the course of the national debate, Social Catholic writers emphasized the complexity of the foundling problem, citing its origins in the combined influences of structural economic conditions and human frailty. While decrying in particular the immorality of parents who abandoned their legitimate children to foundling homes, they continued to defend society's obligation to foundlings and the mothers who gave birth to them. They attempted to fulfill part of this obligation through the Société de Saint-François-Régis by urging parents to reclaim any children whom they had left in foundling homes. However, it was the state, and not the church or private charity, that under the terms of the 1811 decree had responsibility for the children's welfare.[31] Social Catholics' support for state aid thus seems to have stemmed more from the legislative realities of the situation created by the 1811 decree than from an ideological commitment to a state system of aid. As debates would show, they were not strongly attached to the institution of the *tour* per se, but rather to a policy that recognized society's obligation to children who had been abandoned.

However, Social Catholics' construction of the foundling problem and its putative solution came under increasingly well-argued attack by moral economists inside and outside central and regional administrations who criticized both the Social Catholic analysis of the foundling problem and its implied administrative solution. These moral economists would show that the Social Catholic position was hopelessly outmoded, since it failed to take into consideration fundamental changes at work within French society in general and within working-class family life and psychology in particular. Moral economists undermined key aspects of the Social Catholic position by providing new

---

as newborns reached age fifteen months, and a fifty-franc bonus when the child reached twelve. The latter bonus also existed in the Haut-Rhin. See, respectively, prefect of the Haut-Rhin to the minister of the interior, 5 January 1836, AN, F15/2541; "Règlement concernant le service des enfants trouvés et abandonnés placés en nourrice dans les campagnes," 5 June 1822, contained in the Commission administrative des hospices de Rouen to the prefect, 5 March 1836, ADSM, 1 XP/260; and F. Bouriaud, "De la réduction des tours d'exposition des enfants trouvés dans le département de la Vienne," *Annales d'hygiène publique et de médecine légale* 17 (1837): 200.

30. In 1828, the conseil général of the Nord, under the prefect's guidance, decided that it would be impossible to allocate financial responsibility equitably among communes, and therefore decided that the monies would be taken strictly from the department's general fund. Conseil général du Nord, "Délibérations," session of 1828, p. 33, ADN, N2/15.

31. There is mention of one local chapter of the Société de Saint-Vincent-de-Paul near Toulon whose members visited wet nurses who had received foundlings, but this appears to have been an exceptional case. See Albert Foucault, *La société de Saint-Vincent de Paul: Histoire de cent ans* (Paris, 1933), p. 110.

analyses of the dangers of infanticide that were imputed to the restriction of foundling services, the relation of working-class parents to welfare institutions designed to receive the children, and finally, the impact of foundling institutions on working-class family life. The clarity and simplicity of their analysis, which they supported with empirical data, gradually gave them an extraordinary advantage over their Catholic interlocutors, in no small part because it was easier to deduce practical policy from their analysis of the problem.

Articulating the essential causes that accounted for the large number of foundlings and abandoned children was, of course, one of the cruxes of the debate. Social Catholics emphasized that sheer poverty was the most fundamental: "It is too evident for those who know the condition of the class that contributes the whole quota of foundlings that it would be impossible for unwed mothers as well as legitimate parents to be able . . . to make provision for the care and feeding of these sad victims."[32] Indeed, the Social Catholics' greatest defender in the Chamber of Deputies, Alphonse de Lamartine, argued that the mere fact of abandoning a child proved the individual's or family's total desperation and financial distress.[33] The instinct of maternal love, he argued, was so strong as to prevent recourse to abandonment except in the direst of financial circumstances—constraints imposed by society itself. Leading moral economist commentators and administrators, however, could not accept this argument, since "every day we see the unhappy wives of workers whose poverty is nearly absolute reject bad advice and worse examples. They nurse their children with their own milk and with the help of private charity. . . . This poor child does not die of starvation in its family. Neither is it abandoned. The love of its mother protects it as Providence watches over."[34] The authors of this study, whose experience at the foundling hospital in Lyon put them close to the grass roots of the problem, demonstrated that subsistence crises there could not be positively correlated with increases in the number of foundlings.[35]

Regional administrators in the Nord and the Seine-Inférieure were not so hasty in dismissing the Catholics' main argument, that the essential foundations of the foundling problem lay in overall economic conditions. In the late 1820s, the conseil général of the Seine-Inférieure seems to have accepted the prefect's view that local economic crises were bound to increase the number

32. Emmanuel de Curzon, *Etudes sur les enfants trouvés au point de vue de la législation, de la morale, et de l'économie politique* (Poitiers, 1847), p. 116.

33. Speech before the Chamber of Deputies in *Moniteur*, no. 151, 31 May 1838, p. 1466. See also his comments on the *tour*, cited in Fuchs, *Abandoned Children*, p. 44.

34. Terme and Monfalcon, *Histoire*, p. 245. On the foundling question under the July Monarchy, see Donzelot, *The Policing of Families*, pp. 26–30, and Fuchs, *Abandoned Children*, pp. 34–40.

35. Terme and Monfalcon, *Histoire*, pp. 191–92.

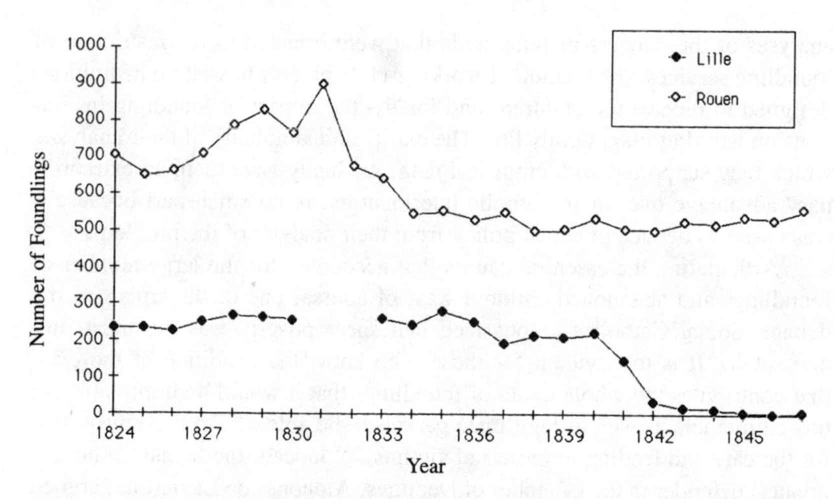

Figure 4.1 Number of Foundlings Received Annually, Lille and Rouen, 1824–1847. Sources: AN, F15/982, 985, 987–88, 1149–51, 2529, 2531, 2540–41; ADSM 2 LP/77–78, 81–97; P. S. Lelong, *Rapport sur les enfants trouvés* (Rouen, 1835), Table 2; Aimé Houzé de l'Aulnoit, *Enfants assistés* (Lille, 1879), appendix I; Lucien Denis, "Notes sur les enfants trouvés," *Revue sociétés savantes de Haute Normandie*, no. 42 (1966).

of foundlings.[36] Similarly, in an 1830 letter to the minister of commerce and public works, the prefect of the Nord indicated "that the lack of work and the high price of necessities . . . contributed one of the causes of these distressing abandonments."[37] (See Fig. 4.1 and 4.2.) The prefect of the Seine-Inférieure had much the same thing to say, citing "public misery" as the cause of the increasing number of foundlings in his department.[38]

However, the relationship between poverty and child abandonment in the Haut-Rhin was difficult to discern because of that department's failure to construct a service for foundlings similar to those in most of the rest of France. The department of the Haut-Rhin resembled the Nord and Seine-Inférieure by its important concentrations of working-class populations dependent on the health of the cotton industry, whose fortunes fluctuated widely. Like sev-

36. Conseil général de la Seine-Inférieure, "Délibérations," 1828, p. 107, ADSM, 1 NP/16.

37. Letter of 30 June 1830, AN, F15/2529.

38. Prefect of the Seine-Inférieure to the minister of commerce and public works, 19 November 1831, AN, F15/2531. See also the letter from the prefect of the Nord to the same minister, dated 27 July 1832 (AN, F15/2540): "The [growth in the number of foundlings] must be attributed to the prolonged distress of the indigent class, resulting from the lack of work and the high price of necessities, circumstances which must bring with them a greater number of abandonments than in ordinary times." He also cited the epidemic of cholera in the Nord as well as the ease with which local administrations admitted children to the hospitals. The return of better economic conditions was held responsible for a decline in abandonments. See the report of the prefect to the conseil général du Nord, service de 1833, AN, F15/2540.

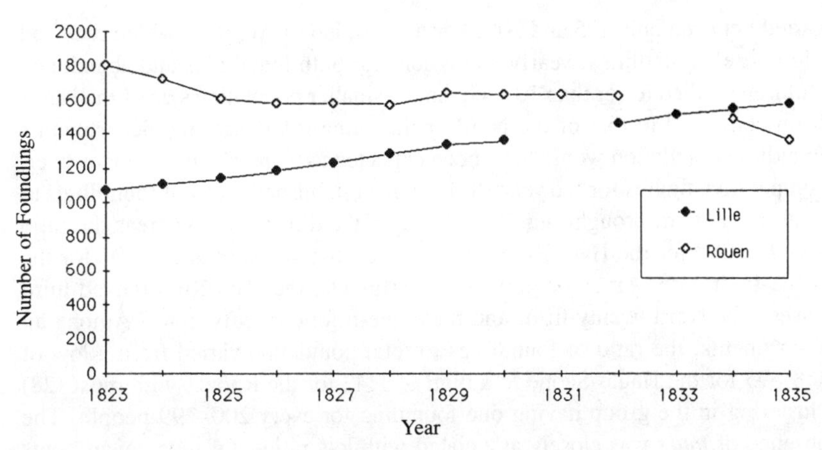

Figure 4.2 Total Number of Foundlings on Rolls at Year End, Lille and Rouen, 1823–1835. Sources: See Fig. 4.1.

eral other departments, however, it had never conformed to the provision of the 1811 decree that required one receiving hospital, with a *tour,* in each arrondissement. No *tours* were ever established there, although several departmental hospitals did care for the few foundlings that there were. The hospital in the city of Altkirch was responsible for administering aid to foundlings from all areas of the arrondissement, including Mulhouse. In contrast to most departments with *tours,* admission to aid was based on an inquiry into the background of the child, and it was the prefect and not local hospital officials who routinely ruled on whether specific foundlings would be admitted to departmental assistance.[39] The principle of local responsibility for dependent children had a long history in the area. No *hôpital-général* had ever been established in the Haut-Rhin, and consequently, local hospitals usually restricted the wide variety of their services to their own inhabitants. The agreement of the directors of the hospice of Colmar to receive the department's foundlings during the Revolution was extracted only under concerted pressure from the central administration.[40]

The failure of departmental authorities to establish *tours* was pointed to as one of the main reasons why there were so few foundlings in the Haut-Rhin. Between 1825 and 1839, years for which there are reliable records, the total number of foundlings and abandoned children on the department's rolls

39. Prefect of the Haut-Rhin to the minister of the interior, 5 January 1836, AN, F15/2541.

40. Département du Haut-Rhin, "Etat des lits fondés dans les hospices du Haut-Rhin," 24 Frimaire An XI, AN, F15/1075. The unwillingness of hospitals, including Mulhouse's, to receive such children stemmed in part from the failure of the department to allocate funds from its budget to them, which contrasted with grants to Colmar's hospital. See the prefect of the Haut-Rhin to the minister of the interior, 30 August 1810, AN, F15/1075.

varied between only 175 and 200. For the hospital of Altkirch, which received Mulhouse's foundlings, yearly admissions for both foundlings and abandoned children totalled fewer than 10.[41] Given the smaller population size of the Haut-Rhin compared to that of the Nord or the Seine-Inférieure, the department's foundling population would have been expected to be much smaller. However, comparative figures for the year 1841, which established ratios of foundlings to total population, brought out the salience of the difference. Whereas the ratio was 1:2,082 for the Haut-Rhin, it was 1:485 for the Nord and 1:291 for the Seine-Inférieure. Among eighty-six departments, the Haut-Rhin ranked third lowest, the Nord twenty-fifth, and the Seine-Inférieure fifty-first.[42] Among all departments, the ratio of foundlings to total population varied from a low of 1:8,695 for the Haute-Saône to a high of 1:42 for the Rhône, with most (28) clustering in the group having one foundling for every 200–299 people. The absence of *tours* was closely associated with low ratios. Of nine departments having no *tours,* seven were among the twenty departments with the lowest ratios.[43]

Comparative data on the widely varying ratios of foundlings to total population and the different levels of repressiveness in regional policy helped to dispel the notion that foundlings were an inevitable fact of life, particularly in industrial areas. Moral economists would take these and other data to show that prudent administrative policy could be used to end abuses of the system. One of the primary abuses, substantiated by empirical evidence, was that some of the children left as foundlings were legitimate. However, secrecy surrounding *tours* up to the middle of the 1830s in Lille and Rouen and in most other places prevented observers from precise knowledge on this score, fueling debates about the provenance of children who were being received. Attempts to assess proportional responsibility for the abandonment of children among different groups thus proliferated. One source ranked the following groups in order from the least to the most important: families which had neither the means nor will to raise another child; women "carried away by passion who

41. The total number of foundlings and abandoned children in the Haut-Rhin declined from 247 in 1825 to 216 in 1829, increased to 250 in 1835, and then declined again to 174 in 1839. For the years 1825–28, see AN, F15/1079–81; for 1829–30, F15/2530; for 1832–35, F15/2541; and for 1836–39, ADHR, 1X/84.

42. Baron Ad. de Watteville, *Du sort des enfants trouvés* (Paris, 1846), pp. 42–43, compared foundling populations in 1844 with the census populations of 1841. The raw figures were 223:464,466 for the Haut-Rhin, 2,243:1,085,298 for the Nord, and 2,528:737,501 for the Seine-Inférieure. At an earlier date, the minister of the interior had brought both the Haut-Rhin's low ratio of foundlings to population and the fact that it had no *tours* to the attention of other prefects. See Ministère de l'Intérieur, "Du déplacement et de la fermeture des tours" (1836?), p. 6, ADSM, 1 XP/260.

43. In addition to the Haute-Saône and the Haut-Rhin, these included Vosges, second lowest; Bas-Rhin, seventh; Jura, eighth; Côte d'Or, fourteenth; and Meuse, nineteenth.

seek to save at least the appearance of honor"; women who "were taken by the first man who came along—who belong to everyone and no one, who have neither food nor shelter except that which public charity gives them"; and women who became pregnant "heedlessly."[44] A similar evaluation summarized the argument: "All those who have studied this question . . . agree that there are three [causes of abandonment]: debauchery, shame, and poverty—in other words disorder of mores, fear of opinion, and the impoverishment of mothers."[45] Nevertheless, it was not so clear that "everyone" agreed on the relative importance of these different causes.

The issue of shame was deeply rooted in the history of foundling institutions, creating an important source of disagreement between moral economists and Catholics of all stripes. One of the original rationales for the *tour*'s secrecy was to prevent unmarried women's shame from leading them to commit infanticide. The conseil général of the Seine-Inférieure appeared to concur with this belief, at least in theory. Their minutes indicated that "the shame which is always associated [with an illegitimate birth] does not fall only on the woman who has erred, but on the whole family."[46] Indeed, as one observer noted, shame was "an eminently moral sentiment . . . that we must encourage rather than weaken. It is an indirect homage to good conduct and exemplary regularity in life. There is more hope for changing unwed mothers who fear the divulging of their secret than for those who withstand their public dishonor without great repugnance."[47] Moral economists believed, however, that an increasing proportion of lower-class women, particularly in large industrial towns, felt little shame in their illegitimate pregnancies.[48] Infanticide still existed, but only in a marginal fashion relative to the large number of foundlings, and according to the researches of Bernard-Benoît Remacle, was the crime of rural women.[49] Information on the place of residence of those accused of infanticide during the years 1843–47 confirms Remacle's judgment. Of 809

44. G. Symphor Vaudoré, *De la suppression des tours établis dans les chefs-lieux d'arrondissement* (Caen, 1838), p. 10.

45. Laget, "Extrait," p. 27.

46. Conseil général de la Seine-Inférieure, "Délibérations," session of 1835, AN, F15/3897.

47. Laget, "Extrait," p. 36.

48. Terme and Monfalcon, *Histoire*, p. 195. R. Vignes, *Mémoire sur les enfants trouvés et les mesures administratives qui leur ont été appliquées dans le département du Gers* (Auch, 1838), p. 47, criticized the lack of shame among unwed mothers, but without limiting it to the case of urban women.

49. *Rapport à M. le Ministre, Secrétaire d'Etat à l'Intérieur concernant les infanticides et les mort-nés dans leur relation avec la question des enfants trouvés, par M. Remacle* (Paris, 1845), p. 18. The rural background of women accused of infanticide was also emphasized in Abbé A. H. Gaillard, *Résumé de la discussion sur les enfants trouvés et observations sur la loi proposée au Corps législatif* (Paris, 1853), p. 10. But cf. *Rapport au Roi sur les hôpitaux, les hospices et les services de bienfaisance, par M. de Gasparin* (Paris, 1837), p. 68.

accused, 677, or 83.7 percent, were listed as residing in rural communes, and 128, or 15.8 percent, in urban communes.[50] Although all parties to the foundling debate believed that official statistics on infanticide grossly underestimated its incidence, moral economists took these figures and data on the mortality of foundlings to show that one of the other purposes of foundling institutions—the preservation of infant lives—was emphatically not being served by current arrangements. A national summary showed that between 1824 and 1836, when there were approximately 360,000 foundlings left in hospitals designed to receive them, 230,000, or nearly 64 percent, died sometime before their twelfth birthday.[51] Age-specific data showed 50 to 70 percent mortality during the first year of life.[52] The decimation of the foundling population came first at the hospital, where many infants arrived already weakened; from the fact that in many cases hospitals chose or were forced to attempt artificial feeding for want of wet nurses; from the rigors of infants' journey to the home of rural wet nurses; and finally from the variety of accidents and diseases that awaited them once they arrived there.

Although foundling mortality in the three areas under observation is impossible to calculate on the basis of age, data from annual reports filed between the mid-1820s and mid-1830s do permit the calculation of annual mortality rates for some years (see Table 4.3). Only aggregate figures for the Haut-Rhin are included in Table 4.3 because of the small numbers of cases, and even figures aggregated at the departmental level are suspect for the same reason. Indeed, in 1820, the minister of the interior had questioned the very low mortality figures submitted to him by the prefect of the Haut-Rhin, which showed that of an average population of foundlings and abandoned children of 216, only 6 had died during 1819. The prefect responded that the data were in fact accurate.[53] It is clear that mortality rates of foundlings in the Haut-Rhin varied widely from year to year because of the small numbers of children involved. Figures from Lille and Rouen are more worthy of confidence, however.

Rouen's hospital commission attributed the high mortality of foundlings there to the children's poor health, which they saw as "the inevitable result of the depravity of the lower class, especially within the population employed by

50. Of the total, 743, or 91.8%, were women. France, Ministère de la Justice, *Compte général de l'administration de la justice criminelle en France* (Paris, 1843–47); *Rapport à M. le Ministre*, table XII.

51. Cited in Conseil général de la Seine-Inférieure, "Délibérations," session of 1838, ADSM, 1 NP/22.

52. Watteville, *Du sort*, p. 33; Louis-René Villermé, "De la mortalité des enfants trouvés," *Annales d'hygiène publique et de médecine légale* 19 (1838), tables 1 and 2. On the Parisian hospice, see Fuchs, *Abandoned Children*, pp. 141–48.

53. Minister of the interior to the prefect of the Haut-Rhin and the latter's response, dated respectively 2 June and 16 June 1820, in AN, F15/1077.

Table 4.3. Annual Rate of Mortality among Foundlings, Haut-Rhin, Rouen, and Lille, 1824–1835, and Proportion of New Foundlings in Mid-Year Foundling Populations of Rouen and Lille

	Haut-Rhin	Rouen		Lille	
Year	Mortality rate	Mortality rate	Percentage of new foundlings	Mortality rate	Percentage of new foundlings
1824	—	34.0 (555)	19.9	11.5 (124)	10.7
1825	9.6 (5)	36.8 (582)	19.5	10.1 (112)	10.3
1826	13.8 (6)	36.1 (536)	20.8	8.3 (94)	9.6
1827	5.3 (2)	37.3 (563)	22.4	7.6 (91)	10.3
1828	0	41.2 (634)	24.8	10.3 (126)	10.6
1829	8.7 (2)	37.1 (597)	25.7	10.1 (130)	10.0
1830	7.1 (2)	35.1 (566)	23.4	9.6 (127)	8.7
1831	—	—	—	—	—
1832	7.5 (2)	33.2 (543)	20.7	—	—
1833	6.7 (2)	—	—	8.3 (121)	8.7
1834	0	—	19.3	8.0 (121)	8.0
1835	0	36.3 (511)	—	8.6 (135)	8.9

Sources: For Rouen: AN, F15/1149–51, 2531, 2541; for Lille:AN, F15/982, 985, 987–88, 2529, 2540; for the Haut-Rhin: AN, F15/1079–81, 2530, 2541.

Note: Mortality rates, expressed in percentages, are calculated on the basis of the total number of days lived by foundlings during the years in question, and thus represent true mortality rates. Figures in parentheses indicate the number of foundling deaths per year. The percentage of new foundlings was calculated by taking one-half of each year's new foundlings and dividing that number by the mid-year foundling population.

our numerous factories."[54] Data in Table 4.3 on foundlings in Lille and Rouen, however, suggest that there was also a close association between annual foundling mortality and the proportion of new foundlings in the total population. The higher the proportion of newly admitted, very young foundlings in a foundling population, the higher the mortality would be. Similarly, any policy that restricted the admission of new foundlings would result in mortality declines simply by raising the average age of the foundling population as a whole. As discussed below, this latter factor helps to account for the modest decline in foundling mortality among Lille's children in 1826–27.

Despite the high mortality of France's foundlings, not even the most censorious of moral economist observers truly believed that abandoning a child in the *tour* was intended as an act of infanticide: "Infanticide and child abandonment differed very little for ancient peoples. They ordinarily had the same

54. Commission administrative des hospices de Rouen to the prefect, 5 March 1836, ADSM, 1 XP/260. P. S. Lelong, *Rapport sur les enfants trouvés et abandonnés fait au conseil général de la Seine-Inférieure* (Rouen, 1835), pp. 36–37, cited a 75% mortality rate among Rouen's foundlings in the first three years of life for those admitted between the years 1828 and 1834.

goal—to put the newborn to death. It is not the same for modern societies. Most frequently, the abandonment of a newborn by its father and mother presupposes their desire to save its life. It indicates their hope of being aided by strangers in the accomplishment of their first duties."[55] Count Duchâtel used a similar argument in distinguishing vigorously between social conditions of the Old Regime and those of nineteenth-century France that he believed made Social Catholics' fear of infanticide obsolete. Whereas foundling homes had once been necessary, he argued, French mores had now become more civilized. The greater orderliness of nineteenth-century society thus demanded that outmoded institutions such as *tours* be abolished.[56]

However, the infanticide issue remained a central concern of Catholic observers and regional administrations. Local and departmental administrators were clearly under pressure from two sides. Their services to foundlings had to be sufficient to prevent embarrassingly high numbers of infanticides or other scandals that would shock public opinion and bring down the wrath of the central administration. Yet, any overly generous provision of aid by local hospital authorities led to rising costs decried by conseils généraux and local taxpayers. It was very difficult indeed to steer a middle course between these conflicting demands. In a report to the conseil général of the Seine-Inférieure, one expert noted:

> An absolute refusal to have pity for the unhappiness of others may engender despair and lead to great calamities. Moderate obstacles maintain hope and give vitality, often even energy, to courage about to be extinguished. On the other hand, too great accommodation hastens the hour of discouragement. Let us guard against the two extremes. Let us not tempt the love of the family, the love of work, and the spirit of personal dignity which even the youngest must have in their hearts. . . . We must guard against constructing all kinds of free hostels . . . along the road travelled by the working classes.[57]

Lelong's report expressed a suspicion that grew into a central proposition of the moral economist critique of foundlings institutions: that they themselves were a primary cause of rather than the solution to the problem of child abandonment. The emergence and elaboration of this view resulted from moral economists' increased attention to the values and psychology of parents or lone women

55. Terme and Monfalcon, *Histoire*, pp. 21–22. Cf. Shorter, *The Making of the Modern Family*, p. 173, who emphasizes the fact that abandonment to the foundling home "was tantamount to infanticide."

56. Comte Tanneguy Duchâtel, *Considérations d'économie politique sur la bienfaisance ou de la charité dans ses rapport avec l'état moral et le bien-être des classes inférieures de la société*, 2d ed. (Paris, 1836), p. 262.

57. Lelong, *Rapport*, p. 25.

who abandoned their children. In contrast to Social Catholics, who continued to point out that the number of foundlings being received was holding rather steady, moral economists constructed an analysis of child abandonment that concentrated on projecting foundling numbers into the future.

The main thrusts of the emerging moral economist argument were that *tours* were a positive incitement to child abandonment; that working-class parents both legitimate and illegitimate were using the institutions intentionally to divest themselves of responsibility for their children; and that consequently, large proportions of the younger generation of workers were losing family ties essential both to their own survival and to the survival of the French social order:

> *Tours* are an incessant provocation to the abandonment of foundlings in the areas where they exist. They exert . . . a deplorable influence on the morality of the working classes and must be placed in the first rank of indirect causes which pervert the population of large cities. The mere fact of their existence causes one-half of the abandonments of newborns. . . . In the lower classes of society, especially in large cities, there is a profound indifference towards duty. . . . There are many good mothers and honest hearts among proletarians; but also, how many brutish and perverted souls?[58]

Prefects, conseils généraux, and the central administration gradually concurred in the judgment that many infants received as foundlings had a parent or parents who could have cared for them but who chose to leave them in the *tour* because of a decline in parental, particularly maternal, feeling and parents' desire that the state share in the costs of rearing their children. A report to the conseil général of the Seine-Inférieure noted: "Our department is not the only one . . . that has deplored this tendency towards the weakening of familial affection. If this dangerous and immoral example is allowed to grow and spread, soon a part of our population will no longer have children. They will have produced only offspring from whom they detach themselves more cruelly than most animals . . . , which abandon their young only when they are able to fend for themselves."[59]

Moral economists' concern was not only for the moment but for the implications of the problem for the future of French society. That their fears stemmed from grossly inaccurate demographic projections did nothing to make the sociodemographic future any less frightening for them at the time: "It is nearly certain that our population, about thirty-four million, will double by the beginning of the next century. As it is the indigent classes that undoubtedly

58. Terme and Monfalcon, *Histoire*, p. 251.
59. Lelong, *Rapport*, p. 33.

produce the most children, one could ask with trepidation how we will be able to supply the growing needs of our proletarian masses. There are authors who point out . . . that foundlings and the families they form already compose one-twentieth of the French population."[60] Another source of fear was moral economists' belief that France's foundling institutions were yielding the same consequences as England's Poor Law, which was "devouring England in the midst of the greatest industrial prosperity."[61] And although no one believed that all foundlings were the children of the urban industrial working classes, it was widely believed that the decline of family feeling and the growth of new attitudes towards foundling institutions among this segment of the population were important keys to explaining abuses of the system of aid.[62]

The moral economist portrait of those who abandoned their children emphasized that a new form of rational calculus underlying the behavior of working-class women and men made the foundling problem in the ninteenth century significantly different from what it had been before. Having shown that shame was not an important cause of abandonments among this sector of the population, moral economists found it easier to search for other explanations and to argue that foundling institutions encouraged women to enter illicit sexual unions with insouciance, knowing that they could dispose of their consequences in the *tour*. Such conduct, they believed, demonstrated a kind of twisted rationality that threatened to destroy women's natural instinct to preserve their children.[63] Under this argument, legitimate parents were not guilty of exactly the same calculus, but they too were tempted to abandon their children as a result of the availability of services that, according to Benjamin Delessert, provided conditions better than those in children's own homes. On the floor of the Chamber of Deputies, he argued:

> Many parents, in order to rid themselves of the cares of parenthood, find it convenient to place their children in a hospice, which they view as a free boarding home. And their consciences do not reproach them. When they see these clean cradles, these well-kept dormitories, nuns who are so kindly and sympathetic, they think that their children will be better cared for than in their own home, and they do not calculate the ravages made by sickness and death among this population of abandoned children.[64]

60. L. A. Labourt, *Recherches historiques et statistiques sur l'intempérance des classes laborieuses et sur les enfants trouvés*, 2d ed. (Paris, 1848), p. 198.

61. Terme and Monfalcon, *Histoire*, p. 181; Charles Dupin, *Forces productives et commerciales de la France* (Paris, 1827), 1: 40; Duchâtel, *Considérations*, p. 236.

62. Labourt, *Recherches*, p. 86; Préfecture du Nord, "Enfants trouvés et abandonnés," service de 1833, AN, F15/2540.

63. M. Marchand, "Sur les enfants trouvés et abandonnés," *Annuaire Normand*, 1841, pp. 386–87.

64. *Moniteur*, 31 May 1838, p. 1468.

Regional administrators could lend support to the new emphasis on the rational, calculative element underlying child abandonment by reporting on various manifestations of this frame of mind. Both they and hospital administrators knew that there were elaborate information networks through which hospital workers and wet nurses conspired to pass information to mothers who wished to maintain contact with their children: "Observations of this public service have forced us to recognize that for a long time, abandonments and exposures at the *tour* have not been the results of indigence. That, on the contrary, most are the effect of the cupidity of fathers and mothers whose goal is to have their children cared for . . . at no expense to them, without losing hope of finding them and visiting them at the wet nurse's."[65] There were also mothers who left their children in the *tour* and then returned after a day or two seeking employment as a wet nurse for them: "We see mothers making a game of charity. They present themselves as wet nurses at the hospitals where they left their children and thus claim the pleasures of motherhood as well as the profits of their profession of wet nurse."[66] Practices such as these were cited by moral economists as proof of the extraordinary differences between the causes of child abandonment under the Old Regime and July Monarchy France. Whereas in the past, they argued, children had become dependents of the state as the result of their mothers' shame or the fact of their being absolutely without family to support them, the problem now stemmed from parents' lack of real attachment to their children and their unwillingness to accomplish the fundamental duty of supporting them.

The Background of Foundlings in Rouen

Archival sources on foundlings and abandoned children in Rouen and Lille provide some information with which to assess the relative merits of moral economist and Social Catholic analyses of the causes of foundlings and abandoned children. An examination of information on foundlings in Rouen and abandoned children in Lille reveals the extraordinary diversity of human situations that led to children being separated from their parents.[67]

65. Prefect of the Nord, letter of 20 July 1836, cited in Aimé Houzé de l'Aulnoit, *Enfants assistés: La question des tours* (Lille, 1879), p. 4.

66. Conseil général du Nord, "Délibérations," session of 1834, meeting of 23 July, AN, F15/2540.

67. Because of the large number of cases involved, I have concentrated on foundlings in Rouen and abandoned children in Lille. I rejected my original plan of examining background information on a random sample of Rouen's foundlings, since such a strategy failed to take best advantage of the minority of cases that contained some information on the child. The texts discussed below are thus representative only of those foundlings for whom some information was indicated.

Table 4.4. Age Structure of Foundling Population Received at the *Hôpital-Général* of Rouen, Selected Years, 1831–1846

Year	Number of cases in sample[a]	Highest age	Age (in days)		
			Mean	Median	Mode
1831	41	11 mos.	15.6	2	1
1836	43	18 mos.	19.0	2	1
1841	41	4 yrs.	70.1	1	1
1844	42	2 yrs.	45.5	1	1
1846	44	3 yrs.	47.1	2	1

Source: Hôpital Général de Rouen, Commission Administrative, "Délibérations," 1831, 1836, 1841, 1844, 1846, ADSM, 2 LP/81, 86, 91, 94, 96.

[a]Sample of year's cases obtained by using the first case entered at the weekly meetings of the hospital's administrative commission. A total of 11 cases that fell into the samples were lacking age data.

Figures from the *tour* of Rouen show that in the 1830s and 1840s, as in the past, children were likely to become foundlings soon after their birth (see Table 4.4). Similarly, in the notes they sometimes left with their children, parents, usually mothers, set out their thoughts about what they had done in terms very reminiscent of those of earlier times.[68] The years 1830–31 in particular called forth a relatively large number of explanatory notes from poor couples and lone women who left their children at the Rouen *tour* that contrasted with the relative silence in "normal" times, as if people leaving their children were from groups that never believed that they would take such a step:

> We are two unhappy little children who seek your great goodness. We are not, in reality, abandoned by our parents, but like us they are struggling with the misfortune that seems to pursue the afflicted. . . . Do not let us suffer hunger, cold and all the needs of life any more. Do not send us away, we beg you. If our father and mother can take care of us again, they

68. Léon Lallemand, *Un chapitre de l'histoire des enfants trouvés: La maison de la Couche à Paris, XVIIe-XVIIIe siècles* (Paris, 1885), p. 31; Olwen Hufton, *The Poor of Eighteenth-Century France* (Oxford, 1974), pp. 333–34. Notable studies of eighteenth-century foundling populations, besides those already cited, include François Lebrun, "Naissances illégitimes et abandons d'enfants en Anjou au XVIIIe siècle," *Annales, E.S.C.* 27 (1972): 1183–89; Jean-Pierre Bardet, "Enfants abandonnés et enfants assistés à Rouen dans la seconde moitié du XVIIIe siècle," in Société de démographie historique, *Hommage à Marcel Reinhard: Sur la population française au XVIIIe et au XIXe siècles* (Paris, 1973), pp. 19–47; Alain Molinier, "Enfants trouvés, enfants abandonnés et enfants illégitimes en Languedoc aux XVIIe et XVIIIe siècles," ibid., pp. 445–73; Claude Delasselle, "Les enfants abandonnés à Paris au XVIIIe siècle," *Annales, E.S.C.* 30 (1975): 187–218; and Charles Engrand, "Les abandons d'enfants à Amiens vers la fin de l'Ancien Régime," *Revue du Nord* 64 (1982): 73–92.

will do it in time. But what can a father, sick for a long time and a mother similarly afflicted and weakened under the weight of these sorrows, do for us? You must realize how saddening it is for them to leave us.[69]

To the Directors of the hospice of Rouen . . . Sirs: Unhappy circumstances force us to leave this child at the hospice. We pray the director to have her cared for and educated as well as possible. It is a conspicuous favor that we will remember, to a family as honest as it is unfortunate, which vows to repay you for your care and to make our child a better position in the future.[70]

To the Administrators of the Hospice-Général of Rouen: It is with the greatest pain that I separate myself from my son, after the great suffering I have gone through to keep him in his present state. I fear that the winter will freeze him. Already he is suffering from hunger. This is why I give him up to your generous arms, to give him that which I cannot furnish. I hope that he will stay in this *maison générale,* and I hope to see him again as soon as I can take him back for good. I think that two years would be enough. He has been baptized. His name is Jean Penoux, son of Aimée Barbier, his mother.[71]

That the abandonment was only temporary was a recurrent theme, although Aimée Barbier was unusual in specifying the length of time she wished to have authorities keep her child. She was clearly misguided in her hope that he would be kept in the hospital. Like all of Rouen's foundlings, Jean Penoux would be sent out to a wet nurse, most probably in another arrondissement or department.[72]

These kinds of notes appear to have been intended to serve several purposes: to evoke the sympathy of hospital authorities by eloquent appeal to their compassion or to urge better care for their child by pointing out that he or she was of decent parents who were legitimately married. An indication by unwed mothers or parents that the child had been baptized expressed the same kind of concern. Important, too, were statements that parents or lone mothers were suffering greatly from an act of abandonment that was only temporary. Pieces of cloth or copies of the notes attached to the children were kept as evidence by the parents and hospital officials for the time when the child could

69. Hôpital-Général de Rouen, Commission administrative, "Délibérations," session of 19 January 1831, ADSM, 2 LP/81. This and the following citations are taken from records of meetings of the Hôpital-Général's administrative commission, which took place weekly except during September. Minutes noted the foundlings received since the previous meeting.

70. Ibid., session of 11 May 1831.

71. Ibid., session of 2 November 1831.

72. See note 100, below.

be reclaimed. Attempts to reclaim children were recorded in the deliberations of the administrative commission of Rouen's hospital. The record for the longest time between abandoning a child in the foundling home and attempting to reclaim it seems to have been held by a woman who had abandoned her legitimate child in 1812 and attempted to find him nineteen years later.[73]

Records of the administrative commission also revealed the intricacies of the networks that linked unwed mothers, midwives, and wet nurses in the area.

> Julie Lequesme, seamstress, rue Gerot, tried last week to reclaim a female child whom she had abandoned on 26 March 1830. It was recognized that this child had died on 18 April 1831 at the home of the woman Delarme. . . . After being convinced of her child's death, the girl Lequesme made the following declaration: that she had given birth on 22 March 1830 in the home of the woman Desforges, midwife, rue Prison, who demanded a sum of thirty francs to find the child again once it had been abandoned. Having agreed to this condition, the mother was . . . told by the midwife that the child had been placed at the home of the woman Duclos, commune of Bourneville, arrondissement of Pontaudemer [Eure]. . . . In fact, a child of the same sex and age as Lequesme's child [had been placed there]. Lequesme had been visiting her for two years, brought her a cradle as well as clothing, and seems to have made all the sacrifices which a mother imposes on herself in similar circumstances.[74]

The wet nurse was penalized for having deceived Lequesme and was denied any further charges from the Rouen foundling home.

As in the late eighteenth century, Rouen's Hôtel-Dieu also sent a large number of infants to the *tour*. These cases were no better documented than the majority of normal foundlings, perhaps because hospital authorities wished to help mothers remain anonymous.[75] Some of the most richly documented cases were those sent to Rouen's hospital by mayors of neighboring rural communes, sometimes in the neighboring department of the Eure, where the drama of illegitimacy ran high:

> The year 1831, the ninth of April, I, mayor of the commune of Vindrimaire, . . . department of the Eure, having been informed that a child had been abandoned at the home of Jean-Baptiste Blot, *cultivateur* in this commune, I went there and found a male child whom we believed to have

73. Session of 13 April 1831, ADSM, 2 LP/81.

74. Hôpital-Général de Rouen, Commission administrative, "Délibérations," session of 6 June 1832, ADSM, 2 LP/82.

75. On Rouen in the eighteenth century, see Bardet, "Enfants abandonnés," p. 21, and idem, *Rouen aux XVIIe et XVIIIe siècles: Les mutations d'un espace social* (Paris, 1983), 1: 331–46.

been born today. . . . We asked those present—Herbert Bonaire, Jacques Lebrain, and François Catteville, all three servants living at M. Blot's—if they knew where the baby came from. They responded that it was [the child of] Justine Rabot, a girl without domicile, who gave birth this morning at the home of M. Benoire, agricultural laborer in this commune; that she abandoned it there, saying to Catteville, "Look, here is the fruit of your love," and then she turned and fled. We asked Catteville, a married man, whether he recognized this fact, which he formally denied, after which I had the child removed and ordered it to be transported to the hospice of Rouen.[76]

There were other similar incidents recorded from rural communes in which the simple poverty of the unwed mother was cited by the local mayor as the cause for the child's being sent to Rouen.[77] The *tour* of Rouen also received another small group of children who were already dead, who had been born with physical disabilities, or who were born to mothers who were themselves physically or mentally deficient—observations that were duly noted in the registers.[78]

The very rich but limited information from Rouen's hospice tends to substantiate Catholics' insistence on the heterogeneous conditions—including poverty, sickness, and illegitimacy—that underlay the "foundling problem." The *tour* received illegitimate and legitimate children both rural and urban; handicapped children; children of women seduced and abandoned; and those sent by mayors of rural communes who had neither the means, the desire, nor the mandate to cope with them. One of the obvious problems of interpretation, however, is the inherent bias in any analysis based on records that actually indicated substantive information about the children, since whatever debauched and grasping parents there were would probably have deposited their infants without any notes attached, or concealed their true natures by expressing themselves in humble appeals to the philanthropy of hospital authorities.

Abandoned Children in Lille

The kind of information on abandoned children kept by the hospice of Lille is very different from that on Rouen's foundlings. It can be summarized more

76. Session of 11 April 1831, case 311, ADSM, 2 LP/81.

77. For an additional rural drama like the Catteville case, see session of 27 July 1836. For cases of impoverished rural mothers and their dependent infants, see, *inter alia,* sessions of 27 February 1828, 22 June 1831, 2 November 1836, and 10 February 1841, respectively in ADSM, 2 LP/79, 81, 86, 91.

78. Sessions of 5 January 1831 (child already dead); 8 and 29 June 1836 (child blind); 7 July 1841 (child with deformed legs); 12 May 1841 (mother "imbécile"), in ADSM, 2 LP/81, 86, 91 (for the two 1841 cases).

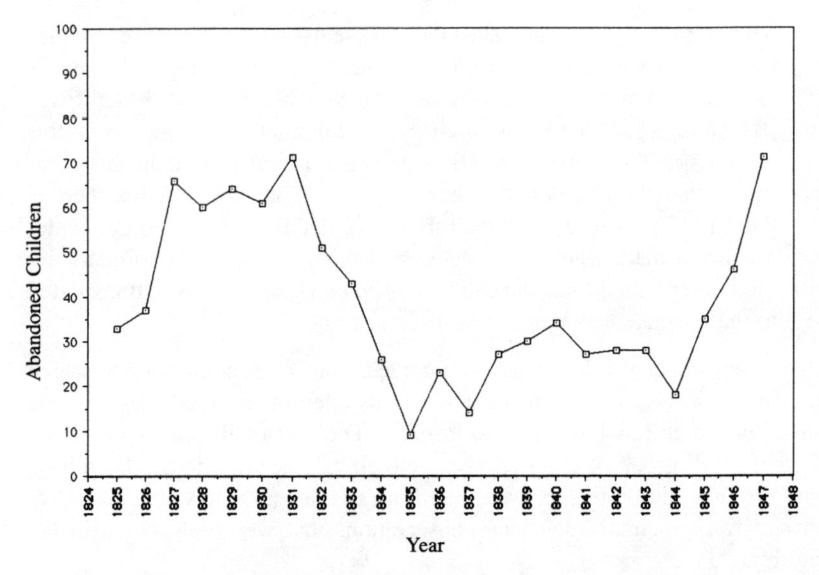

Figure 4.3 Number of Abandoned Children Received Annually, Lille, 1825–1847. Sources: AN, F15/982, 985, 987–88, 2529, 2540; Aimé Houzé de l'Aulnoit, *Enfants assistés: La question des tours* (Lille, 1879), appendix I.

easily but does not provide the same kind of rich historical detail offered by some of Rouen's cases. However, in the range of diverse circumstances that led to children's "abandonment," data on Lille's abandoned children echo findings from Rouen. Abandoned children, it will be recalled, were those whose parents' names were known and who fell into dependency as the result of their parents' disappearance or the inability of the public authorities to have recourse to them. Information on elements of their background is thus more complete. During 1825–47, a total of 902 abandoned children were received by the Hôpital-Général of Lille (see Fig. 4.3). Like foundlings in Rouen, their numbers tended to increase during times of general economic distress, as in the early 1830s and the late 1840s. Hospital records reveal that more than 59 percent of the children whose status was recorded were legitimately born. Although the children's legitimate status was insufficient to keep them from becoming dependents of the state, there were some interesting differences between the legitimate and illegitimate children received.

Four causes or combination of causes accounted for nearly 82.5 percent of the 354 cases of illegitimate abandoned children in Lille during these years, and for nearly 90 percent of those for whom information about causes of their abandonment is clear: the arrest, detention, or imprisonment of the mother; the mother's disappearance or absence; illness of the mother; and the death

Table 4.5. Causes Listed for the Entry of Illegitimate and Legitimate Children to the Rolls of Abandoned Children, Lille, 1825–1847

Cause[a]	Number of children	Percentage of total
Illegitimate Children		
Arrest, detention, or imprisonment of mother	159	44.9
Disappearance or absence of mother	67	18.9
Sickness (mental or physical) or hospitalization of mother	37	10.5
Death of mother	29	8.2
Other causes	44	12.4
Cause(s) unknown or unclear	18	5.1
Total	354	100.0
Legitimate Children		
Death of mother; disappearance or absence of father	117	22.5
Death of father; disappearance or absence of mother	89	17.1
Arrest, detention, or imprisonment of mother	77	14.8
Disappearance or absence of parents	40	7.7
Imprisonment of parents	31	6.0
Imprisonment of mother; disappearance or absence of father	22	4.2
Death of mother; imprisonment of father	14	2.7
Death of father; imprisonment of mother	12	2.3
Other causes	99	19.0
Cause(s) unknown or unclear	20	3.8
Total	521	100.1

Source: Enfants abandonnés, *Registres*, vols. 1–3, AHL, 4467–69.

[a]The listing of more than one cause indicates that both contributed to the child's condition, not that the first listed actually preceded the second in time.

of the mother (see Table 4.5). Causes listed for the reception of legitimate abandoned children were more diverse, entailing circumstances that usually involved both mother and father. The arrest, detention, or imprisonment of mothers led to "abandonment" of both illegitimate and legitimate children in two ways: either the child was taken into custody at the time of the mother's arrest or incarceration, or the child was born while the mother was actually in prison. The greater importance of arrest or imprisonment as a cause of illegitimate abandoned children suggests that pregnancy may have forced many of these women out of work, encouraging the kind of crimes for which they were sent to the Maison centrale de détention at Loos, on the outskirts of Lille, particularly begging, vagrancy, or petty theft. This argument is supported by information on the children's places of birth. Nearly 30 percent of illegitimate abandoned children received were born in Loos, while only a little over 10 percent of the legitimate children were born there (see Table 4.6). Beyond

Table 4.6. Birthplace of Abandoned Children Received, Hospice of Lille, 1825–1847

Place	Number and percentage of children by birth status[a]	
	Legitimate	Illegitimate
Lille[b]	307 (58.9%)	168 (47.4%)
Loos[c]	53 (10.2)	104 (29.4)
Nord[d]	87 (16.7)	41 (11.6)
Total Nord	447 (85.8)	313 (88.4)
Pas-de-Calais	18 (3.5)	7 (2.0)
Other departments	14 (2.7)	12 (3.4)
Belgium	21 (4.0)	8 (2.3)
Other foreign	2 (0.4)	0 (0)
Birthplace unknown	19 (3.6)	14 (4.0)
Grand total	521 (100.0)	354 (100.1)

Source: See Table 4.5.

[a]Percentage of each group's total in parentheses.

[b]Including suburbs of Wazemmes, Esquermes, Fives, and St. André-les-Lille.

[c]Location of the Maison centrale de détention.

[d]Excluding Lille and Loos.

this one difference, however, the birthplaces of illegitimate and legitimate abandoned children were distributed rather similarly. Eighty-five to eighty-eight percent had been born in the Nord, with small numbers from the Pas-de-Calais, other French departments, and Belgium.[79]

Illegitimate abandoned children were on average significantly younger than their legitimate counterparts (see Table 4.7). While 55.4 percent of illegitimate abandoned children were one year old or younger, the corresponding figure for legitimate children was only 18.3 percent. The youth of illegitimate abandoned children resulted in part from the fact that many of the illegitimate children were, so to speak, born "abandoned" in Loos as the result of their mothers' imprisonment. It is likely that for unwed mothers, pregnancy alone created a crisis, while the fate of legitimate children depended on those of both mothers and fathers. Thus, legitimate children seem to have been abandoned more as the result of crises that occurred after their births, while illegitimate

79. Authorities in the Nord were well aware that Belgian children were also being left in the city's *tour*. See the letter from the prefect to the minister of the interior, 16 September 1825, AN, F15/983, and conseil général du Nord, "Délibérations," session of 1829, p. 20, ADN, N2/16.

Table 4.7. "Age" Structure of Population of Abandoned Children, Lille, 1825–1847, by Birth Status

"Age"[b] (in years)	Number and cumulative percentage of children by birth status[a]	
	Legitimate	Illegitimate
< 1	64 (12.3%)	155 (44.0%)
1	31 (18.3)	40 (55.4)
2	30 (24.1)	13 (59.1)
3	32 (30.3)	21 (65.1)
4	32 (36.4)	8 (67.3)
5	35 (43.2)	15 (71.6)
6	36 (50.1)	21 (77.6)
7	42 (58.2)	18 (82.7)
8	38 (65.5)	11 (85.8)
9	43 (73.8)	17 (90.6)
10	41 (81.7)	16 (95.2)
11	25 (86.5)	6 (96.9)
12	27 (91.7)	6 (98.6)
13	17 (95.0)	2 (99.1)
14	13 (97.5)	2 (99.7)
15	4 (98.3)	1 (100.0)
16+	9 (100.0)	
Total	519[c]	352[c]

Source: See Table 4.5.

[a]Cumulative percentages of each category's total in parentheses.

[b]The registers do not indicate true age but only the year of birth and the year of entry into the hospital. "Age" thus refers to the year of reception minus the year of birth. Children received in the calendar year of their birth are thus counted as under age one.

[c]Each group has 2 children with no "age" listed.

children were themselves frequently the cause of a crisis situation in the lives of their mothers.

The limited information on the occupations of parents of abandoned children in Lille confirms what has already been implied in the discussion of Rouen's foundlings—that is, the diversity of lower-class groups that contributed to the problem. A rank order of occupations of mothers of abandoned children shows the importance of day laborers (54) and women in the traditional occupations of dressmaking (37), lacemaking (24), and domestic service (17), while other textile trades (spinners, winders, folders) contributed a total of 14 cases. Even sparser data on the occupations of fathers indicate a wide variety of working-class occupations. The largest number of fathers listed were day laborers (13), workers (11), and weavers (10). The heterogeneity of occupations of parents of abandoned children suggests that workers in the newer industrial sectors were not especially implicated in the diverse human problems that created abandoned children.[80]

Diversity is also a feature of the data on causes of abandonment, even within the categories constructed for Table 4.5. The category "disappearance or absence" of mother, father, or parents may be used as an example. It includes parents who left a child with a wet nurse and were never heard from again; fathers or mothers who had migrated to other communities and were not in the city when something (sickness, hospitalization, death) happened to the remaining spouse; fathers who were in the military when something happened to the mother; and parents who actually abandoned their children on the high road. It should be noted, however, that the last group was a small minority.

Thus, it seems clear that illegitimate children were likely to become dependent on public sources of support in part because of the lack of a second parent to share responsibility for them. However, data from both Rouen and Lille illustrate that the mere fact of having a father was not sufficient to keep a legitimate child from becoming a ward of the state when general economic crisis, the father's absence from the city, or the inevitabilities of sickness and death affected individual couples.

Policies toward Abandoned Children in the Mulhouse Area

Some very limited information on the treatment of abandoned children in the Mulhouse area illustrates how the use of defensive strategies by local officials helped to keep the numbers of dependent children there very small. Besides being unwilling to receive foundlings, local administrators in the Haut-Rhin, including those of Mulhouse, battled to avoid responsibility for abandoned children who were not indigenous to their communities or domiciled there. Several incidents exemplified this state of mind. One case involved a six-year-old child named Jacques David. Jacques had left Mulhouse with his father, a weaver in search of work. Several months later, Jacques and his father returned to the city, unbeknownst to Jacques' twenty-year-old sister, who had remained. The child was found alone on the road just outside the city by a woman who made her own efforts to discover who he was. She took Jacques to her husband's workplace, Blech Fries spinning and weaving mills, "to see if anyone recognized him." He was identified by one of the overseers there, and his sister was called in to confirm his identity. The mayor of Mulhouse

80. Occupations were listed for only 39 of the mothers of legitimate children and for 156 of the mothers of illegitimate children. Enfants abandonnés, *Registres*, vols. 1–3, AHL, 4467–69. Totals cited refer to all mothers, including those of children whose birth status is unknown or unclear.

immediately sent Jacques to the subprefect of Altkirch, who tried to have him admitted to the care of the hospice there. The mayor of Altkirch, however, objected that Jacques couldn't be received "because of the precarious financial situation of the hospice." He added: "I am astounded by the haste with which the mayor of Mulhouse tries to rid himself of the children left in his city, which has a richly endowed hospital, to put them in the care of one that is barely surviving. I confess, with sorrow, that this conduct does not demonstrate feelings of humanity that I expected from the city of Mulhouse. . . . Already [they] have sent us two of these poor creatures." In a letter to the prefect, the subprefect of Altkirch agreed: "In these circumstances [the mayor's] actions do not conform to the feelings of humanity or philanthropy that should inform such a paternal municipal administration. . . . The hasty dismissal of these unhappy children . . . [shows] a kind of cruelty, indifference, and selfishness which have revolted me."[81]

In a later effort to convince the city of Mulhouse to take more responsibility for the arrondissement's dependent children, the subprefect of Altkirch asked the mayor of Mulhouse about the possibility of shifting the arrondissement's foundling administration from the city of Altkirch's hospital to Mulhouse's, a suggestion that was vigorously rejected.[82] The city administration, like many others in the Haut-Rhin, reserved its relief efforts for its citizens. In the case of orphans of parents born in the city, the administration was felt to have an obligation of support. An 1836 letter to the administrators of the city's orphans referred to the case of three children of Frédéric Stiedler. Stiedler, a worker, had abandoned his wife and three children, and the mother had subsequently died. Inquiries among his former employers showed that Stiedler had committed a number of thefts and was not the kind of person whom the city administration would want to bring back to support his children. The children's entitlement to support from the city was evoked on the basis of their parents' having been born there.[83]

Understanding the wide diversity of human situations that led to foundlings and abandoned children makes it easier to comprehend why moral economists and administrators sympathetic to their views began to concentrate so much of their analysis on the final rather than the contributing causes of found-

81. All correspondence on this affair, which occurred in 1833, is contained in ADHR, 1X/76. See also the conflict between the mayors of Mulhouse and the neighboring commune of Dornach concerning the fate of the Schaltenbrand children.

82. Subprefect of Altkirch to the prefect of the Haut-Rhin, 25 May 1847, ADHR, 1X/91. The nonexistence of foundlings in Mulhouse was noted in Achille Penot, *Recherches statistiques sur Mulhouse* (Mulhouse, 1843), p. 64.

83. The letter, by an unidentified source, recounting this set of circumstances is dated 22 August 1836, AMM, Q III/Fa5. Regulations of the city's hospital, which reserved its services to indigenous citizens, are contained in AMM, Q I/Aa12, from 11 February 1841.

lings and abandoned children. Records suggest that what caused foundlings and abandoned children were the conditions of working-class life itself. Had moral economists been willing to entertain this fact, as Catholic commentators did, they would doubtless have been thwarted in what came to be the central government's main policy objective—to reduce the number of children. Concentrating on the final rather than the contributory causes of the problem enabled moral economists and their supporters within the administration to forge ahead with policy solutions that conformed both to administrative exigencies and to the sociopsychological model of causation they had constructed.

Policy Reform: Old Elements and New

Policies based on a moral economist perspective that explained the foundling problem essentially by reference to the value system and mores of parents were quite logically designed to prohibit the behavior to which those values gave rise. In this effort, new policies were sometimes combined with those of longer standing, whose goal was to discourage mothers from abandoning their children by eliminating any possible contact between them and their infants once the children had been left in the *tour*. Mothers were to be convinced that abandonment was a definitive and not merely a temporary break in their relations.

One of the older strategies that was used not only in France but in England and Belgium as well was the attribution of new names to foundlings who had been received in the *tour,* including children whose names were indicated on notes left with them.[84] Charles Dickens portrayed this policy, which in England was incumbent on the "porochial beadle." In the following dialogue with an admiring bystander, one of England's beadles, Mr. Bumble, recounted the tale of a well-known foundling.

> "We have never been able to discover who is his father, or what was his mother's settlement, name, or condition."
>
> "How comes he to have any name at all, then ?"
>
> . . . "I inwented it."
>
> "You, Mr. Bumble !"
>
> "I, Mrs. Mann. We name our foundlings in alphabetical order. The last was a S,—Swubble, I named him. This was a T,—Twist, I named *him*. The next one as comes will be Unwin, and the next Vilkins. I have got

84. This was the practice in Rouen and Bordeaux. On Bordeaux, see Derbigny, *Analyse raisonnée*, pp. 55–56; on Belgium, Hélin, "Une sollicitude," p. 226.

names ready made to the end of the alphabet, and all the way through it again, when we come to Z." [85]

Although renaming foundlings was part of a policy intended to limit abuses of the prevailing system of aid, its implementation was one of the reasons that the abandonment of legitimate children to the *tour* evoked such horror, particularly among moral economists. That foundlings literally lost their names meant that they thereby lost all rights to inheritance.

However, parents were apparently able to circumvent such administrative rules, leading as early as the mid-1820s to more aggressive efforts on the part of the ministry of the interior to repress fraud in foundling services. Particular attention was paid to ensuring both that wet nurses did not attempt to substitute other infants for foundlings sent to them by urban hospitals and that infants were placed with wet nurses far enough away from the hospitals where they had been received so that mothers could have no contact with them.[86] The ministry's decision to send outside inspectors to various departments to ensure that such regulations were being followed was made by the central government on its own or as a result of requests by prefects and conseils généraux, since it was quite obvious to many of them that local hospital administrators and, even more so, their staffs could not be counted on to maintain services to foundlings that avoided such abuses.[87]

These inspections usually succeeded in reducing the numbers of children. The arrival of an inspector in the Nord in 1827 was preceded by rumors planted by the departmental administration into the information networks which they had always deplored, proclaiming that wards of the different hospitals in the department were to be exchanged so that they would be beyond the easy reach

85. Charles Dickens, *Oliver Twist* (London, 1966), pp. 51–52. The Rouen administration was as "inwentive" as Mr. Bumble, using the same alphabetical system for assigning names to foundlings who were left without an indication of their names, and reassigning names to those whose given names were indicated. On the policy of Parisian authorities, see Fuchs, *Abandoned Children*, pp. 120–21.

86. Circular from the minister of the interior to prefects, 20 July 1828, AN, F15/145. The circular referred to previous letters on these two issues, of 20 May 1826 and 21 July 1827. Foundlings were required as early as 1818 to wear an identifying necklace that could not be removed. Some hospitals, including Rouen's hospices, had had such regulations under the Old Regime. Others, however, apparently never did comply with this order. Examples of these necklaces are contained in AN, F15/2531, and depicted in Fuchs, *Abandoned Children*, p. 123. The 1828 circular also set up an inspectorate of hospices, *bureaux de bienfaisance*, and *enfants trouvés*.

87. Complaints about the relative indulgence of local hospital administrators were referred to as early as an undated letter from the *3e division*, Bureau des secours et hôpitaux to the minister of the interior in preparation of the decree of 1811, AN, F15/2533. One later commentator saw hospital commissions in many areas as a "permanent obstacle" to thoroughgoing reforms of foundling administration. See Bondy, *Mémoire*, p. 12.

of mothers who wished to maintain contact with them.[88] As a result of this inspection, over 25 percent of the department's foundlings and abandoned children were claimed either by nurses or parents. The inspection also revealed that most of the children taken off the rolls were children of poor mothers who were serving as nurses for them.[89] However, there were important intradepartmental variations in the number of children claimed. While 87.5 percent of the children from Dunkerque's hospital were reclaimed by their parents, nearly all of them (449 of 513) legitimate children, the corresponding figure for Lille's hospital was only 4.5 percent (61 of 1,365), nearly all of whom were adopted by their nurses. The inspector of foundling services, M. Wallut, attributed Lille's smaller decrease to the fact that the city's hospital services "were well-organized . . . that all precautions had been taken to conceal from parents the name of the commune where [their children] had been placed."[90] The possibility also exists, however, that the mothers of Lille's foundlings were financially unable to reclaim their children. Over the ten-year period from the mid-1820s to the mid-1830s, figures showed that Lille and Rouen's foundlings and abandoned children from Lille and Rouen were generally less likely to be claimed by parents or wet nurses than the foundling populations from other hospitals in their respective departments (see Table 4.8). One commentator on Rouen's foundlings noted that the small number of parents or guardians who claimed the children, particularly the foundlings, "attests only too well to the fact that mothers who abandon their children make a total sacrifice."[91]

Whether and how to permit parents to take back their children had been a problem since the institution of the 1811 decree. Article 21 of the decree

88. The parsimonious conseil général of the Nord refused to vote funds to pay for the 1827 inspection, which was funded by the Ministry of the Interior itself. See Préfecture du Nord, session of 1827, "Rapport fait au conseil général: Enfants trouvés et abandonnés," AN, F15/986.

89. The total number of children taken off the rolls was 1,006 of 3,904 children. See Préfecture du Nord, "Enfants trouvés et abandonnés," service de 1833, AN, F15/2540, and prefect of the Nord to the minister of the interior, 5 October 1827, AN, F15/986. The prefect added that the only way such an abuse could be remedied was by the actual transfer of foundlings to distant departments, since it was always liable to reoccur.

90. Prefect of the Nord to minister of the interior, 5 October 1827, AN, F15/986; M. Wallut to the prefect, 9 August 1827, ADN, X4/1. Wallut believed, however, that an additional 150–200 of Lille's children could be stricken from the rolls "by giving a great deal of publicity to the repressive measures that must be taken." Wallut's upcoming visit to the Seine-Inférieure was also noted in the register of the Hôpital-général of Rouen's administrative commission deliberations. All wet nurses were to be notified that children were going to be exchanged with those in other departments unless parents or nurses adopted them. See Hôpital-Général de Rouen, Commission administrative, "Délibérations," session of 19 December 1827, ADSM, 2 LP/77.

91. Lelong, *Rapport*, p. 17. The same source, pp. 30–31, noted that of the wards of the hospital of Rouen who were reclaimed by their parents in 1829–34, 47% were legitimate children.

Table 4.8. Foundlings and Abandoned Children Reclaimed by Parents or Others, Lille and the Nord, Rouen and the Seine-Inférieure, 1824–1835

Place	Foundlings		Abandoned children	
	Total number received	Number and percentage reclaimed	Total number received	Number and percentage reclaimed
Lille	2,509	157 (6.3)	349	59 (16.9)
Nord[a]	5,129	653 (12.7)	573	159 (27.7)
Total Nord	7,638	810 (10.6)	922	218 (23.6)
Rouen	6,336	472 (7.4)	266	52 (19.5)
Seine-Inférieure[b]	1,699	316 (18.6)	168	129 (76.8)
Total Seine-Inférieure	8,035	788 (9.8)	434	181 (41.7)

Source: See Table 4.3.

Note: "Reclaimed" in the archival sources is followed by "by their parents." However, these figures also include children adopted by their nurses and others. Data for Lille and the Nord are for 1824–30 and 1833–35; data for Rouen and the Seine-Inférieure are for 1824–30, 1832, and 1835.

[a]Excluding Lille.

[b]Excluding Rouen.

had stated the obligation of parents who reclaimed their children to reimburse the administration if they were able. In practice, the central administration seems to have been quite lenient in giving children back at no charge, since a strict enforcement of the article would have failed to take advantage of an opportunity to have the children removed from the rolls.[92] Under the July Monarchy, benevolent persons including the duchesse d'Orléans contributed funds towards this cause. On the occasion of her marriage, she contributed 10,000 francs via the Ministry of the Interior to pay for clothing for children who were to be returned to their parents without charge by various departments. Over one-half of these funds went to the departments of the Seine and Rhône, with the Nord receiving 800 francs and the Seine-Inférieure 405 francs.[93] The gift of the duchess also illustrated that royal traditions had not entirely disappeared, even though expressions of beneficence were increasingly believed to be a cause of rather than a solution to the foundling problem.

92. See the Directeur général de l'administration des communes, hôpitaux et octrois to prefects, 17 November 1813, AN, F15/2533. Rouen's hospital administration returned some children to their parents at no charge, but received indemnities from others. Hôpital-Général de Rouen, Commission administrative, "Délibérations," meetings of 15 October 1828, 9 March, 13 April, 22 June, and 27 July 1831, ADSM, 2 LP/78, 81.

93. "Rapport à M. le Ministre Secrétaire d'Etat au département de l'Intérieur," 8 June 1837, and "Note pour S.A. Royale Mme. la duchesse d'Orléans . . . ," AN, F15/146–47.

There was also a certain contradiction between basic practices of foundling administration and the desire of administrators and inspectors to stimulate the reclaiming of children. On the one hand, efforts to conceal children's whereabouts from their mothers were believed to deter mothers from abandoning their children. But on the other hand, when mothers were denied any contact with their children, they were apparently less likely to reclaim them when the departmental administration wished them to do so.[94]

In any case, the effect of inspections was only temporary, and they had to be repeated. In 1830, the prefect of the Nord explained that the conseil général had to raise the level of funding for foundlings again because abuses ended by the 1827 inspection had already returned.[95] In the middle of the 1830s, when the number of foundlings in the Nord was holding steady, the prefect urged the central administration to send another inspector.[96] In 1834, he was again complaining that foundling services in the Nord were in the same state that they had been before the 1827 inspection, both as a result of the return of abuses within the service and because of a new downturn in economic conditions in the department.[97]

Foundling Exchanges

Inspections did succeed in encouraging parents to reclaim their children and in reducing the proportion of legitimate children in foundling populations. Moreover, although they were only temporary palliatives, inspections of foundling services strongly confirmed moral economists' analysis of the foundling problem and led directly to a more aggressive administrative strategy of coordinating a policy of exchanges of foundlings within different arrondissements of individual departments or among departments. As in the past, the goal was to encourage mothers to take back children whom they had abandoned or, secondarily, to convince wet nurses to adopt them. Interestingly enough, this strategy was based on an administrative wager that maternal love, whose demise moral economists had previously lamented, would be sufficient to encourage either biological or adoptive mothers to claim the children. The prefect of the Nord expressed his belief that since "maternal love never loses its entire hold on mothers, we think that they will resolve to abandon their chil-

94. Esquiros, *Paris*, 2:315–16.

95. Prefect of the Nord to the minister of commerce and public works, 30 June 1830 (?), AN, F15/2529.

96. Prefect of the Nord to the minister of the interior, 31 October 1834, AN, F15/2540. This letter mentions the reestablishment of the inspectorate as of 15 March 1834, which had apparently lapsed in the interim. See also prefect of the Haut-Rhin to the minister of the interior, 5 January 1836, AN, F15/2541.

97. Préfecture du Nord, "Enfants trouvés et abandonnés," service de 1833, AN, F15/2540.

dren . . . with much greater difficulty if they cannot hope to be able to follow and look out for them at the homes of [their] wet nurses. . . . We saw with what haste children were taken back by their parents during the inspection of 1827, when we spread the rumor of an upcoming exchange with departments far away."[98] Exchanges of foundlings and abandoned children were pursued throughout France, particularly in the years 1834–37, yielding the desired administrative results. Of 36,493 children in thirty-one departments involved in the transfers, 16,339 were either reclaimed by parents or adopted by the families in which they were living or by other "charitable persons."[99] In 1838, after the exchanges, the national foundling population was reduced to 95,624, the lowest figure since 1817. The prefect of the Seine-Inférieure believed that his services for foundlings and abandoned children did not require drastic intervention, since children there had for many years routinely been sent to nurses outside the area where they had been abandoned.[100] He did order some transfers during the good weather, but these led to only two children from Rouen's hospital being reclaimed by their parents.[101] The Haut-Rhin was characteristically unaffected by the policy, the prefect admitting quite freely to the minister of the interior that he had ignored circulars advising such a strategy since the late 1820s because they were simply not needed.[102]

In the Nord, however, transfers of children succeeded in reducing the number of foundlings and abandoned children both by encouraging parents or guardians to claim the children and by increasing mortality. During exchanges in 1836–37, for example, the administration effected a 50 percent reduction in their numbers, from 3,800 on 1 July 1836 and 2,638 on 1 January 1837, to 1,952 on 31 December 1837. During the two years of the exchange, a total of 551 children were reclaimed by their parents, which contrasted with a normal

98. Conseil général du Nord, "Délibérations," session of 1829, p. 71, ADN, N2/16. See also session of 1838, AN, F15/3896: "As soon as mothers are certain that children deposited in *tours* will be sent far away immediately, that by leaving their child they will be unable to ascertain the hospital where it has been sent and must remain in total ignorance of its whereabouts, surely many of them will hesitate to leave their children. . . . In this way we will no longer have frauds and our foundling population . . . will tend to decline."

99. *Rapport au Roi*, pp. 69–70. A later, unofficial source indicated a figure of 32,608 children affected by exchanges that involved sixty departments between 1827 and 1839. Laget, "Extrait," p. 17. See also Shorter, *The Making of the Modern Family*, p. 187.

100. Préfecture du département de la Seine-Inférieure, session of 1836, "Rapport du préfet au conseil général," AN, F15/3897. Rouen's children were sent to the arrondissements of Pontaudemer and Neufchâtel, and from there to the departments of the Somme, Oise, Eure, and Calvados. The Parisian hospice had long followed the same kind of strategy. See Fuchs, *Abandoned Children*, p. 41.

101. Commission administrative des hospices de Rouen to the prefect, 8 July 1836, and prefect to same, 13 June 1836, ADSM, 1 XP/260.

102. Prefect of the Haut-Rhin to the minister of the interior, 5 January 1836, AN, F15/2541.

number of approximately 90 per year. The prefect also credited the exchanges with lowering the 1837 figure of children received to 606 for the department as a whole, where in the past there had been 800–1,000 annually.[103]

Figures on mortality during exchanges in the Nord are difficult to pin down, since the minister of the interior demanded information on mortality only during the month that the children were actually exchanged. The prefect informed the minister that only 35 of the 1,424 exchanged had died, representing an excess of mortality two to three times over monthly age-specific mortality in normal years. However, the prefect of the Nord believed that the numbers were too small to make any firm judgments about this aspect of the exchange's impact.[104] As the result of transfers in the Nord, children were claimed by their mothers, but primarily by their nurses.[105]

The minister of the interior was clearly concerned with gathering information from prefects about the effects of this large-scale foundling transfer. He forwarded a circular to each one concerning mortality and the effects of the transfers on the children and on public opinion in the areas affected.[106] He was prepared for the kind of public reaction which the foundling transfers evoked. In fact, reaction came from predictable quarters, reaching the floor of the Chamber of Deputies in 1838 in the course of discussions on the budget. Lamartine threw down the gauntlet on the issue. Reviewing arguments that defended the obligation of the French state to come to the aid of foundlings and abandoned children, he admitted that there were parents of legitimate children who abused the *tour*. However, he reserved his greatest wrath for "this refined barbarism of exchanges, one of the cruelest inventions of our administrative genius, which takes numbers as morality, treats humans like objects and human feelings as quantities. . . . When [adoptive] fathers, mothers, and children resist being separated, you send gendarmes to force them and drive [the children] in convoys from one province to another like criminals guilty

103. All figures and comments on this exchange are contained in a letter from the prefect of the Nord to the minister of the interior, 10 October 1838, AN, F15/3896.

104. Of the children exchanged, 27.6% were under age three, 40% were ages three to six years, 21.6% from six to nine years, and 10.7% from nine to twelve. The minutes of the conseil général contain an undocumented reference to a 19% mortality figure for children involved in the exchanges. Conseil général du Nord, "Délibérations," meeting of 4 September 1839, p. 66, ADN, 2152(1–4).

105. The prefect explained that the relatively small number of mothers who reclaimed their children resulted from the fact that the mothers were domestics or Belgian women who had returned to their country of origin, an explanation rather different from those he had offered previously. Nurses' willingness to adopt foundlings for whom they were caring has been cited by Edward Shorter as evidence for the nurses' adoption of "modern" notions of motherhood. *The Making of the Modern Family*, pp. 186–88.

106. The circular was dated 27 July 1838 and is referred to in the prefect of the Nord's letter to the minister of the interior of 10 October 1838, AN, F15/3896.

of being born [and] of becoming attached to the fathers and mothers you had given them."[107] Some administrators were scornful of reactions such as Lamartine's, arguing that it was naive for people to feel guilty about separating foundlings from their nurses: "Concerning the sum of affection of which some observers find these children deprived when they change residence, one must have strange illusions about the facts. . . . The miserable physical and moral state of the [children] before the transfers reduces these fears to their true value."[108] However, these administrators did have to admit that some of the children had been affected by their transfer: "We cannot deny that some children experienced a great impression of moral [shock] when they were brought back to the hospitals to be exchanged and separated from their first trustees. There were some touching scenes. But generally these feelings did not last long. No one has reported any adverse effects produced on the children as a result of the breaking-off of their affections."[109] Speaking in the Chamber of Deputies, M. Dupin countered criticisms of the exchange policy, scoffing at the notion that children were suffering unduly. To claims that families were being broken up, he pointed out that most of the children were too young to feel the separation. "Among children of three or four years, nostalgia does not exist."[110]

In their effort to solve the foundling problem as it was now constructed, the central and regional administrations had followed a course of action that flowed logically from their analysis of the causes of the problem. In so doing, however, they aroused at least the distaste of large segments of bourgeois opinion.[111] Although many middle-class Frenchmen doubtless concurred with key elements of the moral economist perspective, including its emphasis on the misuse of foundling services by self-interested parents, they were shocked

107. *Moniteur*, 31 May 1838, p. 1467. Lamartine's advocacy of aid to foundlings within the conseil général of the Saône-et-Loire is discussed in William Fortescue, *Alphonse de Lamartine: A Political Biography* (London, 1983), pp. 87–88. Fortescue hypothesizes that Lamartine's defense of the interests of foundlings stemmed from the poet-legislator's guilt over his own illegitimate children. It seems likely that the piety of Lamartine's mother, alluded to in Chapter 3, note 97, and the fact that his only legitimate child died very young also exerted some influence. His stance on this issue was entirely consistent with what was admittedly a ideologically eclectic political career. On Lamartine's attitude towards the foundling problem, see also Ethel Harris, *Lamartine et le peuple* (Paris, 1932), pp. 180–89 and Paul Bert, *Lamartine, "Homme social": Son action dans la région natale* (Paris, 1947), pp. 92–99.

108. Conseil général du Nord, "Délibérations," meeting of 4 September 1839, p. 68, ADN, 2152(1–4).

109. Prefect of the Nord to minister of the interior, 10 October 1838, AN, F15/3896.

110. *Moniteur*, 31 May 1838, p. 1469. This Dupin, a noted attorney and deputy, was the older brother of Baron Charles Dupin.

111. Laget, "Extrait," p. 18; Eugène Buret, *De la misère des classes laborieuses en Angleterre et en France* . . . (Paris, 1840), 1:418–19.

by this aggressive administrative solution based on it. Lamartine had raised an important issue in arguing that foundling exchanges disrupted the only opportunity that many of the children had for some kind of family life. His critique of the exchanges stemmed, in fact, from their anti-family excesses. His adversaries, on the other hand, argued that they were defending the interests of the family by attempting to reduce abandonments in the first place, or at the outer limit by using exchanges to encourage adoptions by wet nurses or the reclaiming of children by parents. For them, the pro-family ends justified the rather distasteful means required to forward them.

Catholic opinion was not to be thwarted quite so easily in its criticism of exchanges. Opponents pointed to evidence that while the immediate effect of the policy was to increase adoptions and the taking-back of children by parents, these effects were only short-lived. Soon after exchanges took place, the primary structural financial problems of caring for the children resumed, and the same children found themselves abandoned again.[112] Whether because of the publicity of the exchanges, Lamartine's eloquence in the Chamber of Deputies, or the repugnance of a significant segment of public opinion, this administrative strategy appears not to have been used again on a large scale after the mid-1830s. However, one of the immediate effects of the exchange strategy and opposition to it was to stimulate the search for an alternative to the system of *tours* provided for in the 1811 decree.

Tour Closings and the Search for New Administrative Solutions

Although sources disagree on the exact number of *tours* closed or modified during the 1830s, they concur in viewing the middle of the 1830s as the beginning of a general trend in this direction. Of an original 250 *tours* established in 273 receiving hospitals as the result of the 1811 decree, 35 were closed between 1823 and 1834, and 73 in the years 1835–37.[113] By 1848, there were 65 *tours* remaining in 48 departments.[114] These figures are difficult to interpret, since even when the name was retained, the nature of the *tour*'s services could

112. In the Nord, for example, the number of foundlings rebounded from 1,952 at the end of 1837 to 2,009 in 1838 and 2,130 in 1839. Conseil général du Nord, "Délibérations," meeting of 31 August 1840, pp. 65–66, ADN, 2152(1–4). That exchanges were only a temporary palliative was discussed in the meeting of 4 September 1839, p. 66, ADN, 2152(1–4).

113. Léon Lallemand, *La question des enfants abandonnés et délaissés au XIXe siècle* (Paris, 1885), p. 19.

114. Laget, "Extrait," pp. 18–21. At this date, there were a total of 141 of the original 273 receiving hospitals still in existence, 76 of which had no *tours*. See the statistical discussion in Baron Ad. de Watteville, *Statistique des établissements de bienfaisance: Rapport à M. le Ministre de l'Intérieur sur la situation administrative, morale et financière du service des enfants trouvés et abandonnés* (Paris, 1849), p. 14.

change. The general trend was to restrict hours of the *tours*' operation and/ or to require identification of children and the adults who brought them to the hospital.[115]

Closing *tours* was not a neat, surgical process. Disagreements still lingered at the local level, leading to fits and starts in implementing such a policy. While some sought a wholesale closure of the institutions, others remained unconvinced of the desirability of such a radical policy. The prefect of the Seine-Inférieure, in contrast to members of the conseil général, was opposed to the wholesale closure of *tours,* although he supported the goals that closure was designed to fulfill: "to obligate unmarried women and families to retain the children [in order] to maintain family ties which create society's morality," and secondly, to diminish expenses.[116] Although *tour* closings in adjacent departments put greater pressure on those in the Seine-Inférieure that remained open, the prefect confessed his own belief that the large majority of foundling cases came from women who would be unable to raise the children.[117] Despite the prefect's opinion, the conseil général voted in 1839 to close one of the department's three *tours,* the one in Dieppe, then went back on its ruling and temporarily compromised by leaving the facility open only during daylight hours.[118] By 1847, however, the *tours* of Dieppe and LeHavre had been closed, leaving Rouen's as the only one in the department.[119] After that date, children were still received, but without the cover of anonymity. The vice-president of Rouen's hospital administration in the early 1850s argued that the greater restrictiveness of this new policy at Rouen's *tour* meant that the children received after its implementation were very likely to be in poor health. When

115. For a discussion of these kinds of changes in the *tour* of Amiens, see R. Burr Litchfield and David Gordon, "Closing the 'Tour': A Close Look at the Marriage Market, Unwed Mothers, and Abandoned Children in Mid-Nineteenth-Century Amiens," *Journal of Social History* 13 (1980): 467–69.

116. Conseil général de la Seine-Inférieure, "Délibérations," 1840, p. 18, ADSM, 1 NP/ 24. The prefect also noted here that there had been more departmental funds spent on foundlings in Year XII, 1809, and 1810 than in 1839.

117. The prefect expressed his own belief that 5/7 of foundlings belonged to prostitutes, 1/7 to domestics who had succeeded in concealing their pregnancy, and 1/7 to poor families. For the first two groups, closing *tours* would have no effect in stimulating the creation of more stable family bonds. See Conseil général de la Seine-Inférieure, "Délibérations," 1840, p. 19, ADSM, 1 NP/ 24. These proportions were later cited in M. L. Nepveur, *De la condition physique et morale des enfants trouvés au XIXe siècle: Observations adressées au conseil général de la Seine-Inférieure* (Rouen, 1849), pp. 9–10.

118. Conseil général de la Seine-Inférieure, "Délibérations," 1839, p. 79; 1840, p. 120; 1843, p. 200; 1846, pp. 158–59, ADSM, 1 NP/23, 24, 27, 30.

119. Ibid., 1847, pp. 191, 323; 1848, pp. 273–78, ADSM, 1 NP/31–32. The prefect announced the imminent closure of Rouen's *tour* in the session of 1847, but reconsidered his decision. The city's *tour* remained open until 1860, though the anonymity of the person leaving the child was no longer guaranteed. See Shorter, *The Making of the Modern Family*, p. 195.

admissions were easier, he argued, hospitals had received children from much better backgrounds.[120]

By a decree of 17 December 1839, the prefect of the Nord ordered that beginning on 1 January 1840, infants there would be admitted to departmental aid only provisionally until an investigation of their background could be accomplished.[121] Lille's *tour* was closed as of 1 January 1842, and by 1844, there were none in the Nord, despite pleas from Lille's municipal administration, which wished the city's institution reopened.[122]

In the midst of this trend, Social Catholics continued to support the obligation of French society to dependent children, but they began to retrench somewhat on the *tour* question. They were unable, for example, to counter the moral economist argument that Saint Vincent-de-Paul himself had never used such a means to help care for foundlings and that a great many more deaths of children occurred as a result of being left in the *tour* than as a result of infanticide.[123] On the floor of the Chamber of Deputies, the minister of the interior ridiculed the idea of speaking of Vincent-de-Paul's and Napoleon's policies on foundlings in the same breath.[124] Exposing the crypto-populationist and militaristic motives of Napoleon's *tour* policy became the order of the day.[125] Beyond these features of the 1811 decree, critics could also point out that it

120. M. L. Nepveur, *De la mortalité des enfants trouvés en France et à Rouen en particulier* (Rouen, 1851), pp. 13–14.

121. Mayors of cities where the *tours* existed furnished the departmental administration with the birth certificates of illegitimate children and reception notices from their hospices, which served as evidence in the investigations, the prefect having final say on admissions to aid. Conseil général du Nord, "Délibérations," meeting of 31 August 1840, p. 67, ADN, 2152(1–4).

122. Ibid., meeting of 2 September 1844, ADN, 2152(5–8). A long, detailed report to the conseil général argued against the desire of the city council by laying out the principal moral economist arguments. See "Rapport sur les enfants trouvés et abandonnés fait au conseil général . . . dans la session de 1844," ADN, 2152(5–8); Houzé de l'Aulnoit, *Enfants assistés*, pp. 5–6; and Watteville, *Du sort*, pp. 39–41. One of the consequences of the closing of the *tour* in Lille was that mothers now had to pay to have their infants transported to other institutions in France and Belgium. Pierre Pierrard, *La vie ouvrière à Lille sous le second Empire* (Paris, 1965), pp. 124–25.

123. On Saint Vincent-de-Paul, see Conseil général de la Seine-Inférieure, "Délibérations," 1838, p. 81, ADSM, 1 NP/22. This point is also brought out in Adolphe Baudon, *De la suppression des tours d'enfants trouvés*, Extrait du *Correspondant* (Paris, 1847), p. 3.

124. *Moniteur*, 31 May 1838, p. 1467. He mocked: "A moment ago, someone [Lamartine] interspersed recollections of Napoleon and Saint Vincent-de-Paul. Sirs, these men proceeded in different ways." The reporter noted that the minister's remarks evoked "hilarité."

125. The relevant articles of the 1811 decree read: "At six years, as many children as possible will be boarded in the homes of farmers or artisans. The price of board will diminish each year to age twelve, when all male children able to serve will be placed at the disposition of the minister of the navy." (title IV, art. 9); "The said children raised at the state's expense are entirely at its disposition. And when the minister of the navy [wishes to] dispose of them, the tutelage of the administrative commissions [of foundling hospitals] shall cease" (title VI,

conflicted with articles of the Code Civil and Code Pénal that required birth declarations from parents or witnesses to a birth and prohibited abandoning a child in either a deserted or public place.[126]

The moral economist cause was also furthered by the work of Bernard-Benoît Remacle on the relation between *tour* closings and infanticide. In a work published in 1838, the author began to formulate an argument that would be expanded later in his 1845 report to the Ministry of the Interior, which showed that there was no positive correlation between *tour* closings and infanticide.[127] Like other works of the period, Remacle's 1838 and 1845 studies attempted to assess the effects of foundling policy by examining ecological correlations between levels of infanticide and departmental *tour* policy. In both publications, the author compared groups of departments that had followed different administrative strategies. In the 1838 work, Remacle compared increases of infanticide in three sorts of departments: those that had closed more than one *tour,* those that had closed all their *tours,* and those that had maintained all of their *tours*. He found that infanticides during the year 1835 had a greater tendency to increase among departments that had maintained their *tours*.[128]

Findings of past discussions and of Remacle's inquiry appear to have weakened Social Catholic attachment to the *tour* as a viable institution. This did not, however, deter them from insisting on the more general thrust of their views, which was that some provision had to be made for the care of children who had previously been left in *tours:* "When one has proven that *tours* place a greater number of children as a burden on society than the number it would be obligated to help in their absence, one has proven nothing against them. Because the point is to know not if society's obligation has

---

art. 16). There is general agreement that after the fall of the Empire, these articles were not applied, according to one observer because the children were physically unfit. See Esquiros, *Paris*, 2:299–300. For a discussion of Napoleon's motives, see Labourt, *Recherches*, p. 76. See also Fuchs, *Abandoned Children*, p. 260, for a discussion of the children's perceived moral unfitness.

126. For discussions of the legal issues involved, see Derbigny, *Analyse*, pp. 44–45; "Mesures de police prises à Paris à l'égard des enfants trouvés," *Annales d'hygiène publique et de médecine légale* 19 (1838): 66–75; and "Rapport sur les enfants trouvés et abandonnés fait au conseil général du Nord," Délibérations, 1844, pp. 160–63, ADN, 2152(5–8).

127. *Des hospices d'enfants trouvés en Europe et principalement en France depuis leur origine jusqu'à nos jours* (Paris, 1838), pp. 212–13, and *Rapport à M. le Ministre*, pp. 1–7.

128. His 1845 report to the minister of the interior increased the categories of departments to four, adding departments that had opened *tours*. This expanded analysis also looked at infanticide data over twenty years and found that the departments which established *tours* showed the greatest increases in infanticide accusations. Critiques of Remacle's work are included in Curzon, *Etudes*, p. 171, and J. J. Rapet, "De l'influence de la suppression des tours dans les hospices d'enfants trouvés sur le nombre des infanticides," *Journal des économistes*, December 1845, pp. 60–68.

become more onerous, but whether it is fulfilled in all its extent. The point is to know whether it is possible to place more obstacles to abandonments while remaining within the limits necessary to conserve children's lives."[129] In fact, such an "obstacle" had existed for many years and had been in place at the very local level. It consisted primarily of home assistance (*secours à domicile*) to mothers and families burdened by small children.

The Problem of Home Assistance and the Family

The growing appeal of home assistance for mothers or families with young children was a consequence of the moral economist victory in delegitimizing *tours* by pointing to their misuse. It also stemmed from their demonstration that foundling institutions were unable to preserve children's lives, and to some extent from Social Catholic retrenchment on the question of the *tour*. The move toward policies of home assistance can also be seen as part of the larger historical movement away from policies based on the idea of what Michel Foucault called "the great confinement"—the seventeenth- and eighteenth-century strategy through which king and church collaborated to gather numerous categories of individuals together in hôpitaux généraux to repress vagrancy; heal the sick; or care for the young, the insane, or the aged whose families were unable or unwilling to care for them.[130] Although only a small part of most foundlings' short lives were spent in hospices or hôpitaux-généraux, their aggregation here had been identified by moral economists as one of the sources of the foundling problem. That hospitals themselves had not borne the brunt of the financial burden of foundlings was, they believed, part of the reason that hospital administrators had frequently shown more indulgence in receiving foundlings than conseils généraux or regional administrators would have liked.

Policies of home assistance to families had existed for centuries, particularly in cities; and Lille, Rouen, and Mulhouse were no exceptions. In Mulhouse, the number of families aided by the Bureau de bienfaisance was 255 in 1847, and included a total of 1,287 persons.[131] Lille's Bureau de bien-

129. Curzon, *Etudes*, p. 76.

130. Critiques of the hospital system had been gaining strength since the end of the Old Regime. During the early stages of the Revolution, there had been a notable resurgence of interest in aiding individuals in their homes. See Harvey Mitchell, "Politics in the Service of Knowledge: The Debate over the Administration of Medicine and Welfare in Late-Eighteenth-Century France," *Social History* 6, (1981): 194, and "Quatrième rapport du comité de mendicité: Secours à domicile à donner à la classe indigente dans les différents âges et dans les différentes circonstances de la vie, par M. de Larochefoucauld-Liancourt," December 1790, reproduced in *Procès-verbaux et rapports du comité de mendicité de la Constituante, 1790–1791*, pub. and annot. Camille Bloch and Alexandre Tuetey (Paris, 1911), pp. 393–96.

131. During that year, private charitable organizations aided another 1,070 individuals; and

faisance distributed home assistance in a variety of forms. Data collected for a census of those receiving aid in 1841 helped administrators reduce the number of individuals aided from 24,383 to 21,447, which included 30.8 percent receiving aid throughout the year, 30.7 percent receiving it only during winter, and 38.5 percent receiving assistance only in case of sickness.[132] Home assistance in Rouen in the 1830s and 1840s routinely involved aid for 6,500 to over 7,000 people, with expenditures ranging from 50,000 to over 100,000 francs.[133] Private efforts frequently seconded those of the *bureaux de bienfaisance,* sometimes specializing in aid to mothers and children. In Rouen, for example, the Société de secours maternel donated aid in both money and clothing to poor, legitimately married women who were having their third or fourth child, on condition that the mother agree to nurse the baby.[134]

Although the practice of assistance to families in general, or to mothers and children in particular, was a long-standing one, the idea of extending it to unwed mothers in order to discourage them from abandoning their children had gone into abeyance since the Revolution.[135] In 1837, however, such a policy was approved by the Ministry of the Interior for use in changing the function of the capital's hospitals and foundling institution. Under the new plan, poor women who came to deliver their children at the city's hospitals were required to nurse them for forty-eight hours and, if they agreed not to abandon them, were granted temporary allowances in the form of clothing and money.[136] Mothers who brought children to the foundling hospital were also

---

a number of *sociétés de secours mutuels* with a total membership of 7,227, assisted 1,284 individuals during the same year. See Département du Haut-Rhin, Bureau de bienfaisance de Mulhouse, exercice 1847, "Renseignements statistiques," AMM, Q I/Aa12, and Yvette Tschill, "Le Bureau de bienfaisance de Mulhouse, 1798–1848," in Georges Livet and Georges Shaff, eds., *Médecine et assistance en Alsace* (Strasbourg, 1976), pp. 248–51.

132. Bureau de bienfaisance de Lille, Commission administrative, "Registre aux délibérations," p. 147, ABBL, E. 72, vol. 17.

133. Records do not always distinguish clearly between the city of Rouen and the arrondissement of Rouen, and the accounts of aid become much sloppier by the 1840s. See the series Statistiques des bureaux de bienfaisance, contained in ADSM, 2 XP/50, for the 1830s and 1 XP/1129, 2 XP/1129, for the 1840s.

134. The provision of aid at the third or fourth child depended on how strapped for funds the organization was. In times of severe demand, aid was extended only to women who already had three children. From the late 1820s through the 1840s, the society annually helped from 232 (1826) to over 400 (1838) mothers with children. Aid was withdrawn when a mother was discovered taking her child to a wet nurse without authorization by a physician who could attest to her inability to breastfeed. Records of the society are contained in ADSM, 20 J/1, 2. See also Victor Duval, *La charité à Rouen: Les oeuvres catholiques* (Rouen, 1895), pp. 5–9.

135. There were some proponents of this strategy for dealing with the foundling problem under the late Restoration. However, they seem to have been in a small minority. See Théodore Legras, *Notice historique sur les hôpitaux et l'asile des aliénés de Rouen* (Rouen, 1827), p. 98.

136. Fuchs, *Abandoned Children*, pp. 71–82.

granted temporary home assistance if they agreed to keep their children. The prefect of police, reporting on these measures, cited the reduction in child abandonments that the policy had effected. He noted:

> These improvements . . . have been obtained without any shocks, with no constraints, with no other efforts than those of an enlightened and sustained zeal, and so to speak, by necessity. . . . [I]t was sufficient to place several very legal barriers to the abandonment of newborns in the interests of these poor creatures [in order] to reawaken . . . in the hearts of mothers who wished to abandon them a natural feeling that had been cooled, and to give to those whose poverty demanded it a layette and some help in the form of money.[137]

But the prefect noted regretfully that the measure had met with some opposition from those who accused the administration of executing an immoral policy based only on considerations of economy. Citing the work of Remacle, the prefect denied any correlation between increases in infanticide and the imposition of some restrictions on receiving foundlings. The fact that recent months had witnessed a small increase in infants abandoned in the streets of the capital he ascribed to the activities of people who were hoping to see the new policy defeated. Similarly, in a debate with Lamartine during the following month, Benjamin Delessert, who supported the new policy, would vigorously deny that babies were being left on the steps of the Chamber of Deputies.[138] Defenders of the new policy, including the prefect of police, denied that it constituted a real closing of the Parisian *tour* and viewed it only as a small modification whose result would be "not to increase infanticides . . . but rather to preserve the lives of numerous children left to their mothers' care and to assure them a name, a status, [and] a family." The interests of society, of humanity, and of public morality, he argued, had thus been reconciled by the new policy.

Nevertheless, the idea of extending assistance to unwed mothers was laden with its own moral implications. Critics of the idea included the only Catholic clergyman who wrote extensively on the foundling problem during these years, the Abbé A. H. Gaillard. He expressed his opposition to such a policy by reminding Social Catholics and moral economists alike of the contagion of vice that would ensue from allowing children to stay with such mothers.[139] In his publications, one of the moral economists' arguments came

137. "Rapport du préfet de police au ministre de l'Intérieur . . . ," *Moniteur*, 2 April 1838, p. 758.

138. *Moniteur*, 31 May 1838, p. 1469.

139. Gaillard, *Recherches*, pp. 333–34.

back to haunt them in the abbé's judgment that home assistance to unwed mothers would encourage illegitimate pregnancies. As another critic noted, "We reject payment to unwed mothers, not because it will create a larger burden than the one we bear now, but because it is an endeavor whose result will be to establish a kind of illegitimate family in the face of the legitimate." [140] The author argued that the presence of an illegitimate child would prevent its mother's "rehabilitation." [141]

These judgments were insufficient to reduce the growing appeal of assistance to unwed mothers when seen against the system of *tours* to which it was inevitably compared. Although administrators of the central government vaunted the economies that could result from payments to mothers to prevent them from abandoning their children, they were eager, too, to defend the policy's moralizing influence on family life. In an influential report of 1837, the minister of the interior explained one of the key advantages of this strategy: "As for the moral implications, there is no need to observe how important it is not to separate the child from the mother and to avoid breaking the family bond, to the great prejudice of both [child and mother]." [142] The minister laid out the policy's financial advantages by urging the adoption of home relief for mothers for the first two years of the infant's life. Under this system, departments would avoid the obligation to pay for the care of the children during the next ten years that they would have continued to be wards of the state.

Other proponents of home assistance rejected the Abbé Gaillard's argument that it would serve to encourage vice. They believed that the presence of a child in the home would serve to moralize the mother, and among married couples to restrain fathers from abandoning their families while the child was young. Thus began a curious rehabilitation of the reputation of unwed mothers, who were now seen as capable of moral regeneration within a family setting. From long experience with unwed mothers, one administrator wrote:

> These are not women among whom all maternal feelings have been extinguished. They are women who resemble all the women of their class and who differ only by their position. They have lacked wholesome ideals of morality and religious sentiments not obvious from the outside but deeply engraved in their souls to influence their conduct, to guide their judgment, hasten reflection and prudence in all their actions. . . . [T]hey lack family traditions, supervision, and parental advice. . . . I am persuaded that . . . the general reprobation hurled indiscriminately against all unwed

140. Curzon, *Etudes*, p. 235.

141. Ibid., p. 217.

142. *Rapport au Roi*, p. 74. The importance of this report as an expression of the changing view of the central administration is cited in Lallemand, *La question*, p. 60.

> mothers is applied justly . . . only to certain hot-beds of corruption in large cities.[143]

Other proponents even cited the success of the Convention's policy of home assistance to unwed mothers in restraining them from abandoning their children.[144]

Earlier proponents of home assistance, such as the Baron de Gérando, had urged that some supervision accompany these grants, and at the beginning of the implementation of the 1837 policy change in Paris, one of the members of the administrative commission of the Paris hospitals charged with the foundling services carried out this duty.[145] Although he discovered a "low level of morality" among several of the 155 mothers whom he visited, he also reported his judgment that children were better cared for than they would have been by nurses hired by the Parisian foundling home. His comments were tempered by the observation that most of the infants whose mothers received home assistance had been sent out to wet nurses because their mothers, both married and unmarried were working women.[146] However, the pro-family goal of the policy was arguably being fulfilled, since mothers were now permitted contact with their infants, a factor that the commissioner believed helped ensure proper care.[147]

By 1845, systems of home assistance to unmarried mothers existed in fifty-two departments, involving nearly 45,000 children. Several commentators noted that in departments where this funding was available, the ratio of foundlings to births was 1 to 49, while in the thirty-four departments where it did not exist, the ratio was 1 to 32.[148] However, special funding of this kind by departmental authorities appears to have remained very modest. In the Nord, a budget of 2,000 francs for home assistance to unwed mothers appeared for the first time in 1841. Funding stayed at or near this level through the late 1840s, rising as high as 3,900 francs in 1848, a sum distributed to only fifty women in the entire department. Expenses for services to foundlings

143. T. M. Curel, *Parti à prendre sur la question des enfants trouvés* (Paris, 1845), pp. 158–59. Baudon, *De la suppression*, pp. 10–11, discussed the effects of home assistance on fathers and pointed out that restoring illegitimate children to their families would also serve to encourage the work of the Société de Saint-François-Régis.

144. Esquiros, *Paris*, 2:375, referring to the law of 28 June 1793.

145. Baron J. M. de Gérando, *Le visiteur des pauvres* (Paris, 1820), pp. 86–87.

146. This problem was also encountered in the home assistance policy for unwed mothers established in the Hautes-Alpes. Curel, *Parti*, p. 157.

147. "Rapport fait au conseil-général des hospices par le membre de la commission administrative chargé du service des enfants-trouvés," *Moniteur*, 2 April 1838, p. 759.

148. Laget, "Extrait" p. 37; Watteville, *Statistique*, p. 21. Watteville commented: "This result is extraordinary. It seems impossible to attribute it exclusively to the adoption of the [home assistance] measure."

and abandoned children declined concomitantly, from 146,000 francs in 1841 to 90,000 francs by 1845.[149] Aid in Lille came not only from departmental funds, but also from city coffers. In 1842, the prefect ordered Lille's Bureau de bienfaisance to grant a stipend of six francs per month to unwed mothers who took their children from the hospice-général. By 1844, he had to counter the reluctance of some members to granting aid to unwed mothers and ordered them to stifle their objections by "muting their repugnance or their scruples, [and] listening only to the voice of humanity and true charity."[150] This kind of aid persisted through the 1840s, continuing the grants of six francs for six months.[151] In 1845, one observer noted the success of Lille's home assistance program in reducing mortality among infants who were given back to mothers.[152] In the Seine-Inférieure, the desirability of a transition to a system of home assistance was set forth in the 1847 session of the conseil général, although specific levels of funding for this new effort were not articulated.[153]

Policy Changes in Perspective

The complex of policy changes related to foundlings and abandoned children that characterized the period from the end of the 1820s to the end of the 1840s did not eliminate this category of children. *Tour* closings in many areas and the transition to more flexible systems of home assistance, however, were symptomatic of a change in attitudes. Solutions based on care for children outside their families were shown by moral economists to be wasteful of money and

149. In 1833, the same service had consumed nearly 300,000 francs. See Conseil général du Nord, "Délibérations," meeting of 30 August 1841, ADN, 2152(1–4); 30 August 1843, 2 September 1844, ADN, 2152(5–8); 3 September 1845 and undated meeting, session of 1847, ADN, 2152(9–11). In the meeting of 30 August 1843, it was noted that "aid accorded to unwed mothers maintains family ties." The costs of the Seine-Inférieure's services to foundlings and abandoned children in the decade from 1824 to 1833 had averaged nearly 200,000 francs per year, reaching their highest level in 1831, when the figure was 215,886 francs. Lelong, *Rapport*, table 2.

150. Bureau de bienfaisance de Lille, Commission administrative, "Registre aux délibérations," meetings of 1 February 1842 and 19 March 1844, pp. 187, 393–94, ABBL, E. 72, vol. 17.

151. Unwed mothers were also granted one-time aid of 20–25 francs to marry the fathers of their children. See the meetings of 27 May 1845, 5 May 1846, and 17 August 1847, in Bureau de bienfaisance de Lille, Commission administrative, "Registre aux délibérations," pp. 68, 224, 454, ABBL, E. 72, vol. 18.

152. *Rapport à M. le Ministre*, p. 17. For the same effects in the Hautes-Alpes, see Curel, *Parti*, pp. 155–56.

153. Conseil général de la Seine-Inférieure, session of 1847, p. 331, ADSM, 1 NP/31. In his 1849 report, *De la condition*, p. 9, M. L. Nepveur noted the novelty of such a practice in the department—one of which he disapproved—and stated that no money had yet been awarded to unwed mothers there.

human life, to be positive incentives to dependency, and to be counter to the establishment of working-class parent-child relations informed by feelings of affection and bonds of solidarity.

Moral economists' success in delegitimizing older strategies of delivering aid to foundlings resulted in part from their successful introduction of a full-blown sociopsychological portrait of the effects of the *tour* on working-class communities, and especially on working-class mothers. Beginning from a model of mothers whose rational calculation of advantages accruing to them from an abuse of foundling institutions, critics of the *tour* were consistently led back to their fundamental belief that maternal feelings could be rekindled. As has been shown, foundling "exchanges" were based on such a wager. However, the "exchange" policy, based on a moral economist reading of the foundling problem, foundered in the face of both public opinion and the realities of working-class family life. The later 1830s and the 1840s witnessed a sort of policy retrenchment in which moral economists compromised with these realities while still defending their construction of the causes and consequences of the foundling problem and its relation to working-class family life. Moral economists' support for the policy of home assistance to unwed mothers emerged as a viable means for reconciling the goals of encouraging parent-child bonds with the task of building a moral economy at the family level.

Seen in the longer historical perspective, the debate over the proper care of foundlings and abandoned children in the late Restoration and July Monarchy represented the successful shifting of attention from the obligations of state and administration to working-class children to the obligations of parents. In the seventeenth century, when the monarchy began to intervene actively and systematically in the problem of abandoned children, policy was intended to fulfill obligations of royal paternalism, Tridentine piety, and *raison d'état*. The growth of eighteenth-century Enlightenment ideals gave new legitimacy to royal policy, although the source of these obligations now included the demands of "nature" or the values of "humanitarian" ideals. In this transition, obligations to children were still believed to rest with the king and his administration, and to a lesser extent with seigneurial authorities. By the end of the Old Regime, obligations of "enlightened" or even Tridentine piety, humanitarianism, and royal paternalism converged to lend ideological support to the provision of aid to foundlings and abandoned children. Necker's critique of foundling homes was not a lone voice at this time, but it was still very much in a minority.

The moral economist perspective on the foundling problem and its relationship to the working-class family by the 1830s and 1840s was symptomatic of a breakdown of this heterogeneous constellation of values and practices that had earlier legitimized the monarchy's obligations towards foundlings. Moral economists' argument that the primary obligation to children rested with their parents and that the nuclear family stood as the proper vehicle for the fulfillment of this obligation clearly had links to the kind of mentality change traced by Brinton to the years of the Directory and Consulate. At this time, legislators had already begun to frame the exigencies of "natural" obligations in terms of concrete civil law rather than abstract notions of "humanitarianism" and to place greater emphasis on the need to balance humanitarianism with the demands of economy and order within civil society.

The moral economist position developed this line of argument. By the time of the foundling debate under the July Monarchy, the notion of "natural" obligation had little do with a rationally understood law of nature that counseled enlightened obligations to the poor. Rather, it referred to the biologically based and socially approved obligation of mothers or parents to their own children. The *mère dénaturée* who abandoned her child when she could have kept it was one whose corrupted and twisted economic rationality had helped to extinguish those maternal feelings of affection that lay at the foundation of the nuclear family.

The increase in the numbers of foundlings and abandoned children and in the funds spent to provide for them doubtless helped to stimulate policy innovation. Just as important, however, was the success of moral economist observers and administrators in linking the problem of foundlings and abandoned children to the perceived erosion of parental obligation, particularly among France's urban working classes. An examination of the records of foundlings and abandoned children in the industrial areas under study has lent little support to moral economists' judgment that the nineteenth-century foundling problem had historically new causes that were associated with the particular values of urban industrial workers. What seems to have changed more than the causes of child abandonment was its newer interpretation.[154]

If Social Catholics were correct in continuing to insist on the variety of social conditions that produced foundlings and abandoned children, moral economists were undoubtedly correct in arguing that large numbers of working-class mothers were using the *tour* welfare system to help them care for their children. The available sources, including parental responses to exchanges of foundlings and abandoned children, confirm the moral economist judgment that parents sought to utilize these institutions much as they would have used a nurse whom they themselves had hired. The efforts by many mothers to maintain contact with their children despite efforts by administrators to make this impossible were evidence of ongoing parental concern.

154. Jean Sandrin, *Enfants trouvés, enfants ouvriers: XVIIe–XIXe siècle* (Paris, 1982), p. 69, also sees a greater change in bourgeois attitudes towards foundlings than in the causes precipitating their abandonment.

However, moral economists' demonstration that by abandoning their infants, mothers or fathers consigned them to institutions from which it was unlikely that they would emerge alive, was an essential part of an argument that questioned parental feelings of "humanity." Significant differences between the mortality rates of foundlings and French children in general raised in their families supported them on this issue.[155] In this part of the debate, Social Catholics, who were generally less adept at analyzing statistical data than their moral economist interlocutors, lost a real opportunity to defend their point of view. Although a few of them pointed out that the most meaningful statistical comparison for foundling mortality lay not with the overall mortality of France's children but rather with working-class figures, their legislative defenders never made this point with the zeal it deserved.[156] Similarly, the argument that foundling mortality might be reduced by raising the wages of wet nurses to whom foundlings were given was never made with much vigor, since Social Catholics probably judged, quite rightly, that such an argument was unlikely to win support for their position.[157] The much narrower difference between working-class infant and child mortality and foundling mortality, however, may help to explain why working-class mothers had recourse to foundling institutions to help them raise their children. For many of them, particularly the mothers of illegitimate children, there simply was not that much difference in mortality between infants whom they left in the *tour* and those they would have had to consign to inferior wet nurses whom they could rarely afford to pay.

Although moral economists were successful in delegitimizing the *tour* on a number of scores, including its link in weakening parent-child bonds, the implementation of home assistance was not necessarily successful in encouraging mothers to nurse their own children. Like previous generations of urban, working-class women, those of early industrial France were frequently constrained by the demands of their work to use a wet nurse. This was hardly a novel social invention of the nineteenth century.[158] What was perhaps newer was that industrialization was expanding the number of working-class women who both needed the services of a wet nurse and who were unable to pay for one. Although archival sources have revealed no evidence that female fac-

155. Duchâtel, *Considérations*, p. 247, cited mortality figures of 60% to age twelve for foundlings and 30% for children "raised in their families." More recently, Edward Shorter has also made this argument in *The Making of the Modern Family*, p. 181.

156. This point was raised in Baudon, *De la suppression*, p. 10.

157. The argument that wages paid to wet nurses of foundlings were so low that only the poorest women would agree to accept the position was, however, made in Baudon, *De la suppression*, p. 32.

158. On the link between women's work and the need for wet nurses, see Maurice Garden, *Lyon et les Lyonnais au XVIIIe siècle* (Paris, 1970), pp. 135–37.

tory workers were more likely than other working women to abandon their infants to the *tour,* it seems premature to argue, as Shorter did, that female factory workers entirely rejected the employment of wet nurses to raise their infants.[159] What seems to have been happening was that factory women, like other working women, were attempting to adapt foundling institutions to their own needs.

Moral economists' willingness to accept a home assistance policy for unwed mothers as well as for legitimate parents represented a compromise of some of their fundamental beliefs. In an ideal world, they would have lobbied vigorously against the provision of aid to unwed mothers on the basis of its encouragement of vice. In practice, however, the virtues of economy and the advantages of children being under the care of their mothers or parents outweighed the specter, raised most vigorously by the Abbé Gaillard, of children living with parents whose morality left much to be desired.

Moral economists' analysis of working-class parents and their culture had once again evolved through two distinctive phases. Their argument had begun with an effort to expose the deep moral division that lay between working-class parents and the rest of society, and between working-class parents of the nineteenth century and poor parents in the past, who were portrayed as having had recourse to child abandonment only in the direst of circumstances. Moral economists of the 1830s and 1840s decried the decline of natural human sentiment among mothers and the substitution in their hearts of a grasping, rational calculus that caused their misuse of outdated welfare institutions. However, confronted with the continued resonance of Social Catholic values, with larger public opposition to policies such as the infamous "exchanges" of children, and with the practical need to create *some* kind of policy to substitute for the one left by the 1811 decree, moral economists were increasingly attracted by the appeal of home assistance to mothers of illegitimate children. Their rehabilitation of the reputation of unwed mothers was part of a new argument that emphasized that home assistance could itself encourage family life. Although restoring infants to their unwed mothers or unmarried parents was in no way a guarantee that children would be taught proper mores, moral economists increasingly argued that placing children back into their families was a critical step towards spreading values of a domestic moral economy among France's working classes.

159. Shorter, *The Making of the Modern Family*, p. 177, citing English and late-nineteenth-century French evidence.

5

Children's Industrial Work and the Family

The Problem of Child Labor Reform

Like concubinage and child abandonment, child labor had significant links with France's past. Moral economists and Social Catholics of the Restoration and July Monarchy were well aware of the importance of children's work to the household economies of peasants of the distant past and to more recent protoindustrial households.[1] But their systematic examination of the character and significance of child labor took place during the demise of the protoindustrial system and its replacement by a more urbanized industrial economy that was gradually moving the work of children, like that of adults, outside the family. Many of the participants in the debate over child labor viewed the significance of changes in children's work against this background of economic transformation and defended their arguments for intervention as legitimate responses to larger currents of social change.

Moral economist and Social Catholic proposals for intervening into the organization of child labor centered on industrial work places and entailed vigorous efforts to articulate the differences that distinguished children's work in small shops from labor in larger, more mechanized work places. One of the primary differences, in the view of moral economists and Social Catholics alike, was that industrial or factory labor removed children from a family or family-like setting and transformed them into workers, with the habits and attitudes of adults, at a very young age. In the eyes of the two main advocates of child labor reform, the problem that needed to be addressed was not so much one of children working as of child workers.

In the effort to understand children's involvement in the labor processes

1. For an analysis of children's labor under protoindustrialization, see Hans Medick, "The Proto-Industrial Family Economy," in Peter Kriedte, Hans Medick, and Jürgen Schlumbohm, *Industrialization before Industrialization: Rural Industry in the Genesis of Capitalism* (Cambridge, 1981), p. 55.

of France's industrial work places, observers would grasp for analogies with the past. The most obvious comparison was with the age-old experience of apprenticeship. However, it became increasingly apparent during the 1830s that the only real similarity between the situation of apprentices in an older economic regime and the industrializing economy was the ages of those working. Even in this regard, it could be pointed out that child workers, particularly those in France's new textile industries, frequently began to work at ages far below those typical of apprentices. This difference and the characteristics of industrial work places in which children now undertook their labors would be used by critics to lay out their construction of child labor as a problem.

The configuration of the ideological landscape that emerged in debates over legislation to restrict children's industrial labor was unsurprising in its broad outlines. The voice of moral economists was raised most systematically and efficaciously as the force for interventionist and innovative social policy. Social Catholics, with their inherent distaste for urban life and factory labor, were willing allies, though they were followers rather than leaders once legislation became the preferred vehicle for policy intervention. Their preference for voluntaristic organizations in mediating relations between bourgeoisie and working class led to their sponsorship of activities for young workers and apprentices. However, the ideological predispositions of the Social Catholic movement in favor of older forms of work organization continued to mark their attitudes. In 1850, the head of the Société de Saint-Vincent-de-Paul was still lamenting the demise of apprenticeship and decrying its effects on the family:

> Every epoch has its own character, its most urgent needs, its special plague. The plague that [now] devours society is the destruction of family feeling and paternal authority. We must . . . attack this problem and work to prevent the decomposition of the family. . . . [I]n our relations with children and with parents in the family, in the schools, and in apprenticeship organizations, we must everywhere repeat the truths that tend to strengthen paternal authority and tighten family bonds. We must follow attentively the . . . behavior of our children, of our apprentices, of our young workers. To reinforce these views it would be desirable to train young people for their fathers' careers. Apprenticeship carried out in the family would be far preferable to that in the workshop. Unfortunately, things do not happen this way in the majority of cases. Sons take a career different from that of their fathers.[2]

2. Speech by Adolphe Baudon to the General Assembly of the Parisian *conférences* of the Société de Saint-Vincent-de-Paul, reprinted in the *Bulletin de la Société de Saint-Vincent-de-Paul*, no. 17 (1850): 125–27.

Baudon's address expressed the society's continuing distaste for the economic changes brought on by industrialization, particularly as they affected relations within the family. Indeed, the society would continue to try to mitigate what it saw as the disruptive moral effects of social change by sponsoring organized activities for both apprentices and young workers. In Lille in particular, the society helped to look after children from the families they aided. In a report from the late 1840s, local records of the society indicated that "our apprentices, or rather our young factory workers (because apprenticeship contracts strictly speaking are no longer used in this area), gather together each Sunday evening . . . where they are the object of the care and oversight of members of the chapter. We entertain and instruct them. Furthermore, each member has under his patronage a child whom he is responsible for following and supervising in his family and in the [work place]."[3] Apparent in both Baudon's speech and the work of the society, however, was a growing sense that they were fighting a rear-guard action against the forces of social change.

The impetus for intervention into child factory labor emanated not from Social Catholics, who lamented the passing of an old economic and moral order, but more clearly from those who shaped and helped to define the new. The notion that child labor was becoming an economic and moral problem originated most vigorously from elements within the Alsatian *patronat,* who were entirely familiar with the technical peculiarities of newer industrial work places, and the moral economist ideologues, who were helping to articulate the economic and moral aspects of an industrial capitalist system in the making. It was this cluster of men who gradually shaped what was to become the dominant mode of conceptualizing children's industrial labor as a problem that lay properly within the purview of state authorities. Although moral economists had only lukewarm affection for state intervention that restricted rights of property, their analysis of child labor led them to ascribe new importance to moral considerations that suggested a reconsideration of the state's role.

The story of child labor reform in France, culminating in legislative approval of the nation's first child labor law in 1841, began and ended in controversy, exposing once again interesting fissures of opinion and attitude among the drama's diverse participants. Discussions about the reform of child labor entailed a number of contentious issues concerning the relative exploitation of children within industrial work places, the relation of children's work to family life, and the moral and financial implications of government intervention. Factory owners, prefects, legislators, and the families of child workers

3. By 1850, local manufacturers had become actively involved in this effort, which involved 150 "apprentices." "Bulletin statistique de la conférence de Lille," undated, but probably 1849, and "Tableau statistique de la conférence de Lille," 1850, both contained in ASVP, Paris, Dossier 1.

were all affected by the process of policy formulation and implementation, though not necessarily in ways intended by leaders of the reform effort.

Efforts to implement reform were similarly laden with contention. Here, the persistence of competing ideological dispositions about child labor would be most obvious, exposing not only reluctance within the industrial bourgeoisie to accept the actualization of moral economists' plans for a more orderly and disciplined industrial world, but workers' own adherence to values about the family economy and children's place in it that appeared to deviate sharply from the wisdom that social policy would attempt to impart.

The Nature and Extent of Children's Work in Industry

Grasping the dimensions of children's industrial labor in the period under study is quite difficult, since some of the available data refer to children's work in particular sectors of the economy, such as cotton weaving or spinning, while others refer only to children's work in the kinds of work places that came under the jurisdiction of the child labor law of 1841 at the time of its passage. (See Appendix A, article 1.) In an article published in 1872, Baron d'Eichtal estimated the total number of children employed in the cotton industry in the late 1830s at 100,000–150,000. Two years later, Armand Audiganne estimated the number of children under sixteen who had come under the jurisdiction of the 1841 law at 80,000, working in a total of over 6,000 work places. A more contemporary estimate, of 1846, put the number of French children working in the production of cotton goods at 150,000, within a labor force in this sector that totalled over one million.[4]

Work places that employed children fell under the jurisdiction of the law of 1841 both because of the size of their work force and the presence in the work place of steam engines or continuous-process furnaces.[5] Many of Lille's cotton-twisting mills (*retorderies*) and linen-thread-spinning shops (*filteries*) and most of Rouen's weaving establishments fell only into the first category, although handloom weaving employed relatively few young children. On the

4. Baron Eugène d'Eichtal, "Les lois sur le travail des enfants dans les manufactures en France," *Revue des deux mondes* 100 (15 July 1872): 422. His figure corresponds with one cited in 1839 in the Chamber of Deputies, referring to children ages seven to fourteen. Figures for other industries cited in the Chamber included 200,000–300,000 children in the wool industry and 180,000 in silk. See the report of M. Billaudel in *Moniteur*, 16 June 1839, p. 990, and Hilde Rigaudias-Weiss, *Les enquêtes ouvrières en France entre 1830 et 1848* (Paris, 1936), p. 48; Armand Audiganne, *La nouvelle loi sur le travail des enfants et la famille ouvrière depuis 35 ans* (Paris, 1874), p. 6; Dr. Thouvenin, "De l'influence que l'industrie exerce sur la santé des populations dans les grands centres manufacturiers," *Annales d'hygiène publique et de médecine légale* 36 (1846): 21.

5. See article 1 of the law in Appendix A.

Table 5.1. Age Distribution of Child Workers Affected by the Law of 22 March 1841, Seine-Inférieure, Early 1840s

Age of children	Number of children	Percentage of total
< 8	9	0.1
8–12	1,279	19.0
12–14	2,720	40.4
14–16	2,719	40.4
All children	6,727	99.9

Source: A. Corneille, *La Seine-Inférieure commerciale et industrielle* (Rouen, 1873), p. 506.

Note: The ambiguity caused by overlapping age categories cannot be resolved, either here or in Tables 5.2–5.5 below, because the data are presented in this form in their original. One might conjecture that the category "8–12" actually included only children ages 8–11, while twelve-year-olds were placed in the following category.

other hand, cotton- and linen-spinning as well as cloth-printing establishments usually fulfilled both criteria for inclusion.

Local and regional data give some insight into the size and age structure of the child labor force (see Table 5.1). In the early 1840s, children's factory labor in the department of the Seine-Inférieure was concentrated in the age group twelve to sixteen. However, this total of more than 6,000 child workers, which also appeared in archival sources, was ascribed to the "Rouen area." In an 1843 report, for example, the prefect of the Seine-Inférieure cited the results of that year's inspection of 650 establishments covered by the law; these work places employed approximately 6,000 children in the arrondissement of Rouen and the neighboring canton of Grand'Couronne alone.[6] Industrial statistics compiled in the mid-1840s, which included workshops employing at least ten workers, showed a total of 5,362 workers under sixteen in industrial establishments of the arrondissement of Rouen, the vast majority (5,289, or 98.6%) in textiles. According to this same source, the two largest employers were cotton mills (2,513) and cloth-printing shops (1,124). The third largest, cotton weaving, employed only 365 children.[7]

6. Préfecture de la Seine-Inférieure, "Rapport sur les résultats des inspections," AN, F12/4713; "Procès-verbaux d'inspection," November 1843, ADSM, 10 MP/1362. By a decree of 27 January 1842, the minister of agriculture and commerce ordered that the Grand'Couronne be included in Rouen's child labor inspections. ADSM, 10 MP/1361.

7. France, Statistique générale, *Statistique de la France publiée par le Ministère de l'Agriculture et du Commerce*, ser. 1, 12 (Industrie, vol. 3) (Paris, 1847): 26–47.

Table 5.2. Age Distribution of Child Workers Affected by the Law of 22 March 1841, Lille, 1848

Age of children	Number of children	Percentage of total
8–10	96	7.1
10–12	328	24.3
12–16	928	68.6
All children	1,352	100.0

Source: "Tableau du nombre d'enfants employés dans les manufactures de Lille et assujettis à la loi sur le travail dans les fabriques," ADN, M611/13. This document reported that there were 919 boys and 333 girls, for a total of 1,252, but supplied age data for 1,352.

In the Nord, figures on the number of child workers affected by the law aroused some skepticism. Both the mayor of Lille and the prefect concurred that information gathered showed totals of child employment that were far below the reality. An inquiry made in 1842 of the "Lille area" showed a total of 1,727 children employed in establishments covered by the law: 625 (or 36.2%) ages eight to twelve and 1,102 (or 63.8%) ages twelve to sixteen. Of these children, 926, or 53.6 percent, were working in the cotton mills as piecers or bobbin tenders. The mayor opined, "To anyone who knows the importance of our industrial establishments . . . these figures seem suspicious."[8] The wider Lille arrondissement showed a labor force of 4,023 children covered by the law; 1,253, or 31 percent, of them ages eight to twelve, and 2,779, or 69 percent, ages twelve to sixteen, employed in a total of 288 work places.[9] The prefect echoed the mayor's skepticism about figures on child employment in the area's industrial work places, but felt that "further investigation by the [inspection] commission should prove this." Further investigation of Lille's child labor force yielded no such information, however. In an 1845 inspection, there were a reported 1,300 children at work in eighty of the city's work places covered by the law.[10] By January 1848, the total was nearly the same, the child workers' ages distributed as shown in Table 5.2. The *Statistique de la France* of the mid-1840s reported 1,736 children under sixteen in the textile work

8. The figures and the mayor's response are cited in Pierre Pierrard, "Le patronat et le travail des enfants en 1848," *Economie et humanisme*, no. 117 (1959): 55.

9. Préfecture du Nord, "Travail des enfants dans les manufactures. Installation de la commission d'inspection. Discours de M. le préfet," AN, F12/4712. The same figure for the number of children employed is cited in André Lasserre, *La situation des ouvriers de l'industrie textile dans la région lilloise sous la monarchie de Juillet* (Lausanne, 1952), p. 153. However, the author counted 272 establishments, noting that three-fourths of the children were employed in textiles.

10. M. Kolb-Bernard to the prefect of the Nord, 20 December 1845, ADN, M611/11.

places in Lille with ten or more workers; 876, or 50 percent, of them were in cotton spinning, and 476 (27%) were in the city's many linen-thread-spinning establishments.[11]

Data on the size and structure of Mulhouse's child work force are more voluminous than those for either Lille or Rouen, but pose interpretive difficulties for comparisons over time because of the different age categories used to organize them. Age categories dictated by the terms of the 1841 law divided children into two groups, ages eight to twelve and twelve to sixteen. However, these groupings were not used in early records from Mulhouse. As early as 1825, there were 1,578 children ages ten to sixteen employed in the city's cotton mills, cloth-printing works, and weaving establishments.[12] By the time of the 1841 law's implementation, there were 3,369 children, ages eight to sixteen, employed in industries of Mulhouse and its neighboring commune of Dornach, composing 26.5 percent of the city and suburb's total labor force.[13] Cloth printing and cotton spinning remained the principal employers of child labor, the *Statistique de la France* from the mid-1840s indicating a total of 1,812 children under sixteen in the former and 1,249 in the latter industry.[14]

Although children in all three cities, but particularly Lille and Rouen, continued to be employed in a variety of small workshops not covered by the law, the work places that attracted the greatest attention of observers and legislators were the new, large cotton mills of July Monarchy France. Although modern factories constituted a minority of work places employing children in Lille and Rouen, they were numerous in Mulhouse. They were also places where children composed a large proportion of the mill work force. (See Table 3.1.) The following description of a cotton mill reflects the kind of awe that contemporaries felt when confronted with a new technological spectacle. It is worthy of lengthy quotation:

11. France, Statistique générale, *Statistique de la France publiée par le Minstère de l'Agriculture et du Commerce*, ser. 1, 10 (Industrie, vol. 1) (Paris, 1847): 16–39. Lille's suburban communes of Esquermes, Wazemmes, Fives, and Moulins are included in these totals.

12. "Etat sommaire des enfants travaillant dans les fabriques de la ville de Mülhausen," AMM, R I/Cb2. In his *L'enseignement à Mulhouse de 1798 à 1870* (Strasbourg, 1961), p. 72, Raymond Oberlé cites this same source, but calculates a figure of 1,817 children under age thirteen. My calculations show that of the total, nearly 39% of the children listed in age groups ten to thirteen and thirteen to sixteen were employed in spinning, slightly over 59% in cloth printing, and only slightly more than 2% in weaving. Several of the industrialists who supplied figures for this inquiry said that they employed younger children in cloth printing, but did not specify the exact numbers.

13. Oberlé, *L'enseignement*, p. 74. In 1844, children made up 26.1% of the factory labor force of the arrondissement of Altkirch and 21.5% of that for the department of the Haut-Rhin. See "Nombre d'ouvriers de fabrique travaillant dans les manufactures du Haut-Rhin en 1844," ADHR, 1M 127/5.

14. France, *Statistique de la France*, 10:136–49.

What is called a spinning mill is usually one or two brick buildings of three or four stories. The special shops contained in these buildings are lighted on both sides by large, closely spaced windows that distribute light evenly.

The neat and regular arrangement of the machines creates an imposing impression even when the factory is at rest. But when it is running, it is certainly one of the strangest and most grandiose spectacles industry can present. All is movement and noise. The driving belts crisscross, the fly wheels turn, the gears mesh, the bobbins unwind, the rollers turn, the steel teeth tear up their prey, the heavy carriages filled with spindles go back and forth.

Sometimes the speed is so frightening that it escapes our glance, dazzling us. It appears that there is a mad acceleration, the prelude to a catastrophe. And yet it is regulated by an implacable precision. . . .

What a beautiful picture of force is [presented] by this powerful machinery, which triumphs over all, yet regulates itself!

Its voice is no less extraordinary than its activity. It is not a sound that tires or tortures the ear . . . it is a dreadful murmuring that fills the head, swells and softens it like metal being forged. In the midst of all this [there is] a strange whistling, produced by rapid movements and suddenly relaxed compression, which is like the moans of the suffering, or matter in revolt.

But what makes the machine's noise more extraordinary is the impression caused by the absolute silence of the human voice. (It is prohibited under penalty of a fine to talk in the shops.) This contrast makes you understand even more that here the machine is the master and man its humble slave.[15]

Children's and young people's work within cotton mills was concentrated in several tasks. In the most modern mills, the mechanization of labor processes had, in the judgment of many, reduced the inherently unhealthful effects of such processes as batting. As Dr. Thouvenin, Lille's eminent moral economist noted,

Mechanized batting is used for spinning coarser and medium-grade threads and is today used almost exclusively in Alsace, the Vosges, and

15. Emile Bosquet, *Le roman des ouvrières* (Paris, 1868), pp. 49–50. Pierrard, "Le patronat," p. 57, has noted that Lille's cotton mills *intra muros* in the 1840s were generally less modern than those in the suburbs and were frequently houses refurbished for their new use. Illustrations of mills in the Mulhouse area, contained in Société industrielle de Mulhouse, *Histoire documentaire de l'industrie de Mulhouse et de ses environs au XIXe siècle* (Mulhouse, 1902), vol. 1, plates XVII–XXII, show that factories here conformed more to the images purveyed in Bosquet's novel, which was concerned with the period of the 1830s and 1840s.

> the Seine-Inférieure. However, in the Nord, where a large quantity of fine cotton is spun for use in the production of tulles and lace, manual batting is still in use in a large number of spinning mills. Mechanical batting is done by a kind of drum, into which the younger worker (of either sex) continuously puts small amounts of cotton. This work is not tiring. The amount of work performed by the machine is equivalent to that of five or six men.[16]

By contrast, the doctor regarded hand batting as one of the most unhealthful occupations in spinning or cotton-twisting mills because of the quantity of dust and down released by the continuous impact of the bat on the cotton. The mechanization of batting, which permitted the replacement of adult males with children, resulted in a less unhealthful occupation.

Carding had long been performed by women and the young and remained essentially a child's or young adult's task after it too was transformed into machine tending. The process consisted of putting batted cotton into machines that elongated and thinned out the cotton filaments. The carding room gathered together the work of young adult women (*soigneuses*), usually ages fifteen to twenty-five, and younger males as "doffers" and card cleaners (*débourreurs de cardes*).[17] During the 1830s and 1840s, however, the greatest number of child workers in the mill were employed as "piecers" for the "mule" spinner, who was nearly always an adult male. Depending upon the number of machines he was tending, the mule spinner employed anywhere from one to four young workers, whose job it was to tie up threads broken during the spinning process. Child workers were responsible for keeping bobbins clean and free of waste and for replacing them when they were empty. These children also helped with machine cleaning, which took place at the end of the work week, usually on Saturday or on Sunday morning.[18]

Of all the textile industries employing children in factory labor, cotton-spinning mills assembled the greatest diversity of ages, though different age groups and the two sexes were not evenly distributed throughout the work place. Children and young people of both sexes were employed in the preparatory processes, particularly when these processes were mechanized, and as piecers working directly in spinning. Young women predominated in the less mechanized finishing processes and in working drawing frames. In nearly all

16. Thouvenin, "De l'influence," p. 21.

17. Ibid., p. 22; Chambre consultative des arts et manufactures de Roubaix to the minister of public works, 17 August 1837, ADN, M611/1. The latter remarked that young workers were employed here because they cost less than adult male workers.

18. See the letter from the pharmacist Dupuis of Maromme, near Rouen, to the minister of commerce, 27 January 1847, AN, F12/4617, which warned of the dangers of cleaning the machines during operation. Dupuis had written to interest the minister in a plan for reducing industrial accidents through the implementation of covers for the gears of spinning machinery.

Table 5.3. Age Distribution of the Child Labor Force in Selected Industries of Lille, Early 1840s

Type of industry	Number and percentage of children by age[a]		
	8–12	12–16	All ages
Cotton spinning	328 (36.1%)	580 (63.9%)	908 (100.0%)
Linen spinning	90 (35.9)	161 (64.1)	251 (100.0)
Cotton twisting (*retorderies*)	63 (50.4)	62 (49.6)	125 (100.0)
Linen-thread spinning (*filteries*)	88 (44.0)	112 (56.0)	200 (100.0)
Weaving	16 (35.6)	29 (64.4)	45 (100.0)
Wool spinning	17 (54.8)	14 (45.2)	31 (100.0)
Cloth printing	7 (43.8)	9 (56.2)	16 (100.0)
Bonnet making	2 (16.7)	10 (83.3)	12 (100.0)
All industries	611 (38.5)	977 (61.5)	1,588 (100.0)

Source: "Travail des enfants dans les manufactures: Etat des établissements auxquels la loi pourrait être appliquée," ADN, M611/7.

[a]Percentage of the total in each industry in parentheses. Figures for some establishments have been eliminated because of faulty data—i.e. figures for the two age groups did not correspond to the totals indicated.

cases except the spinner-piecer relationship, groups of young workers were supervised by male overseers.

By contrast, other industries employing children were more segregated by sex. Work in cotton-twisting mills, at least in Lille, was primarily a male occupation, employing young boys who worked alongside adult males winding threads onto the twisting machines.[19] It appears that the child labor force in Lille's cotton twisting mills was one of the youngest. According to figures from one source, in that city 40 to over 50 percent of the children working in the cotton-twisting and linen-thread-spinning shops that came under the jurisdiction of the 1841 law were in the eight- to-twelve-year-old category, while the corresponding figures for cotton mill and linen mill children were 36.1 and 35.9 percent (see Table 5.3). Mechanized linen spinning, a relatively new but growing industry in Lille in the 1840s, provided a variant on the processes of cotton spinning and was predominantly a female occupation. Only two of Lille's eight linen-spinning mills affected by the 1841 law employed males as workers. One observer noted that while two-fifths of the labor force of cotton-spinning mills were women, the corresponding figure for linen spinning was two-thirds.[20]

19. Charles Engrand, "Les ouvriers lillois de 1829 à 1832" (Diplôme d'études supérieures, Université de Lille, 1957), p. 160; Jean-Baptiste Dupont, *Mémoire sur les moyens d'améliorer la santé des ouvriers à Lille* (Lille, 1826), p. 37.

20. M. Loiset, "Les accidents du travail, "*Bulletin médical du Nord*, 1850, p. 63. Dr. Thouvenin noted with approval that in linen-spinning mills that did employ workers of both sexes, the sexes tended to work in different shops. "De l'influence," p. 30.

The cloth-printing industry, which was so important to Mulhouse's economy, employed children to work alongside the printer, spreading mordants on the chassis that supplied them to the printing surface, which was either wooden blocks or cylindrical rollers.[21] Like piecers employed in cotton spinning, the children (known as *tireurs*) who worked alongside the adult printers were integral to the production process. Their responsibilities included not only spreading the mordants, but seeing that the printing surfaces and basins that contained the mordants were kept clean. One source noted: "The best printer could do nothing if his tireur were negligent or dirty."[22] Although printers and their tireurs could be either male or female, Villermé noted that men predominated in the newer mechanized cylinder printing. Both techniques coexisted in cloth-printing mills of July Monarchy France, although mechanized printing was increasingly the norm, especially in the Mulhouse area.[23]

Formulating the Problem of Child Labor

Concerted efforts to define and articulate the problem of child labor did not begin with a sharp distinction between the work of adults and children in the factory. In particular, discussions within the Société industrielle de Mulhouse, stimulated by a petition from the industrialist J. J. Bourcart, first centered on factory labor as a whole and on the fifteen-hour workdays that involved all workers. In his 1828 address to the industrial society Bourcart proposed that factory labor for all workers should be limited to twelve hours, thereby emulating an 1825 English law.[24] In his address, Bourcart also initiated consideration of the close association between the moral and physical effects of industrial

21. Mordants are chemical substances that make the dyeing material, usually, in the nineteenth century, a vegetable root such as madder or woad, adhere to the cloth, making it resistant to fading. Mordants such as aluminum or iron acetate were produced in the printing establishment by combining metal salts or oxides with acids. The resulting chemical reaction freed the metal, the acid volatizing or being washed away, leaving a metallic ion that bonded with the dye. See C. L. and A. B. Berthollet, *Elements of the Art of Dyeing*, trans. Andrew Ure (London, 1824), p. 84, for a description of the different steps involved in the process of cloth printing.

22. Maurice Daumas et al., *Histoire générale des techniques* (Paris, 1968), 3:721.

23. Louis-René Villermé, *Tableau de l'état physique et moral des ouvriers employés dans les manufactures de coton, de laine et de soie* (Paris, 1840), 1: 9–10.

24. J. J. Bourcart, "Proposition de M. Jean-Jacques Bourcart, de Guebwiller, sur la nécessité de fixer l'âge et de réduire les heures de travail des ouvriers des filatures," *Bulletin de la Société industrielle de Mulhouse*, no. 5 (1828): 327. In 1840, Bourcart was mentioned in the Chamber of Deputies as the owner of the largest spinning mill in France. *Moniteur*, 25 December 1840, p. 2517. On Bourcart's petition, see Francis Hordern, "L'évolution de la condition individuelle et collective des travailleurs en Alsace, XIXe siècle (1800–1870)" (Thèse de doctorat, Université de Paris, Faculté de droit et des sciences économiques, 1970), pp. 386–87; William M. Reddy, *The Rise of Market Culture: The Textile Trade and French Society, 1750–1900* (Cambridge, 1984), pp. 169–70.

labor. He argued that the moral well-being and the health of all workers, both young and old, would be enhanced by a limitation of work hours. Furthermore, he believed that there were financial advantages for industrialists who limited work hours, since workers laboring shorter hours would produce more efficiently. He argued that even if the end result of such a regulation were a diminution in the overall quantity of cotton output, the vexing problem of overproduction would thereby find at least a temporary solution. The result would be a more robust work force for industrialists and more robust soldiers for the state.[25] Bourcart's address and the response of the commission appointed by the society to comment on it were couched in the language of philanthropy, evoking the moral obligation of industrialists to "look after the happiness and well-being of workers, well-being that would be enhanced by the limitation of work hours of all workers to twelve hours a day."[26] The commission's response to Bourcart's remarks was generally quite favorable.

In its response, the commission brought the question of children's work to center stage. The miserable state of young workers, their long working days of fifteen to seventeen hours, and the need for some of them to leave home for work at 3 or 4 A.M. in order to walk the distances between their homes and the factory were all noted, as was the social impact of these facts for detractors of industry, who accused factory owners of crass materialism, especially when workers' poverty was contrasted with the wealth of the "directors of industry." The commission of the Société industrielle de Mulhouse was happy to counter such attacks by bearing witness that "industrialists also know how to reconcile their interests with that sweet philanthropy that forms one of the most beautiful of man's attributes."[27]

In its report, however, the commission of the society sadly concluded that appeals to philanthropy would be unlikely to result in an effective limitation of work hours. The problem was that not all factory owners were equally honorable or susceptible to arguments of philanthropy. Dishonorable owners of industry who violated a gentlemen's agreement to limit work hours would be abetted by the working classes themselves, whose poorest members, particularly those in cotton spinning, would seek work in mills where hours were not limited.[28] For these reasons, members of the industrial society gradually concluded that the means to their end lay with legislative intervention. They believed that legislation, however, would raise contention over two basic principles: the principle of paternal authority and the principle of the freedom of

25. Bourcart, "Proposition," pp. 327–28.

26. "Rapport de la commission spéciale, concernant la proposition de M. Jean-Jacques Bourcart," *Bulletin de la Société industrielle de Mulhouse*, no. 5 (1828): 330.

27. Ibid., p. 330.

28. Ibid., pp. 332–33.

industry. Although the commission believed that restricting children's work to twelve hours a day and establishing a lower age limit of nine years would not interfere with paternal authority, they were not yet prepared to support such an idea wholeheartedly.

Therefore, the Société industrielle de Mulhouse sought expert opinion on the two principles. It received few responses, but one of these few, from the liberal *économiste* Charles Dunoyer, was to have an important impact. While Dunoyer rejected the legitimacy of a law to limit adults' freedom to form labor contracts for whatever duration they wished, he argued that a similar limitation on children's work hours did not pose the same problem of principle, since paternal authority was already circumscribed in a number of ways.[29] At the same time that the society was considering Dunoyer's response, it considered other strategies for improving the moral and physical condition of factory workers, including the legalization of certain kinds of workers' coalitions. However, such alternatives were rejected.[30] Dunoyer's response and the slim appeal of other approaches to improving the labor conditions of factory workers were thus critical in launching the society's efforts to defend the interests of child workers as separate and distinct from those of their parents.

This reorientation of Bourcart's idea for reform towards an exclusive concentration on children's labor was not universally applauded by the membership of the Mulhouse industrial society. The idea of limiting children's work was felt by some to handicap mills in isolated areas where child laborers were often scarce. Important too was the objection of one member, M. Reber, who ascribed workers' poor physical condition to causes extraneous to the labor process—including bad housing, bad food, and the debauchery of young workers.[31] Poor economic conditions in the cotton trade in the late 1820s, which Bourcart had seen as an encouragement to social experimentation, were now cited as a reason for caution.

When the question of child labor reform was again raised within the Société industrielle de Mulhouse, it was as the result of inquiries from the Ministry of Public Education and was now couched in terms that restricted the discussion explicitly to child labor—a feature that would remain unchanged until final passage of the child labor law in 1841. The changed terms of the debate apparently permitted a speedier response by the society's members. Although a minority of a new commission appointed to study the matter shared the sentiments expressed earlier by Reber, the majority concurred with Dunoyer's opinion that admitted the legitimacy of legislative intervention into

29. M. Kestner-Rigau, "Rapport fait au nom de la commission spéciale chargée d'examiner les questions relatives au travail des jeunes ouvriers des fabriques," *Bulletin de la Société industrielle de Mulhouse*, no. 28 (1833): 343.

30. Ibid., p. 345.

31. Ibid., p. 347.

the work of children. The commission now stated its belief that the length of the workday was itself a central problem and argued strongly that the state had not only the right but the duty to defend the general interests of society against excesses of individual interests that resulted in the exploitation of young workers.[32]

By comparison with what was to come, the commission reports and deliberations of the Société industrielle de Mulhouse, which were so critical in initiating the examination of child labor as a social problem, were notable by their austere and understated tone. By the action of one of their number, the society had launched on a set of deliberations that might have led to support for the wholesale reduction of work hours for both adults and children.[33] However, the interest of public authorities in the more narrowly drawn subject of child labor and the objections of principle by such men as Dunoyer helped lead them away from this path of intervention. Moreover, refocusing the factory-labor problem on the question of children alone seems to have been partly responsible for raising the rhetorical stakes of the discussion. Nowhere was this more evident than in the work of Daniel Legrand, a coreligionist of Mulhouse's *patronat* but one who began to frame the "problem" of child factory labor in terms much stronger than those admitted within public discussions of the industrial society.

Whereas the industrialists of Mulhouse expressed their own arguments within an understated version of moral economist precepts, Legrand's writings on the problem of child labor added brimstone to the discussion. In his *Lettre d'un industriel des montagnes des Vosges*, Legrand changed not only the tone but the moral stakes of the game.[34] The idea that English laws might serve as models for French legislation, explicitly acknowledged within the Société industrielle de Mulhouse, became in Legrand's work a challenge to the moral integrity of France's leaders. In the powerful opening remarks of his text, Legrand argued that even England, which "subordinated its political to its financial interests" and (as all Frenchmen knew) was obsessed with maintaining the competitiveness of its industry in world markets—even England "ha[d] found that *all its interests, without exception,* imperiously demanded the *intervention of legislation* in order to fix the age, working hours and schooling of its factory workers in order to save them from *ruin* and *perdition.*"[34] The English, Legrand argued, had already seen a vision of a totally unregulated industrial economy. This and their greater religiosity, he believed, lay at the source of

32. Ibid., pp. 349–50.

33. In this they would not have been alone. Throughout debates on child labor legislation, the Chamber of Commerce of Lille would defend just this kind of bill.

34. Daniel Legrand, *Lettre d'un industriel des montagnes des Vosges à MM. Gros, Odier, Roman et comp. à Wesserling, distribuée aux membres des deux chambres et du ministère* (Paris, 1838), p. 3.

their otherwise puzzling departure from principles of laissez-faire economics in agreeing to intervene into the problem of child labor.[35] For Legrand, the underlying cause of the child labor problem lay fundamentally in an economic system based on competition and a corresponding if erroneous concentration of many French industrialists on short-term economic gain.[36] This financial shortsightedness, he argued, was exacerbated by the cupidity of parents in selling the labor of their children, the whole process resulting in one of the most deplorable consequences of large-scale industry—its destruction of family life: "The development of family life is one of the greatest benefits of Christianity and the element on which it can exercise its most beneficent influence. Whatever tends to weaken [these] sacred bonds and family life slowly undermines the social edifice and the bases of morality."[37]

Legrand strongly believed that unlike factory industry, children's work in small-scale or familial work settings reinforced family life and protected children from the immoral behavior of adults that they were liable to encounter both within the factory and on the way to and from work. He differed from most Alsatian moral economists who supported the principle of child labor legislation from within the Société industrielle de Mulhouse, not only by his advocacy but also by his practice of small-scale industry in which parents worked directly with their children.[38] Legrand's defense of small-scale family industry supported by the family's possession of land was, in fact, strongly reminiscent of Social Catholic critiques of factory production. In his portrait of France's factory children, whom he considered to be "poor and sad victims," Legrand emphasized the moral depredations that factory production had unleashed on both owners of industry and their workers.[39] He argued that the moral, financial, and social interests of all classes militated in favor of legislative intervention in preparing the nation's future, and provided empirical and practical as well as moral arguments for his position. He supported Bourcart's ideas that workers—both adults and children—were more productive during shortened working hours and that shortening work hours might help avoid crises of overproduction that seemed to plague French industry every seven years.[40]

35. Ibid., p. 4. The growing intervention of English state agencies into society, accompanied by a seemingly contradictory ideological defense of the values of laissez-faire, is illuminated in Philip Corrigan and Derek Sayer, *The Great Arch: English State Formation as Cultural Revolution* (Oxford, 1985), pp. 118–30.

36. Ibid., pp. 5–6.

37. Ibid., p. 11.

38. Legrand's own ribbon-making operation in the Vosges was founded on this type of work organization. Raymond Weiss, *Daniel Legrand (1783–1859): Son oeuvre sociale et internationale* (Paris, 1926), pp. 25–26. Weiss believed that Legrand was not particularly familiar with the actual working conditions of factory children in such places as Mulhouse (p. 65).

39. Legrand, *Lettre*, p. 3.

40. Ibid., p. 13.

In Legrand's work, nearly all of his arguments were subsidiary to his overriding concern with the moral dimensions of the child labor problem and with the future implications of legislators' failure to intervene in it. To illustrate his concern, Legrand raised one of the more horrifying specters of an unregulated future, a picture that exposed another side of child workers, those sad victims whose vulnerability called out for reform:

> These young boys of six to twelve years old, a pipe already in their mouth, swearing and obscene words on their lips, brandy for their drink . . . becom[e] fathers when they should still be schoolboys [and] have families with many children by the most shameful and pernicious of speculations, in order to give themselves over that much faster with their equally depraved companion to laziness and drunkenness—to be fed in their turn by their children at an age when they should feed them themselves, thus overturning all the bases of paternal authority.[41]

The kind of defiant toughness that Legrand deplored was familiar at least to Alsatian factory owners. They experienced it during work stoppages organized by local piecers in sympathy with the spinners with whom they worked. Work stoppages by Mulhouse's spinners in March 1827 in response to firings and wage reductions had been accompanied by organized gatherings of piecers in their support. Similarly, a strike by spinners in nearby Ste. Marie-aux-Mines in March of 1834 resulted in spinners' and piecers' banding together to demand back wages and an end to attempts by owners to substitute inferior cotton that was more difficult to spin.[42] However, Legrand and other moral economists chose to emphasize the estrangement between working-class parents and their children, arguing that industrial conditions led greedy parents to speculate on their children's labor power, thus setting up a vicious intergenerational cycle.

Like their English predecessors, who had lobbied for legislative intervention, Legrand and his coreligionists from the Mulhouse area eagerly defended the goal of educating working-class children in specialized institutions such as schools and *salles d'asile* (day-care centers), which they believed could begin to fill the educative functions that factory parents neglected. The development of legislative intervention and the establishment of such new institutions, Legrand implied, could begin to extirpate the more menacing features of child workers that stood in contrast to their status as victims.[43]

Legrand was something of an anomaly among Alsatian proponents of child labor legislation, particularly in his defense of small-scale industry and his inflated rhetorical style. However, his emphasis on the familial and moral

41. Ibid., p. 14.

42. For police and administrative correspondence on these activities, see AMM, J II/Hf 1 and 3. The 1827 agitation is discussed in Paul Leuilliot, *L'Alsace au début du XIXe siècle*, 2:499–500.

43. Ibid., pp. 15–16.

dimensions of the child labor problem placed him squarely within the mainstream of a moral economist position in the making. His writings, even in their flawed French, helped to stimulate government interest in child factory labor and its broader implications, particularly for the family.

The Familial Dimensions of Child Factory Labor

In 1837, a circular from the minister of agriculture, commerce, and public works was sent out to local chambers of commerce, *conseils des prud'hommes,* and mayors in order to gain information about children's factory labor. It also attempted to gather information about the family by asking whether and to what extent children who worked in factories were likely to be employed in the same establishment as their parents.[44] One finding that emerged from this inquiry was that the youngest children were likely to go to work if their parents were themselves working in the same mill. J. J. Bourcart had first pointed to this phenomenon: "Spinning workers are employed from the age of eight. In places where the population is sparse, even children of seven are employed, especially if they [work] with their father in the same shop."[45] This observation was supported by a number of responses to the ministerial circular:

> Very frequently, fathers employ their sons or daughters. We can estimate this number to be at least ⅓. It is they who employ them at the earliest age.[46]
>
> In factories that employ young workers, notably those that spin cotton, wool, and linen, such as *retorderies,* children generally enter at age eight to ten. The latter accompany their parents and run errands, etc. They have no fixed wages and receive a gratuity that varies between 50 centimes and 1.50 francs per week, according to their strength and skill.[47]
>
> In the spinning mills, about ⅛ of the children employed are ages 7 to 9½. The children of this age are often brought by their parents and work

44. The circular—no. 39, 31 July 1837—is contained in AN, F12/4704. Question 7 asked, "Do [the children] belong most often to workers who are themselves employed in the factory, and in what proportion?"

45. J. J. Bourcart, cited in Hordern, "L'évolution," p. 254. In the debate in the Chamber of Peers, M. Humblot-Conté argued that manufacturers allowed children under eight into their mills simply because parents ask them to. *Moniteur*, 7 March 1840, p. 433.

46. "Mémoire du conseil des prud'hommes de Rouen," AN, F12/4704.

47. "Extrait de la délibération de la chambre de commerce de Lille," meeting of 29 September 1837, AN, F12/4705. Children's wages in the Nord ranged from 50 centimes to 1 franc per week for children up to age eight; 1.5–3 francs from ages eight to ten, 3–4 francs from ten to twelve, and 4–6 francs from twelve to sixteen. One historian has estimated that these wages would purchase from one to three kilos of bread a day in "normal times." Lasserre, *La situation*, p. 152.

> almost always under their direction. The second group, from ages 10 to 12, composes ⅝. Finally, those from 12 to 14 compose ⅜ of the total . . . about ⅛ of the children belong to workers in the same shop and the rest to workers of all occupations.[48]

The question originally asked by the ministry was not whether children worked directly with their parents, but only whether the children were employed in the same establishment as the parents. Lille's chamber of commerce pointed out this important distinction: "In most factories, especially spinning mills, there are children who belong to workers in the same shop, without their being placed constantly under the immediate supervision of their parents."[49]

Several sources explained why children might not be working either directly under their parents or indeed within the same establishment. Conseils des prud'hommes and chambers of commerce believed that workers were aware that they were more likely to deal harshly with their own children than with those of other workers and thus eschewed working directly with them.[50] More importantly, it appears that when parents had a choice, many wished to disperse their children among different work places when the children were old enough so that if work stopped in one factory, the household's economy would not be entirely devastated. This strategy of placing children in different mills was felt to be most typical of urban workers who had a wider selection of work places.[51] The mayor of the city of Elbeuf, a textile center twenty kilometers southwest of Rouen, noted: "Few children are personally attached to their parents at work. They could and should be. However, workers prefer to disperse their children to ensure that work stoppages in one factory do not leave the entire family without work. [Thus] they assure themselves of some wages in all circumstances."[52] From the standpoint of some observers of child factory labor, it would have been better for parents to work directly with their children, thus reinforcing family bonds and the educative functions of parenthood. On the other hand, the fact that children went to work earlier when they were with their parents and were reported to receive harsher discipline from

48. Société libre pour concourir aux progrès du commerce et de l'industrie de Rouen, "De l'état des enfants dans les manufactures," AN, F12/4705.

49. "Extrait de la délibération," AN, F12/4705.

50. Report of Th. Barrois to the Chamber of Commerce of Lille, AN, F12/4705, and "Mémoire du conseil des prud'hommes de Rouen," AN, F12/4704, both documents in response to the circular of 31 July 1837.

51. "Rapport à la chambre de commerce de Rouen, séance du 27 octobre 1837: Réponses aux demandes du ministre du commerce et des travaux publics sur l'emploi des enfants dans les fabriques et la durée de leur travail," AN, F12/4705.

52. "Rapport du maire d'Elbeuf sur la question relative à l'emploi des enfants au travail," 12 September 1837, ADSM, 10 MP/1362. This point was also noted by Villermé in *Tableau*, 2:112.

them than from other adults made the protection of direct parent-child bonds in the factory less desirable.

As it stood, the work of piecers in cotton spinning and tireurs in cloth printing was controlled and organized essentially by adult workers and not by factory owners. "Workshop heads have few dealings with the children, since the majority are paid by the spinners, just as those employed by rug manufacturers are paid by the weavers."[53] After the child labor law was passed, manufacturers complained that conformity to it was rendered difficult by the persistence of this practice: "MM. Daniel Eck and Company complained to us about the difficulty they had in obeying the law in their cloth-printing works. These difficulties stem from the fact that the children are not really their workers but rather those of the printers who choose and pay them, and hire them as they wish."[54] These latter practices, of course, existed whether or not mule spinner and piecer, or printer and tireur, were linked by family ties. While it appears likely that parents preferred to have their youngest children working for them, especially if this was the condition for their admission to work, it is unlikely that mule spinners, who frequently needed the services of several piecers, would have had the number of young children required.[55] Interestingly enough, despite lamentations about the large number of children whom factory workers produced, it appears that in many areas piecers in particular were frequently in short supply.[56]

The persistence of elements of family work organization within the mills was thus insufficient to counter critiques of the hardships of factory work

53. Chambre consultative des manufactures de Tourcoing to the minister of commerce, 16 August 1837, ADN, M611/1.

54. Préfecture du Haut-Rhin, arrondissement de Belfort, "Rapport des inspections dans le canton de Cernay," 19 January 1844, AN, F12/4712; Peter N. Stearns, *Paths to Authority: The Middle Class and the Industrial Labor Force in France, 1820–1848* (Urbana, 1978), pp. 82–83. On the persistence of links between family and labor both in hiring practices and in the work process, see William M. Reddy, "Family and Factory: French Linen Weavers in the Belle Epoque," *Journal of Social History*, Winter, 1975, pp. 102–12. Reddy shows that the parent-child work bond was strongest when boys were serving an "apprenticeship" under their fathers. See also idem, "The Language of the Crowd at Rouen, 1752–1871," *Past and Present*, no. 74 (1977): 78–79.

55. This point is made by Michael Anderson, *Family Structure in Nineteenth-Century Lancashire* (Cambridge, 1971), p. 115.

56. Response of the Conseil des prud'hommes de Lille to the circular of the minister of agriculture and commerce of 14 September 1840 concerning the proposed child labor law, ADN, M613/5. The council argued that the shortage would be exacerbated by the formation of reduced-hour shifts of the younger group of child workers. See also Thouvenin, "De l'influence," *Annales d'hygiène publique et de médecine légale* 37 (1847): 99, who argued that the problem was more acute in Lille and Rouen than in Alsace. However, bad commercial conditions in Mulhouse in spring of 1845 were cited as a cause of a shortage of child workers there. Prefect of the Haut-Rhin to the minister of agriculture and commerce, 14 May 1845, AN, F12/4712.

for children no matter for whom the child worked. Indeed, the responsibility of parents for the early introduction of their children into their own work place was used to demonstrate the implication of parents in the exploitation of their own children. Furthermore, though the issue of internal factory discipline reached public debates only sporadically, there was some contemporary evidence of a newer trend that would reduce familial authority in the larger mills where children were employed. Revolutionary movements of 1830 and 1848, in particular, appear to have encouraged new efforts to organize and proclaim more standardized forms of work discipline for adult workers (see Appendixes B–D). The evidence of factory regulations must be treated with care. Very few of these documents are available for study in the areas under observation, and it is not clear how innovative they really were.[57] Similarly, as this study has emphasized, the promulgation of laws and regulations is not synonymous with their enforcement. However, the few available regulations do imply the desire of both owners and public authorities to place stricter controls over the relationship between spinners and piecers as well as over general relations between workers and management. Elements of older forms of work organization appear explicitly in these regulations. The notion of apprenticeship was still apparent.[58] Spinners were held responsible for damage done by their piecers.[59] Spinners were still obligated to find their own piecers, although relations between them were now more controlled by factory regulations, as well as by the law of 1841 itself.[60]

However, a comparison of regulations promulgated in the Rouen area as a result of worker actions during the Revolution of 1830 with the later regulations from Lille shows that the latter tended to become more elaborate and even didactic, containing homilies that sought to explain the benefits of regulations for both workers and owners and the reasons why particular rules were in order.[61] Under these more explicit systems of factory discipline, children were less susceptible, many argued, to the kind of arbitrary, emotionally based

57. William M. Reddy has emphasized that pre-1830 rules in the Roubaix area tended to be concerned more with technical aspects of the work process than with controlling workers' behavior per se. *The Rise of Market Culture*, pp. 103–4. For an example of Alsatian work regulations from 1837, see Georges Poull, "L'industrie textile vosgienne, des origines à 1978," *Le pays de Remiremont* 2 (1979): 30. These regulations stressed the supervisory authority of overseers and owners in machine maintenance and cleaning, and provided for searches of workers and the imposition of fines. No mention is made in them of relations between adult and child workers.

58. Appendix B, art. 17.

59. Appendix B, art. 20.

60. Appendix C, art. 4; Appendix D, arts. 10 and 11; Appendix A, art 8.

61. See, for example, Appendix D, art. 5, for the justification of penalties for lateness and absences. On the events surrounding the promulgation of Rouen's 1830 work rules, see Reddy, *The Rise of Market Culture*, pp. 114–25.

discipline that they received from parents or older family members. This is what Léon Faucher may have been getting at when he wrote: "If the young factory worker is a kind of regimented pariah, at least the discipline he obeys is not particularly arbitrary. It is at least something to have rules—even if they are harsh."[62] Although family bonds within the work place doubtless persisted through the nineteenth century and indeed up to the present, it was also apparent that one of the goals of newer forms of factory regulation was to destroy one-to-one authority relations between workers and their young helpers by substituting that of management. One of the effects of such regulations was to weaken remnants of family work organization that remained much longer in smaller, artisanal shops.[63]

Making a Law on Child Labor

By the time the child labor question was debated in both legislative houses in 1840, it bore the effects of prior formulations within the work of Alsatian moral economists, the examples of English legislation, the widely read work of Villermé on the condition of the French working classes, and the results of several government inquiries. Petitions from the Société industrielle de Mulhouse and the Société pour l'encouragement de l'instruction primaire parmi les protestants de France were not the first to be brought before the Chambers of Peers and Deputies concerning the problem of child labor, but they were the ones that stimulated the discussions that ultimately resulted in France's first substantial law regulating child labor.[64] Petitions pointed to children's youth, the long hours children worked in France's mills, and their poor physical health. Premature and continuous work, the petitioners argued, deprived children of "affections that could have been developed in their families" and of religious training. Lobbying efforts were undertaken "in favor of the unfortunate whose age and the negligence of their parents have deprived of all protection."[65]

In the principal legislative debates, which took place during the spring of 1840 in the Chamber of Peers and at the end of the year in the Chamber

62. "Le travail des enfants à Paris," *Revue des deux mondes*, 15 November 1844, p. 661.

63. Stearns, *Paths*, pp. 83–85.

64. Earlier pleas for regulation had come from, *inter alia*, the rector of the Academy of Strasbourg. In a letter of 27 November 1832 to the minister of public education, ADHR, 1M/123b, he had urged that France emulate England's intervention into the problem of children's labor. See also Lasserre, *La situation*, p. 155. For a more detailed account of the various groups involved in pressuring the government for the reform of child industrial labor, see Lee Shai Weissbach, *Assuring the Future Harvest: Child Labor Reform in France, 1827–1885* (Baton Rouge: Louisiana State University Press, forthcoming), chs. 2 and 3.

65. *Moniteur*, 16 June 1839, p. 989.

of Deputies, proponents of a law very early gained possession of the moral high ground, even though nearly all participants expressed their belief that "something" had to be done about the problem of child labor. The government was initially loath to support legislation as the proper vehicle for reform, defending instead its own plan for local administrative regulations. It expressed its hesitation in the Chamber of Peers through ministerial skepticism about the likelihood of a law's enforceability. However, the government's reluctance to support legislation quickly met with the disgust of the opposition press as well as that of the commission of the Chamber, headed by Baron Charles Dupin, demonstrating that the government was somewhat out of touch with opinion within the upper house.[66] A newly appointed minister of commerce, M. Gouin, announced the government's acceptance of the commission's proposal for a law very soon after the debate began.[67]

Showing that legislative intervention into children's industrial labor was needed required that the plight of factory children be demonstrated to differ significantly and powerfully from that of children in other kinds of work places. This was not entirely easy to accomplish. Of course, several features of children's industrial labor had caught the attention of French observers as early as the 1820s. One of the most important was the long hours that children and young people had to work. The working day in cotton mills during the 1830s when the mills were in full operation generally lasted from 5 A.M. to 7 P.M., broken by rest periods of one to two hours' duration. The hours of operation for cloth-printing works, however, varied considerably, since cloth printing required natural light. While summer work typically extended to eleven or twelve hours a day, in the winter, hours were reduced to eight.[68] Another aspect of

66. The *National*'s editors were particularly critical of the government's original plan for solving the child factory labor problem through administrative regulation alone. The replacement of the minister of agriculture and commerce, Cunin-Gridaine, shortly before the March 1840 debates in the Chamber of Peers, they believed, was related to the government's rapid abandonment of this strategy. However, their argument that the government's plan to reform child labor conditions by administrative regulation rather than legislation was supported only by such lackeys of Guizot as the Count Rossi was exaggerated, as debates would show. See *Le National*, 5 March 1840.

67. For Gouin's announcement of the government's decision, see *Moniteur*, 5 March 1840, p. 417. The previous minister, Cunin-Gridaine (see n. 66 above), a wealthy industrialist from Sedan, was back in his old job as minister of agriculture and commerce by the time of the debate in the Chamber of Deputies. Despite his cabinet's preference for administrative regulation over legislation, he was cited as one of the greatest supporters of the 1841 law in Armand Audiganne, *La nouvelle loi*, p. 9.

68. Notes from the inspection of Blech, Steimbach, and Mantz, contained in "Extrait des délibérations de la commission d'inspection de l'arrondissement d'Altkirch pour l'exécution de la loi du 22 mars 1841, séance du 20 décembre 1843," AN, F12/4712; prefect of the Haut-Rhin to the minister of agriculture and commerce, 14 May 1845, AN F12/4712; the mayor of Darnétal (near Rouen) to the prefect of the Seine-Inférieure, 5 January 1838, ADSM, 10 MP/1361.

children's work in cloth printing that evoked the criticism of some observers was the use of strong chemicals in mordants handled by the children.[69]

Yet, long working hours were hardly limited to large factories nor to those that were most highly mechanized. Children working at home or in small familial workshops could be shown to be working at least as long, even if they were not working at the continuous pace characteristic of work in mechanized factories. In a society accustomed to thinking of labor as the appropriate activity of its working classes during most of their waking hours, the length of the working day for factory children was not at first glance a persuasive argument in favor of restricting legislation to industrial establishments. Furthermore, military recruitment data that had long been used as evidence to demonstrate the poor physical condition of the industrial work force were ambiguous, as opponents of the legislation were delighted to show. For certain areas where small-scale industry was prevalent, opponents could demonstrate that the physical state of the working class was equally poor as, if not more deplorable than, the state of workers in areas where textile factories abounded.[70]

To counter these kinds of arguments, moral economists such as Dupin would emphasize that since the advent of steam power, children's work, like that of adults, had been thoroughly revolutionized. Work in mechanized mills had led not only to the extension of work hours, but to a kind of work that was both more continuous and faster-paced. Without arguing that long work hours were entirely unique to mechanized mills, he and his supporters tried to articulate the complex of features that distinguished industrial work processes. As leader of the moral economist offensive in the Chamber of Peers, Dupin brought to the debate his immense technical knowledge of industrial processes and his expertise on recent child labor legislation in other nations that had chosen to focus on factory labor. He urged French legislators to support reform that would concentrate on large industrial work settings: "We have refused to worry about conditions peculiar to [particular] workshops or boutiques where the same skills and routines have been practiced for centuries

69. Louis-René Villermé, *Tableau*, 1:9–11, noted the pungent odor of acetic acid in the cloth-printing works he visited in Mulhouse. Concern about the presence of chemicals was expressed, *inter alia*, in Préfecture du Haut-Rhin, "Rapports d'inspection pour l'exécution de la loi du 22 mars 1841," AN, F12/4712, and the letter from the mayor of Darnétal to the prefect of the Seine-Inférieure, 5 January 1838, ADSM, 10 MP/1361.

70. The most active proponents of this argument were representatives Barbet of Rouen and Lestiboudois from the Nord in the Chamber of Deputies. Barbet, in particular, led the battle to show that it was the habits of workers themselves and not conditions of work that were responsible for the moral and physical degeneration of the working class. *Moniteur*, 16 June 1839. p. 990, For Lestiboudois's comments concerning the proportion of conscripts rejected for physical infirmity in regions of small-scale industry, see *Moniteur*, 22 December 1840, p. 2484. A report to the conseil général of the Seine-Inférieure in its 1840 session argued that the city's handloom weavers were in much worse physical condition than the factory spinners. Conseil général de la Seine-Inférieure, "Délibérations," session of 1840, p. 175, ADSM, 1 NP/24.

without any more abuses now than there were formerly. We wished to restrict ourselves to the new manufacturing industry that abuses the inferiority of the human constitution by subordinating and sacrificing it . . . to mechanical engines."[71] Proponents of specialized legislation also emphasized the novelty of the child industrial labor problem by arguing that children's work in cloth printing or cotton spinning began at younger ages than those typical of apprentices under an old regime of work organization, in many cases well before their first communion.[72] Moreover, apprenticeship was not an adequate standard of comparison either, since the kind of training that young factory workers received was apt to fit them only to replace the ranks of the semiskilled labor force that accounted for most of the workers in textile mills. The argument was that unlike previous generations of handicraft apprentices, child factory workers really weren't learning anything of value. This was particularly the case with cotton-mill piecers. As the Baron de Gérando argued in the Chamber of Peers, the piecer "will have learned to practice the trade of a brute, which you could have carried out as well by an inattentive monkey."[73] Conservative Catholics such as Gérando needed little persuasion to believe that factories entailed a distressing and qualitatively new kind of labor that was in and of itself deleterious to the morality and health of France's child workers.

A wholesale rejection of factory labor, however, was somewhat attenuated in the work of Villermé. Although he lent his critical support to the idea of regulation or legislation of children's industrial labor, he was very much opposed to legislation that would include limits on the work of adults.[74] While he acknowledged the deplorable moral and physical conditions of many adult factory workers, Villermé distinguished clearly between them and their children, whom he saw "very frequently as the victims of the debauchery and lack of foresight of their parents."[75] He characterized children's factory work as a kind of "torture" and discussed approvingly the efforts of Bourcart and the Société industrielle de Mulhouse to improve children's working conditions despite their own "interests."[76] Villermé also supported the system of reduced-hour shifts for young child workers that had been organized in En-

71. *Moniteur*, 6 March 1840, p. 426.

72. In many observers' minds, first communion seems to have been a rite of passage associated with the transition to an age when apprenticeship might begin. In his study based on the memoirs of the Rouen weaver Charles Noiret, Georges Guérif has noted that in the early July Monarchy, weaving apprenticeships usually began when the child was twelve to fifteen years old. However, the practice of weaving apprenticeships was declining because of the low wages to be expected from handloom weaving. Parents preferred to send their children to work in spinning mills "or other establishments." See "Charles Noiret et l'enquête de 1848 sur la profession de tisserand," *Revue d'histoire économique et sociale* 49 (1971): 102.

73. *Moniteur*, 8 March 1840, p. 442.

74. *Tableau*, 2:108.

75. Ibid., p. 86.

76. Ibid., pp. 95–96, 367.

gland to accommodate the labor law of 1833, and showed that it had already been implemented in some Alsatian mills to allow children to attend school.[77]

The greatest of France's moral economists thus put his enormous personal prestige behind the principle of administrative regulation of or legislation for reforming children's industrial labor. His voluminous findings left some ambiguities, however, over the primary causes of children's exploitation in industry and its long-term solution. For Villermé, the extended hours of children's factory labor coupled with parental influence, and not factory labor per se, were the main structural causes of children's suffering. His travels through France's industrial centers had led him to associate factory labor and immoral behavior and to point out the general desirability of work in small familial establishments.[78] Nevertheless, he had also pointed out that drunkenness, illegitimacy, and poverty varied widely by region and were not limited to factory workers; these problems also afflicted certain elements of the artisanal working class, whose high wages, he believed, frequently led to drunkenness, exploitation of children, and other symptoms of immorality. Thus, the mores of the adults who worked in factories, and not the technological circumstances of factory labor, were ultimately most critical in leading to the exploitation of France's child workers. Villermé in no way shared either the Social Catholics' or Legrand's horror at the factory in and of itself.[79]

Villermé's findings that workers in many areas were not badly off, or that their lives had improved since the 1820s, were in fact used by legislators skeptical of various elements of the law under debate. In the Chamber of Deputies, Villermé was cited at the first reading of the petitions as having shown that workers were not universally debilitated or immoral.[80] His study was also used in the Chamber of Peers by those who wished to fend off demands for legislation. Count Rossi, one of the government's early legislative allies, cited Villermé's findings on the vast regional differences among France's working classes—results that in Rossi's argument made a uniform law on child labor inappropriate.[81] Gustave de Beaumont, in his effort to keep the state out of the work place and away from an ill-defined protection of mores, also appealed to Villermé's argument that industry had gradually improved the lives of workers.[82] Finally, Villermé's work was used as evidence against the pending legislation by a deputy who wished child labor legislation to be extended to all industries.[83] In retrospect, it is clear that the argument that children's

77. Ibid., pp. 104–5, 123.

78. Ibid., 1:443.

79. William Coleman, *Death Is a Social Disease: Public Health and Political Economy in Early Industrial France* (Madison, 1982), pp. 207–19.

80. *Moniteur*, 16 June 1839, p. 990.

81. *Moniteur*, 6 March 1840, p. 424.

82. *Moniteur*, 22 December 1840, pp. 2487–88.

83. *Moniteur*, 24 December 1840, p. 2505. This last argument was gradually interpreted as

labor in factory industry was inherently more oppressive than work they were doing in smaller shops was not entirely convincing. Legislators were simply better informed about abuses of children in larger factories than about abuses in smaller shops, given the amount of attention that had been devoted to the subject.

Dupin's preference for legislation restricted to types of work places that were regionally concentrated and marginal to the experience of most of the nation was clearly part of the legislation's appeal to many peers and deputies. Although moral economists like Dupin believed that factories presented qualitatively new working conditions as well as historically unique forms of physical and moral degradation, they also believed that a law limited in scope would have a higher likelihood of passage and enforcement. Limiting legislation to larger, more technically developed establishments would also mitigate objections expressed most forcefully by the Social Catholic Montalembert. Voicing his critique of industry in the Chamber of Peers, Montalembert cautioned: "I am not speaking of home industry exercised in the cottage, the *foyer paternel*. This is a blessing. But what I am attacking, what I do deplore is large-scale industry . . . spinning mills and other industries of this kind that uproot the poor man, his wife and children from family customs and . . . rural life and put them in unhealthy barracks, veritable prisons where all ages and sexes are condemned to systematic and progressive degradation."[84] Similar arguments had been brought to the attention of the government in response to a ministerial circular of 1840 concerning different proposals for regulating child factory labor. A summary of these responses showed a widespread belief that

> inspection [of small-scale industry] would interfere with its operation. But it would interfere also with something more precious and sacred in these families by substituting daily intervention by the [state's] authority for paternal power. . . . Is it necessary for the worker's home to be open day and night to the inspector's investigations? The child will become used to viewing his father as an enemy who is being constantly watched by the law and its magistrates. Certainly the evils are great, but it is not by such a remedy that we will cure them. If the law prevented certain individual failures, it would more profoundly disturb the moral sense of the working classes by introducing a new element of defiance and discord into their families.[85]

---

profoundly hostile to viable legislation, for reasons discussed below. At least one historian has also viewed it in this light. See Lasserre, *La situation*, p. 158.

84. *Moniteur*, 5 March 1840, p. 419.

85. "Analyse des observations présentées par les chambres de commerce, les conseils de prud'hommes, les chambres consultatives des arts et manufactures, des conseils généraux et les

Intervention into small-scale industry would thus have had to confront the objections of those who saw it as a clear violation of paternal authority within the work place.[86]

The Question of Paternal Rights

Perhaps the greatest defender of the moral reputation of France's industrialists in the debates in both the Chamber of Peers and Deputies was the chemist Gay-Lussac.[87] He, more than anyone else, criticized the idea of a law that would constrain factory owners rather than appealing to their sense of humanity and justice. After criticizing the proposed legislation for purveying a prejudicial view of the factory owner, he invited his colleagues "to see in the manufacturer a useful and honorable citizen providing for the needs of society, assuring work to the working class and presenting himself in their midst, making himself beloved like a true father."[88] This was too much for Dupin, who doubtless sensed where Gay-Lussac's arguments were leading. He objected: "Some are always likening a manufacturing establishment to the *foyer paternel*. This is a blatant error. A manufacturing establishment that brings together 200 or 400 people is completely different from the interior of the family. It is an establishment which by the simple multiplicity of workers presents more than a private aspect, one in which the public authorities have a right to intervene in a certain manner."[89] Elements of Gay-Lussac's point of view nonetheless resurfaced in the Chamber of Deputies in an argument proposed by the representative Lestiboudois. He suggested that the French government, by intervening into children's labor, was undermining paternal responsibility for children. This, he argued, would have some of the same consequences as foundling legislation, making all factory children essentially the wards of

---

préfets sur les trois projets de loi relatifs au travail des enfants dans les manufactures," AN, F12/4706.

86. For a while, it even seemed as if the Chamber of Deputies would raise the number of workers required to qualify work places for inclusion under the law from 20 to 40. However, this amendment was ultimately defeated, even though it was supported by the commission of the Chamber and the government alike. *Moniteur*, 24 December 1840, pp. 2506–7, and 25 December 1840, pp. 2511–13.

87. Gay-Lussac had been elected to the Chamber of Deputies in 1831, 1834, and 1837, and in 1839 accepted a peerage.

88. *Moniteur*, 10 March 1840, p. 458. Gay-Lussac objected to the law because it did not appeal to the "generous sentiments" of factory owners, but instead implied that factories were "the scourge of the human race," a locution that raised the hackles of Victor Grandin later in the debate in the Chamber of Deputies. Grandin, the only industrialist on the commission of the Chamber, heard that such a statement had been made in the Chamber of Peers and protested it in the name of France's industrialists. He appears not to have realized that Gay-Lussac had expressed it disapprovingly. For Grandin's remarks, see *Moniteur*, 23 December 1840, p. 2497.

89. *Moniteur*, 10 March 1840, p. 458.

the French state. In his view, the reason that the English could legitimately proceed with their intervention into child labor was that their Poor Law had already admitted that it was ultimately the state and not poor families that had responsibility for the care and maintenance of children—a principle that Lestiboudois vigorously opposed.[90]

Lestiboudois's argument was supported in the Chamber of Deputies in a speech by M. Taillandier, who showed that the intervention of the state would in fact violate the paternal home: "When one has once recognized in public power the right to cross the threshold of the *foyer domestique* and to intervene in family affairs, what barrier may we oppose to deviations from the principle?"[91] What happened next was quite interesting. For, in his response to Taillandier's objection, Villemain, the minister of public education, took up Dupin's line of argument, denying that the law would interfere with paternal authority or violate the sanctity of the *foyer domestique,* since factory owners did not stand in the same relation to their factories as fathers did to their homes. The proposed legislation could not violate paternal authority because owners of industry had no paternal rights in such establishments: "There is no analogy between the interior of a family and these large units created by our society, which should serve the public good without detriment to morality and humanity."[92] What was conspicuously absent was any discussion of whether the paternal rights of factory children's *fathers* might be violated by legislative intervention. On this single occasion when a discussion of the issue seemed to be imminent, the minister Villemain had interpreted Taillandier's argument as referring to the "paternal" rights of factory owners and refuted this claim with Dupin's argument that there were no relevant paternal rights worthy of consideration within work places to be affected by the law.

The notion that regulating child factory labor could constitute a violation of the rights of fathers of factory children elicited little support except by tacit deduction from the highly polemical and minority arguments of principle voiced by Lestiboudois and Taillandier. Several deputies pointed out that restrictions on child labor were likely to result in a decline in working-class families' income, but this was merely a regrettable empirical fact, insufficient to detract from the legitimacy of pending legislation. The English Poor Law scare tactic was also apparently losing some of its rhetorical force. Indeed, reference to it was faced head on by one Alsatian legislator in the Chamber of Deputies, M. Diétrich, who argued that a French Poor Law would become more necessary if the Chamber of Deputies failed to intervene to improve the physical and moral condition of the French working classes.[93]

90. *Moniteur*, 22 December 1840, pp. 2483–84.
91. *Moniteur*, 23 December 1840, p. 2495.
92. Ibid.
93. *Moniteur*, 22 December 1840, p. 2488.

As leader of moral economist opinion in favor of the legislative route to reform, Charles Dupin wished to put the paternal authority question to rest. He did this very skillfully by making it appear self-evident that a model of paternal obligation he and other moral economists would put forward was traditional and unexceptionable, violated only by fathers whose control over their children now amounted to little more than a role as a labor broker. Speaking of paternal authority, Dupin argued:

> Far from us to deny this sacred authority! On the contrary, in our opinion it is strengthened by laws that circumscribe it, surrounding its free exercise by a social bulwark. We proclaim *paternal rights*. By these words we understand first, the right to supply [children] with food, clothing, and lodging, and to provide for the health of their children; further, the right to take care of their souls as well as their bodies and to educate them in the love of work as well as virtue. But we wish the law to prohibit the right to sell the strength, health, and lives of children without control.[94]

He criticized those opponents of the law who continued to believe that parents should be the arbiters in the matter of their children's work.

> It is the fathers, before the children, who are demoralized. And [critics of legislation] ask us to refer ourselves to the fathers, when it has been proven that it is precisely the fathers who sin . . . and who disdain instruction for themselves and their children. . . . Alas! It is they whose precious feelings of tender love, of vigilance and solicitude for their children are often extinguished. Thus, it is necessary that the law become a kind of father when the real father fails [the dictates] of both nature and society.[95]

One of the arguments espoused by proponents of the law in the Chamber of Peers was thus a newly emerging model of the relationship between the working-class father and his children, one that deemphasized the idea of paternal control, since control over children's wages was one of the problems, and substituted a model of stewardship. Dupin's recital of the obligations of fatherhood was not in itself contentious. In highly idealized form it could be interpreted as a timeless and universal portrait of fatherhood. In its specific setting, however, his formulation functioned not primarily as an idealized or sentimentalized version of the "good father" to which mere mortals could

94. Charles Dupin, *Du travail des enfants qu'emploient les ateliers, les usines et les manufactures consideré dans les intérêts mutuels de la société, des familles et de l'industrie* (Paris, 1840), p. li. In the introduction to his book, Dupin elaborated on themes addressed in debates in the Chamber of Peers. The main body of the text reproduced arguments made in his speeches in the Chamber in March 1840.

95. Ibid., p. 87.

only aspire, but rather as a new standard of actual paternal behavior by which the fathers of factory children had been measured and found wanting. His interpretation was echoed in the Chamber of Deputies, later on in the debate:

> When it is a question of removing children from the dangers of premature or excessive work—to protest in the name of paternal power—isn't this to abuse an important term? Oh, doubtless the father's authority is a respectable and sacred thing, but [only] when the father understands and respects his mission; when, like a second Providence he watches over the frail body and innocent soul of his child; when he is devoted to keeping him from all evil and corruption in order to prepare the future of a happy being, an honest man. Only then is he realizing the fullness of his right because he fulfills all the sanctity of his duty. But if he is brutalized by ignorance or poverty and is not aware of the considerations owed to this tender age; if in order to satisfy real or artificial needs he hastens to traffic in his child, or to send him to a job that tires and brands him; if he coldly cashes in on the future of this unhappy creature—oh, then he has stripped himself of the power that was given him towards a whole other end. And society has the right to say to him: "This child no longer has a father. It is I who shall protect him."[96]

Such images of working-class fathers were not unanimously accepted. In the Chamber of Deputies, Villeneuve-Bargemont refrained from a wholesale indictment of the fathers of factory children and characteristically viewed the problem of workers in industry as a whole. His support for regulating the work of children alone was based, he argued, on a practical consideration. He saw it as only a first step towards controlling the competitive system of industry that England had unleashed upon the world.[97] For him, the goal of the law was not merely to restrain fathers and some factory owners from exploiting the labor power of children, but the broader one of shoring up the family as a group. Villeneuve thus favored a wide variety of measures: separation of the sexes in the factories, abolition of Mondays as holidays, payment of workers in midweek and not on Saturdays, and the abolition of loans to workers—all measures that had been recommended by Villermé.[98] However, Montalembert's and Villeneuve's support of the short-term goals of child labor legislation provided crucial support for moral economists like Dupin.

96. Speech by M. Corne, reported in *Moniteur*, 22 December 1840, p. 2485. Corne also noted sardonically that it was unusual for the Chamber to hear talk about the absolute freedom of industry from those who so frequently sought government protection.

97. Villeneuve supported the proposal put forward by the Chamber of Commerce of Lille for the limitation of work hours for adults and children alike to twelve hours.

98. *Moniteur*, 23 December 1840, pp. 2492–94.

The goal of moralizing the families of the working classes drew Social Catholics and moral economists closer together than they had ever appeared before. The argument that the moralization of the working classes was an overriding goal of child labor legislation came from familiar quarters early in the discussion in the Chamber of Peers. Dupin, the Baron de Morogues, and the Baron de Gérando all made this position quite clear. After citing the numerous social indicators of immorality in factory towns, including high levels of illegitimacy, Dupin summarized his view of this goal: "Especially in those parts of the kingdom that are most given over to the mechanical arts and the richest in manufacturing, places where great numbers of children are employed, we have a great interest in recalling the working class, from its tender youth onwards, more and more to principles of order and morality, to the respect for persons and property, to the veneration of laws and of religion."[99] Baron de Morogues, for his part, believed that improving the mores of the working class was even more important than maintaining its health, and he cited figures on "immorality" indicating that it was two to ten times as high in factory towns as in rural areas.[100] The Baron de Gérando shared this emphasis on the goal of moralization, seeing it as a key to improving working-class well-being.[101]

It became clear that a key to changing the mores of the working classes was the encouragement within the family of the same kind of long-range thinking that moral economists hoped to encourage among factory owners and legislators opposed to the principle of interventionist legislation. The main task of moral economist legislators was thus to show that reducing working-class parents' dependency on the wages of their children would help lead to a future in which families' short-term interests would be modified so as to accord with the longer-term interests of both families and the French social order. Speaking of the child labor law, the deputy Corne argued: "Nothing is more apt to awaken ideas of order, a concern with the future among a class that poverty renders too unconcerned. . . . I have no doubt that we are already rendering this service to humanity—to prevent many troubles born of lack of foresight . . . which arise afterwards with threatening urgency."[102] In the minds of such deputies, provisions of the law would serve a pedagogic function, limiting the boundaries of parental and industrialists' power in the interests of the future of French society as a whole. The law would coordinate and reconcile interests that appeared to conflict only because the views of some parents and industrialists were short-sighted, lacking in values of *prévoyance* both financial and moral.

99. *Moniteur*, 23 February 1840, p. 353.
100. *Moniteur*, 5 March 1840, p. 418.
101. *Moniteur*, 8 March 1840, p. 442.
102. *Moniteur*, 22 December 1840, p. 2485.

Here, moral economist proponents of child labor legislation supported the idea that the long-term interests, if not the short-term interests, of France's factory owners militated in favor of legislation. It was these long-term interests that Dupin characterized as their "true interests." [103] In his systematic summary of the debates, Dupin expanded on this theme, arguing that the law was essentially saving some industrialists from their own shortsightedness. Moreover, the goal of the law was to make the working class "stronger, more enlightened, more moral. Far from these precautions being a source of ruin for the masters who gain advantage from this class, they will become, to the contrary, a cause of fortune in their favor. We are thus working for the manufacturers, not harming them." [104] In the Chamber of Deputies, M. Diétrich cited the example of industrialists within the Société industrielle de Mulhouse who best understood what those interests were: "These are enlightened industrialists, those who do not seek to increase their fortunes in a few days by means of immoderate work and the false enticement of excessive profits." [105] Not all legislators concurred with this portrait of Mulhouse's industrialists. Some legislators, particularly in the Chamber of Deputies, believed that the main reason the push for child labor legislation had originated in Alsace was that conditions for child workers were worst there.[106] A number of deputies, however, appear to have shared in the view that lessons of moral economy sometimes had to be taught to unenlightened members of the industrial bourgeoisie as well as to the working class.

The argument that values of moral and financial prudence were to be strengthened among all classes affected by the law was tactically useful in that it provided proponents of legislation a way to show that the law was in the financial and moral interests of factory owners as well as the children and families that worked in them. This argument clearly incorporated some of the most cherished values that had informed earlier moral economist positions on other policies intimately related to working-class families. In addition, the idea that the law would have moralizing effects on working-class families may have been one of the few on which nearly all legislators could agree.

103. *Moniteur*, 10 March 1840, p. 459.

104. Dupin, *Du travail*, p. 49.

105. *Moniteur*, 22 December 1840, p. 2488.

106. M. de Ressigeac made this point rather late in the discussion in the Chamber of Deputies, arguing that children were particularly bad off not merely because of working conditions within the mills of the Mulhouse area, but also because of the long commute that many children had to make. *Moniteur*, 25 December 1840, p. 2515. For a similarly critical view of working-class conditions in Mulhouse, see Louis Levrault, "Mulhouse et le vieux Mülhausen," *Revue d'Alsace*, no. 1 (1836), and the rejoinder, attributed to Dr. Achille Penot, in the *Industriel Alsacien*, 23 January 1836.

Divisions in Opinion on Elements of Legislation

Between discussions of the law in the Chamber of Peers in March of 1840 and debates in the Chamber of Deputies in December of that year, the minister of agriculture and commerce had solicited the opinion of local groups about various provisions of the law. While the results showed a great deal of support for the principle of legislation, substantial differences on particulars remained. The Chamber of Commerce of Lille continued to advocate its proposal for a twelve-hour limit on the work of adults as well as children and was supported in this position by the city's Conseil des prud'hommes. Their insistence on this strategy was now interpreted as principled opposition to the pending legislation. Other groups who were identified as opponents of the law included the Chambers of Commerce of St. Etienne and Cherbourg, the Chambre consultative des arts et métiers of St. Quentin, and the Conseil des prud'hommes of Roubaix. Groups from the regions under study here that were cited as having accepted the *principle* of the law included the chambers of commerce of Mulhouse and Rouen, the two cities' conseils des prud'hommes, and the conseils géneraux of the Haut-Rhin and the Seine-Inférieure.[107]

However, even among those who accepted the "principle" of legislation, there were still disagreements about work hours and age categories. The conseil général of the Seine-Inférieure wanted the minimum age of child workers raised to twelve. The chamber of commerce of Mulhouse wanted children eight to twelve years old to be able to work eleven hours a day, and the older children twelve hours a day. Mulhouse's chamber of commerce also felt that very few children under twelve were employed in spinning or weaving mills, and that the youngest children tended to be employed in cloth-printing mills, where they were working directly with their parents. They felt that prohibiting this kind of work would create both financial and moral problems, since children would no longer be under direct parental supervision.[108] The conseils des prud'hommes of both Mulhouse and Rouen wanted children to be able to work twelve hours a day from age ten on.[109] The Alsatian deputy Diétrich also proclaimed that Daniel Legrand himself did not favor the reduced-hour shifts for child workers that were used in England. Rather, he preferred a law that enabled children to work twelve hours a day beginning at age ten.[110] The inten-

107. For a discussion of these different responses, see Renouard's report in the *Moniteur*, 17 December 1840, p. 2456.

108. Chambre of Commerce of Mulhouse to the minister of commerce, 19 September 1840, ADHR, 1M/123b.

109. See Renouard's report in the *Moniteur*, 17 December 1840, p. 2456, and "Analyse des observations présentées par les chambres de commerce, les conseils des prud'hommes, les chambres consultatives des arts et manufactures et les conseils généraux, sur le projet de loi relatif au travail des enfants dans les manufactures," *Moniteur*, 21 December 1840, p. 2477.

110. *Moniteur*, 25 December 1840, p. 2517.

tion of these shifts was to provide especially for the needs of the younger child workers. It was believed by many, however, that this system would disrupt the factory work process and thus be difficult to implement and enforce.

The issue of who would be entrusted with inspecting establishments subject to the law also stimulated a great deal of disagreement. One of the problems was that the government had simply not thought out this issue before allowing discussion to come to the floor of the legislative chambers. Dupin preferred to emulate the British system by establishing a special corps of paid inspectors.[111] The commission he headed and the peers as a whole favored the involvement of department-level authorities, particularly prefects and subprefects, in choosing appropriate inspectors, even though legislators feared that local interests would be powerful enough to thwart the law's enforcement. This was, in fact, one of the reasons that many peers had opposed the government's original plan to reform child labor through departmental regulations.[112] The idea of having school inspectors fulfill the task of factory inspection was supported by some peers but was rejected by Victor Cousin, the minister of education.[113] This proposal resurfaced later in the Chamber of Deputies in its commission's report but was again rejected, since it was thought to be difficult to find men with expertise in both domains who had the time to do a good job in both roles.

Members of the Chamber of Deputies as well as local groups were sharply divided on the inspection issue. In late spring 1840, the commission of the Chamber of Deputies received objections to the participation of some local authorities, particularly mayors, since they were alternately viewed as possible business rivals or as lackeys of factory owners. There were widespread fears, too, that mayors lacked the requisite technical expertise to carry out factory inspections.[114] One member of the Chamber of Deputies, M. Thil, argued that the powers of the inspectors should not be discussed until deputies were sure of what their "social position" was; in so arguing, he was expressing the fear of many members that inquisitorial inspections were to be carried

111. On the enforcement of the English Factory Acts, see Bernice Martin, "Leonard Horner: A Portrait of an Inspector of Factories," *International Review of Social History* 14 (1969): 412–43; and the more recent debate over enforcement between A. E. Peacock, "The Successful Prosecution of the Factory Acts, 1833–1855," *Economic History Review*, 2d ser., 37 (1984): 197–210, and Peter Bartrip, "Success or Failure? The Prosecution of the Early Factory Acts," *Economic History Review*, 2d ser., 38 (1985): 423–36.

112. See the comments of Victor Cousin, the Baron de Morogues, and Montalembert on this issue in the *Moniteur*, 5 March 1840, p. 418.

113. Comments by the Comte de Cholet and Victor Cousin in the *Moniteur*, 11 March 1840, p. 467.

114. M. Renouard, "Rapport fait au nom de la commission chargée de l'examen du project de loi relatif au travail des enfants dans les manufactures, usines ou ateliers," *Moniteur*, 5 June 1840, p. 1295.

out by low-level bureaucrats or even by members of the *police judiciaire*. The minister of agriculture and commerce tried to calm these fears by suggesting that *négociants* and manufacturers who were personally unaffected by the law might serve, and that inspectors could also be recruited from among retired economists who would bring technical expertise to the task.[115] Given the level of disagreement, the commission of the Chamber of Deputies ultimately decided to leave the inspection issue to the government to resolve.[116]

The question of how violations of the law were to be treated also stimulated vigorous debate. In discussions in the Chamber of Peers, the Marquis de Laplace argued that since it was cupidity that led parents to exploit their children, their punishment for violating the law should also be pecuniary.[117] However, Charles Dupin objected to this argument by reminding his colleagues that working-class parents would be unable to pay even modest fines. The suggestion that factory owners should be required to pay a 16–100 franc fine and to appear before the *police correctionnelle* to answer violations of the law aroused the repugnance of some legislators, who believed that workers might take advantage of such a provision and falsely accuse owners just to see them brought before the tribunal. Such appearances, they believed, could weaken owners' authority over their workers. The Chamber finally decided to enact a simple fine for a first violation and to provide for a fine of up to 200 francs for owners' recidivism—a solution already approved by the Chamber of Peers.[118] The Chamber of Deputies also decided against either imprisonment or fines for parents who violated the law, under the pleas of Lamartine and one other supporter.[119] Despite lingering divisions over the details of the law, final passage of the child labor law took place in February 1841 in the Chamber of Peers, by a vote of 104 to 2, and in March 1841 in the Chamber of Deputies, by a vote of 218 to 17.[120]

115. Discussion contained in the *Moniteur*, 29 December 1840, pp. 2544–45. *Le National* was particularly vigorous in supporting the participation of doctors and *conseils de salubrité* in the inspection process, arguing that they were best qualified to assess the physical and moral condition of child workers. See the issues of 29 and 30 December 1840 for articles authored by an anonymous "savant consciencieux et respectable."

116. See Appendix A, art. 10, below, and remarks by M. Guilhem in the *Moniteur*, 29 December 1840, p. 2546.

117. *Moniteur*, 11 March 1840, p. 467.

118. See Renouard, "Rapport," *Moniteur*, 5 June 1840, p. 1295.

119. Comments of Lamartine and M. Thil in *Moniteur*, 30 December 1840, pp. 2553–54. Lamartine also opposed fines for factory owners.

120. Weissbach, *Assuring the Future Harvest*, ch. 4, notes that these votes on a final bill were much stronger than those counted on the previous reading of the bill in both chambers. A preliminary version of the law was passed in the upper house on 11 March 1840, by a vote of 91 to 35, and in the lower house on 30 December 1840, by a vote of 185 to 50. Weissbach and Jean Sandrin, in his *Enfants trouvés, Enfants ouvriers: XVIIe–XIXe siècle* (Paris, 1982), pp. 165–66, point to the indifference of approximately half of the members of both houses, who failed to cast

Enforcing the Law: The Problem of "Free Time" and Schooling

The limitation of children's work hours had originally been defended as a step towards encouraging school attendance, a goal cherished in particular by the Alsatian Protestants. More than any other proponents of child labor legislation, the Alsatians were concerned with the academic aspects of schooling, while the majority of observers both inside and outside the legislative chambers and administration placed greater emphasis on the priority of moral education.[121] Schooling of factory children was thus intended to fulfill several goals: to help guard against the creation of a caste of working-class children uniquely deprived of schooling, to initiate children to proper lessons of morality, and to teach literacy.[122]

Sending factory children to schools or to salles d'asile was designed to mitigate the specter of "free time" for the youngest child workers and to substitute for it an introduction to moral education: "After having accorded free time to the children, you must keep up with them during every instant of this freedom. You must include a provision which assures a useful and moral employment of this time."[123] Deputy Diétrich, among others, supported the creation of salles d'asile to address this problem: "The necessary complement to a good child labor law is the general organization of salles d'asile in the factory areas. The evil is that in these places family life does not exist. The

---

their votes on the preliminary or final versions of the legislation. Without a complete count of the proportion of membership present for other legislative votes during this period, it is impossible to assess how typical these absences were. It may be that some who supported the law were convinced that the laws would pass and failed to show up for the vote for this reason. However, as both Sandrin and Weissbach argue, these figures may also suggest that a sizable proportion of the membership of both the Chambers of Peers and Deputies were not vitally concerned by the child labor issue.

121. See, for example, the letter from the prefect of the Haut-Rhin to the minister of public works, 16 November 1837, ADHR, 1M/123b, in which he argued that the main problem created by children's early entry into factory employment was the neglect of their schooling. On the need for moral education among factory children, see the letter from the Chamber of Commerce of Lille to the minister of agriculture and commerce, 21 August 1840, *Archives de la chambre de commerce de Lille*, 1:510; Honoré Frégier, *Des classes dangereuses de la population dans les grandes villes* (Paris, 1840), 2:62.

122. The argument that factory children would be left behind other children in their schooling was expressed by M. Renouard, reporter of the commission on the law in the Chamber of Deputies in *Moniteur*, 5 June 1840, p. 1294. François Furet and Jacques Ozouf have noted that rapid demographic growth and industrialization did tend to depress urban literacy in the late eighteenth and early nineteenth centuries, and that literacy rates were particularly low among workers in textiles, not merely because of the recruitment of many workers from rural areas of depressed literacy, but also because of the demands of work itself. François Furet and Jacques Ozouf, *Lire et écrire: L'alphabétisation des Français de Calvin à Jules Ferry* (Paris, 1977), 1:235–38, 241, 257–58, 261.

123. Remarks by M. Humblot-Conté in the Chamber of Peers, *Moniteur*, 8 March 1840, p. 442.

children are raised in the factory. It is this vicious and savage education that must be replaced by a moral and religious one. . . . In this way we may hope for [their] true regeneration."[124] Legislators' sentiments were seconded by local authorities: "Forcing the children to leave the factory after a certain time while the fathers and mothers are still there is to encourage truancy and laziness among them during the rest of the day. . . . it is certain that they will not go to school unless they are taken and kept there."[125] Filling the "free time" of children ages eight to twelve who were to be released from their factory duties after only eight hours of work represented a real problem for legislators and for local administrators, who were aware of factory children's fondness for wandering the streets when liberated from work: "Among the worst tendencies [of youth] the most formidable . . . is this passion for vagrancy. It leaves us no peace. . . . Often appeased somewhat during . . . bad weather, we suddenly see it reawakened by the merest circumstance and inevitably by the first rays of spring sunshine."[126] From Mulhouse, there were similar reports: "When they are not employed in the factories, a large number of children of poor workers pass their day pilfering, either on the canal bridge or in neighboring gardens and orchards. This is their school. Despite their paternal concern to extend education, local authorities do not have the means of obligating parents to make them attend a better one."[127]

Legislators had lamented working-class parents' lack of interest in sending their children to school, but believed that resistance to schooling could be broken down by making it a requirement for children's employment: "Once schooling of children is a condition for their employment, the apathy of fathers, their contempt for schooling that they themselves have not had, will be counteracted by their interests. Today, it is cupidity that makes a father refuse school for his child."[128] In the early 1840s, however, there were insufficient places for factory children in local salles d'asile. As of 1840, Lille had

124. *Moniteur*, 22 December 1840, pp. 2488–89.

125. Commission d'inspection du travail des enfants dans l'arrondissement de Rouen, Résolutions du 25 août 1843. The prefect of the Seine-Inférieure sent this observation to the minister of agriculture and commerce in a letter of 20 November 1843. See also the letter from the commission to the prefect of the Seine-Inférieure, 25 November 1843, AN, F12/4713.

126. The journal *Providence*, cited in Eugène Buret, *De la misère des classes laborieuses en Angleterre et en France* (Paris, 1840), 2:5.

127. Chamber of Commerce of Mulhouse to the minister of commerce, 19 September 1840, ADHR, 1M/123b. See also "Rapport du Bureau des manufactures sur les réponses à la circulaire du 31 juillet 1837 relative à l'emploi des enfants dans les fabriques," AN, F12/4704. Fear of vagrancy among factory children whose work hours had been reduced was also expressed in a letter from the prefect of the Nord to the minister of agriculture and commerce, 21 December 1844, AN, F12/4712.

128. M. Renouard, reporter for the commission on the child labor law in the Chamber of Deputies in the *Moniteur*, 5 June 1840, p. 1294.

only 480 places for all children. Mulhouse's institution had grown from 130 places in 1834 to 450 in 1844, but this was still inadequate for dealing with child factory workers.[129] Mulhouse's conseil municipal had originally urged the establishment of a salle d'asile with the argument that mothers and older sisters of young children "could contribute to the well-being of their families by working. The children would be better watched, fed, and warmed there than at home." [130] Lille's welfare commission intended a wide range of results from its salle d'asile. They believed that

> by caring for the education of children, their hearts and thoughts will be directed towards religion and the love of human attachments. . . . Having acquired some instruction, the younger generation will have more lofty sentiments and as a result will no longer be able to bring themselves to live in filth. . . . Brought up in Christian morality, they will want to practice the domestic virtues and will become bound to each other by family ties. We will no longer see as many depraved parents or ungrateful children.[131]

Public authorities clearly believed that factory children's free time would be turned to public disadvantage and that familial sources of supervision were lacking primarily because of the work of mothers. Although authorities frequently decried the absence of mothers from the home to work, they also believed that this labor was regrettably in the financial, if not the moral, interests of the family. Moreover, founders of Mulhouse's salle d'asile had implied that young children received a better upbringing there than in their homes. The problem was that salles d'asile were designed for the youngest children and were not equipped to care for older child factory workers or to see to their instruction.

For some areas, it was possible to demonstrate the high levels of illiteracy and lack of schooling specific to the semiskilled elements of the factory labor force, even within the Mulhouse area and Alsace as a whole, which were known for their concern for primary education. Using records of conscription,

129. On Lille, "Travail des enfants dans les manufactures: Observations addressées à M. le Ministre de commerce et à la commission de la chambre des Deputés au sujet du project de loi présenté aux chambres," 27 April 1840, *Archives de la Chambre de commerce de Lille*, 1:474–75. On the overcrowding problem in the salle d'asile in the Saint-Sauveur quarter, see Bureau de bienfaisance de Lille, Commission administrative, "Registre aux délibérations," meeting of 30 October 1838, p. 267, ABBL, E. 71, vol. 16. On Mulhouse's establishment, see AMM, R VII/Aa1, Q II/D, Q V/Ca 1.

130. Conseil municipal de Mulhouse, "Procès-verbaux," 4 April 1832, p. 332, AMM, D I/A1. At its inception, the institution was opened from 5 A.M. to 8 P.M. to children of both sexes, but only to those ages three to six.

131. Bureau de bienfaisance de Lille, Commission administrative, "Registre aux délibérations," meeting of 24 August 1841, p. 151, ABBL, E. 72, vol. 17.

one historian has shown that in the decade 1841–50, nearly 50 percent of Mulhouse's cotton spinners and piecers were illiterate, while cloth printers, engravers, and workers in machine industry were less than 10 percent illiterate. Levels of illiteracy also varied from nearly 8 percent for conscripts born in Mulhouse to 23 percent for those born in areas of the Haut-Rhin outside the city and over 30 percent for conscripts born in the neighboring department of the Bas-Rhin and other French departments.[132] Another, more recent study has shown that within Mulhouse's working class of the July Monarchy, literacy was positively correlated with high skill levels, Protestant religious affiliation, and birth in the city. Workers who migrated in from the outside tended to be less skilled, more illiterate, and Catholic.[133] At least in Mulhouse, however, it was not easy to argue that illiteracy rates for factory workers were significantly different from those for French males as a whole. Whereas illiteracy among all conscripts in Mulhouse for the year 1841 was 28.2 percent, for those native to the city it was 19.1 percent, and for France as a whole, 46.6 percent.[134] Although the Mulhouse data showed positive correlations among migration, unskilled work, and illiteracy, they did not support the contention that factory workers were significantly disadvantaged when national figures were taken into consideration.

Preliminary inquiries among the Nord's children employed in factories covered by the 1841 law revealed that of some 4,000 canvassed, more than half said that they had received no schooling.[135] Data for Lille also suggested that children working in cotton- and linen-spinning mills were less likely to have attended school than children in the city's other kinds of workshops (see Table

132. Raymond Oberlé, "Etude sur l'analphabétisme à Mulhouse au siècle de l'industrialisation," *Bulletin du musée historique de Mulhouse* 67 (1959): 105–9.

133. See Arthur Borghese, "Industrialist Paternalism and Lower-Class Agitation: The Case of Mulhouse, 1848–1851," *Histoire Sociale / Social History* 13, no. 25 (1980): 60–61. Gay L. Gullickson, in her study of a village near Rouen, found that by the 1840s adult factory spinners and children working in the local mill had, respectively, the highest levels of illiteracy and the lowest levels of schooling in the village. See *Spinners and Weavers of Auffay: Rural Industry and the Sexual Division of Labor in a French Village, 1750–1850* (Cambridge, 1986), p. 122.

134. Oberlé, "Etude," p. 110.

135. Préfecture du Nord, "Travail des enfans dans les manufactures. Installation de la commission d'inspection, discours de Monsieur le Préfet," undated, but early 1840s, AN, F12/4712. The prefect of the Nord misquoted the document from which these figures were drawn. He wrote that there were 1,253 children from ages eight to twelve and 2,770 from twelve to sixteen, "in total 4,043." The actual figures were 1,273 and 2,770, for a total of 4,043. Of these totals, 72.3% of the eight- to twelve-year-olds and 69.6% of the twelve- to sixteen-year-olds had received no schooling. Figures for establishments in the cantons of Lille, which included 1,755 children, showed that 78.8% of the eight- to twelve-year-olds and 73.8% of the twelve- to sixteen-year-olds had received no schooling. The original figures for establishments inspected in 1842, are contained in "Travail des enfants dans les manufactures (loi du 22 mars 1841). Etat des établissements auxquels la loi pourrait être appliquée," ADN, M611/7.

Table 5.4. School Attendance among Lille's Child Workers, Early 1840s (percentages)

Type of industry	Children ages 8–12 not attending school	Children ages 12–16 who had not attended school	Total children ages 8–16 with no schooling
Cotton spinning	83.5	81.9	82.5 (N = 908)
Linen spinning	90.0	82.6	85.3 (N = 251)
Cotton twisting	60.3	48.4	54.4 (N = 125)
Linen-thread spinning	69.3	67.9	68.5 (N = 200)
Weaving	81.3	48.2	60.0 (N = 45)
All industries	79.8	69.5	78.2 (1,529)

Source: See Table 5.3.

5.4). Information on Rouen's child factory workers also showed high levels of illiteracy and a lack of schooling among them. A November 1843 inspection of ten spinning mills within the city limits, for example, revealed that the majority of the 246 children working in them had received no schooling. Those who told inspectors that they had gone to schools "for a while" still, in the opinion of the inspector, were "absolutely without primary instruction." [136]

The problems of implementing an educational system to fill the hours of the younger children released from work after eight hours, providing minimum schooling for the older children, and enforcing the eight-hour work provision of the law proved to be most intractable. The law of 1841 required that factory children ages eight to twelve attend school, and those twelve to sixteen only if they had not previously received primary instruction. However, the law was not definite on the way that schooling was to be organized. Local differences thus emerged.

In Lille, efforts to comply with the schooling provisions of the law entailed sending the younger group of children to school for half-day sessions, either morning or afternoon. Parents were given the choice of sending their children to classes taught by lay or Catholic teachers. In the communal school, factory children were segregated from the rest of the group, given the "impossibility of their following all the exercises." [137] The twelve- to sixteen-year-olds had to be accommodated, too. Since regular school classes lasted from 8 to

136. "Procès-verbaux des inspections," ADSM, 10 MP/1362. One of the factory owners questioned, M. Guibel Montreuil of the rue d'Elbeuf, was unable to tell the inspectors the actual number of child workers he employed, estimating them at "about 50." This figure has been used to calculate the total number of children involved in the inspection. The mean number of children employed per mill was 24.6, with a standard deviation of 14.7, showing the widely diverse sizes of Rouen's mills that employed children at this date. The number of children employed ranged from a high of 50 in Montreuil's mill to a low of 6 in the mill operated by the Veuve Prunier in the rue St. Hilaire.

137. Prefect of the Nord to mayors of the department, 10 October 1844, AN, F12/4712.

11 A.M. and from 2 to 4 P.M., the solution was to have the older group of children attend from noon to 2.[138]

The individual most responsible for trying to enforce the schooling provisions of the 1841 law in Lille was Charles Kolb-Bernard, one of the leaders of Lille's Société de Saint-Vincent-de-Paul, who viewed factory owners and children alike as contributors to the difficulties of enforcement. His vigorous efforts to oversee the enforcement of the schooling provisions of the law entailed a variety of strategies, all of them designed to combat local habits: "Child labor inspectors in Lille have to exercise their surveillance over more than 80 establishments and nearly 1,300 children, whom we must follow individually. It is only by exact and so-to-speak military discipline that we will be able to achieve a proper application of the law. The failings we have noted should demonstrate in how many ways factory owners and children may violate this discipline *with impunity*." [139] One of the "failings" that most concerned Kolb-Bernard was that children changed schools as they changed work places, which apparently took place very frequently. In this way, they tried to circumvent penalties instituted by a prefectural regulation of 1844. By virtue of articles 19 and 20 of the May 1844 regulation, children who had missed school six times during two consecutive fortnights without a legitimate excuse could be excluded from work for one week: "They cannot be readmitted [to work] until, during the same period of time, they have attended classes during the morning and afternoon at the communal or private school *designated by the child labor inspectors* and until proof of such attendance is noted on the children's *livret* by the teacher." [140] Kolb-Bernard desired an extension of these penalties to absences from Sunday school, as well as a more systematic application of penalties for lateness (after fifteen minutes) and insubordination at school, which was reportedly so acute that the city administration had to assign several policemen to maintain order in the classrooms. It was beginning to be questionable whether it was worse to have the children miss school or attend it:

> Experience has shown that besides absences from school, children going . . . with some regularity may commit acts . . . of a reprehensible nature, acts which more than absences need to be repressed with severe penalties: bad conduct during class, refusal to take part in lessons taught by the

138. Département du Nord, ville de Lille: "Etat des établissements communaux et privés destinés à l'enseignement élémentaire des deux sexes," AN, F12/4712.

139. Charles Kolb-Bernard to the prefect of the Nord, 20 December 1845, ADN, M611/11. Kolb-Bernard was president and then vice-president of the child labor inspection commission for the arrondissement of Lille.

140. On the prefectural regulation and its demise in 1845, see Lasserre, *La situation*, pp. 161–62, and Kolb-Bernard to the prefect of the Nord, 4 July 1845, ADN, M611/11.

> teachers, habitual and systematic lack of discipline, and the most sinful outrages directed towards school directors or members of the clergy who come to give religious instruction.[141]

Besides the difficulties of enforcing the schooling provisions of the law, enforcing the eight-hour work day for the younger group of children presented its own difficulties.[142]

What was worse, news was spreading that the law was not being enforced in the Nord. To complaints expressed within the Chamber of Deputies about this problem, the prefect of the Nord responded to the minister of agriculture and commerce that bad commercial conditions made him hesitant to repress existing abuses vigorously.[143] Under pressure from both the central administration and local inspectors such as Kolb-Bernard, the prefect ordered in 1844 that smaller shops that had previously escaped the scrutiny of inspectors be more vigorously examined. The sparse correspondence on this offensive, however, revealed the reluctance of local authorities in the department to send inspectors into what were essentially familial establishments.[144]

Kolb-Bernard's desire to extend the work-exclusion penalty of the May 1844 regulation to children guilty of bad conduct in class and to absences from Sunday schools also met with resistance on the part of the prefect, who believed that such punishments exceeded the power of child labor inspectors, falling rather within the purview of the local school committee.[145] Children were apparently penalized as the result of the prefectural regulation of 1844, although their numbers were not documented.[146] However, the small amount of information available on penalties for Lille's manufacturers who were found to have violated the law showed that legislators' fears of inquisitorial and repressive inspections were quite unfounded. Of three documented cases from the mid-1840s, two involved owners' refusal to allow inspectors to examine

141. Kolb-Bernard to the prefect of the Nord, 4 July 1845, ADN, M611/11. On policemen in the schools, André Lasserre, *La situation*, p. 162, observed: "This is not surprising, given that about fifteen classes were supposed to contain 1,300 badly-raised children." While Lasserre accepted the 1,300 figure as a reflection of the number of children actually attending classes, Pierrard, "Le patronat," p. 63, has argued that it referred only to the number enrolled, which was much larger than the number attending.

142. Kolb-Bernard to the prefect, 5 February 1844, ADN, M611/8.

143. Letter to the minister of Agriculture and commerce, 6 July 1843, AN, F12/4712. The prefect noted that compliance was least advanced in the city of Roubaix.

144. See, for example, the letter from the mayor of Wervicq-sud, in the arrondissement of Lille to the prefect of the Nord, concerning local *filteries*, ADN, M611/10.

145. Kolb-Bernard to the prefect of the Nord, 20 December 1845, and the prefect's responses, undated, in ADN, M611/11.

146. In February(?) 1845, the mayor of Lille designated special schools to receive children who had been penalized and who were now out of work. *Arrêté* of the mayor of Lille, ADN, M611/11.

children's livrets, and one involved the failure of factory children to attend school. Fines for these cases were three francs.[147]

In important ways, Mulhouse's authorities were better prepared to deal with the schooling requirements of the law of 1841. The city had had a system of night classes for factory children since 1831, started under local initiative. However, the classes had been poorly attended, reputedly because of parents' lack of concern for their children's education and the fact that parents needed the children's wages.[148] Factory children began to appear at the night school during initial attempts to implement the 1841 law, but they did not stay very long. This is exactly what the school director had feared; he wrote the mayor: "I have the honor of sending you two lists concerning the state of the night school during the month of May [1842]. You will note that my fears were all too well founded when I said that the children would come to receive their certification, and having obtained it, would appear no more."[149] The mayor conveyed this information to the industrialists of the city, reminding them of their moral obligation to see that the younger children attended school. Things quickly became complicated, however. In a letter to the mayor, the owners of Dolfuss-Mieg, one of the largest employers of child workers, complained: "For several days, admission to the night school has been refused to our piecers on the pretext that they should have been there at 6 P.M. and not 7 P.M. We ask you to observe that given the distance of our establishment from the center of the city, it is impossible for our piecers to be at school before 7 P.M. even though we have them stop work one-half hour before the other workers."[150] A letter from the schoolmaster, however, revealed that the children had been lying to their employers: "Those who *wish* to come have plenty of time. No one ever asked the children to come at 6 P.M. In fact, it would not suit us at all to have the pupils waiting outside the school for one hour, fighting."[151] Pupils, he argued, could enter the school until 7:25 P.M. In July of the same year, the schoolmaster sent the mayor a summary of information about levels of attendance in the city's classes for factory children that showed that approximately half of those registered were attending regularly.[152]

147. List of infractions, ADN, M613/11.

148. Mayor of Mulhouse to the rector of the communal school, 13 June 1832, cited in Oberlé, *L'enseignement*, p. 72. Oberlé's fine study of Mulhouse's educational history has served as a source for the discussion of Mulhouse's classes for factory children. In studying the implementation of the 1841 law in the Mulhouse area, I have used many of the same documents as Oberlé. My conclusions about the level of enforcement of the law here are in general accord with his.

149. Letter to the mayor of Mulhouse, 1 June 1842, AMM, F VI/Ea1.

150. Letter of 8 June 1842, AMM, F VI/Ea2.

151. Letter of 10 June 1842, AMM, F VI/Ea2.

152. Oberlé, *L'enseignement*, p. 77.

By October 1842, the schoolmaster was already writing about the period of enforcement of the child labor law in the past tense: "Before the vacation, the number of children at the night school was considerable, especially during the execution of the law on child factory labor. . . . For a while we sometimes had up to 250 boys and 140 girls. The former have gradually diminished to 150–160 and the latter to 100." But, he noted, since the end of the vacation, there were only 80–90 boys and 60 girls.[153]

Given these problems, the schoolteacher and the Mulhouse administration planned to implement a new system of daytime classes, which appears to have gone into effect in April 1844.[154] Factory children were divided into eight "divisions," with children in each division attending school for two hours every other day. Four sessions of two-hour classes were held each day from 8 A.M. to noon and from 2 to 6 P.M. A system of reduced-hour work shifts was also instituted so that children could substitute for one another while different groups were attending classes. These special classes were set up in schools in Mulhouse and the neighboring village of Dornach, and were paid for by the factory owners.[155] The schoolmaster in Mulhouse made provision for 500 children divided into two rooms of 250, further divided into 4 groups of 62 children. He also noted the need for three new masters for the reorganized system.[156] However, differences between the number of students enrolled and the number of children actually attending remained a problem. As of March 1845, there were 372 children attending the two factory schools in Mulhouse and Dornach, whereas the schoolmaster believed that the number should have been triple this figure.[157] Factory inspections confirmed that the probable cause of school absences was that the children were continuing to work beyond the limits set by the law. At the beginning of the enforcement period in

153. AMM, R I/Cb2. The hiring of a third schoolmaster and two other aides for the night-school classes for factory children was also discussed and approved by the conseil municipal. Conseil municipal de Mulhouse, "Procès-verbaux," 13 October 1842, AMM, D I/A1.

154. Préfecture du Haut-Rhin, "Extrait d'une lettre du maire de Mülhausen à M. le sous-préfet de l'arrondissement d'Altkirch," 26 January 1844, AN, F12/4712. In April of the same year, the mayor wrote to local factory owners to inform them that the new system would be implemented "presently." Letter of 3 April 1844, AMM, F VII/Ea4.

155. Préfecture du Haut-Rhin, "Extrait d'une lettre du maire de Mulhouse à M. le sous-préfet de l'arrondissement d'Altkirch," 26 January 1844, AN, F12/4712. In a letter to the prefect of the Nord, the prefect of the Haut-Rhin acknowledged that the system of reduced-hour shifts of child workers was not working well, but said that it provided the best means for trying to comply with the 1841 law. See the correspondence between them, dated 11 January and 22 January 1844, in ADHR, 1M/123b. The prefect of the Nord had noted that the law was most difficult to enforce among children working in his area's cotton mills.

156. "Etat des enfants fréquentant l'école communale du soir en décembre 1843," AMM, F VI/Ea3.

157. Schoolmaster of Dornach to the mayor of Mulhouse, 13 March 1845, AMM, F VI/Ea5.

1842, factory inspectors had found a number of errors in factory registers and children's livrets. Registers of child workers tended to be sloppily kept. They sometimes listed fewer children than the number who had received the school certificates now required for work. Occasionally, they contained the names of children who had received no certification. Information in children's livrets on the length of time they had attended school was often incorrect—for example, stating that the children had attended for six or eight years rather than months. Errors in first names on school certificates also led inspectors to believe that younger children were passing them on to older brothers and sisters. A list of directions for future inspection plans indicated the need to pay closer attention to children's ages, to end work by children under age eight, and to attempt to convince parents to abide by the schooling provisions of the law.[158]

Inspections in the spring of 1843 showed some progress in the bookkeeping aspects of the law's enforcement as well as increasing pressure from the central administration.[159] In a number of instances, however, children were still working beyond the hour limitations set by the law and admitted to the inspectors that they did not return to school once they received certification.[160] By late 1843, inspectors were warning industrialists in the Mulhouse area that the time of "amiable warnings" was passing.[161] Fines appear to have been meted out beginning in 1844 after the prefect himself began to involve himself personally in the inspection process. In late 1844, for example, fifteen fines were handed out to factory owners in Mulhouse: eight fines of fifteen francs each for those whose youngest employees were working more than eight hours a day and whose child workers were lacking livrets, and seven fines of five francs each for factory owners whose younger workers were laboring more than eight hours.[162] Additional correspondence during that year showed par-

158. Record of the *comité d'inspection* for the arrondissement of Altkirch, undated, but probably 1842, AMM, F VI/Ea3. At this time, the inspection commission also suggested that all parents be required to send their children to school in order to get them off the streets and that the Bureau de bienfaisance refuse aid to any parent who refused.

159. The Société industrielle de Mulhouse had complained about the nonenforcement of the law to the Chamber of Deputies. In a letter to the prefect of the Haut-Rhin, it explained that it had directed its complaint to the Chamber and not to the administration since the law had originated there. The society believed that it was particularly in the smaller communes that the law was being avoided. See its letter of 8 April 1843, ADHR, 1M/123b. See also the letter from the minister of agriculture and commerce to the prefect of the Haut-Rhin, 16 June 1843, informing him that it was time for the law to be enforced, ADHR, 1M/123b.

160. Child labor inspectors to the subprefect of Altkirch, 12 August 1843, AMM, F VI/Ea3.

161. "Extrait du registre des délibérations de la commission d'inspection de l'arrondissement d'Altkirch, séance du 20 décembre 1843," ADHR, 1M/123b.

162. Département du Haut-Rhin, "Exécution de la loi du 22 mars 1841. Contraventions constatées pendant le 4e trimestre de 1844," ADHR, 1M/123b. In an earlier letter, the subprefect

ticular ministerial concern for enforcement of the law in the arrondissement of Altkirch.

By spring of 1845, many of the bookkeeping problems seem to have been corrected. An inspection in late April of that year among thirteen spinning, cloth-printing, and weaving establishments showed that copies of the law were now generally displayed and registers of child workers were well kept, although inspectors noted that many employers were still failing to keep a record of the dates when children entered their employment. Inspectors' biggest complaints were that owners still could not back up their assertions that children were attending school, and that children were still working longer hours than those permitted by the law. At the Dolfuss-Mieg spinning mill, the owner freely admitted that the older children were working thirteen hours a day during the days they did not attend school, a comment the inspectors appreciated for its rare frankness. Inspectors, including Dr. Achille Penot, Mulhouse's noted moral economist, were not always welcomed. Some of the children, such as those at the Heilmann-Mantz cloth-printing works, were defiant, arguing that they were not obligated to attend school, while others at Hirn-Guth spinning mills told inspectors that they were attending night schools that no longer existed. In the Schlumberger cloth-printing mill, an employee tried to impede the inspection and gave inspectors what they considered evasive answers to their questions.[163] Inspectors were especially concerned over violations of work-hour regulations for the younger group of children, and appear to have been more likely to hand out violations for this infraction than for the nonverifiability of older children's assertions that they were attending school.[164]

Children's failure to attend special classes set up for them confounded prefects from the different departments, who vented their feelings of frustration to each other. In correspondence between the prefects of the Nord and of the Seine-Inférieure, the former confessed the difficulties of enforcing the law, particularly among children working in the department's cotton mills. The latter shared his pessimism, lamenting that "the artisans' families resist depriving themselves of a part of their youngest members' wages. When factory owners send them away, either they become vagrants in the countryside

---

of Altkirch had noted that there were no violations registered for the first three months of the same year. Letter to the prefect of the Haut-Rhin, 14 May 1844, ADHR, 1M/123b.

163. Firms included in this inspection employed a total of 5,150 adults, 297 children ages eight to twelve, and 721 children ages twelve to sixteen. ADHR, 1M/123b.

164. Firms given violations included Heilmann-Mantz, Katz Frères, Schlumberger et Cie., and Mathieu Paraf. The firm of Josué Hofer seems to have escaped citation because of the owner's expressed desire to set up his own factory school, and that of Dolfuss-Mieg because of its owner's ingenuousness, noted above.

instead of going to school, or else if they do go to school, the teacher of the commune where the children do not live refuses to give them free instruction. Nearly all the children employed in our factories are illiterate."[165]

Attempts to enforce the schooling provisions of the 1841 law in Rouen read like a familiar story. As in Mulhouse, the Rouen area apparently had night schools that were reserved for young workers as well as for children engaged in agricultural labor. But even in towns where schools did exist, they were not well attended.[166] The idea that parents in the Rouen area were reluctant to send their children to school because of financial need was reinforced by evidence from at least one inspection. The inspectors found in their visit to one small weaving establishment employing only five children that all the children were illiterate, and that several of them were working directly with their parents, one of them a widow with three children. When the inspectors urged these parents to send their children to school, the parents stated their refusal and "alleged that they couldn't feed them if they didn't work."[167] Rouen's chapter of the Société de Saint-Vincent-de-Paul was well aware of violations of the 1841 law and attempted to encourage parents to send their children to school rather than to work by paying them to do so.[168]

Between April 1843 and April 1846, the city administration of Rouen delivered 1,448 special livrets to the city's working children, 1,034 to boys and 414 to girls. Of these children, 69.4 percent of the boys and 61.6 of the girls had "attended school." If the level of their schooling was commensurate with that of Elbeuf's working children, approximately 70 percent of those who had attended would have done so for less than four years.[169] By 1846,

165. Letters dated 11 and 15 January 1844, ADSM, 10 MP/1362. The prefect of the Seine-Inférieure was referring to the fact that many children in the Rouen area were working in mills not located in the commune where they were domiciled.

166. Prefect of the Seine-Inférieure to the minister of agriculture and commerce, 13 June 1844, ADSM, 10 MP/1362. See also the report of the mayor of the city of Elbeuf to the prefect of the Seine-Inférieure concerning schooling among factory children in his town, dated 21 July 1843. He lamented the reluctance of parents to send their children to school, even though the institutions were free and the most assiduous students were rewarded with clothing. He noted: "In order for such largesse to remain without effect among poor workers, they must have a pressing need for their [children's] hands in helping them to raise their family." ADSM, 10 MP/1362.

167. Results of the inspection by MM. Lemire and Desbois of the establishment of MM. Auber et Cie, Rouen, ADSM, 10 MP/1362.

168. Part of the document describing this program is illegible, but it appears that such payments to parents were first distributed rather indiscriminately, but were thereafter targeted to families whose children were particularly deserving of such aid because of their good conduct. Letter accompanying the *Bulletin statistique des conférences de Rouen*, 1845, ASVP, Rouen, Dossier 5. The author noted that this effort, among ninety school children, consumed 900 francs of the chapter's budget.

169. Data on children's livrets is contained in "Mairie de Rouen: Livrets délivrés," ADSM,

the prefect of the Seine-Inférieure noted that there was still a pressing need for schools in the Madeleine, St. Hilaire, and St. Sever quarters, where there were a large number of work places and working children.[170]

Beyond the hostility of children and the reluctance of working-class parents to conform to the law, it was clear that many factory owners were also part of the problem. In Lille, a number of these manufacturers had closed ranks to protest the 1844 school regulation which penalized children by excluding them from work. They calculated that excluding a child from work for a week was equivalent to stealing forty-five francs from them, because many spinners were necessarily idle during the children's absence.[171] In Rouen, younger children were being forced to lie upwards about their ages because a number of factory owners were not conforming to the spirit of the 1841 law: "Several factory owners, believing themselves to be in conformity to the law, have fired children ages eight to twelve and have retained only those ages twelve to sixteen." [172] In an 1845 letter to the minister of agriculture and commerce, the prefect of the Haut-Rhin noted that a recent inspection of child labor in Mulhouse had revealed the same trend. The only effect of the law, he argued, was to exclude younger children from the mills, while the older children were still working eleven to a now-illegal thirteen hours a day.[173] A rise in the ages of Mulhouse's child factory work force from the mid-1820s to the period shortly after the implementation of the 1841 law is impossible to prove with any certainty. However, data in Table 5.5 are presented for the purposes of rough-and-ready comparison. In 1826, children under age ten were simply not included in totals of children employed in cotton spinning and cloth printing, though it is certain than there were many working, especially in the latter industry. At that date, 49.5 percent of child workers listed were thirteen and younger. By the time that the law began to be implemented in the city, approximately 25 percent of children listed as working in Mulhouse's cotton mills were twelve and younger. Even with the different boundaries of these age categories, it seems very likely that younger children were being forced

---

10 MP/1362. The amount of schooling received by Elbeuf children who had attended was calculated from the report of the mayor cited above in note 166. Of the total of Elbeuf's children referred to in the mayor's report, only 49% had attended school at all.

170. Letter to the vice-president of the Comité de l'instruction primaire de l'arrondissement de Rouen, 5 February 1846, ADSM, 10 MP/1362.

171. Pierrard, "Le patronat," p. 62.

172. Commission des inspecteurs du travail des enfants pour l'arrondissement de Rouen to the prefect of the Seine-Inférieure, 25 November 1843, AN, F12/4713.

173. Children ages twelve to sixteen were working eleven hours a day three days a week when they were at school and thirteen hours each of the other three days. Prefect of the Haut-Rhin to the minister of agriculture and commerce, 14 May 1845, AN, F12/4712; Stearns, *Paths*, p. 70.

Table 5.5. Age Distribution of the Child Labor Force in Selected Industries of Mulhouse, 1826 and Early 1840s

A. 1826

Type of industry	No. and % of children by age[a] 10–13	13–16	All ages
Cotton spinning	228 (49.5%)	233 (50.5%)	461 (100.0%)
Cloth printing	557 (61.8)	344 (38.2)	901 (100.0)

B. Early 1840s

Type of industry	No. and % of children by age[a] 8–10	10–12	12–16	All ages
Cotton spinning	28 (3.0%)	209 (22.3%)	702 (74.8%)	939 (100.1%)
Cloth printing	268 (30.5)	251 (28.6)	359 (40.9)	878 (100.0)
Cotton weaving	0	13 (4.2)	298 (95.8)	311 (100.0)
Wool spinning	4 (1.7)	22 (9.3)	210 (89.0)	236 (100.0)
Machine construction	0	0	94 (100.0)	94 (100.0)
Cloth bleaching	0	1 (6.2)	15 (93.8)	16 (100.0)
Cotton twisting	1 (1.7)	13 (22.0)	45 (76.3)	59 (100.0)

Source: For 1826, figures from AMM, R I/Cb2; for early 1840s, figures from "Travail des enfants dans les manufactures, loi du 22 mars 1841, ville de Mulhouse. Relevé par nature d'industrie," AMM, F VI/Ea1.

[a]Percentage of total in each industry in parentheses. These figures are not a measure of the exact size of the child labor force, since some establishments had to be eliminated because of faulty data.

out of the mills.[174] Figures on children in cloth printing appear at first glance to have changed less. However, given the absence of children under age ten in the 1826 record, it seems reasonable to conclude that the age distribution of children in cloth printing also shifted upwards as a result of the 1841 law.

Problems in enforcing both the letter and spirit of the law of 1841 emerged clearly in administrative correspondence. In an 1845 letter, the minister of agriculture and commerce reminded the prefect of the Seine-Inférieure that he had asked him for a list of establishments in the department subject to the law four years previously.[175] Two years later, the minister was even more concerned about information, forwarded to him by the prefect, that in the arrondissement of Rouen and the canton of the Grand'Couronne there were still 140 children under age eight employed.[176] The difficulties of enforcing the law

174. It is very possible that the data from the early 1840s also bear the effects of children lying upwards about their ages.

175. Letter of 27 September 1845, ADSM, 10 MP/1362. The minister acknowledged the reception of this information as of 25 October 1845 in a letter of 28 November.

176. Letter of 13 January 1847, ADSM, 10 MP/1362. In a later letter to his subprefects, the prefect mentioned that there were now 204 such children, and a total of 6,988 children employed

of 1841 in Lille came as little surprise, given the long-standing opposition of Lille's industrialists to the system that differentiated the work hours of the two groups of children and distinguished both from the work hours of adults.

In Mulhouse and in Alsace in general, however, factory owners had been in the vanguard of petitioners in favor of legislation. Thus, in 1843 the prefect of the Haut-Rhin had expressed some surprise about the difficulties of enforcing the law in the capital of Alsace's textile industry: "I did not expect that in Mulhouse, the greatest industrial center of the department, the provisions of the 1841 law would be so little advanced; that despite promises made to me, the inspection commission has not renewed its factory visits since last year. We know now that it is in Mulhouse, . . . which . . . produced the strongest wishes for a philanthropic law, that there are the greatest obstacles to the law's enforcement, on the pretext that it is insufficient."[177] As we have already seen, enforcement in the Mulhouse area improved after this statement was made, when the prefect became involved in the inspection process. However, violations clearly remained by the end of the 1840s.

Available archival information suggests that among the three areas under study, the child labor law was most vigorously enforced in the Mulhouse area, although in all three areas, data on inspections, violations, and fines become thinner as the end of the 1840s approached.[178] As noted, the insufficiencies of the law and failures to enforce it had been brought to the attention of the Chamber of Deputies by 1843. In the late 1840s, again under the leadership of Baron Charles Dupin, there was a renewal of interest in the Chamber of Deputies in extending the law to smaller work places and intervening in the work of women.[179] However, no legislation was adopted before the regime was swept away.

---

in the department in work places covered by the law, only 4,452 of whom had been issued the special livrets dictated by article 6 of the law. Letter of 1 October 1847, ADSM, 10 MP/1362. One observer attributed the lax enforcement of the law of 1841 in the Seine-Inférieure to the domination of its conseil général by manufacturing interests. See *Aperçu sur la condition des classes ouvrières et critique de l'ouvrage de M. Buret sur la misère des classes laborieuses, etc., par le Pce D . . . S . . .* (Paris, 1844), pp. 38–39. For a contrasting view of the composition of the conseil général there, see André-Jean Tudesq, *Les conseillers généraux en France au temps de Guizot, 1840–1848* (Paris, 1967), pp. 143–45.

177. Letter to the minister of agriculture and commerce, 7 April 1843, ADHR, 1 M/123b. In another letter, the prefect argued that child labor inspectors in the arrondissement of Altkirch were too lenient and those in the arrondissement of Belfort most rigorous. Prefect of the Haut-Rhin to the minister of commerce, 23 August 1844, AN, F12/4712.

178. Pierre Pierrard has argued that the law was not well enforced in the Lille area until the 1850s after the appointment of a new and vigorous inspector of child labor, F. Dupont. See *La vie ouvrière à Lille sous le second Empire* (Paris, 1965), pp. 339–40.

179. "Rapport fait par M. le baron Dupin, sur le projet de loi relatif au travail des enfants dans toutes les manufactures, fabriques, usines, chantiers et ateliers," *Moniteur*, 2 July 1847, pp. 1839–47; Stearns, *Paths*, pp. 165–66. Weissbach, *Assuring the Future Harvest*, ch. 5 contains a thorough discussion of the proposed legislation and responses to it.

For most of the 1840s, what success the law's enforcement enjoyed seems to have come at the very local level from the combined effort of a very few inspectors, especially when they were supported by the prefect in charge. The noted moral economists Dr. Thouvenin of Lille and Dr. Penot of Mulhouse were members of the inspection commissions in their localities. The prefect of the Haut-Rhin was under special pressure because of the importance of Alsatian pressure for legislation, a genealogy that some factory owners in the Mulhouse area apparently wished to forget when faced by inspectors in the flesh. Factory owners in the Mulhouse area were especially averse to provisions of the law that distinguished between the work hours of children aged eight to twelve and those twelve to sixteen. This stemmed from their view that the system of reduced-hour work shifts for the younger group was most disruptive of factory work processes.

The Place of Child Labor Reform in the Ideology of the Moral Economists

Given differences of opinion expressed in particular in the Chamber of Deputies during debates over the law, the resistance of factory owners themselves should have come as no surprise. Most of the local organizations that expressed an opinion had supported the principle of legislation raising the age of admission for children. However, they had also frequently favored the strategy of permitting children to work the full complement of hours required of adult workers once they were hired, probably because such a law would have been less disruptive of the status quo within the work place. On the other hand, a law like that originally supported by Bourcart or by the chamber of commerce of Lille, which sought to limit the hours of work in general, would have stood little likelihood of passage, in part because of fear of competition with English industry and in part for reasons of principle made clear by Dunoyer's sharp distinction between the legitimacy of the state's intervention into the labor of adults and that of children.

One of the main effects of the law of 22 March 1841 was unintended. That was to drive the youngest children out of factories altogether—not because of their own or their parents' desire, but rather because the reduced-hour shifts designed to accommodate their work were too bothersome for factory owners to organize and supervise. Another important factor in the firing of the younger group of children, at least in the Mulhouse area, was that owners were apparently most likely to be fined for violations of work hours among the younger group of workers. Ironically, then, the law was removing from the factory those children who were most likely to be working alongside their parents. This apparent irony dissolves, however, when it is remembered that legislators had no sense that there were real family interests to be preserved within industrial work places.

The decision to consider children's labor separately from that of their parents became a key feature of the moral economists' approach to the problem of child labor very early in their discussions. Their view that working-class parents, fathers in particular, were engaged in the shortsighted exploitation of their own children led them to emphasize an inherent conflict between the generations, a conflict that we have seen in previous policy discussions based on analyses of parent-child relations within the working-class family. Moral economists' argument that children working in France's new industrial sectors had no defenders of their own special and separate interests except those who spoke for legislation was fundamental. It stemmed from their belief that there were no real family interests to be respected within industrial work places—a conclusion that was itself deduced from paternal failure to protect children from exploitation. Having delegitimized the authority of parents who cooperated in the exploitation of their own children, legislators could more easily arrogate elements of parental authority to themselves. Moreover, moral economists in particular viewed predictable parental resistance to the law as confirmation of parents' financial and moral shortsightedness as well as a lack of affection that had made the law necessary in the first place.

Contemporary descriptions of parent-child work bonds within the factory, although frequently embedded in observations very hostile to working-class parents, contain several elements that may help us to understand the ways workers themselves viewed the labor of their children. Evidence that the youngest children were the most likely to be working with or near their parents, either as piecers or tireurs, seems credible, as does the idea that workers themselves requested permission to bring their young children with them, particularly if both parents were working. It also seems reasonable to conclude that many children, even in urban mills, had actually worked alongside a parent or other relative at some time in their youth. However, information also suggests that parents were not preoccupied with this direct relationship per se, and that when children grew older, urban workers in particular would use the availability of multiple places of employment to help secure the family economy.[180] For parents, ensuring the subsistence of the family unit took precedence over maintaining direct parent-child bonds in the work place. While twentieth-century historians and sociologists have been very keen to emphasize the authority that fathers or mothers were able to wield over their children within industrial work places, it appears that parents' first priority was to sub-

180. In their critique of Neil Smelser's *Social Change in the Industrial Revolution: An Application of Theory to the British Cotton Industry* (Chicago, 1959), M. M. Edwards and R. Lloyd-Jones have argued that the prevalence of family work bonds which Smelser imputed to early-nineteenth-century cotton mills was more typical of rural than urban areas. M. M. Edwards and R. Lloyd-Jones, "N. J. Smelser and the Cotton Factory Family: A Reassessment," in N. B. Harte and K. G. Ponting, eds., *Textile History and Economic History: Essays in Honour of Miss Julia deLacy Mann* (Manchester, 1973), p. 315.

sist by adapting their deployment of familial labor power to the new realities of urban industrial life.[181] Reports that adult workers were more likely to mete out harsh punishment to piecers or tireurs who were family members are also entirely credible, even though they were used by many observers to buttress the case against working-class parents' affection or concern for their children. In parts of preindustrial Europe, we are told, parents frequently wished their children to enter the employ of other adults, not only so they could contribute cash to their own family's income, but in order to avoid the kind of face-to-face parent-child work bonds whose frustrations could and did result in harsh discipline.[182]

As proponents of the views of Michel Foucault have observed, the movement to standardize labor discipline within factories of July Monarchy France could be seen by some moral economists as a force for improving the lives of child workers, since it gradually weakened what was viewed by many as an inherently oppressive relationship between adults and the children who worked directly with them.[183] However, movements to formalize labor discipline within France's industrial work places of the 1830s and 1840s also had consequences largely ignored by this point of view. To the extent that factories of July Monarchy France were viewed as work settings that were increasingly stripped of familial characteristics, they were thought less and less appropriate for the work of children. Although Social Catholics and moral economists alike certainly preferred children to be working in factories than to be wandering the streets of industrial towns, they were far from viewing the growth of rationalized labor discipline as an argument for children's factory employment. While these regulations could be considered effective instruments for moralizing adult workers, moral economists and Social Catholics strongly preferred salles d'asile or schools as more appropriate institutional vehicles for helping to make France's young workers into children who would live as dependents under the stewardship of their fathers.

Although the menacing toughness of France's child workers had been a key part of Daniel Legrand's argument for intervention and an ongoing theme of local administrative reports on efforts to enforce the 1841 law, debate in

181. On families' attempts to ensure their survival by economic diversification, see Richard Wall, "Work, Welfare, and the Family: An Illustration of the Adaptive Family Economy," in Lloyd Bonfield, Richard M. Smith, and Keith Wrightson, eds., *The World We Have Gained: Histories of Population and Social Structure* (Oxford, 1986), pp. 265, 279.

182. Speaking of preindustrial England, Peter Laslett has noted that some parents preferred to have their own children work outside the home while hiring other young people to replace them. He argues: "Parents may have been unwilling to submit children of their own to the discipline of work at home." Peter Laslett, *The World We Have Lost*, 2d ed. (New York, 1971), p. 13.

183. "Les enfants du capital," *Les révoltes logiques*, no. 3 (1977): 3–6, cited in Philippe Ariès, "Le travail des enfants et la famille populaire," *Critère*, no. 25 (1979): 252–53.

the legislative chambers emphasized children's status as victims. This shift in emphasis entailed the same kind of evolution in understanding seen previously in moral economists' ruminations about other policy issues. While their initial apprehension of the nature of the social problem they were investigating emphasized the saliency of working-class deviation from mores fundamental to the social and moral order, their efforts to construct solutions to it gradually entailed their attempt to see latent similarities between the objects of their analysis and themselves. In the case of the child labor problem, this function was fulfilled by an overwhelming concentration on similarities between the needs of child factory workers and those of other children.

Organizing the transformation of France's child factory workers into dependent children, however, posed vast practical difficulties. Plans to reconstitute the family economy of France's industrial workers by making young people dependent on their fathers for their upkeep were rendered illusory not merely because of the reluctance of child workers or parents to cooperate in the plan. Not only parents and children, but many industrialists continued to view the work of children outside the home not as a problem but simply as a fact of life. Moral economists' attempt to demonstrate that such a view was shortsighted could as yet make little real headway in changing a pattern of children's labor that was fully integrated into the production processes and working-class family economies of industrial France. If such were the attitudes of many inhabitants of industrial areas who were to be affected by the law in action, how then could such a law have been voted?

The triumph of the moral economist vision of France's industrial future over the issue of child labor reform can be explained by understanding the specific setting of discussions within the two chambers and the attractiveness of moral economist precepts for an increasing proportion of peers and deputies. Debates within the Chamber of Deputies in particular had, of course, shown that there were differences of opinion about just what the interests of industrialists and the French social order really were. As Peter Stearns has pointed out, wealthier manufacturers of the Mulhouse area had long been known among contemporaries for their innovative and "paternalist" intervention into working-class life in order to make it more orderly and disciplined.[184] For them, regulating child labor was merely another chapter in their continuing efforts to create, at least locally, a secure industrial order. However, in the course of discussions of the child labor problem, deputies such as Barbet or Grandin clearly saw themselves as defenders of those interests by arguing *against* a law that they believed would threaten the authority and the income of factory owners.

It must be remembered that the majority of deputies and, to an even

184. Stearns, *Paths*, pp. 89–90.

greater extent, members of the Chamber of Peers, were not directly implicated in industrial pursuits. Beyond the overblown rhetoric of a Gay-Lussac, there is little evidence that most peers or deputies saw factory owners of July Monarchy France as the benevolent, paternal figures whom the great chemist had extolled. There were, to be sure, limits to what legislators could say on the floor of the two chambers about the role of French factory owners as exploiters of children. In fact, one of the tactics used by proponents of child labor legislation to avoid impugning the moral reputation of French factory owners was to evoke the horrors of factory work for children in England.[185] This strategy helped to avoid public embarrassment of France's industrialists and doubtless assuaged the consciences of some legislators who were embarrassed that a French child labor law had been so long in the making.[186] Proponents of child labor legislation neither could nor did make the argument that French industrialists were as oppressive as their English counterparts. On the other hand, the members of the two houses were not entirely sympathetic to claims that factory owners' interests were being violated to the extent that these claims were understood as the protestation of "special interests." Thus, many deputies and peers were quite susceptible to Dupin and his supporters' fundamental argument that opposition to legislation was based on a shortsighted conception of what industrialists' interests actually were.

The alliance between Alsace's industrialist *patronat* and moral economist theoreticians under the banner of their shared ideology was thus critical to the passage of the child labor reform bill. Although factory owners who adhered to the moral economists' ideology could exert influence over social policy at the local level, it took the support of enlightened experts such as Dupin or Villermé to demonstrate the theoretical and practical attractions of the moral economist view of the world. They helped to demonstrate that this perspective and the kinds of policy it dictated could serve as a means for moralizing the families of France's workers and at the same time reconcile the long-term interests of the diverse elements of France's bourgeoisie with those of the state. The importance of this latter accomplishment should not be underestimated. At a time when French industrial development was highly specific to particular

185. See, *inter alia,* the remarks of Villeneuve-Bargemont, *Moniteur*, 23 December 1840, pp. 2492–93, and Montalembert, *Moniteur*, 5 March 1840, p. 418. The lugubrious features of France's industrial conditions were occasionally brought up. See, for example, remarks by the deputy Corne, *Moniteur*, 22 December 1840, p. 2485.

186. A number of legislators expressed their embarrassment that other governments which Frenchmen felt to be their inferiors in defending values of humanity, morality, and civilization were outdistancing France's in proclaiming measures to protect child workers. Austria and Prussia, as well as England, already had child factory legislation by the time the French legislative debates began. See, *inter alia,* the remarks by Renouard, reporter of the commission for the child labor law in the Chamber of Deputies, in *Moniteur*, 26 May 1840, p. 1181, and M. Goldbéry in *Moniteur*, 23 December 1840, p. 2496.

regions and the presence of industrialists still marginal in many institutions of national scope, "enlightened" industrialists were well-advised to seek out and form alliances with representatives of moral economist opinion in order to bring their own perspective to the attention of political and government authorities at the national level. In demonstrating the compatibility of the long-term interests of France's emerging *patronat* with the interests of more traditional elements within the French bourgeoisie, moral economists also legitimized a more lofty and respected position for themselves, their ideas, and their policy strategies in coping with children's labor reform as well as with other problems of the urban industrial order.

6
Conclusion
Family Policy in Historical Perspective

The investigations, debates, and efforts at policy implementation considered in this study were all parts of a process that began when members of the French bourgeoisie attempted to grasp basic features of working-class family life in early industrial France. A comprehension of the successive stages that followed closely from this initial point of departure has demanded that we take seriously the centrality of the moral dimension of observers' and policy-makers' concerns. Indeed, it would not be an exaggeration to understand the world views and policy recommendations of both Social Catholics and moral economists during this period as part of their effort to discover new means of establishing both the substance and sense of moral community between bourgeoisie and working classes.

Such a proposition is surprising only if we forget how the term *moral* was understood by the main protagonists in this struggle. For Social Catholics, the creation of a new form of moral community between bourgeoisie and working class entailed both a literal and valuative coming-together of the two groups under the auspices of a renewed form of Christianity that placed the "social question" at the center of its concerns. Relations between the home visitors of the Société de Saint-Vincent-de-Paul and "their" families, or the volunteers of the Société de Saint-François-Régis and "their" couples, were clearly marked by basic inequalities of the social order. However, Social Catholics intended to transcend these man-made inequalities and establish a sense of moral community on the basis of renewed values of mutual obligation and reciprocity. Their goals and the fervor that the first generation of Social Catholics brought to their task corresponded quite well to basic tenets of Judeo-Christian thinking about the nature of moral community, which placed high value on the virtues of reciprocity, mutual obligation, and solidarity.

Yet, as I have tried to demonstrate, projects to establish moral community between social classes were also designed to take place very concretely at the level of mores, those habits of daily life and "habits of the heart" which social observers and administrators viewed as emblematic of underlying values. Moral economists devoted their greatest attention to this level. Their notion of moral community also emphasized the reinforcement of values of reciprocity, mutual obligation, and solidarity. It was their belief that these values needed to be firmly entrenched within the family before any larger sense of interclass community could be constructed at the societal level. Like some of their British counterparts of the period, moral economist policymakers of July Monarchy France sought to use instruments of state power to begin accomplishing this task of social reconstruction.[1] Finding the precise terms and mechanisms through which their goal might be reached entailed an ongoing struggle among the diverse bearers of legislative, administrative, and intellectual power and between these men and the working-class families whose lives were the targets of reform.

Ideological and practical leaders of French society in the late Restoration and July Monarchy were faced with severe problems in identifying the institutions upon which to construct a new moral community that would include the first generations of industrial workers. Institutions and ideologies that had previously been fundamental in purveying at least the illusion of community either at the political or social levels were no longer available to serve this critical function. At the political level, leaders of the July Monarchy suffered the consequences of the demise of a divine-right monarchy that had expressed the universality of the state in part by extending its compassionate eye to the poor. As Tocqueville with his usual acumen observed, the demise had occurred just at the moment when the monarchy appeared to be establishing a new capacity for integrating progressive notions of rational humanitarianism into the repertoire of practices that legitimized its existence.[2] Deprived of traditional monarchical sources of legitimacy, political and social leaders grasped for new means of legitimizing their claims to authority. As we have seen, Guizot and other defenders of the political status quo of July Monarchy France consistently sought to base the legitimacy of bourgeois rule as much on its claims to moral authority as on its de facto dominance within the political, economic, and administrative spheres. However, political institutions, organized as they were to restrict the *pays légal* to a small minority of men, were thoroughly inadequate to the task of reestablishing a sense of the state's fundamental role in linking Frenchmen to one another.

Social Catholics of the period, particularly the militant generation of

1. See Philip Corrigan and Derek Sayer, *The Great Arch: English State Formation as Cultural Revolution* (London, 1985), pp. 114–32, a fascinating work that has suggested many comparisons with the French case discussed here.

2. Alexis de Tocqueville, *The Old Regime and the French Revolution*, trans. Stuart Gilbert (New York, 1955), pp. 180–87.

Frédéric Ozanam, were themselves instrumental in evoking the failure of a post-Revolutionary church hierarchy to attend to the spiritual and moral needs of a new industrial working class, arguing that it had thereby forfeited its own traditional claim to providing an institutional means through which bonds of moral community could be forged between upper and lower classes. This factor was the main reason that laymen had to become more involved in the work of nineteenth-century confraternities like the Société de Saint-Vincent-de-Paul or the Société de Saint-François-Régis.

Within working-class culture itself, the bourgeoisie's legal and practical delegitimization of long-standing corporate traditions through revolutionary legislation and ongoing restrictions on trade corporations had been designed to dissolve older forms of community and to reestablish the social order on new notions of economic and social individualism. As William Sewell has demonstrated, French leaders never entirely succeeded in eradicating the substance of these traditions, which continued to function as a powerful force motivating workers' resistance to the bourgeoisie's construction of the moral rules of a new social order.[3] It is nevertheless important to remember that such corporate traditions had lost their legitimacy in the eyes of those who attempted to govern both state and society.

Given these considerations, it seems apparent that the leaders of French society during the July Monarchy were faced with a situation in which the institutional bases of community life, particularly those linking bourgeoisie to worker, had been severely impoverished. Within such a setting, the family appeared to be one of the few institutions likely to serve the function of reinforcing bonds of social solidarity. In fact, the family's importance as a locus of widespread concern cannot be understood in isolation from this political and social setting. The family also assumed a powerful hold over the minds of social commentators and policymakers because it served such a central function in the bourgeoisie's own definition of itself. It stood as a central institution through which the bourgeoisie proclaimed and legitimized its moral fitness to rule. This powerful sense of moral community at the family level stemmed from what was seen as the family's capacity to mediate human needs for affection and individual self-realization with the necessity of providing predictable material resources to manage those aspirations concretely within a society whose recent memory was marked by the specter of social and political disorder.

France's moral economists were heirs of traditions of thinking about the social world that originated in the waning years of the Old Regime. Like those Old Regime progressives who came to share in a vision of a new community

3. *Work and Revolution in France: The Language of Labor from the Old Regime to 1848* (Cambridge, 1980).

based on ideals of humanity and the "rights of man," moral economists appear to have shared a sanguine notion of the possibilities of establishing moral community on the basis of universifiable values. However, they also shared the desire of men like Necker to organize their society in such a way as to reduce to more prudent dimensions the financial obligations of rich to poor.

Moral economists were also heirs of the kinds of thinking and acting upon the social world that emerged under the Directory. During this period, as we have seen, legislators were already retrenching from the optimism typical of an earlier group of revolutionaries in their search for means of reestablishing social peace and habits of subordination. They sought out practical strategies for reconstructing the social order that were less political and more administrative in nature. The experience of radical revolutionary upheaval, and the failure to formulate lasting revolutionary political institutions doubtless made their search more pressing.[4] A quest for new foundations upon which to base social peace led legislators under the Directory and Consulate to consider more closely those social divisions that had given rise to radical revolution. Moral economists also inherited this legacy of the Revolution, one that reflected a growing awareness of the power of "sociological" differences to disrupt the social order. Like the men of the Directory and Consulate, moral economists of the late Restoration and July Monarchy believed that the source of universifiable values on which to construct a society in their image lay not primarily in the atrophied realm of politics, but rather in the increasingly complex realm of civil society.

The advent of industrialization lent new urgency to the task of mediating real and perceived social divisions between classes and of finding new institutional bases of social solidarity. Social Catholic activists went into the trenches of working-class domestic life with their own agenda and ideas for the proper means of reassociating upper and lower classes. As a group, the first generation of lay activists within the Société de Saint-Vincent-de-Paul felt little personal implication in the class struggle they feared. Instead, they viewed themselves as social mediators between industrial capitalists and workers. Although it appears that later in the nineteenth century such Social Catholic activist organizations lapsed into purely charitable functions, the militant fervor of Ozanam's generation should not be underestimated. The policy solutions they advocated were predicated on spiritual terms, depending for their success on the establishment of individualized, face-to-face relationships between workers and bourgeois. This generation's desire to maintain the lay character of its work and to organize it outside the influence of a church hier-

4. On the failure of liberal politics and its institutional bases, see Lynn Hunt, David Lansky, and Paul Hanson, "The Failure of the Liberal Republic in France, 1795–1799: The Road to Brumaire," *Journal of Modern History* 51 (1979): 734–59.

archy that remained generally committed to its Gallican traditions helped to maintain the autonomy and spiritual purity of Social Catholic efforts. Their activities also earned them the admiration of other Catholics committed to the liberation of the church from the constraints of complicity with the state. While their voluntarism obviously placed severe limits on the efficacy of Social Catholic organizations as vehicles for the spiritual and moral regeneration of an increasingly secular society, such a conclusion must be tempered by recalling the success of the Société de Saint-François-Régis in restoring France's workers to the community bounded by legitimate marriage, a success crowned by the willingness, even eagerness, of the state administration to contribute towards its efforts.

Social Catholics' horror at the materialism and social estrangement exacerbated by industrial capitalism and defended in the lessons of classical political economy was the most powerful but clearly not the only example of a wider French rejection of visions of a social order based on models borrowed from the English experience. In the period examined in this study, an English style of laissez-faire, even in its narrow economic version, appears to have enjoyed little support among the politically powerful bourgeois who dominated the state's legislative and administrative institutions. Most French bourgeois of the period really did believe that with the horrifying exception of the Poor Law, English society was ruled by state institutions that were committed to a widely propounded ideology of laissez-faire. For moral economists and Social Catholics, the idea of reducing the state's concern for the economic and social order according to these precepts appeared to be elevating a dangerous kind of social negligence to the pedestal of moral philosophy. The principles of orthodox laissez-faire seemed to them to offer few means for resolving problems of social and moral disorder. As we have seen in the discussion of child labor legislation in Chapter 5, there were spokesmen for a laissez-faire point of view, especially within the Chamber of Deputies, men who criticized the illegitimacy of state intervention into child labor conditions, but such a view of the proper role of state administration could and did lead to their colleagues' irony or rebuke. During the period under study, leaders of French bourgeois opinion did not accept that what they viewed as an English vision of the world was either appropriate or adequate to resolving working-class family problems that they believed bore deep social and moral significance.

Imbued with a belief in the value of empirical inquiry, moral economist investigators of national and local reputation travelled some of the same paths as Social Catholic activists and emerged from their inquiries with a body of information about family-related mores that served to inform contemporaries of the precise nature and causes of social division. Gathering, analyzing, and disseminating this information helped not only to acquaint members of the bourgeoisie with specific information on "sociological divisions" in early industrial France but also to crystallize a greater sense of the bourgeoisie's own virtues. Although the information they created about working-class families provided moral economists and their readers with a portrait of social and moral disorder, further explorations and policy efforts gradually revealed latent features of working-class families that could be acted upon and used by policy administrators to help close the gap between the values and mores of working and middle classes.

The success of moral economist observers in gaining support for their views thus lay in their ability to find a middle course between the militancy of early Social Catholicism and the equally innovative precepts of English political economy. Their ideological stance and policy strategies paid serious attention to the French state's need to perform traditional functions of mediation in the affairs of the society it governed while avoiding excess. Moral economists both inside and outside state and administrative power showed how government agencies at both the national and local levels could intervene in the family lives of workers, but in ways they believed would reduce the necessity of sustained or systematic intervention in the future. Under their policies, the state and its administration would retain their historic functions of equilibrating the social order. However, they believed that the establishment of working-class families as independent islands of moral and financial community would help to prepare individual workers and working-class families for integration into a new moral order based on shared adherence to values that would minimize the necessity of future state intervention. Moral economists' ideal was thus to use the vehicles of administrative and state intervention in order to make such intervention ultimately unnecessary.

The adoption of the views and language of moral economy helps to explain why "enlightened" industrialists like those within the Société industrielle de Mulhouse were able to succeed in their own reform agenda on the issue of child labor. Through their adherence to this powerful world view, they demonstrated to more traditional elements within the French bourgeoisie that industrialists had legitimately earned the right to share power and help govern the society they were beginning to shape. Their conception of the *long-term* interests of French industrialists showed that these interests were entirely reconcilable with those of the older bourgeoisie and the state. The language and practice of moral economy thus provided a means through which owners of industry could move from the fringes to a more central role in governance, both political and social. Moral economy helped them to demonstrate that they were not merely a "special-interest" group whose lust for short-term gain constituted the totality of their concerns. It showed that they, too, were concerned with the larger problems of order and community. This process of self-legitimation was a critical one. For although industrialists in their role as local notables frequently enjoyed high status and power within the confines of their own provinces and were gradually gaining membership in the central organs of state and legislative power, their status and reputation lagged behind those of traditional elements of the French bourgeoisie who were more accustomed to governing.

The appeal of moral economist ideology at the center of state power has been explained in several ways. Part of its appeal lay in moral economists' ability to provide guidance in the practical problems of administration. However, I have also shown that the capacity of moral economist policy to evolve over time, even to become more flexible in adapting to certain features of working-class family life, heightened its attractions. The rehabilitation of the reputation of mothers of illegitimate children, which helped to legitimize the repression of older forms of assistance to foundlings and a changeover to a more economical system of home assistance, was only one example of the adaptive qualities of moral economist policy in action. This adaptiveness was in turn based on the capacity of moral economist observers to seek grounds of social and moral reconciliation even as they decried the valuative distance that they believed separated industrial workers' families from those of the bourgeoisie. Although moral economists' initial emphasis on deviation was critical in arousing interest in policy reform among uninformed bourgeois with little personal knowlege of industrial society, their articulation of some of the latent if embryonic similiarities between industrial workers and the bourgeoisie functioned to make the enterprise of policy intervention seem more viable.

When it came time to implement policies based on principles of moral economy at the local and regional level, however, its adherents inside and outside of administrative institutions faced a variety of challenges. As this study has shown, the urban administration of Mulhouse had adopted elements of a moral economist vision of the world well before that view was proclaimed in classic texts of the July Monarchy. Mulhouse's bourgeoisie, like many others in Germany and Switzerland, had ruled along a preindustrial version of these lines for many years, literally granting membership in the urban community on the bases of people's allegiance to mores of which they were the paragons. In the 1820s, the Mulhouse administration's version of a moral economist approach could shock representatives of the regional and central government by its zealous adherence to values that seemed both excessive and somewhat foreign to French traditions of governance. By the 1830s and 1840s, however, as industrialization proceeded, the principles and policies of moral economy as practiced in Mulhouse began to appear rather more appealing to certain elements within governing circles. This resulted both from the capacity of moral economist policy to evolve into less militant forms and from the growing fear of social division that economic change was fostering.

However, Mulhouse's urban traditions were quite different from those of Lille or Rouen. Evidence from these two towns showed their leaders' familiarity with preindustrial urban poverty and a correspondingly less dramatized estimation of industrialization as the source of entirely novel social conditions or working-class mores. Because of the persistence of older trades in Lille and Rouen and the slower pace of urban industrial growth, there seems to have been a greater continuity between preindustrial past and industrial present. Information from the archives of the Bureau de bienfaisance of Lille, for example, has shown the persistence in that city of workers' belief that they were entitled by a kind of hereditary right to public assistance. And though city leaders and departmental prefects, including Villeneuve-Bargemont, would attempt to delegitimize such a view, their struggle seems to have been a protracted one. Indeed, it is doubtful that city or welfare administrators in these two cities ever fully adopted the kind of militant moral economist view of the world so apparent in Mulhouse. The administrators of Lille's Bureau de bienfaisance were clearly concerned about the problem of common law unions, yet they attempted to deal with it in the same manner as volunteer members of the Société de Saint-François-Régis, that is, through the use of moral suasion rather than the force of law. Although the precise mentality of Rouen's city administration on this issue remains more obscure, there is no evidence that urban officials there ever envisaged the kind of militant moral economist policy used in Mulhouse.

In the administration of the foundling problem, prefects in the Nord and Seine-Inférieure were clearly caught between a variety of pressures. They, their conseils généraux, and the central administration all wished to diminish costs. However, prefects were responsible for seeing to it that changes in administrative policy not arouse public opinion or create scandals. Local hospital officials who were closer to the grass roots of the foundling problem had their own concerns and generally tried to urge against substantial innovation. While departmental policy on foundlings and abandoned children did change as the result of initiatives from the central government, these changes were hardly successful in ending the problem of child dependency. Although *tours* in the Nord and Seine-Inférieure were closed or modified sufficiently to reduce administrative costs, the new strategy of home assistance to unwed mothers demonstrated the necessity of adapting moral economist ideals to some of the realities of urban working-class life.

Opposition to the enforcement of child labor legislation involved both workers and factory owners in all three regions. Although the idea of legislation had great appeal on the eve of parliamentary debates, implemention of an actual law foundered in the face of opposition to its inconveniences, even in the Mulhouse area. Well-known moral economists such as Penot and Thouvenin and leading Social Catholics such as Kolb-Bernard lent their hand to local enforcement, but it would be difficult to see the law's attempt to transmit principles of moral economy into the industrial social order as much of a success.

Such considerations stand as a challenge to the value of historical approaches that seek to understand the intervention of "the state" into family life by concentrating essentially on the discourse of theoreticians of social policy or on plans for intervention. An examination of ideological divergences within the bourgeoisie who controlled basic institutions of government and administration helps us to understand better why state-driven policies towards the family frequently experienced such tentative fits and starts when it came time to implement them. Policies directed towards the domestic sphere were laden with contention, arousing at different times the opposition of "public opinion," irate factory owners, dissenting voices within administrative bureaucracies, and workers themselves. A study of the problems inherent in devising and implementing family policy under the late Restoration and July Monarchy also nuances any portrait of a triumphant and unified bourgeoisie by analyzing how different world views among makers of opinion and policy placed obvious limitations on the state's power to translate policy theory into social action in a smooth or unmitigated fashion.

One of the consequences of this analysis is to argue for an understanding of the French bourgeoisie of the period as a group that was still grasping for the best ways to create a society in its own image, particularly in its struggle to understand and control the new forces of industrial society. Part of the barrier to this enterprise, as we have seen, was the lethargy of most bourgeois, who had little interest in contemplating any part of the "social question" until the barricades went up. The fact that factory workers were generally less likely than artisans to be manning those barricades made the task of moral economists and Social Catholics that much more difficult. Both groups were often hampered in their efforts to arouse widespread interest in their points of view in part because French industrial society was evolving so slowly. Moreover, the menacing features of industrial society, obvious mainly to those who were actually interested in documenting or understanding the mores of industrial workers, lay in a realm of human behavior removed from the public theaters in which working-class challenges to the status quo usually took place.

The view of working-class family life that emerges from archival sources left by efforts to implement policy is one that shows extremely strong resemblances to patterns of external behavior that had existed for many years. The rise in concubinage and illegitimacy began well before before the onset of industrialization. However, the breakdown of rurally based systems of proto-industry in the three areas and the currents of labor migration that this breakdown stimulated seem to have increased the incidence of both phenomena. Evidence from the work of Social Catholic organizations and from administrative records has suggested my argument that labor migration in the 1830s and 1840s probably had a more disruptive impact on working-class marriage practices than some historians, generally writing about the later nineteenth century, have implied. Yet this disruption was not so much a consequence of radical changes in values as of the difficulties that migrant working-class men and women encountered in attempting to conform to the legal requirements of legitimate marriage. Future research on the family origins of the European factory proletariat may well show that rural-to-ubran migrants emerged from a milieu in which concubinage and illegitimacy were already familiar occurrences. In this case, migrants' tendency to enter common law unions would rightly appear as a familiar experience, one that was not essentially the result of conditions specific to urban residence. My hunch is that such a finding is very likely indeed. Nonetheless, the removal of people from their places of birth seems to have hastened the decline of community controls on legitimate marriage that had long been central in the rural world. My concern to emphasize some of the disruptive effects of urban migration stems also from my belief that census and vital registration records, those rightly treasured documents for the study of working-class marriage and family, tend to underestimate the stresses and strains on family life exacerbated by migration during the early industrial period.

Some of these strains were clearly apparent in the records of institutions for foundlings and abandoned children. However, they too had significant links with the past. Working-class mothers and fathers in nineteenth-century factory towns were not historically unique in experiencing the wide range of problems that led to children's becoming foundlings or abandoned children. Not only did rural female workers of the period contribute their share of children to urban *tours,* but the kinds of problems these institutions received had long been endemic to lower-class families living on the margins of subsistence. In the period I have examined, working-class women did attempt to use foundling institutions as a way of having the state help care for their infants while they went to work. Their actions attested to their continuing belief in the legitimacy of this obligation and their attempt to adapt an older form of social welfare policy to their needs in a situation of continuing poverty. There was really very little social innovation here.

The problem of child factory labor was a newer one, and it is possible to see this feature of industrial working-class family life as representing the greatest break with the past. As Michael Anderson has pointed out, however, it is misleading to overemphasize urban factory workers' own concern to maintain the kind of one-to-one family work bonds typical of a rural, protoindustrial past.[5] By the period under study, urban industrial workers in France, as in England, seem to have been adapting quite rapidly to an economic situation in which work and family roles were necessarily differentiated. Industrial work places did continue to incorporate a certain familial dimension, particularly in hiring practices and in the employment of child workers. However, parental

5. Michael Anderson, "Sociological History and the Working-Class Family: Smelser Revisited," *Social History* 3 (1976): 322–25.

behavior seems to indicate that once children could be admitted to factory work on their own, the main priority of both parents and children was to contribute wages towards the maintenance of a family economy. If this goal could be furthered by distributing wage earners among different work places, then that step was taken. Maintaining a family economy, not surprisingly, took precedence over maintaining one-to-one family bonds within the work place.

At the highest level of abstraction, industrial workers of the Restoration and July Monarchy would have found little reason to dissent from the family values that underlay moral economist or Social Catholic policy. There was little in workers' behavior to show that they rejected the notion, for example, that families were institutions that ideally combined bonds of affection and the search for some measure of material stability. In fact, although many bourgeois commentators identified these values with their own social class, they were probably more correct at the point at which they came to articulate latent similarities between industrial workers and bourgeois on this and other valuative issues. The problem was that moral economists in particular were seeking industrial workers' conformity to an increasingly restrictive range of behaviors by which widely accepted family values were now to be realized. This growing sense of restrictiveness, illustrated among other examples in Dupin's model of fatherhood, was partly a function of the general importance ascribed by bourgeois commentators to the close link between mores and morality or, put another way, between the specific habits of daily life and workers' fitness to join a newly conceived moral community. It also resulted from the fact that workers' domestic life was the object of more sustained scrutiny, thus permitting a greater awareness of specific deviations from behaviors identified with the proper realization of family values.

In the study of the effects of family policy, we have seen some modification of workers' behavior with regard to concubinage, child abandonment, or child labor under the compulsion of administrative or legislative constraints and moral suasion, changes that were greeted as signs of success by moral economists and Social Catholics alike. We have also seen signs that this conformity was often reluctant and coerced. Although family policies sometimes forced working-class mothers, fathers, or children to change their behavior, the persistence of concubinage or of child dependency on state and private assistance to this day reminds us that changes traced to the success of policies were not final. Of the three policy issues with which this study has dwelt, child labor practices probably underwent the greatest modification under the July Monarchy, although a recent study clearly shows the persisting difficulties authorities encountered in formulating, enacting, and enforcing child labor legislation up until the very end of the nineteenth century.[6] The main

6. Lee Shai Weissbach, *Assuring the Future Harvest: Child Labor Reform in France, 1827–1885* (Baton Rouge: Louisiana State University Press, forthcoming), chs. 6–10.

conclusion suggested by these observations is that under the conditions of early industrialization, workers' family behavior was changing much less radically than moral economists or Social Catholics believed. The family life of France's industrial workers under the late Restoration and July Monarchy shows a clear resemblance to earlier kinds of behavior that workers had developed to maintain both individuals and the family group. In this respect it had the same *general* goals as family policies implemented throughout the years of the late Restoration and the July Monarchy. The critical difference, of course, was that family policy created at the top of the social pyramid sought to dictate the precise means to be used to achieve those goals.

For reasons elaborated in this study, Social Catholics of the generation of Frédéric Ozanam would reject entirely the argument that their efforts sought to transmit bourgeois values of family life to the families of industrial workers, since what they intended was a spiritual revolution designed to link bourgeois to worker under a set of universifiable values that transcended man-made class divisions. However, in arguing that the importance Social Catholic activists ascribed to the family stemmed as much from their lay as their religious values, and in examining the similarities between their concerns and those of the secularly minded moral economists, I have tried to show that the family's centrality to the task of constructing new foundations for an interclass community of mores was widely shared within the social class to which most Social Catholics activists belonged.

It is interesting to conjecture what moral economists might think of my argument that they represented a vanguard of bourgeois social thought and action designed to bring working-class family behavior into line with the requirements of a new moral community they were attempting to construct. My suspicion is that they would have been delighted with such a characterization. Unlike many analysts and implementors of family policy in the late twentieth century, moral economists and Social Catholics of late Restoration and July Monarchy France had an extraordinary confidence in the values their policies were intended to teach and a sanguine belief in their ability to discern which family behaviors were most desirable both for individuals and for their society as a whole. Moreover, they shared a clear and powerful belief in the capacity of attitudinal changes to inspire systematic changes in behavior. Although both groups shied away from a previous generation's emphasis on using universalistic notions of the "rights of man" or politics to forge new forms of social and moral solidarity, their published works and policy innovations resonated with the kind of ideological and practical fervor one associates with those who have designated themselves as leaders of the moral and social order.

Appendices
Bibliography
Index

Appendix A. The Law of 22 March 1841 on the Work of Children Employed in Factories and Workshops

Art. 1: Children may be employed only under conditions determined by the present law:

1. in manufacturing establishments, factories, and workshops and their auxiliary [buildings] that contain a mechanical motor or continuous-process furnace;
2. in all factories that employ more than twenty workers assembled in the workshop itself.

Art. 2: To be admitted, children must be at least eight years old.

From eight to twelve years of age, they may not be at work for more than eight of twenty-four hours, with work time divided by a rest period.

From twelve to sixteen years of age, they cannot be at work more than twelve of twenty-four hours, with work time divided by rest periods.

Work may occur only between 5 A.M. and 9 P.M.

The ages of children will be attested to by a certificate delivered without charge by the *officier de l'état-civil*.

Art. 3: All work between 9 P.M. and 5 A.M. is considered night work.

All night work is forbidden to children under age thirteen.

If stoppages of hydraulic motors or urgent need for repairs demand it, children older than thirteen may work during the night, counting two hours as three, between 9 P.M. and 5 A.M.

Night work for children over thirteen, similarly calculated, will be tolerated if it is recognized as indispensable in establishments with a continuous-process furnace whose functioning cannot be suspended any time during the course of the day.

Art. 4: Children under sixteen may not be employed on Sundays or on holidays recognized by law.

Art. 5: No child under twelve may be admitted to work without parents or guardians proving that he is currently attending one of the public or private schools in the area. All children admitted must attend school until age twelve.

Children over 12 will be exempted from attending school if they bear a certificate from the mayor of their place of residence attesting that they have received primary, elementary instruction.

Art. 6: Mayors are required to deliver a livret to the father, mother, or guardian bearing the age, names, birthplacc, and domicile of the child and the time during which he has received elementary instruction.

The directors of the work places shall inscribe

1. on the livret of each child, the date of his entry into the establishment and of his departure from it;
2. on a special register, all the information referred to in this article.

Art. 7: Administrative regulations may

1. extend the application of the provisions of this law to other manufacturing establishments, factories, or workshops besides those alluded to in article 1;
2. raise the minimum age and reduce the work hours determined in articles 2 and 3, as concerns the kinds of industries where children's labor may exceed their strength or compromise their health;
3. determine those work places where children under age sixteen may not be employed because of danger or unhealthful conditions;
4. forbid children to do certain dangerous or harmful kinds of work where they are admitted;
5. rule on the indispensable kinds of work to be tolerated by children on Sundays and holidays in factories with continuous-process furnaces;
6. rule on cases of night work provided for in article 3.

Art. 8: Administrative regulations should

1. provide for measures necessary to the execution of this law;
2. assure the maintenance of good conduct and public decency in workshops, factories, and manufacturing establishments;
3. assure the primary instruction and religious education of the children;
4. prevent all misuse or abusive punishment of children;
5. assure healthful and secure conditions necessary to the children's lives and health.

Art. 9: In each workshop, directors must display a copy of this law, relevant administrative regulations, and internal work place regulations they are required to make to assure [the law's and regulations'] execution.

Art. 10: The government will establish inspections to oversee and assure the execution of the present law. In each establishment, the inspectors may examine the registers relevant to the execution of this law, internal regulations, children's livrets, and the children themselves. They may be accompanied by a doctor appointed by the prefect or subprefect.

Art. 11: In case of an infraction, inspectors shall draw up a report which shall stand as evidence until contradicted.

Art. 12: In case of infractions of the present law or of administrative regulations handed down for its execution, the owners or managers of the establishments will be called before the justice of the peace of the *canton* and punished by a fine *de simple police* which cannot exceed fifteen francs.

Infractions that result either from the admission of under-age children or from excessive work shall result in as many fines as there are children improperly admitted or employed. The combined fines may not exceed 200 francs.

If there is a repeated infraction, the owners or managers of the establishment will be called before the court of the *police correctionnelle* and be given a fine of 16 to 100 francs. In cases provided for by the second paragraph of this article, the combined fines may not exceed 100 francs.

Recidivism is declared if in the twelve previous months the party has received a first judgment for infraction of this law or of the administrative regulations it authorizes.

Art. 13: This law will not become obligatory until six months after its promulgation.

Appendix B. Spinning-Mill Work Regulations, Rouen Area, 1830

The following regulations applied in mills located in Maromme owned by MM. Vallée and Chollet. Promulgated in 1830, they are located in ADSM, 10 MP/1302.

1. From the moment they are admitted to work in the shops, all workers are required to behave honestly and to submit to established rules. They are expected to go to their respective shops in the morning as well as during the rest of the day and after meals—five minutes after the sound of the bell. They cannot leave until the bell has rung for this reason, unless permission has been obtained from the director or overseer, under penalty of a fine equal to the time lost.

2. The hours both for the beginning of work and for meals will be regulated by the time of sunup and sundown. Workers will be informed of changes.

3. No workers will be received without a livret in good order. Work days and days of rest will be designated by the director. No requests for quitting during the current fortnight will be accepted. The request will be registered only on the Saturday (payday) following. Those given their fortnight's severance pay at the same time are one overseer of accessory jobs, one spinner of fine threads, one piecer, one reeler, one picker, etc., and if on the Saturday of the same fortnight period there are two workers of the same type who wish their severance pay, the first who signs up will be released after two weeks, the second after a month, and so forth.

4. No one may be absent during work hours without the permission of the director. Those who do not come to work and who have not notified the director in time will pay a fine equal to the wages for work lost during the absence.

5. The worker who fails to keep his machine and work place clean and in good order, who fails to oil the machine before beginning work and before dinner, or who causes damage to any materials will pay a fine equal to double the cost of the damage done.

6. Those who come to work drunk, or who cause disturbances either by forming coalitions or insulting the overseer, will be fired as of the next day and will pay a fine of one day's wages. If the offense is one meriting exemplary punishment, the worker will be brought before the appropriate tribunals.

7. A worker starting on a new machine should, during the first hour, make an inspection of it to see that no pieces are missing. He should make a declaration of this fact because after a certain time he will be held responsible for paying for replacements.

8. Pickers who fail to clean their cotton well and reelers who wind their thread badly either by letting knots pass, making skeins of less than five *sous,* or not attaching threads in the prescribed manner will pay a fine of ten centimes each time [bad work] is discovered.

9. No worker shall receive his livret until he has cleaned his machine and work place. If he refuses, he will pay a fine of one franc.

10. Smoking, whistling, singing bawdy songs, communicating between workers at different machines, interrupting tranquility and work order in whatever manner, are prohibited under penalty of a fine proportional to the offense.

11. Pay day is every Saturday for the earnings of a fortnight's work. Workers will receive no cotton after the Thursday of the current two-week period.

12. The lighting of stoves, lamps, candles, or paper inside the workshops is expressly forbidden under penalty of a fifty-centime fine.

13. Those who fail to keep their lights clean and covered with a chimney will pay a fine of twenty-five centimes.

14. Those who break windows, light chimneys, large or small brooms, rollers, or other objects will pay for their replacement.

15. Those found sitting on baskets or tin pots or who break them by throwing them or by any other means will pay the value of the damage, or double if the offense is repeated.

16. Workers will receive their cotton by weight, and at the final weighing they must give back a weight equal to that received, wastage included. They are responsible for the quantity lacking.

17. Workers entering as apprentices cannot request severance pay until one year after entering unless they pay the following indemnities: spinning apprentices, forty francs; piecers, carders, or slubbers, fifteen francs.

18. Damage done to the outside or inside of the workshops will be paid for by all workers if they do not reveal the name of the delinquent responsible.

19. Every Sunday, there will be an inspection of the machines. On Monday, the names of those receiving fines will be announced.

20. Spinners are responsible for damage done by their piecers and bobbin tenders. Cotton ruined by negligence or lack of care, either by being left on the floor or swept up with the dust, will be paid for by all workers in the shop if the delinquent is not known.

21. Workers will be searched every time it is deemed appropriate. Those guilty of stealing will be handed over to the law.

22. Workers are reminded that art. 415 of the Penal Code prohibits all coalitions on their part under penalty of imprisonment for at least one and no more than three months; for leaders and instigators, the penalty is imprisonment for at least two but no more than five years.

23. Art. 386 of the Penal Code [states]: Shall be punished by imprisonment any individual guilty of theft committed in the following cases: (no. 3) If the thief is a domestic, servant, *compagnon,* or apprentice of a house, shop, or store of his master.

24. Art. 21 of the same Code [states]: Any individual of either sex, sentenced to imprisonment, will be held in a workhouse. The duration of this sentence will be at least five but no more than ten years.

25. Art. 22 of the same Code [states]: Whoever is sentenced to imprisonment and before serving this sentence will be placed in the pillory where he or she will remain exposed to the view of the people during one hour. Over his or her head will be placed a sign indicating in large, legible letters: the name, occupation, domicile, sentence, and its reasons.

26. A worker caught hitting another for whatever reason will pay the equivalent of one day's wages.

27. Those disobeying the director or overseer will pay a fine of one-half a day's pay, and a whole day's pay if disobedience is accompanied by insult. (This does not imply legal action.)

28. The porter is prohibited from letting any worker leave without authorization by the director, under penalty of a two-franc fine.

29. The director and overseer should be the first to arrive and will make their rounds after the end of work. They are each responsible for the lack of execution of these regulations.

30. If, by his bad conduct, ill will, or laziness a worker leaves those other workers he is supplying idle, or lets his machine sit idly, he will lose his right to demand severance pay.

31. Mutilating or ripping up these regulations, of which a copy has been sent to the mayor's office, is prohibited under penalty of a fine of three francs, borne by the workers of each shop if the party responsible is not known.

Appendix C. Work Regulations Declared at the Prefecture of the Seine-Inférieure, Rouen, 13 September 1830

The following regulations are found in ADSM, 10 MP/1380.

Art. 1: In the morning, the bell will announce the entry of workers. This entry time shall follow the hours of sunrise so as to diminish night work as much as possible. The work day shall be 14½ hours, of which 13 shall be work time.

Art. 2: The door will be closed ten minutes after starting time.

Art. 3: It is expressly forbidden to any worker to bring anyone into the workshops without the head's permission.

Art. 4: All spinners are required to find piecers, and it is expressly forbidden to beat them.

Art. 5: The master shall furnish oil for greasing and burning. Workers shall pay for it out of their wages.

Art. 6: Variations in wages, up or down, shall be announced two weeks in advance at pay time.

Art. 7: Fire is one of the greatest dangers to the establishments. Footwarmers and heating pots are prohibited, as are touching the stoves, lamps, or lights without the master's permission. Smoking is particularly forbidden in the workshops, stairways, and courtyards under penalty of a three-franc fine. The offending workers may be fired as a result. Bringing wine or spirits . . . or any kind of liquor into the shops is forbidden under penalty of a two-franc fine—as well as confiscation of the liquor and container. The worker may be fired.

Art. 8: In taking over a machine, each worker shall examine it on the first day. If he finds pieces missing, he shall so declare to the master or overseer, because after one day he shall be required to pay the costs.

Art. 9: No coarse or fine spinner shall change the tension, separation, or angle of his machine.

Art. 10: Any worker who breaks or smashes something, ruins wood, iron, or copper through error or malevolence shall pay the value of his damage. This article shall not be considered [as pertaining to] sums ordinarily kept out of wages but rather as restitution to the master.

Art. 11: Only one worker for each fifteen [working on] the same [kind of] machines shall be permitted to leave each fortnight. In case there are numerous requests, workers will leave in the order in which they requested it. Work time lost or bad conduct by a worker during the current fortnight may delay the handing over of his livret.

Art. 12: If *force majeure* stops all or part of the work, the master is in no case forced to pay workers an indemnity.

Art. 13: There are no specific sums set for infractions of articles 2, 3, 4, 5, and 9. As it is the workshop director who best knows the usages and abuses of his area, it is he who decides on the greasing, cleaning, and good order of the shops, the cleaning of machines, etc. He shall fix the sums to be retained for each of these [offenses] as long as combined they do not exceed one day's pay for each fortnight.

However, since the indemnity for errors committed during a fortnight are light, the master is always free to fire a worker if after reaching the limit [of fines] he continues his offenses.

Art. 14: In no case may the sums retained [from workers' wages] be kept for the profit of the master. Each fortnight's payday, a detailed list of fines levied, except those resulting from articles 5, 8, and 9, will be displayed in the shop. This money shall be used for sick workers who have been in the establishment for at least four months.

Each payment shall be inscribed on the list of fines of the nearest payday so that all workers can verify the recipients of this money.

Art. 15: Since this new contract between master and worker is different from that agreed to by workers entering the workshops, each mill owner is obligated, the same day as its promulgation, to return the livrets of workers who request them.

It is understood that this time period shall not exceed twelve hours. But to avoid disputes about the lapse of time between the promulgation of this regulation and requests for livrets, each workshop head shall write on the bottom of the regulation the hour at which it was posted; and in the presence of the workers and overseer, care should be taken to note the hour at which the livrets are requested.

This policy shall be affixed during the first hour of work.

Appendix D. Work Regulations in Cotton-Spinning Mills of Lille, 1849

The regulations for Lille were reprinted in Henri Loyer, *Recueil pour servir aux archives du comité ou chambre syndicale des filatures de coton de Lille* (Lille, 1873), pp. 13–23. They were "adopted unanimously by the Committee of Cotton Mill Owners of Lille and its suburbs in its meeting of 11 october 1849." They are headed by the motto "Peace and Work." Pages 13–17, which contain factory rules, are excerpted here. The rest of the document contains detailed information on the mutual funds created by the regulations.

Regulation: Aid and Discipline

1. In order to aid sick workers and maintain morality and discipline at work, [which are] as profitable for the worker as the owner, a *mutual fund* shall be established in each cotton mill of Lille and its suburbs.

2. This fund is maintained by sums retained each Saturday from the wages of each worker and from disciplinary fines.

3. The fines cannot be considered an advantage to the owner, since they are meant to aid the sick, even though the cause leading to the fine has nearly always affected the owner prejudicially.

4. The amount of sums retained, fines, and aid is proportional to the size of wages. Thus, spinning workers are divided in to three classes or categories as follows:

   1. 1st Class: Men
   2. 2d Class: Women and piecers over sixteen
   3. 3d Class: Pickers working in the mill and apprentices or piecers under sixteen

Lateness and Absences

5. Lateness and absences result in partial or total unemployment in the establishment, inactivity of large amounts of capital, and the loss of large sums such as costs of coal, employees' salaries, etc.

The absence of even one worker or his negligence at work may in certain cases result in keeping all others from working, in other words, *compromising the interests of workers themselves as well as those of the owner*.

6. The only possible punishment is to apply disciplinary fines.

Fines

7. Lateness and absences are punished by the following fines:

Class	*Late to enter*	*Absences*				*2d day, etc.*
		1½ hrs.	*3 hrs.*	*6 hrs.*	*1st day*	
1st	15 c.	30 c.	50 c.	1 F.	2 F.	2.5 F.
2d	10	15	20	.40	.80	1.0
3d	5	10	15	.25	.50	.60

The labor of a large number of workers depends on the work of the firemen and coarse spinners. These workers may be fired after one day's absence.

All other workers are fired only after two days.

Ordinary Fines

8. Ordinary offenses are punished with the same fines as lateness. Serious offenses are punished in proportion to the damage caused.

9. Ordinary fines are applied for the following:[1]

- Firemen: for insufficient water in the boiler, irregular functioning of the machine, lateness in starting up, negligence in machine maintenance, lack of gas, and tardiness in cleaning the refiner.
- Scutchers: for bad work in making laps, insufficiency in the number, dimensions, and weight of these laps.
- Pickers: for badly picked cotton or cotton with too much waste.
- Carding workers: for unsatisfactory work in tying up, weights, fleece, and laps, imperfections in the reels, . . . and negligence in work done.
- Doffers: for not observing instructions given.
- Frame spinners: for badly made bobbins, waste on the bobbins, double or single threads, bad ties, mixing bobbins, waste badly sorted, machine badly maintained.
- Spinners: for beads in the thread, bad ties, unraveling threads, . . . machines badly maintained, loose threads, . . . negligence resulting in imperfections in the thread.
- Piecers (old and young): for disorder or waste on the bobbins, faulty sorting or labelling of waste, beads, bad ties, single and double threads, etc.
- Fine spinners, piecers (female), and water-frame spinners: For badly made bobbins, single threads, bad knots, waste on the bobbins, ties at the ends, threads insufficiently twisted, loose threads, lack of order and mixing bobbins or negligence in work. . . .

10. The ordinary fine is applied also:
    1. To any worker who has not cleaned his machine . . . and work place at the appropriate time.
    2. To the worker who has not greased the machines for which he is responsible

1. Only part of an extensive list has been included.

at the appropriate time or who has not conformed to instructions given for greasing.

3. To any piecer who has refused to obey his spinner during work or [machine] cleaning time or who has answered him back with an insult.
4. To any worker who has been found away from his machine during work hours.

General Provisions

11. The spinner who hits his piecer shall pay a fifty-centime fine.

12. Workers who fight in the factory shall pay the same fine as if they had been absent during a whole day.

13. Any worker who enters the factory with a pipe insufficiently extinguished or out of its pouch pays a fifty-centime fine. If he holds a lighted pipe in his mouth, the fine is two francs.

14. Any worker who comes to work drunk must leave the establishment. The fine incurred is counted in proportion to the time absent. If he resists the owner or overseer in leaving the factory, the fine is doubled.

15. All arguments among workers in the factory and all obscene words and actions will result in the imposition of a fine whose size is determined by the seriousness of the case.

16. The fireman is dismissed immediately if, at the time when the steam engine should be operating, he is drunk; or if by error or negligence he has compromised the security of the establishment.

Sums Retained

17. Sums retained as the result of faulty work are established in proportion to the degree of bad production. Like fines, they enter into the mutual fund.

Compensation

18. A bonus of twenty francs is given each year by the owner at the time of the festival of the Broquelet to any worker who has received no fines during the year. The bonus is shared if several workers are in this situation.

Two-Week Work Periods

19. For the reciprocal security of owner and worker, it is the practice that when the worker wishes to leave the establishment or when the owner dismisses the worker, each will inform the other a fortnight in advance.

20. During this fortnight, the worker must, as formerly, conform to the regulations of the factory and bring the same care and zeal to his work. The owner must also treat the worker the same way as in the past.

21. The worker who wishes to leave the factory must give notice at the factory's office on Saturday from 10 A.M. to noon.

22. The last fornight's work is composed of two weeks of actual work. The worker receives back his livret after machine cleaning of the second week.

23. If a worker does not appear at the factory for two weeks, his livret is deposited at the central police bureau of the town hall of his domicile. Before so depositing it, the owner will charge the livret for sums owed [the owner] as the result of pay advances, fines, or bad work.

Bibliography

Archival Sources

Most of the archival sources used in this study come from records of public administration at the central, regional, and local level. Archival sources for the study of foundling administration are found at the Archives Nationales in series F15, Hospices et secours. My debt to this series is obvious in the text. Records from the period of the Directory and Consulate are rather spotty. Readers interested in the question of foundlings and abandoned children under the Revolution and archival sources for their study should consult Alan Forrest's fine study, *The French Revolution and the Poor*. From the middle of the 1820s, series F15 contains yearly reports, by department, in a standardized, tabular format listing numbers of foundlings and abandoned children received, their total numbers, and their costs, accompanied by a rich administrative correspondence in which prefects communicate both their own attitudes and those of their conseils généraux towards the administration of foundlings and abandoned children. One source of frustration was the fact that for Lille and Rouen at least, there were several years (in the early 1830s) for which there were no annual reports to be found. Similarly, the modification or elimination of foundling services in the late 1830s seems to have obviated the need for these reports. In the establishment of statistical series of foundlings, I have thus supplemented information from the Archives Nationales with information from published studies based on local sources.

Departmental archives also contain information relevant to an understanding of foundling administration, though these holdings tend to be less rich than the holdings of the Archives Nationales. For the Haut-Rhin and the Nord, this information is contained in series X, Assistance publique; for the Seine-Maritime, series XP, Hospices et secours.[1] The very detailed records of the hospitals that received foundlings and abandoned children are found at the Archives départementales de la Seine-Maritime

1. Documents in several series of the Archives départementales de la Seine-Maritime have recently undergone reclassification. The archives holds a published list of correspondences between old and new classification numbers. I have used the old classification numbers throughout this book.

in series 2 LP, containing the deliberations of the administrative commission of the Hôpital-Général de Rouen, and series 2 QP, the actual foundling registers. For Lille, registers of foundlings and abandoned children received at the Hospice-Général are held by the Archives hospitalières. There, I consulted foundling registers nos. 4–7, AHL, 4467–69. Deliberations of the conseils généraux of the Nord and Seine-Inférieure were also consulted for information concerning departmental policy toward foundlings and abandoned children. Deliberations for the Nord are contained in ADN, N2/14–26, for the late 1820s to the late 1830s and are continued in registers 2152(1–14) for the sessions of 1840 to 1847. Records of the conseil général of the Seine-Inférieure are held in ADSM, 1 NP/16–32, for the late 1820s to the late 1840s.

Archives Nationales, series F12, Administration générale de la France, provides documentation on the preparation and implementation of the law of 1841, including correspondence between the central government and regional authorities. For any regional study of the child labor question, these sources need to be supplemented with materials from departmental and/or local archives. At the Archives départementales du Nord, the problem of child labor is documented in series M, Administration générale, and in particular in M611 and M613. At the Archives départementales de la Seine-Maritime information on child labor and the execution of the law of 1841 is contained in series 10 MP. At the Archives départementales du Haut-Rhin, information on child labor conditions and the enforcement of the 1841 law is contained in series 1M. Mulhouse's Archives municipales contain additional information on industrial establishments, their young workers, and the difficulties of enforcing the law of 1841. These materials are contained primarily in series F V; information on the schooling provisions of the 1841 law is also contained in series R I, Instruction publique. Those interested in any aspect of the holdings of the Archives municipales de Mulhouse are well advised to consult the varied and always valuable publications of M. Raymond Oberlé, for many years director of the archives.

The Archives de la Société de Saint-Vincent-de-Paul, used extensively by Pierre Pierrard in his magisterial *La vie ouvrière à Lille sous le second Empire*, are less voluminous for the period before 1850. Archival records here are organized by diocese, and the process of extracting relevant documentation is a slow one, since material is often not arranged in strictly chronological order. As indicated in the text, however, the archives contain valuable information on the works of the society's members, as well as some limited statistics on personnel and the minutes of local chapters, regional meetings, and the society's central council.

The richness of the Fonds Joly de Fleury at the Bibliothèque Nationale is illustrated in Jean-Pierre Gutton's *La société et les pauvres: L'exemple de la généralité de Lyon, 1534–1789* and Olwen Hufton's, *The Poor of Eighteenth-Century France*. I consulted series related to the administration of the Parisian foundling hospital and administrative correspondence on the care of foundlings in the provinces under the Old Regime, contained in numbers 1211, 1221, 1223, 1236, 1237, 1270 and 1271. Those wishing to use the collection are advised to consult Camille Bloch, *Inventaire sommaire des volumes de la collection Joly de Fleury concernant l'assistance et la mendicité*.

Other archival series used in the preparation of this study in include Archives Nationales, series F20, Statistique, for data on population in the three areas examined. This series also contains a bit more information on numbers of dependent children from the mid-1840s to the mid-1850s, contained in F20/282 39–40. The records of the deliberations of Lille's Bureau de bienfaisance, held by the Archives du Bureau de bienfaisance de Lille, provide a wealth of insights, both qualitative and quantitative, into the mentality and extensive relief efforts of the city's welfare administration. Records from the mid-1830s to the late 1840s are contained in vols. 16–18, ABBL, E. 71–73. Other sources of interest at the Archives départementales de la Seine-Maritime included the Fonds Stackler, assorted records of a noted cloth-printing establishment near Rouen from the 1820s to the beginning of the twentieth century, contained in series 4J, and the records of the Société de charité maternelle, contained in series 20J. At the Archives municipales de Mulhouse, I also consulted records of the deliberations of the city's *conseil municipal*, contained in series DI; the records "Police, hygiène publique, justice," contained in series J I and J II; series Q I, Assistance et prévoyance; series Q II, Oeuvres charitables; series Q III, Etablissements hospitaliers; and series Q V, Caisses de secours.

Printed Sources and Secondary Works

Aminzade, Ronald. "Capitalist Industrialization and Patterns of Industrial Protest: A Comparative Urban Study of Nineteenth-Century France." *American Sociological Review* 49 (1984): 437–53.

Anderson, Michael. *Family Structure in Nineteenth-Century Lancashire*. Cambridge, 1971.

Anderson, Michael. "Sociological History and the Working-Class Family: Smelser Revisited." *Social History* 3 (1976): 317–34.

Aperçu sur la condition des classes ouvrières et critique de l'ouvrage de M. Buret sur la misère des classes laborieuses, etc., par le Pce D . . . S . . . . Paris, 1844.

Ariès, Philippe. "Le travail des enfants et la famille populaire." *Critère*, no. 25 (1979): 251–55.

Arriaza, Armand. "Mousnier and Barber: The Theoretical Underpinnings of the 'Society of Orders' in Early Modern Europe." *Past and Present*, no. 89 (1980): 39–57.

Audiganne, Armand. *La nouvelle loi sur le travail des enfants et la famille ouvrière depuis 35 ans*. Paris, 1874.

Bader, Clarisse. *La femme française dans les temps modernes*. Paris, 1883.

Baker, Keith Michael. "French Political Thought at the Accession of Louis XVI." *Journal of Modern History* 50 (1978): 279–303.

Bardet, Jean-Pierre. *Rouen aux XVIIe et XVIIIe siècles: Les mutations d'un espace social*. 2 vols. Paris, 1983.

Bartrip, Peter. "Success or Failure? The Prosecution of the Early Factory Acts." *Economic History Review*, 2d ser., 38 (1985): 423–30.

Bastid, Paul. *Les institutions politiques de la monarchie parlementaire française: 1814–1848*. Paris, 1954.

Baudon, Adolphe. *De la suppression des tours d'enfants trouvés et des autres moyens à employer pour la diminution du nombre des expositions*. Paris, 1847.

Baudrillart, H. *La Normandie, passé et présent*. Paris, 1880.

Beck, Thomas D. *French Legislators, 1830–1834: A Study in Quantitative History*. Berkeley and Los Angeles, 1974.

Benoiston de Châteauneuf, Louis-François. *Considérations sur les enfants trouvés dans les principaux états de l'Europe*. Paris, 1824.

Benoiston de Châteauneuf, Louis-François. "Sur les enfants trouvés." *Annales d'hygiène publique et de médecine légale* 21 (1839): 88–123.

Benton, Ted. *The Rise and Fall of Structural Marxism: Althusser and His Influence*. New York, 1984.

Bergasse, Alphonse. *Recherches sur la consommation de la viande et du poisson depuis 1800*. Rouen, 1852.

Berger, Brigitte, and Berger, Peter L. *The War over the Family: Capturing the Middle Ground*. New York, 1983.

Bergues, Hélène, et al. *La prévention des naissances dans la famille: Ses origines dans les temps modernes*. Paris, 1960.

Berlanstein, Lenard R. "Illegitimacy, Concubinage, and Proletarianization in a French Town, 1760–1914." *Journal of Family History* 5 (1980): 360–74.

Berriat Saint-Prix, M. "Observations relatives aux *Recherches statistiques sur Mulhouse*." *Séances et travaux de l'Académie des sciences morales et politiques*, 1843, pp. 126–30.

Bert, Paul. *Lamartine, "Homme social": Son action dans la région natale*. Paris, 1947.

Berthollet, C. L., and Berthollet, A. B. *Elements of the Art of Dyeing*. Translated by Andrew Ure. London, 1824.

Bertier de Sauvigny, Guillaume de. *Au soir de la monarchie: La Restauration*. 3d ed. Paris, 1974.

Bigot de Morogues, Pierre-Marie-Sébastien, Baron. *De la misère des ouvriers et de la marche à suivre pour y remédier*. Paris, 1832.

Bigot de Morogues, Pierre-Marie-Sébastien, Baron. *Du paupérisme, de la mendicité et des moyens d'en prévenir les funestes effets*. Paris, 1834.

Blanchard, Raoul. *La Flandre: Etude géographique de la plaine flamande en France, Belgique et Hollande*. Paris, 1906.

Blanqui, Jérôme-Adolphe. *Des classes ouvrières en France pendant l'année 1848*. Paris, 1849.

Blanqui, Jérôme-Adolphe. "Tableau des populations rurales de la France en 1850." *Journal des économistes* 28 (1851): 9–27; 30 (1851): 1–15.

Bloch, Camille. *L'assistance et l'état en France à la veille de la Révolution: Généralités de Paris, Rouen, Alençon, Orléans, Châlons, Soissons, Amiens: 1764–1790*. Paris, 1908.

Bloch, Camille. *Inventaire sommaire des volumes de la collection Joly de Fleury concernant l'assistance et la mendicité*. Paris, 1908.

Boltanski, Luc. *Prime éducation et morale de classe*. 2d ed. Paris, 1977.

Bondy, François-Marie Taillepied, Vicomte de. *Mémoire sur la nécessité de réviser la législation actuelle concernant les enfans trouvés et abandonnés et orphelins pauvres*. Auxerre, 1835.

Bonfield, Lloyd; Smith, Richard M.; and Wrightson, Keith, eds. *The World We Have Gained: Histories of Population and Social Structure*. Oxford, 1986.

Borghese, Arthur. "From Riot to Strike: A Study of the Working Class of Mulhouse, 1847–1870." Ph.D. dissertation, University of Rochester, 1978.

Borghese, Arthur. "Industrialist Paternalism and Lower-Class Agitation: The Case of Mulhouse, 1848–1851." *Histoire Sociale / Social History* 13, no. 25 (1980): 55–84.

Bosquet, Emile. *Le roman des ouvrières*. Paris, 1868.

Bossy, John. *Christianity in the West: 1400–1700*. Oxford, 1985.

Bossy, John. "The Counter-Reformation and the People of Catholic Europe." *Past and Present*, no. 47 (1970): 51–70.

Bourcart, J. J. "Proposition de M. Jean-Jacques Bourcart, de Guebwiller, sur la nécessité de fixer l'âge et de réduire les heures de travail des ouvriers des filatures." *Bulletin de la Société industrielle de Mulhouse*, no. 5 (1828): 325–28.

Bourdon, Mathile. *Marthe Blondel, ou l'ouvrière de fabrique*. Paris, 1863.

Bourguet, Marie-Noëlle. "Race et folklore: L'image officielle de la France en 1800." *Annales, E.S.C.* 31 (1976): 802–23.

Bouriaud, F. "De la réduction des tours d'exposition des enfants trouvés dans le département de la Vienne." *Annales d'hygiène publique et de médecine légale* 17 (1837): 173–200.

Boyer, Adolphe. *De l'état des ouvriers et de son amélioration par l'organisation du travail*. Paris, 1841.

Brinton, Crane. *French Revolutionary Legislation on Illegitimacy, 1789–1804*. Cambridge, Mass., 1936.

Buret, Eugène. *De la misère des classes laborieuses en Angleterre et en France. De la nature de la misère, de son existence, de ses effets, de ses causes, et de l'insuffisance des remèdes qu'on lui a opposés jusqu'ici; avec l'indication des moyens propres à en affranchir les sociétés*. 2 vols. Paris, 1840.

Burger, Adolf. *Beiträge zur Statistik der Stadt Mülhausen*. Mulhouse, 1914.

Burguière, André. "Le rituel du mariage en France: Pratiques ecclésiastiques et pratiques populaires (XVI–XVIIIe siècle)." *Annales, E.S.C.* 33 (1978): 637–49.

Cameron, Rondo, and Freedeman, Charles E. "French Economic Growth: A Radical Revision." *Social Science History* 7 (1983): 3–30.

Carter, Edward II; Forster, Robert; and Moody, Joseph N., eds. *Enterprise and Entrepreneurs in Nineteenth- and Twentieth-Century France*. Baltimore, 1976.

Caspard, Pierre. "L'accumulation du capital dans l'indiennage au XVIIIème siècle." *Revue du Nord* 61 (1979): 115–23.

Caspard, Pierre. "La fabrique au village." *Le mouvement social*, no. 97 (1976): 15–37.

Cazeneuve, Dr. Valentin. *Rapport adressé à M. le Préfet du Nord sur les opérations du conseil de révision pendant l'année 1841*. Lille, 1842.

Chaline, Jean-Pierre. "La banque à Rouen au XIXe siècle." *Revue d'histoire économique et sociale*, no. 3 (1974): 384–420.

Chaline, Jean-Pierre. *Les bourgeois de Rouen: Une élite urbaine au XIXe siècle*. Paris, 1982.

Chaline, Jean-Pierre. "Les contrats de mariage à Rouen au XIXe siècle: Etude d'après l'enregistrement des actes civils publics." *Revue d'histoire économique et sociale* 48 (1970): 238–75.

Chaline, Jean-Pierre, ed. *Deux bourgeois en leur temps: Documents sur la société rouennaise du XIXe siècle*. Rouen, 1977.

Chaline, Nadine-Josette. "Attitude et action sociales de l'Eglise dans le diocèse de

Rouen au XIXe et au début du XXe siècle." *Revue des sociétés savantes de Haute-Normandie*, no. 67 (1972): 65–78.

Chaline, Nadine-Josette, ed. *Le diocèse de Rouen-LeHavre*. Paris, 1976.

Chambers, Clarke A. "Toward a Redefinition of Welfare History." *Journal of American History* 73 (1986): 407–33.

Chamoux, Antoinette. "L'enfance abandonnée à Reims à la fin du XVIII siècle." *Annales de démographie historique*, 1973, pp. 263–85.

Charbit, Yves. *Du malthusianisme au populationnisme: Les économistes français et la population, 1840–1870*. Paris, 1981.

Charpentier, Jehanne. *Le droit de l'enfance abandonnée: Son évolution sous l'influence de la psychologie, 1552–1791*. Paris, 1967.

Chassagne, Serge. "La diffusion rurale de l'industrie cotonnière en France (1750–1850)." *Revue du Nord* 61 (1979): 97–114.

Chassagne, Serge. *Oberkampf: Un entrepreneur capitaliste au siècle des lumières*. Paris, 1980.

Chevalier, Louis. *Labouring Classes and Dangerous Classes in Paris during the First Half of the Nineteenth Century*. Translated by Frank Jellinek. London, 1973.

Clément, Ambroise. *Recherches sur les causes de l'indigence*. Paris, 1846.

Coleman, William. *Death Is a Social Disease: Public Health and Political Economy in Early Industrial France*. Madison, 1982.

Corneille, A. *La Seine-Inférieure industrielle et commerciale*. Rouen, 1873.

Corrigan, Philip, and Sayer, Derek. *The Great Arch: English State Formation as Cultural Revolution*. Oxford, 1985.

Courthéoux, Jean-Paul. "Naissance d'une conscience de classe dans le prolétariat textile du Nord?" *Revue économique*, no. 1 (1957): 114–39.

Crafts, N.F.R. "Economic Growth in France and Britain, 1830–1910: A Review of the Evidence." *Journal of Economic History* 44 (1984): 49–67.

Crouzet, François. "Quelques problèmes de l'histoire de l'industrialisation au XIXe siècle." *Revue d'histoire économique et sociale* 53 (1975): 527–40.

Curel, T. M. *Parti à prendre sur la question des enfants trouvés*. Paris, 1845.

Curzon, Emmanuel de. *Etudes sur les enfants trouvés au point de vue de la législation, de la morale, et de l'économie politique*. Poitiers, 1847.

Dansette, Adrien. *Religious History of Modern France*. Translated by John Dingle. 2 vols. Freiburg, 1961.

Daumard, Adeline, in collaboration with Codaccioni, Felix; Dupeux, Georges; Herpin, Jacqueline; Godechot, Jacques; and Sentou, Jean. *Les fortunes françaises au XIXe siècle: Enquête sur la répartition et la composition des capitaux privés à Paris, Lyon, Lille, Bordeaux et Toulouse d'après l'enregistrement des déclarations de succession*. Paris, 1973.

Davis, Natalie. *Society and Culture in Early Modern France*. Stanford, 1975.

"Debate: Natural Decrease in Early Modern Cities." *Past and Present*, no. 92 (1981): 169–80.

Delasselle, Claude. "Les enfants abandonnés à Paris au XVIIIe siècle." *Annales, E.S.C.* 30 (1975): 187–218.

Delumeau, Jean. *Catholicism between Luther and Voltaire: A New View of the Counter-Reformation*. Translated by Jeremy Moiser. London, 1977.

Delzons, Louis. *La famille française et son évolution*. Paris, 1913.

Demier, Francis. "Les ouvriers de Rouen parlent à un économiste en juillet 1848." *Le mouvement social*, no. 119 (1982): 3–31.

Denis, Lucien. "Notes sur les enfants trouvés à Rouen." *Revue des sociétés savantes de Haute-Normandie*, no. 42 (1966): 35–42.

"Le département du Nord sous la Restauration: Rapport du Préfet de Villeneuve-Bargemont en 1828." *Revue du Nord* 25 (1939/42): 243–79; 26 (1943): 21–45.

Derbigny, Henri. *Analyse raisonnée des ouvrages de MM. l'Abbé Gaillard, Terme et Monfalcon, Remacle et de Gérando sur la question des enfants trouvés*. Bordeaux, 1840.

DesAlleurs, Ch. *Histoire de la société de charité maternelle de Rouen*. Rouen, 1854.

Deschamps, Marie-Odile. "Le dépôt de mendicité de Rouen (1768–1820)." *Bulletin d'histoire économique et sociale de la révolution française*, 1977, pp. 81–93.

Desloges, Louis. *Des enfants trouvés, des femmes publiques et des moyens à employer pour en diminuer le nombre*. Paris, 1836.

Deyon, Pierre. "La diffusion rurale des industries textiles en Flandre française à la fin de l'Ancien Régime et au début du XIXe siècle." *Revue du Nord* 61 (1979): 83–96.

Dickens, Charles. *Oliver Twist*. London, 1966.

Donzelot, Jacques. *The Policing of Families*. Translated by Robert Hurley. New York, 1979.

Dreyfus, Hubert, and Rabinow, Paul. *Michel Foucault*. 2d ed. Chicago, 1983.

Dubosc, Georges. *Par ici, par là: Etudes d'histoire et de moeurs normandes*. Rouen, 1922.

Duchâtel, Tanneguy, Comte. *Considérations d'économie politique sur la bienfaisance ou de la charité dans ses rapports avec l'état moral et le bien-être des classes inférieures de la société*. Paris, 1829.

Dupâquier, Jacques, and Dupâquier, Michel. *Histoire de la démographie: La statistique de la population des origines à 1914*. Paris, 1985.

Dupin, Charles, Baron. *Forces productives et commerciales de la France*. 2 vols. Paris, 1827.

Dupin, Charles, Baron. *Du travail des enfants qu'emploient les ateliers, les usines et les manufactures, consideré dans les intérêts mutuels de la société, des familles et de l'industrie*. Paris, 1840.

Dupont, Jean-Baptiste. *Mémoire sur les moyens d'améliorer la santé des ouvriers à Lille*. Lille, 1826.

Dupont, Jean-Baptiste. *Topographie historique, statistique et médicale de l'arrondissement de Lille*. Paris, 1833.

Duroselle, Jean-Baptiste. *Les débuts du catholicisme social en France, 1822–1870*. Paris, 1951.

Duval, Victor. *La charité à Rouen: Les oeuvres catholiques*. Rouen, 1895.

Earle, Edward M., ed. *Modern France: Problems of the Third and Fourth Republics*. New York, 1964.

Eichtal, Eugène, Baron d'. "Les lois sur le travail des enfants dans les manufactures." *Revue des deux mondes* 100 (15 July 1872): 415–38.

"Les enfants du capital." *Les révoltes logiques*, no. 3 (1976): 3–6.

Engrand, Charles. "Les abandons d'enfants à Amiens vers la fin de l'Ancien Régime." *Revue du Nord* 64 (1982): 73–92.

Engrand, Charles. "Les industries lilloises et la crise économique de 1826 à 1832." *Revue du Nord* 63 (1981): 237–51.

Engrand, Charles. "Les ouvriers lillois de 1829 à 1832." Diplôme d'études supérieures, Université de Lille, 1957.

Esquiros, Alphonse. *Paris, ou les sciences, les institutions et les moeurs au XIXe siècle*. 2 vols. Paris, 1847.

Esterno, F.C.P. d'. *De la misère, de ses causes, de ses remèdes*. Paris, 1842.

Faucher, Léon. "Le travail des enfants à Paris." *Revue des deux mondes*, 15 November 1844, pp. 643–65.

Feinstein, C. H., ed. *Socialism, Capitalism, and Economic Growth: Essays Presented to Maurice Dobb*. Cambridge, 1967.

Feller, Elise, and Goeury, Jean-Claude. "Les archives de l'Académie des sciences morales et politiques, 1832–1848." *Annales historiques de la révolution française*, nos. 219–22 (1975): 567–83.

Feuer, Lewis S., ed. *Karl Marx and Friedrich Engels: Basic Writings on Politics and Philosophy*. New York, 1959.

Fix, Théodore. *Observations sur l'état des classes ouvrières*. Paris, 1846.

Flandrin, Jean-Louis. *Families in Former Times: Kinship, Household, and Sexuality*. Cambridge, 1979.

Forrest, Alan. *The French Revolution and the Poor*. New York, 1981.

Fortescue, William. *Alphonse de Lamartine: A Political Biography*. London, 1983.

Foucault, Albert. *La société de Saint-Vincent-de-Paul: Histoire de cent ans*. Paris, 1933.

Foucault, Michel, and Farge, Arlette. *Le désordre des familles: Lettres de cachet de la Bastille au XVIIIe siècle*. Paris, 1982.

Fox, Edward Whiting. *History in Geographic Perspective: The Other France*. New York, 1971.

Fox-Genovese, Elizabeth, ed. *The Autobiography of DuPont de Nemours*. Wilmington, 1984.

Fox-Genovese, Elizabeth. *The Origins of Physiocracy: Economic Revolution and Social Order in Eighteenth-Century France*. Ithaca, 1976.

France. Ministère de la Justice. *Compte général de l'administration de la justice criminelle en France*. Paris, 1827–47.

France. Statistique générale. *Statistique de la France publiée par le Ministère de l'Agriculture et du Commerce*, ser. 1, vols. 10 and 12 (Industrie, vols. 1 and 3). Paris, 1847, 1850.

Frégier, Honoré. *Des classes dangereuses de la société dans les grandes villes et des moyens de les rendre meilleures*. 2 vols. Paris, 1840.

Frey, Michel. "Du mariage et du concubinage dans les classes populaires à Paris (1846–1847)." *Annales, E.S.C.* 33 (1978): 803–29.

Fuchs, Rachel Ginnis. *Abandoned Children: Foundlings and Child Welfare in Nineteenth-Century France*. Albany, 1984.

Furet, François, and Ozouf, Jacques. *Lire et écrire: L'alphabétisation des Français de Calvin à Jules Ferry*. 2 vols. Paris, 1977.

Gaillard, Adolphe-Henri, Abbé. *Recherches administratives, statistiques et morales sur les enfants trouvés, les enfants naturels et les orphelins en France et dans plusieurs autres pays de l'Europe*. Paris, 1837.

Gaillard, Adolphe-Henri, Abbé. *Résumé de la discussion sur les enfants trouvés et observations sur la loi proposée au Corps législatif*. Paris, 1853.

Garden, Maurice. *Lyon et les Lyonnais au XVIIIe siècle*. Paris, 1970.

Gaylin, Willard; Glasser, Ira; Marcus, Steven; and Rothman, David J. *Doing Good: The Limits of Benevolence*. New York, 1978.

Gérando, J. M., Baron de. *Le visiteur du pauvre*. Paris, 1820.

Geuss, Raymond. *The Idea of Critical Theory: Habermas and the Frankfort School*. Cambridge, 1981.

Gillet, Marcel, ed. *L'homme, la vie et la mort dans le Nord au 19e siècle*. Lille, 1972.

Girardin, Saint-Marc. "De la pairie en France depuis la révolution de juillet." *Revue des deux mondes* 12 (1845): 537–62.

Glass, D. V., ed., *Introduction to Malthus*. London, 1953.

Goetz-Girey, Robert. *Croissance et progrès à l'origine des sociétés industrielles*. Paris, 1966.

Goffman, Erving. *Asylums: Essays on the Social Situation of Mental Patients and Other Inmates*. New York, 1961.

Gordon, Colin, ed. *Power/Knowledge: Selected Interviews and Other Writings, 1972–1977, Michel Foucault*. Translated by Colin Gordon, Leo Marshall, John Mepham, and Kate Soper. New York, 1980.

Gossin, Jules. *Manuel de la Société charitable de Saint-Régis de Paris*. Paris, 1851.

Gossin, Eugène. *La vie de M. Jules Gossin*. Paris, 1907.

Gougenot des Mousseaux, Roger. *Des prolétaires*. Paris, 1846.

Grasserie, Raoul de la. "Du rôle moral de la dot." *Revue de morale sociale*, 1900, pp. 437–65.

Grob, Gerald N. "Welfare and Poverty in American History." *Reviews in American History*, no. 1 (1973): 43–52.

Guérif, Georges. "Charles Noiret et l'enquête de 1848 sur la profession de tisserand." *Revue d'histoire économique et sociale* 49 (1971): 94–112.

Grün, Alphonse. *De la moralisation des classes laborieuses*. Paris, 1851.

Gullickson, Gay L. *Spinners and Weavers of Auffay: Rural Industry and the Sexual Division of Labor in a French Village, 1750–1850*. Cambridge, 1986.

Gutton, Jean-Pierre. *La société et les pauvres: L'exemple de la généralité de Lyon, 1534–1789*. Paris, 1970.

Harris, Ethel. *Lamartine et le peuple*. Paris, 1932.

Harte, N. B., and Ponting, K. G., eds. *Textile History and Economic History: Essays in Honour of Miss Julia deLacy Mann*. Manchester, 1973.

Heers, Jacques. *L'Occident aux XIVe et XVe siècles: Aspects économiques et sociaux*. Paris, 1963.

Hélin, Etienne. "Une sollicitude ambiguë: L'évacuation des enfants abandonnés." *Annales de démographie historique*, 1973, pp. 225–29.

Henaux, Evelyne B. "Paupérisme et assistance à Lille au XVIIIe siècle." Maîtrise d'histoire, Université de Lille, 1968.

Higgins, Joan. "Social Control Theories of Social Policy." *Journal of Social Policy* 9 (1980): 1–23.

Higonnet, Patrick L. R., and Higonnet, Trevor B. "Class, Corruption, and Politics in the French Chamber of Deputies, 1846–1848." *French Historical Studies* 5 (1967): 204–24.

Hinrichs, Ernst; Schmitt, Eberhard; and Vierhaus, Rudolf, eds. *De l'ancien régime à la révolution française*. Göttingen, 1978.

Histoire générale des techniques. Published under the direction of Maurice Daumas. Vol. 3, *L'expansion du machinisme*. Paris, 1968.

Hodern, Francis. *Les crises industrielles en Alsace au XIXe siècle (1800–1870) et leur répercussion sur l'emploi des travailleurs*. Aix-en-Provence, 1970.

Hordern, Francis. "L'évolution de la condition individuelle et collective des travailleurs en Alsace, XIXe siècle (1800–1870)." Thèse de doctorat, Université de Paris, Faculté de droit et des sciences économiques, 1970.

Houdoy, Jules. *La filature de coton dans le Nord de la France*. Paris, 1903.

Houzé de l'Aulnoit, Aimé. *Enfants assistés: La question des tours*. Lille, 1879.

Hué, Dr. François. *Histoire de l'hospice général de Rouen, 1602–1840*. Rouen, 1903.

Hufton, Olwen. *The Poor of Eighteenth-Century France*. Oxford, 1974.

Hunt, Lynn; Lansky, David; and Hanson, Paul. "The Failure of the Liberal Republic in France, 1795–1799: The Road to Brumaire." *Journal of Modern History* 51 (1979): 734–59.

L'impossible prison: Recherches sur le système pénitentiaire au XIXe siècle réunies par Michelle Perrot: Débat avec Michel Foucault. Paris, 1980.

Institut Royal de France. *Statistique: Mariage civil et religieux des pauvres*. Paris, 1846.

Isaac, Joseph; Fritsch, Philippe; and Battegay, Alain. *Disciplines à domicile: L'édification de la famille*. Fontenay-sous-Bois, 1977.

Jardin, André. *Alexis de Tocqueville*. Paris, 1984.

Johnson, Christopher H. *Utopian Communism in France: Cabet and the Icarians, 1839–1851*. Ithaca, 1974.

Jones, Gareth Stedman. *Languages of Class: Studies in English Working-Class History, 1832–1982*. Cambridge, 1983.

Julien-Laferrière, François. *Les députés-fonctionnaires sous la monarchie de Juillet*. Paris, 1970.

Kahan-Rabecq, Marie-Madeleine. *L'Alsace économique et sociale sous le règne de Louis-Philippe*. 2 vols. Paris, 1939.

Kaiser, Thomas E. "Politics and Political Economy in the Thought of the Ideologues." *History of Political Economy* 12 (1980): 141–60.

Kaplan, Steven L. *Bread, Politics, and Political Economy in the Reign of Louis XV*. 2 vols. The Hague, 1976.

Katz, Michael B. *Poverty and Policy in American History*. New York, 1983.

Kent, Sherman. *Electoral Procedure under Louis-Philippe*. New Haven, 1937.

Kertzer, David I. "A Life-Course Approach to Coresidence." *Current Perspectives on Aging and the Life Cycle* 2 (1986): 1–22.

Kestner-Rigau, M. "Rapport fait au nom de la commission spéciale chargée d'examiner les questions relatives au travail des jeunes ouvriers des fabriques." *Bulletin de la Société industrielle de Mulhouse*, no. 28 (1833): 339–51.

Kettler, David; Meja, Volker; and Stehr, Nico. *Karl Mannheim*. Chichester, 1984.

Knodel, John. "Law, Marriage, and Illegitimacy in Nineteenth-Century Germany." *Population Studies* 20 (1967): 279–94.

Kriedte, Peter; Medick, Hans; and Schlumbohm, Jürgen. *Industrialization before Industrialization: Rural Industry in the Genesis of Capitalism*. Cambridge, 1981.

LaBerge, Ann. "Public Health in France and the French Public Health Movement, 1815–1848." Ph.D. dissertation, University of Tennessee, 1974.

Labes, Lucien. *Les pairs de France sous la monarchie de Juillet*. Lorient, 1938.

Labourt, L. A. *Recherches historiques et statistiques sur l'intempérance des classes laborieuses et sur les enfants trouvés*. 2d ed. Paris, 1848.

LaCapra, Dominick. *Rethinking Intellectual History and Reading Texts*. Ithaca, 1983.

Laget, Ulysse. "Extrait de l'histoire des enfants trouvés." *Société de la morale chrétienne* 2, no. 3 (1853): 1–62.

Lallemand, Léon. *Un chapitre de l'histoire des enfants trouvés: La maison de la Couche à Paris, XVIIe–XVIIIe siècles*. Paris, 1885.

Lallemand, Léon. *La question des enfants abandonnés et délaissés au XIXe siècle*. Paris, 1885.

Lallemand, Léon. *La révolution et les pauvres*. Paris, 1898.

Lambert-Dansette, Jean. *Origines et évolution d'une bourgeoisie: Quelques familles du patronat textile de Lille-Armentières, 1789–1914*. Lille, 1954.

Lamberti, Jean-Claude. *Tocqueville et les deux démocraties*. Paris, 1983.

Landes, David S. "French Entrepreneurship and Industrial Growth in the Nineteenth Century." *Journal of Economic History* 9 (1949): 45–61.

Laslett, Peter. *The World We Have Lost*. 2d ed. New York, 1971.

Laslett, Peter; Oosterveen, Karla; and Smith, Richard M., eds. *Bastardy and Its Comparative History*. Cambridge, Mass., 1980.

Lasserre, André. *La situation des ouvriers de l'industrie textile dans la région lilloise sous la monarchie de Juillet*. Lausanne, 1952.

Laufenberger, Henry. *Cours d'économie alsacienne*. Vol. I. Paris, 1930.

LeBras, Gabriel. *Etudes de sociologie religieuse*. 2 vols. Paris, 1955–56.

Lebrun, François. "Naissances illégitimes et abandons d'enfants en Anjou au XVIIIe siècle." *Annales, E.S.C.* 27 (1972): 1183–89.

Lecanuet, R. P. *Montalembert: D'après son journal et sa correspondance*. 3 vols. Paris, 1899–1902.

Leclerc, Gérard. *L'observation de l'homme: Une histoire des enquêtes sociales*. Paris, 1979.

Lefebvre, Georges. *Les paysans du Nord pendant la révolution française*. Lille, 1924.

Legoyt, Alfred. *La France statistique*. Paris, 1843.

Legrand, Daniel. *Lettre d'un industriel des montagnes des Vosges à MM. Gros, Odier, Roman et comp. à Wesserling, distribuée aux membres des deux chambres et du ministère*. Paris, 1838.

Legras, Théodore. *Notice historique sur les hôpitaux et l'asile des aliénés de Rouen*. Rouen, 1827.

LeGuillou, Louis. *L'évolution de la pensée religieuse de Félicité Lamennais*. Paris, 1966.

Lelong, P. S. *Rapport sur les enfants trouvés et abandonnés fait au conseil général de la Seine Inférieure*. Rouen, 1835.

Lentacker, F. "Les ouvriers belges dans le département du Nord au milieu du XIXe siècle." *Revue du Nord* 38 (1956): 5–14.

LeParquier, E. *Une enquête sur le paupérisme et la crise industrielle dans la région rouennaise en 1788*. Rouen, 1936.

LePlay, Frédéric. *La réforme sociale en France*. 2 vols. Paris, 1864.

Lequin, Yves, ed. *Histoire des Français, XIXe–XXe siècles: La société*. Paris, 1983.

Leroux, Hugues. *Les filles, qu'en ferons-nous?* Paris, 1898.

Leuilliot, Paul. *L'Alsace au début du XIXe siècle: Essais d'histoire politique, économique et religieuse: 1815–1830*. 3 vols. Paris, 1959–60.

Leuilliot, Paul. "Bourgeois et bourgeoisies." *Annales, E.S.C.* 11 (1956): 87–101.

Leuilliot, P. "La 'situation morale et politique' de l'arrondissement d'Altkirch en 1821." *Revue d'Alsace* 79 (1932): 27–34.

Levainville, J. *Rouen: Etude d'une agglomération urbaine*. Paris, 1913.

LeVan-Lemesle, Lucette. "La promotion de l'économie politique en France au XIXe siècle jusqu'à son introduction dans les facultés, 1815–1881." *Revue d'histoire moderne et contemporaine* 27 (1980): 270–94.

Levasseur, Emile. *La population française*. 3 vols. Paris, 1889–92.

Levine, David, ed. *Proletarianization and Family History*. Orlando, 1984.

Levrault, Louis. "Esquisses du Haut-Rhin," *Revue d'Alsace*, ser. 2, no. 1 (1836): 23–49.

Lévy, Edouard. *Les difficultés du mariage*. Paris, 1923.

Lévy-Leboyer, Maurice. *Les banques européennes et l'industrialisation internationale dans la première moitié du XIXe siècle*. Paris, 1964.

Lhomme, Jean. *La grande bourgeoisie au pouvoir, 1830–1880: Essai sur l'histoire sociale de la France*. Paris, 1960.

Litchfield, R. Burr, and Gordon, David. "Closing the 'Tour': A Close Look at the Marriage Market, Unwed Mothers, and Abandoned Children in Mid-Nineteenth Century Amiens." *Journal of Social History* 13 (1980): 458–72.

Livet, Georges, and Shaff, Georges, eds. *Médecine et assistance en Alsace*. Strasbourg, 1976.

Loiset, M. "Les accidents du travail. "*Bulletin médical du Nord* (1850).

Lottin, Alain. "Naissances illégitimes et filles-mères à Lille au XVIIIe siècle." *Revue d'histoire moderne et contemporaine* 8 (1970): 278–322.

Loyer, Henri. *Recueil pour servir aux archives du comité ou chambre syndicale des filatures de coton de Lille*. Lille, 1873.

Luckács, Georg. *History and Class Consciousness: Studies in Marxist Dialectics*. Translated by Rodney Livingstone. Cambridge, Mass., 1968.

Lynch, Katherine A. "Marriage Age among French Factory Workers: An Alsatian Example." *Journal of Interdisciplinary History* 16 (1986): 405–29.

McCloy, Shelby T. *The Humanitarian Movement in Eighteenth-Century France*. Louisville, 1957.

McLellan, David, ed. *Karl Marx: Selected Writings*. Oxford, 1977.

Mairesse, Jacques, ed. *Pour une histoire de la statistique*. Paris, 1977.

Mannheim, Karl. *Ideology and Utopia: An Introduction to the Sociology of Knowledge*. Translated by Louis Wirth and Edward Shils. New York, 1946.

Marbeau, Jean-Baptiste-Firmin. *Du paupérisme en France et des moyens d'y remédier, ou principes d'économie charitable*. Paris, 1847.

Marchand, M. "Sur les enfants trouvés et abandonnés." *Annuaire Normand*, 1841, pp. 353–427.

Maréchal, Christian. *Lamennais et Lamartine*. Paris, 1907.

Margerie, Eugène de. *La société de Saint-Vincent-de-Paul: Lettres, entretiens, récits et souvenirs*. 2 vols. Paris, 1876.

Martin, Bernice. "Leonard Horner: A Portrait of an Inspector of Factories." *International Review of Social History* 14, pt. 3 (1969): 412–43.

Martin Saint-Léon, Etienne. *Histoire des corporations de métiers depuis leurs origines jusqu'à leur suppression en 1791*. 4th ed. Paris, 1941.

Marx, Karl. *The Eighteenth Brumaire of Louis Bonaparte*. New York, 1969.

Mayeur, Jean-Marie. "Le catholicisme social en France." *Le mouvement social*, no. 77 (1971): 113–21.

Medick, Hans, and Sabean, David Warren, eds. *Interest and Emotion: Essays on the Study of Family and Kinship*. Cambridge, 1984.

Meinenger, Ernest. *Essai de description, de statistique et d'histoire de Mulhouse*. Mulhouse, 1885.

Mendels, Franklin. "Protoindustrialization: The First Phase of the Industrialization Process." *Journal of Economic History* 32 (1972): 241–61.

Merriman, John, ed. *French Cities in the Nineteenth Century*. New York, 1981.

"Mesures de police prises à Paris à l'égard des enfants trouvés." *Annales d'hygiène publique et de médecine légale* 19 (1838): 66–73.

Metzger, Albert. *La république de Mulhouse*. Basel, 1888.

Mireaux, Emile. "Un chirurgien sociologue: Louis-René Villermé." *Revue des deux mondes*, no. 2 (1962): 201–12.

Mitchell, Harvey. "Politics in the Service of Knowledge: The Debate over the Administration of Medicine and Welfare in Late-Eighteenth-Century France." *Social History* 6 (1981): 185–207.

Moch, Leslie Page. *Paths to the City: Regional Migration in Nineteenth-Century France*. Beverly Hills, 1983.

Mousnier, Roland. *Les hiérarchies sociales de 1450 à nos jours*. Paris, 1969.

Muraskin, William A. "The Social-Control Theory in American History: A Critique." *Journal of Social History* 9 (1975/76): 558–69.

Murphy, Terence D. "The French Medical Profession's Perception of Its Social Function between 1776 and 1830." *Medical History* 23 (1979): 259–78.

Naville, François-Marc-Louis. *De la charité légale, de ses effets, de ses causes, et spécialement des maisons de travail et de la proscription de la mendicité*. 2 vols. Paris, 1836.

Nepveur, Albert-Marie-Louis. *De la condition physique et morale des enfants trouvés au XIXe siècle et du système qu'il convient d'adopter comme règle unique du service de ces enfants: Observations adressées au conseil général de la Seine-Inférieure*. Rouen, 1849.

Nepveur, Albert-Marie-Louis. *De la mortalité des enfants trouvés en France et à Rouen en particulier*. Rouen, 1851.

Nepveur, Albert-Marie-Louis. *De la suppression des tours et de l'admission à bureau ouvert des enfants trouvés*. Rouen, 1848.

Nizard, Alfred. "Droit et statistiques de filiation en France: Le droit de la filiation depuis 1804." *Population* 32 (1977): 91–122.

Noiret, Charles. *Mémoires d'un ouvrier rouennais*. Rouen, 1836.

Norberg, Kathryn. *Rich and Poor in Grenoble, 1600–1814*. Berkeley and Los Angeles, 1985.

Oberlé, Raymond. *L'enseignement à Mulhouse de 1798 à 1870*. Strasbourg, 1961.

Oberlé, Raymond. "Etude sur l'analphabétisme à Mulhouse au siècle de l'industrialisation." *Bulletin du musée historique de Mulhouse* 67 (1959): 99–110.

O'Meara, Kathleen. *Frederic Ozanam: His Life and Works*. New York, 1891.

Ouin-Lacroix, Charles. *Histoire des anciennes corporations d'arts et métiers et des confréries religieuses de la capitale de la Normandie*. Rouen, 1850.

Panel, G. *Documents concernant les pauvres de Rouen: Extraits des archives de l'Hôtel-de-Ville*. 3 vols. Rouen, 1917.

Parekh, Bhiku. *Marx's Theory of Ideology*. Baltimore, 1982.

Peacock, A. E. "Factory Act Prosecutions: A Hidden Consensus?" *Economic History Review*, 2d ser., 38 (1985): 431–36.

Peacock, A. E. "The Successful Prosecution of the Factory Acts, 1833–1855." *Economic History Review*, 2d ser., 37 (1984): 197–210.

Penot, Achille. *Discours sur quelques recherches de statistique comparée faites sur la ville de Mulhouse*. Mulhouse, 1828.

Penot, Achille. *Recherches statistiques sur Mulhouse*. Mulhouse, 1843.

Perrot, Michelle. *Enquêtes sur la condition ouvrière en France au 19e siècle: Etude, bibliographie, index*. Paris, 1972.

Pierrard, Pierre. "Le patronat et le travail des enfants en 1848." *Economie et humanisme*, no. 117 (1959): 53–64.

Pierrard, Pierre. *La vie ouvrière à Lille sous le Second Empire*. Paris, 1965.

Pillorget, René. *La tige et le rameau: Familles anglaise et française, XVIe–XVIIIe siècles*. Paris, 1979.

Pinkney, David H. *The Revolution of 1830*. Princeton, 1972.

Piven, Frances Fox, and Cloward, Richard. *Regulating the Poor: The Functions of Public Welfare*. New York, 1971.

Poulantzas, Nicos. *L'état, le pouvoir, le socialisme*. Paris, 1978.

Poulantzas, Nicos. *Political Power and Social Classes*. Translated by Timothy O'Hagan. London, 1973.

Poull, Georges. "L'industrie textile vosgienne, des origines à 1978." *Le pays de Remiremont*, no. 2 (1979): 27–50.

Pouthas, Charles. *La population française pendant la première moitié du XIXe siècle*. Paris, 1956.

Preston, Samuel H., and van de Walle, Etienne. "Urban French Mortality in the Nineteenth Century." *Population Studies* 32 (1978): 275–97.

Price, Roger. "Recent Work on the Economic History of Nineteenth-Century France." *Economic History Review*, 2d ser., 37 (1984): 417–34.

Procès-verbaux et rapports du comité de mendicité de la Constituante, 1790–1791. Published and annotated by Camille Bloch and Alexandre Tuetey. Paris, 1911.

Rapet, J. J. "De l'influence de la suppression des tours dans les hospices d'enfants trouvés sur le nombre des infanticides." *Journal des économistes*, December 1845, pp. 51–72.

Rapport à M. le Ministre Secrétaire d'Etat à l'Intérieur, concernant les infanticides et les mort-nés dans leur relation avec la question des enfants trouvés, par M. Remacle. Paris, 1845.

Rapport au Roi sur les hôpitaux, les hospices et les services de bienfaisance, par M. de Gasparin. Paris, 1837.

"Rapport de la commission spéciale concernant la proposition de M. Jean-Jacques Bourcart." *Bulletin de la Société industrielle de Mulhouse*, no. 5 (1828): 328–38.

Reddy, William M. "Family and Factory: French Linen Weavers in the Belle Epoque." *Journal of Social History*, Winter 1975, pp. 102–12.

Reddy, William M. "The Language of the Crowd at Rouen, 1752–1871." *Past and Present*, no. 74 (1977): 78–79.

Reddy, William M. *The Rise of Market Culture: The Textile Trade and French Society, 1750–1900*. Cambridge, 1984.

Remacle, Bernard-Benoît. *Des hospices d'enfants trouvés, en Europe, et principalement en France, depuis leur origine jusqu'à nos jours*. Paris, 1838.

Remacle, Bernard-Benoît. *Des hospices d'enfants trouvés, en Europe, et principalement en France, depuis leur origine jusqu'à nos jours: Documents statistiques officiels*. Paris, 1838.

Richardson, Nicholas. *The French Prefectoral Corps, 1814–1830*. Cambridge, 1966.

Rigaudias-Weiss, Hilde. *Les enquêtes ouvrières en France entre 1830 et 1848*. Paris, 1936.

Rogron, Joseph-André. *Codes français expliqués par leurs motifs, par des exemples et par la jurisprudence*. 2d ed. 2 vols. Paris, 1843.

Rolants, Edmond-Jules. *Notes sur l'histoire médicale de Lille et de sa région: L'état sanitaire de Lille en 1832*. Lille, 1926.

Rolley, J. "La structure de l'industrie textile en France en 1840–1844." *Histoire des entreprises*, no. 4 (1959): 20–48.

Rosanvallon, Pierre. *Le moment Guizot*. Paris, 1985.

Rossi, Alice S., ed. *Gender and the Life Course*. New York, 1985.

Sandrin, Jean. *Enfants trouvés, enfants ouvriers: XVIIe–XIXe siècle*. Paris, 1982.

Schall, Abbé J. *Un disciple de Saint Vincent de Paul au XIXe siècle: Adolphe Baudon, 1819–1888*. Paris, 1897.

Schofield, R., and Coleman, D., eds. *The State of Population Theory: Forward from Malthus*. Oxford, 1985.

Seillière, Ernest. *Une académie à l'époque romantique*. Paris, 1926.

Semichon, Louis-Ernest. *Histoire des enfants abandonnés depuis l'antiquité jusqu'à nos jours: Le tour*. Paris, 1880.

Sewell, William H., Jr. *Structure and Mobility: The Men and Women of Marseille, 1820–1870*. Cambridge, 1985.

Sewell, William H., Jr. *Work and Revolution in France: The Language of Labor from the Old Regime to 1848*. Cambridge, 1980.

Sharlin, Allan. "Natural Decrease in Early Modern Cities: A Reconsideration." *Past and Present*, no. 79 (1978): 126–38.

Shorter, Edward N. "Female Emancipation, Birth Control, and Fertility in European History." *American Historical Review* 78 (1973): 605–40.

Shorter, Edward. *The Making of the Modern Family*. New York, 1975.

Simon, Jules. *La liberté civile*. Paris, 1872.

Simonde de Sismondi, Jean-Charles. *Nouveaux principes d'économie politique*. 2 vols. Paris, 1819.

Simonde de Sismondi, J.C.L. *Political Economy*. New York, 1966.

Simonds, A. P. *Karl Mannheim's Sociology of Knowledge*. Oxford, 1978.

Sion, Jules. *Les paysans de la Normandie orientale: Pays de Caux, Bray, Vexin normand, vallée de la Seine: Etude géographique*. Paris, 1909.

Skinner, Quentin. "Motives, Intentions, and the Interpretation of Texts." *New Literary History* 3 (1972): 393–408.

Smelser, Neil J. *Social Change in the Industrial Revolution: An Application of Theory to the British Cotton Industry*. Chicago, 1959.

Smith, Bonnie. *Ladies of the Leisure Class: The Bourgeoises of Northern France in the Nineteenth Century*. Princeton, 1981.

Société de démographie historique. *La France d'Ancien Régime: Etudes réunies en l'honneur de Pierre Goubert*. 2 vols. Toulouse, 1984.

Société de démographie historique. *Hommage à Marcel Reinhard: Sur la population française au XVIIIe et au XIXe siècles*. Paris, 1973.

Société de Saint-Vincent-de-Paul de Lille. *Notice historique sur la Société de Saint-Vincent-de-Paul à Lille, 1838–1883*. Lille, 1883.

Société Industrielle de Mulhouse, *Histoire documentaire de l'industrie de Mulhouse et de ses environs au XIXe siècle*. 2 vols. Mulhouse, 1902.

Société libre d'émulation de la Seine-Maritime. *Le textile en Normandie: Etudes diverses*. Rouen, 1975.

Société savante d'Alsace et des régions de l'Est. *La bourgeoisie alsacienne: Etudes d'histoire sociale*. Strasbourg, 1954.

Spagnoli, Paul G. "The Demographic Work of Charles Pouthas." *Historical Methods Newsletter* 4 (1971): 126–40.

Spagnoli, Paul G. "High Fertility in Mid-Nineteenth-Century France: A Multivariate Analysis of Fertility Patterns in the Arrondissement of Lille." *Research in Economic History* 2 (1977): 281–336.

Spagnoli, Paul G. "Industrialization, Proletarianization, and Marriage: A Reconsideration." *Journal of Family History* 8 (1983): 230–47.

Stearns, Peter N. *Paths to Authority: The Middle Class and the Industrial Labor Force in France, 1820–1848*. Urbana, 1978.

Stearns, Peter N. "Patterns of Industrial Strike Activity in France during the July Monarchy." *American Historical Review* 70 (1965): 371–94.

Suzuki, Hiromasa. "L'évolution de l'industrie cotonnière dans la région rouennaise au XIXe siècle: 1789–1880." Thèse du 3e cycle, Université de Rouen, 1969.

Tapprest, J. "Antoine-Eugène Buret (1810–1842) et la médecine du travail." *Archives des maladies professionelles* 25 (1964): 172–77.

Terme, Jean-François, and Monfalcon, Jean-Baptiste. *Histoire des enfants trouvés*. Rev. ed. Paris, 1840.

Thompson, E. P. "The Moral Economy of the English Crowd in the Eighteenth Century." *Past and Present*, no. 50 (1971): 76–136.

Thompson, F.M.L. "Social Control in Victorian Britain." *Economic History Review*, 2d ser., 34 (1981): 189–208.

Thouvenin. Dr. "De l'influence que l'industrie exerce sur la santé des populations dans les grands centres manufacturiers." *Annales d'hygiène publique et de médecine légale* 36 (1846): 16–46, 277–96; 37 (1847): 83–111.

Tilly, Louise A.; Scott, Joan W.; and Cohen, Miriam. "Women's Work and European Fertility Patterns." *Journal of Interdisciplinary History* 6 (1976): 447–76.

Tilly, Louise A., and Tilly, Charles, eds. *Class Conflict and Collective Action*. Beverly Hills, 1981.

Tocqueville, Alexis de. *Democracy in America*. Edited by J. P. Mayer. Translated by George Lawrence. 2 vols. New York, 1966.

Tocqueville, Alexis de. *The Old Regime and the French Revolution*. Translated by Stuart Gilbert. New York, 1955.

Tocqueville, Alexis de. *Recollections*. Edited by J. P. Mayer and A. P. Kerr. Translated by George Lawrence. New York, 1971.

Trattner, Walter I., ed. *Social Welfare or Social Control? Some Historical Reflections on Regulating the Poor*. Knoxville, 1983.

Tudesq, André-Jean. *Les conseillers généraux en France au temps de Guizot, 1840–1848*. Paris, 1967.

Turin, Yves. "Enfants trouvés, colonisation et utopie: Etude d'un comportement social au XIXe siècle." *Revue historique*, no. 496 (1970): 329–56.

van de Walle, Etienne, and Preston, Samuel H. "Mortalité de l'enfance au XIXe siècle à Paris et dans le département de la Seine." *Population* 29 (1974): 89–107.

Vaudoré, Gaétan-Symphor. *De la suppression des tours établis dans les chefs-lieux d'arrondissement*. Caen, 1838.

Vedrenne-Villeneuve, Edmonde de. "L'inégalité devant la mort dans la première moitié du XIXe siècle." *Population* 16 (1961): 665–98.

Vignes, R. *Mémoire sur les enfants trouvés et les mesures administratives qui leur ont été appliquées dans le département du Gers*. Auch, 1838.

Villeneuve-Bargemont, Alban de. *Economie politique chrétienne, ou recherches sur la nature et les causes du paupérisme en France et en Europe, et sur les moyens de le soulager et de le prévenir*. 3 vols. Paris, 1834.

Villermé, Louis-René. "De la mortalité des enfants trouvés." *Annales d'hygiène publique et de médecine légale* 19 (1838): 47–60.

Villermé, Louis-René. "Rapport de M. Villermé sur l'ouvrage intitulé *Recherches statistiques sur Mulhouse*." *Séances et travaux de l'Académie des sciences morales et politiques*, 1843, pp. 115–25.

Villermé, Louis-René. *Tableau de l'état physique et moral des ouvriers employés dans les manufactures de coton, de laine et de soie*. 2 vols. Paris, 1840.

Watteville, Adolphe, Baron de. *Du sort des enfants trouvés et de la colonie agricole du Mesnil-Saint-Firmin*. Paris, 1846.

Watteville, Adolphe, Baron de. *Essai statistique sur les établissements de bienfaisance.* 2d ed. Paris, 1847.

Watteville, Adolphe, Baron de. *Rapport à Son Excellence le Ministre de l'Intérieur sur la situation du paupérisme en France et sur l'administration des secours à domicile.* Paris, 1855.

Watteville, Adolphe, Baron de. *Statistique des établissements de bienfaisance. Rapport à M. le Ministre de l'Intérieur sur la situation administrative, morale et financière du service des enfants trouvés et abandonnés.* Paris, 1849.

Weber, Eugen. *Peasants into Frenchmen: The Modernization of Rural France, 1870–1914.* Stanford, 1976.

Weill, Georges. *Histoire du catholicisme libéral en France, 1828–1908.* Paris, 1909.

Weiss, Raymond. *Daniel Legrand (1783–1859): Son oeuvre sociale et internationale.* Paris, 1926.

Weissbach, Lee Shai. *Assuring the Future Harvest: Child Labor Reform in France, 1827–1885.* Baton Rouge: Louisiana State University Press, forthcoming.

White, Hayden. "Foucault Decoded: Notes from Underground." *History and Theory* 12 (1973): 23–54.

White, Ruth L. *"L'Avenir" de Lamennais: Son rôle dans la presse de son temps.* Paris, 1974.

Yeo, Eileen, and Thompson, E. P. *The Unknown Mayhew.* New York, 1971.

Zeldin, Theodore. *France, 1848–1945: Love, Ambition, and Politics.* Vol. 1. Oxford, 1973.

Zuber, Paul-René. "La famille bourgeoise mulhousienne vers la fin du 18e siècle." *Revue d'Alsace* 83 (1936): 254–63.

Index